The
GENEROUS
PRENUP

HOW TO SUPPORT YOUR MARRIAGE
AND AVOID THE PITFALLS

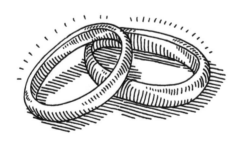

LAURIE ISRAEL

INTEGRITY REGISTRY PRESS

Integrity Registry Press, LLC
1318 Beacon Street
Brookline, MA 02446
(617) 277-3774
www.laurieisrael.com

ISBN 978-0-9998287-0-0
eBook ISBN 978-0-9998287-1-7

Cover and book design by Barbara Aronica-Buck
Cover image by Frank Ramspott
Author photo by Ryuji Suzuki

Manufactured in the United States of America

More Advance Praise:

Laurie Israel raises critical issues in her book, and brings a welcome new perspective on the challenges of a premarital agreement. Her focus on generosity – rather than greed – sets the perfect tone and reorients us to the goals of the marriage. She tells enlightening stories and shares her knowledge and suggestions with a clear mind and a gentle hand, making this a vital resource for attorneys and clients alike.

— Frederick Hertz, Attorney/Mediator, Oakland, California

The Generous Prenup opens an important new door for couples, their friends and families, and their professional advisors as well, providing a wise and experienced perspective on prenuptial and postnuptial agreements that has never before been available. Laurie Israel shows you how you might negotiate an agreement more creative and generous than most lawyers have ever imagined possible. This is a major piece of work that will fill an important need.

—Pauline H. Tesler, Collaborative Lawyer,
Mill Valley, California

This is about to become the "go-to" book for couples contemplating marriage and considering a prenup, as well as lawyers and mediators who work in this field. Laurie Israel's comprehensive book fills the need for something that has been missing for a long time – namely, one volume that covers every conceivable question that one could raise and how the process can remain a "generous" one. I look forward to giving the next couple who contacts me copies of Laurie's book so that I may truly help them go through the process in the most "generous" way.

— Ken Neumann, Mediator, New York, New York

For Elaine and Ben

CONTENTS

THE PRENUP MYTH

I t's March, wedding season for prenuptial-agreement lawyers. People are in love and are preparing for their June and summertime weddings.

It is five o'clock on a Friday afternoon. I'm in my office wrapping up some work before the weekend when I receive a phone call from a young woman – let's call her Anna Smith. She says that she is supposed to be exchanging vows with her fiancé, Greg, in three months. But Greg has just told her that he will not get married without a prenup and that his lawyer has drawn one up. He said that he'll give it to her in a few days, and he wants her to take a look at it as soon as it arrives.

Although there had been some mention of the idea in the past, Anna thought that Greg had abandoned the notion of a prenup. Meanwhile, the wedding has already been planned, and the invitations are stamped and ready to go. Anna and her family are now distraught and angry. In fact, her parents are outraged at Greg. They have totally lost respect for him to have even considered such a thing.

This is how the prenup client contact typically begins for me. For the clients, it's not a good way to start a marriage. It sets up a dynamic where the future husband and future wife are in an adversarial situation. And this is happening right before the wedding. When attorneys get involved, the situation gets worse, and positions become intractable. Often the couple has been in a relationship for a number of years, so terminating the relationship at this point is generally not an acceptable option.

People may think it's fair to separate economic assets and income in a marriage. But as most people in long marriages will tell you, money and finances are an important part of marriage, and become more important as time goes on. Providing security to a loved one, just as providing comfort and a good meal, is important to the maintenance of a loving bond.

Because of the power of the internet, many people are accepting the hype that prenuptial agreements are necessary to all marriages. Prenups are overused, are negotiated in a painful way, are often unnecessary, and can be extremely destructive. Many lawyers have bought into the hype and relentlessly perpetrate prenups as a necessary premarital step for their clients. They describe the agreement primarily as a vehicle for "risk control." They fail to see how it might affect the health of the marriage.

Marriages with prenups (especially in first marriages) often embark with a raw history of harsh negotiations by dueling attorneys that may never be forgotten. Many spouses who are a party to prenups feel they've been taken advantage of. They believe that their assumed premise of what their marriage would be when they said yes had been damaged. The process also harms the more moneyed spouse, who often feels like a bully and is perceived to be one.

The myth about prenups is that they are necessary, that they improve marriages, and that they are a fair way for spouses to deal with each other. In my experience, they usually are unnecessary (in first marriages) and often have the opposite result than what was intended. They detract from marriage because they are unfair. This is what I call the great "prenup myth."

Most prenups are inequitable at the onset of a marriage and become more unfair as the marriage goes on. They create corrosiveness. They have the potential to fray the bond that people have when they enter into marriage in order to make a lifelong commitment to each other. But done under the appropriate circumstances, and with fairness and generosity, prenups can have a positive impact on a married couple. That's what the message of this book is. That's why this book is titled *The Generous Prenup*.

At its basis, this book is about marriage and money. Despite what newly-wed couples might prefer to believe, marriage and money are inextricably intertwined. Money and security are crucial to a healthy marriage. Prenups have the potential and power to distort and weaken the marital relationship.

Of course, marriage is about more than just money. But along with family, sex and companionship, money and financial security are part of the bedrock of marriage. I leave it to other commentators to address the other major elements. But in my experience as a practicing divorce attorney, it is apparent that money issues affect all other qualities of a marriage. They are often the reason marriages are unhappy and often the reason that they end in divorce. I'm writing this book because I believe in marriage, and I want to help people make their marriages as healthy and satisfying as possible.

The book offers couples and their family members information and guidelines on how to avoid prenup-related problems, both before and after the wedding. It helps couples navigate the pros and cons of prenups, and determine whether or not to sign one.

And if a prenup is both desired and appropriate, it identifies a path to obtaining an agreement that is constructive rather than destructive, both in process and content. It also describes how prenups interact with many substantive areas of law, such as estate planning, businesses, immigration, and elder law. It also discusses the enforceability of prenups.

The Generous Prenup also covers postnuptial agreements, which are signed during an ongoing marriage.

The aim of this book is to assist couples considering marriage, engaged couples, their financial advisors, attorneys, and their friends and family members in thinking about prenups. The book will also help married couples who are wondering about the issue of money and security in their marriage.

The Generous Prenup is intended to help people determine what might be in their prenup, if they decide to have one. The book suggests specific methods and provisions that are not often contemplated in a prenup. These "out of the box" ideas can create a prenup that is fair to both parties and that can help rather than hurt a marriage. In this way, thinking about prenup (even it if does not result in a signed agreement) can be a useful lens for awareness of each future partner's needs and values, projected through a long marriage.

I have written the book without footnotes. The reader can find the source material by an internet search of the case, statute, or web article cited in the text. Although some of the cases I've cited are from Massachusetts (I'm a Massachusetts attorney), they are illustrative examples. They may differ from the laws of the reader's home state, or may be similar. I have also included many case and statute citations from other states to give readers a flavor of the laws (both case law and statutory) that exist in many places in the U.S.

The Generous Prenup is designed so that you do not need to read all chapters (or the chapters in order) to acquire the information you need from the book. Take a look at the table of contents to see what interests you and what applies to your situation. You may want to read those chapters first. Many of the general chapters (Chapters 1–6, 16–17, and 20–21) will be helpful to most readers. Some of the chapters (or parts of them) are necessarily more technical than others. If it suits you, and the topic is not high on your list, feel free to skip the chapter or the technical parts within the chapter. If you would like to start with an entertaining chapter, start with Chapter 14 (Lifestyle Prenups).

The material for this book is drawn from a composite of client situations (and solutions) from my 30 years of experience in practicing law. I have changed the names and identifying personal and factual information in the situations utilized herein. The fact patterns (a term used frequently by attorneys to refer to clients' situational profiles) contain elements common to many people seeking prenuptial agreements. Any resemblance to a particular individual's situation or any specific couple's situation is purely coincidental.

The contents of this book are presented for general information purposes only. This book cannot and does not take the place of personal legal advice, but is intended only to provide information to readers interested in the topic of prenuptial agreements. A prenup is often the most important financial document a person will ever sign, and anyone contemplating using a prenuptial agreement should seek the advice of and representation by an experienced attorney before negotiating, drafting, and/or signing one.

— Laurie Israel
December 4, 2017

CHAPTER 1:

WHY I CHANGED MY MIND ABOUT PRENUPS

I've been a divorce lawyer for many years. Not the kind typically encountered in books and movies (and sometimes in life). Not the kind who tries to use every single advantage to get better deals for their individual clients at the expense of their soon-to-be exes. I'm the type that envisions an equitable divorce, one that respects the laws governing marriage and divorce that have been developed over many generations.

These laws reflect the values of fairness and evenhandedness embodied in our states' statutes and previously decided court cases. They reflect a cultural construct of what marriage is in our society. In my work, I practice negotiation, cooperation, collaboration, and mediation in order to achieve civilized divorces with fair results.

Lawyers have historically been called *counselors* for good reason, though it's a different type of counseling than that practiced by a psychologist or psychotherapist. A lawyer not only gives legal advice but, through knowledge and experience in addressing clients' problems, can provide practical guidance on other kinds of life choices and difficulties.

In this regard, people started coming to me some years ago to discuss the strains that were troubling them in their marriages. I began to give private legal counsel to my clients experiencing marital problems on an individual basis. I also began meeting as a neutral mediator with couples to help them solve marital problems.

When people began approaching me about their marital problems, I was in a very good position to understand what some of their issues were about. Some of these, if not all, were caused by financial situations. After all, when you come right down to it, in many respects lawyers are "money doctors," so I was an appropriate resource for these clients.

Lawyers are also very expert interpreters of language – both words and body language. I found that when I met with a couple as mediator, I was able to see quickly the disconnects and misunderstandings in their communication. Often I saw problems that they did not realize were present in their inter-changes, and I was able to point these out to my mediation clients.

My marital mediation practice soon began to include couples who were about to wed, asking me to help them define the financial terms of their upcoming marriages to be reflected in a prenuptial agreement. I also started meeting with clients who were interested in finding out about mid-marriage agreements individually, or as mediator with the couple. These are typically called "postnuptial" agreements in which a couple can set financial terms between them *during* their marriage.

These experiences as well as the many divorce cases in which I have par-ticipated as a client attorney (as well as other aspects of my career, and my per-sonal experience as a spouse in a long-term marriage) have educated me in the importance of financial issues in marriage. I also believe that when financial issues become problematic, other aspects of the marriage (including sex) gen-erally suffer. My clients tell me this is so. The flip side of this is that the ability for a couple to resolve financially-based marital issues can be key to resuming a loving marriage. Reports from my clients also tell me that this is true.

If financial issues are important to the health of a marriage, shouldn't prenups (and postnups), designed primarily to govern finances in a marriage, be a good thing? Unfortunately, in my experience, this is not typically the case.

The Problem with Prenups

As this book will reveal, a prenup distorts the economics of marriage and can thus have an extremely detrimental effect on a couple and their marriage. They can have a huge impact on marriages, especially first marriages.

Prenups are complex and are influenced and affected by various areas of substantive law. So, in a sense, this book is a primer of laws, concentrating on the laws that affect marriage. You'll learn a lot by reading it, even if you are already married or cohabitating, and even if you are already married and not thinking of divorce.

The thrust of this book is threefold. First, the book identifies the dangers of certain prenup terms that are often heedlessly included in prenups. Second, it suggests many possible prenup terms and provisions that can reduce the potential damage of prenups and can even help nurture marriages. And finally, the book contains many ideas and guidance that can mitigate the harm caused by the *process* of getting a prenup, which itself tends to be extremely corrosive.

• • •

Prenuptial agreements always seem to be in the news these days. Whether it's a recent article about the latest celebrity breakup and what the less-famous or less-wealthy spouse received in the divorce, or "click-bait" internet articles promising the "dirt" on celebrity marriages with "weird," "horrifying," or "outrageous" prenup clauses, our fascination with celebrities and their marriages draws in large numbers of us.

Of course, some less well-known people also get prenups – generally people with inherited wealth or high incomes. But these are not the only types of people that get prenups before they marry. As you will see in Chapter 2, there are many reasons people may consider prenups other than wealth. There are also many reasons for people to reject having prenups. But this latter concept is not very strongly reflected in the media.

The news and entertainment media are replete with personal finance pundits and financial planning professionals who push prenups like candy to a child, touting them as the next "best thing." Articles such as "Why I Decided to Get a Prenup – and So Should You" and "Here's Why Every Couple Should Get a Prenup Before Marriage" are legion in the mainstream media and read hungrily by the public. Such commentaries and reports advise readers that it is crucial for couples embarking on marriage to have a prenup – or at least consider getting one.

For example, citing the high divorce rate and comparing a prenup with automobile insurance, personal money guru and media-proclaimed finance "wizard" Suze Orman advises us that virtually everyone considering marriage should have one. This type of web-based information builds up a market and interest in prenups, resulting in more people thinking more often about whether they should have one before their marriage. One might reasonably call it "fake news."

Lately, individual attorneys and law firms have also boarded the prenuptial (and postnuptial) agreement bandwagon. One law firm, for instance, phrases it this way:

> A prenuptial agreement is a smart financial planning tool. A marriage is not just a physical, mental, and emotional union, but a financial one too. Entering into a prenuptial or postnuptial agreement can provide a sense of security couples require.

Another firm states the following:

> Consider us your trusted legal advisor. We'll meet your need to ensure this matter is taken care of – so you can move forward with your wedding day without worry, concern, or regret later. There is no obligation after that first meeting with us. But you deserve to think through your situation before rushing into the next chapter of your life.

These firms promote prenups with little thought as to what changing the financial terms of the marriage might do to the physical, mental, and emotional union of the couple.

Once the notion of a prenup is in a person's mind, it becomes an idée fixe, a preoccupation. The person will often start feeling compelled to follow through on the idea, and the thought begins to become reality. (See Chapter 2 and The Bee-in-the-Bonnet Syndrome.) That person will be very suggestable to an attorney's view that a prenup should be in place before the marriage.

Some attorneys attempt to make their internet ads more balanced. Here's an excerpt from one such firm:

There is a common misconception that prenuptial agreements are one-sided. In reality, these documents are designed to provide protection to *both* [emphasis added] parties entering into a marriage. They can address property division, alimony and other financial issues.

But are prenups really designed to protect both parties entering into a marriage? In general, the answer is a resounding no. They are almost always one-sided, typically designed to protect the person with greater wealth or income – the "more moneyed" spouse. They operate almost invariably to diminish the rights that accrue upon marriage to the other, "less moneyed" spouse. It doesn't sound like a very good deal for the less moneyed spouse, whose rights are diminished, does it? That's because it isn't. Worsening this is that the process is done at the most romantic time in their relationship, right before the marriage.

When people enter into premarital agreements, they are seeking to change the basic rules of money and marriage that have been developed through generations, and even centuries. These rules reflect cultural values and economic morality that have been imbedded in laws affecting marriage, divorce, and inheritance. That's what the law is at its core.

This book is partly about how tampering with the laws disturbs values and ideals involving money and marriage. When you sign a prenuptial agreement, it can alter and destabilize your marriage. Not that every prenup is unreasonable, or that it should never be used. There are good reasons to have one. This book also discusses what can be done to mitigate damage and even create value in cases when signing a prenup is a reasonable and rational thing to do.

But first, here's a typical scenario. I get this fact pattern over and over again, with variations. What's wrong with this picture?

● ● ●

One party of an engaged couple calls me. They are getting married in a few months. They are both in their early thirties (now a common age for first marriages). Both are fully employed, and they each have some household assets typical of young professionals of their age group. They've known each other for five years and have been engaged for the past year. This would be a first marriage for both of them, and they plan to have children soon after marrying.

John is self-employed in a small but growing business. He earns three times as much as Stacey, his fiancé, who is a public school teacher. John has accumulated a modest retirement savings account during his nine years of full-time work. Stacey comes from a family with lesser financial means than John. They couldn't help her through college (as John's parents helped him). She is still paying off her student loans. Because she earns less and has the student loan payments, she has not been able to save for retirement.

John's parents (who did not have a prenup) have been married for forty years. They are in their sixties and in good health. They have accumulated a fair amount of assets but are not exceedingly wealthy. John expects an inheritance. Stacey does not.

John's sister recently went through a divorce and believes she was "burned" by the divorce terms. She has been encouraging John to get a prenup. John begins to search online and starts reading about prenups. He finds dozens of law firm websites characterizing prenups as a must-have before marriage, and now he's convinced that he needs one. He can't get it out of his mind. It is now an obsession.

John broached the idea of a prenup with Stacey, and now she is very angry at him. She has already spent five years with John, but she feels he's being selfish about this. She is now questioning whether she still wants to marry him. Her premise in entering the engagement was that they would share everything after marriage and that all their efforts would be on behalf of the marriage and their future family. Now she wonders if she should really just start all over with someone else.

In this case, despite the advice he's received from the attorney he consulted with (who has already began drafting it), perhaps John doesn't actually need to protect himself with a prenup. Presenting this demand at all, especially so close to the wedding date, may be doing irreparable harm to his and Stacey's relationship. It might possibly cause it to end, if not now, then years later, when the results of the contract he is asking her to sign are fully manifested.

As a prenup attorney I get phone calls like this one fairly frequently. They are from both men and women who are feeling angry, hurt, and frightened and can't see a solution that could make things right again.

Sometimes, however, it's a phone call or email from someone whose marriage might actually benefit from a well-conceived prenup. Perhaps the family of one of the future spouses is truly wealthy, or a future spouse is involved (or might later become involved) in a closely held family business. Perhaps one (or both) of the future spouses had been married before and has children from a previous marriage. It may be a marriage (first or subsequent) of people in their forties or fifties or sixties – or even older. In these and other such situations, a prenup, if done in a thoughtful and nuanced fashion, can be a way to ensure fairness to each of the future spouses. It can serve to create marital harmony and peace within the extended family.

Not only has the media convinced many people that prenups are common and a necessary prerequisite for any marriage. Media outlets also spread the fallacy that a significant segment of the population currently enters into one prior to marriage. This is simply not true. The percentage of couples with prenuptial agreements is actually very low – one could say they're rare – actually extremely rare – particularly in a first marriage between younger people. (See Chapter 5.) And for good reason.

Aside from attorneys promoting their services to "protect" marriages, it may be that a business associate or an estate-planning advisor will strongly suggest one to an engaged person. Perhaps they have taken continuing education courses in which an expert has represented these contracts as necessary. Or, like John's sister, a family member with a subjectively bad experience might encourage an engaged relative to get one.

Often those professionals advising a client to get a prenup are young and have no experience in long marriages. In many instances, they themselves have no such agreements in their own marriages. But invariably, they feel compelled to suggest one because they were taught that prenups provide "risk containment." They believe that they are not serving the client well if they don't recommend it.

Invariably, these "advisors" are insensitive to the negative dynamics and memories that even negotiating a prenup can generate. In almost every prenup I see with young people marrying, tears are shed during the process.

One person feels unloved and starts to question the commitment of their future spouse. Actually signing a prenup can be worse, because the economic terms often have a strong potential to upset the balance of fairness and mutual support in the upcoming marriage.

When I was a young lawyer, I didn't reflect much on the results of sending a young client (male or female) into a marriage with a typical generic prenup. Only one basic template existed at the time. That template, still often used, specified that any potential financial sharing during the marriage would be at the choice of the more moneyed spouse. Further, it provided that there would be no guaranteed inheritance rights, even if the marriage remained intact at the death of that spouse many years in the future.

In using the off-the-shelf template I found in my forms book, I believed I was following good legal practice. But I didn't fully comprehend at that time what marriage was, particularly a long-term marriage. I simply did not understand the financial and personal implications of what I had drafted.

As I grew older and became experienced in the law and in life, I began to realize more fully the importance of the financial sharing and security in the health of a long-term marriage – especially for young people embarking on a first marriage. I started thinking about prenups in a different way, and my drafting reflected this.

The other great problem with prenups is that they do not generally reflect and value the full range of non-monetary contributions to a marriage. (See Chapter 4.) They value the financial contributions of the more moneyed or "earner" spouse more than the nonfinancial contributions of the other spouse.

As will be explained in later chapters, in virtually all states in the U.S., the contributions of the two spouses are valued equally – whether monetary or not – if they both give their efforts fully in support of the marriage.

The law reflects the reality. No one can set a price on the value of a spouse who works in the home, raises children, and also often puts a career in second place (with a lifetime negative earnings effect) in order to support the earner spouse's career and the family as a whole. No law will devalue the spouse that works as a public school teacher with a wife or husband who is an investment fund manager. Courts will assume (generally correctly) that the decision to engage in these two careers was acceptable to the two spouses, and sometimes, even made as a mutual decision.

And yet, prenups often devalue the efforts of the non-earner (or lower-earning) spouse. They put the non-earner spouse in a financially precarious situation, because the usual protections of the law now no longer apply to this spouse. The sting of this devaluation and the negative practical result is felt by both parties and typically has an effect on the marriage that is detrimental to its happiness and success.

Prenups can also set up a hoarding problem. If a prenup sets aside separate property for one spouse, there is a natural tendency for that spouse who owns it to increase it and hoard it as much as possible. This can be very apparent to the other spouse as the marriage proceeds.

Hoarding is to the detriment of the well-being and security of the other spouse. Very bad feelings can result. If one spouse spends his or her time thinking about and actively engaged in protecting and increasing separate property, the marriage will be destabilized, particularly if the other spouse is giving 100 percent to the marriage. This is not rocket science. It is borne out by the facts underlying many divorces that I and other attorneys have dealt with during our careers.

Typical prenups drafted by many attorneys are often extreme, especially when they affect young people embarking on a first marriage. They go far beyond what might be needed or helpful in certain situations. They become monolithic, passed around in Word documents from law firm to law firm, from lawyer to lawyer. They tend to be used over and over again for any and all marriages. This is the legal equivalent of applying an ax to a piece of fish on your plate. Because they are not customized to a particular situation, they often are not reflective of the intent of the future spouses. They can imbalance a marriage and cause actual harm.

The other significant harm posed by prenups is the corrosiveness of the process as it is usually practiced by attorneys. Let's say that one future spouse (as is often the case) doesn't want to sign a prenup. That person might believe in a concept of marriage as sharing everything and might perceive the separation of assets and other limitations to sharing as antithetical to this concept. How can that person's values be accommodated when a prenup is presented to him or her? Generally, it is not.

Prenup contract negotiations are often harsh and inflexible, creating negative interactions at what is normally a very loving and tender time. The memory of such negotiations is permanent. Echoes of these debates can have serious lingering effects on the level of trust between the engaged couple. This is a harm that can reverberate throughout the future marriage.

Often a future spouse may *think* he or she wants a prenup but doesn't understand its effects or implications. That person's attorney may support the client's request without reflection or discussion. There may be no counseling on the downsides of having a prenup. (See Chapter 16.)

It's important for lawyers to take a step back and help clients contemplate and keep an open mind as to whether or not a prenup is needed. And if it's advisable to have one, it's important to consider with a fresh mind what kind of prenup it will be and what provisions it will contain. Unlike what typically comes out of many lawyers' offices, diverse types of prenups are possible, with multiple options for terms. The variations are virtually endless. The more thoughtful and customized a prenup is, the more nuanced it will be and the fairer and more acceptable to the non-initiating spouse. As a result, it can actually be helpful to the upcoming marriage.

But once set into play in an adversarial atmosphere, the implication is often "Marry me with a prenup or not at all." This is a conflict and dilemma going to the very heart of the upcoming marriage. If the future spouse who doesn't want a prenup also doesn't wish to face starting all over in another relationship, he or she must now deal with this implied "Take it or leave it!" ultimatum.

This is not a very loving way to begin a marriage. The parties are now thrust into a tense situation, with emotional and financial ramifications involving their future union that they cannot even imagine or understand, especially if they are relatively young and each embarking on a first marriage. They are now dealing with lawyers in this negotiation. Some pro-prenup attorneys representing more moneyed spouses are very harsh and will brook little or no compromise. They might view a prenup as a "business deal." They'll tell the other side that "the prenup can just be tucked away in a drawer" and "hopefully it will be never used."

But marriage is not just a business deal. The future spouse who doesn't want the prenup, or who wants a less extreme one and can't get the other side to budge, is now facing a difficult and stark choice: Marry with *this* prenup or do not marry at all. If it's signed, it is likely that it will be taken out of the drawer someday.

I have met and heard of very few people who have reached the stage of engagement when a marriage is planned who are willing to abandon the marriage when given this choice. Most engaged couples have made a significant personal investment in their relationships by that time. Often there is a long history of dating; many have cohabited for significant periods; and often they are already considered members of each other's families of origin. So the prenup is usually signed, and its terms then reverberate throughout the marriage itself.

The following chapters offer couples considering prenuptial agreements, as well as their friends and families, guidance on how to handle these pressures and issues, whether a prenup is only being contemplated or is already underway. The book proposes options to make prenups more customized to each situation. It explains how to look ahead into the future in a prenup, illustrating how important that is. It also describes dangerous formulations in prenups that can cause an imbalance in valuing contributions (both economic and noneconomic) to a marriage.

We will start with descriptions of the major factual situations in which people seek to have prenups, followed by some general information about prenups, marriage, and what happens when you marry without one. Then the book will focus on a number of topics, such as prenups to protect businesses, "gray" prenups, immigrant prenups, etc. Then finally, the book addresses how to find a prenup lawyer or mediator, and how to mitigate the damage that can result from the process.

I hope you enjoy the ride!

CHAPTER 2

WHO MIGHT THINK THEY NEED A PRENUP? THE GOOD, THE BAD, AND THE UGLY

With so much media coverage of prenups these days, many people seem to be laboring under one of two opposing misconceptions. One of these ideas stems from simple misinformation, and the other springs principally from unwarranted fears. The first is that only rich people need prenups before marrying, and the other is that practically all engaged people need them, to protect themselves from a host of disasters. As with many such broad but unproven assumptions, the truth lies somewhere between the two extremes.

Just as there are good and bad reasons to get a prenup, there are certain categories of people who should probably have them and others who don't really need them. Although the ongoing media blitz may make it seem that everyone should have one before marrying, it is not true. Prenups are sometimes suitable for people who are not affluent. However, it's generally true that prenups are most appropriate for four basic groups: the wealthy; older people; people with children from a previous relationship; and those with significant premarital assets. (See Chapter 3.) People of more modest means, especially younger couples entering a first marriage, often do not need a prenup at all.

These days some people may wonder whether they should get a prenup even when there is really not a very good reason for getting one. They may become very anxious about it, especially when those they care about and trust (like John's sister in Chapter 1) are telling them that they should have one. In some instances, a financial planner or a similar advisor may raise the issue. Nonetheless, on account of the potential downsides of prenups (see Chapters 4 and 16), it is important to determine carefully whether or not such an agreement might actually be right for you.

The idea that everyone should have a prenup to ward off disaster reminds me of a story told by a woman who was a famous self-help guru in the early part of the twentieth century. Her name was Elsie Lincoln Benedict, and she authored a series of lessons entitled *How to Get Anything You Want*. She gave public lectures across the country, and after one of her talks on positive thinking, an elderly man came up to her and said, "I've had lots of troubles in my life, but most of them never happened."

Some people seeking prenups are like that old man, imagining the worst in everything, including their upcoming marriages. Yes, it's true that many marriages end in divorce – but many don't. The greater truth is that if a marriage does end in divorce, state laws provide very equitable results for most people. (See Chapter 7.) In fact, there are many ways to get a divorce nowadays that are quite civilized and don't involve full-blown litigation. (See Chapter 6.)

As mentioned in the previous chapter, a prenuptial agreement is one of the most important documents a person will ever sign. It's a financial contract with great reverberations affecting the nature and health of their upcoming marriage. Prenups have a great potential to distort a marriage by applying terms that can turn out to be unfair over time and corrode a relationship, so future spouses should have very good and well-considered reasons to pursue one.

After some examination, people preparing for marriage may discover that their perceived need for a prenup might have arisen either from lack of information and knowledge or from anxiety about the future, not based in reality, like Elsie Lincoln Benedict's elderly man, quoted above. It's important to think clearly and act wisely before taking such a major step, and anyone who decides to proceed should do so only with sufficient thought and care.

In Chapter 3, we'll review the most common and sensible reasons various people get prenups. Let's now look at some of the reasons people without great wealth might think they need prenups. Some of these reasons are legitimate and some rather weak. Most of these can be resolved effectively without a prenup, whether the marriage ends in divorce or in the eventual death of a spouse.

1. The Bee-in-the-Bonnet Syndrome.

In the example from Chapter 1, John's sister felt that she had been burned in her divorce, so she told John that he should have a prenup. That got John thinking. To educate himself he started surfing the web for information. He found all sorts of ads promoting prenups, as well as pro-prenup articles written by financial planners and lawyers. Even though this would be a first marriage for both people, and even though his financial situation was more or less average for someone of his age in terms of assets, income, and potential inherited wealth, he became convinced that he needed a prenup.

So John started ruminating. Although he was soon obsessed with the idea, he waited before telling Stacey, his betrothed. The thought that he needed a prenup before marrying soon became his mental reality, and he became quite emotional as a result. When he finally told Stacey they "absolutely had to have a prenup before marrying," the harm was done – even if they eventually decided not to get one.

It's important for everyone thinking about a prenup to evaluate whether or not they really need one and what the potential downsides may be. In fact, it's a good idea for all of us to identify our recurring fears and name them for what they are – just thoughts, not realities. Otherwise we're likely to be governed by them and not act in our own best interest or that of those we love.

2. Inequality of financial contribution.

In this category of couples, one of the future spouses is a very strong earner. Generally (though not always) the more moneyed spouse is a professional or businessperson. Perhaps they're a doctor or have a successful business. Maybe they work in the software industry. Whatever the case may be, they earn more than the other spouse – much more.

The other future spouse may have a more typical financial situation for someone their age. Perhaps they have a nine-to-five job working in a service industry or an office. In any event, they earn quite a bit less than their future life partner.

Perhaps that future spouse works in a charitable organization or as a teacher in a public school. The couple may collectively agree that both their efforts are valuable – to society, the common good – as well as to support their family. A future spouse's greater earning power could be viewed as a necessary balance to provide economic stability and a more comfortable lifestyle that they both want during their marriage. It will also permit them to have a family in which one spouse generally takes on more homemaking and child-care duties. This will likely diminish one of the spouse's potential earnings during his or her lifetime.

Generally, the higher-earning spouse is fine with this arrangement in which one of them earns more, but sometimes they are not. Especially in first marriages, however, legally separating income earned after the marriage in a prenup can create great emotional difficulties between the spouses. When a higher earner wants to separate his or her income (which happens sometimes in prenups), it almost invariably leads to very hurt feelings and is almost never resolved satisfactorily for both parties. Whether or not a "no earned-income sharing" clause ends up in the final prenup draft, even the discussion and negotiations can be quite damaging.

3. Gender-role pride: He doesn't want anything to do with money he didn't earn. She doesn't want to be seen as a gold digger.

In some marriages where there might otherwise be a questionable need for a prenup, a future husband or future wife may want to voluntarily disclaim the earnings or wealth of the more moneyed partner before the marriage. I hear this all the time, both from men and women clients. They want to disclaim marital rights even if the lack of sharing might put them in a precarious situation in the future.

The male partner may say, "I don't need her money. I can make it on my own." The female partner almost always insists, "I'm not a gold digger, and I don't want to be seen as one." I call this type of agreement the "gender-role prenup."

He has been taught that he is the one that needs to make money in the family. To rely on her money (or her family's money) would be embarrassing to him and certainly a romance-killer. In fact, relying on her money or earnings in this culture generally puts a damper on romance for both the man and the woman. (The opposite, interestingly, is generally not true.)

The male partner has been taught to be in control and to be capable – in short, to "be a man." She is attracted to him because of these attributes. Her money (or her success in earning money) upsets these mutual expectations. In order to nip this problem in the bud, he's willing to sign a very restrictive prenup. He will usually sign virtually anything to resolve this issue – no matter what's in the prenup and how restrictive it is. I have heard real horror stories about the results of this particular fact pattern for the man when a divorce occurs.

The problem with such a proposed solution is that situations change during a long marriage. It's unfair for a man to end up after thirty or thirty-five years with nothing to show for his work after having contributed all his earnings to a marriage. Maybe it seemed okay to him when he got married at thirty, but now that he's sixty or older and a divorce is happening, it doesn't seem fair, and he's understandably worried about his future. Because of the prenup, he will be left with few assets and little income to retire on. He wishes he hadn't signed that prenup and feels like he was a fool. He's right. He was foolish to sign it.

There is ample case law already addressing this type of situation to cover people who *didn't* sign prenups. The general outline of these cases is this: The man provided all his earnings to support the family. The couple's mutual expectation was that the wife's family wealth (inherited and/or gifted) would provide for both their retirements. The divorce interfered with those expectations.

In cases like this where there is a divorce with no prenup, the wife often insists in the divorce action that the wealth derived from her family inheritance should not be shared with her husband but instead remain within the bloodlines. In these cases, courts will generally try to build equity into the situation by giving the husband some of the wife's inherited or gifted assets, or perhaps a disproportionate share of marital assets in his favor, in order to secure his financial future.

But if the couple had signed a prenup to the contrary, he would have waived this equitable right, and the prenup would likely be enforceable, leaving him in the lurch after working all those years and supporting his family.

On the other side of the gender divide, I often represent women who are in the process of marrying very prosperous men. This is not surprising, because even in this era of employment advances for women, the data show that women still earn less than men on average, even for the same jobs. Men generally do not have a problem marrying and supporting women who have less lucrative career paths than they do. I've seen men enter into second marriages without prenups, even if they're still paying alimony from their first divorces and even with second wives who are not actively engaged in the job market. As they say, "love is blind."

Frequently the women who initiate prenups under these circumstances have been dating and cohabiting with their male partners for a long time. They insist that they love them for who they are, not for their money. Often the terms of the prenups they are about to sign will make things worse for them than if they married someone *without* money but *without* a prenup. At many points during these negotiations, the women will state that they don't want to be seen as gold diggers. At these moments, they tend to back away from terms that would benefit them and that are quite reasonable, even in a prenup.

Remember, prenups change the normal rules of marriage, generally to the detriment of the less moneyed spouse. A female spouse-to-be who is trying to eliminate the perception that she is a gold digger by signing a very restrictive prenup is putting herself in a very financially precarious situation.

4. They've known each other for six months or less.

Generally future spouses seeking prenups know each other quite well, often having cohabited for a significant period. But some of them barely know each other at all. Most of the people I see who are looking for prenups after a short engagement fall into one of three categories:

(1) the sex hormones are raging; (2) the wife-to-be is pregnant; or (3) the person wanting a prenup is marrying someone from another country, perhaps someone whose visa is about to expire. Sometimes they fit into more than one category.

Short engagements pose many problems in properly formulating and executing prenuptial agreements. There is often a lack of lead time before the wedding, which may have been planned already, with deposits paid and invitations sent out. This raises the issue of potential duress and coercion, which can possibly invalidate a prenup after the fact. (See Chapter 18.) Also, people in a rush may fail to consider the importance of what they are signing and may not pay sufficient attention to the details. I have seen this happen many times when people come to me later and ask if their prenups can be made unenforceable. Or they ask if they can amend their prenups by themselves, without the mutual consent of their spouse. (No, they can't.)

Prenups are highly technical contracts that are typically replete with "legalese." There may be a difference in education and/or English language proficiency between future spouses. This can affect one's ability to understand an agreement and its significance. Also, many people from other countries and cultures have never heard of prenups and have no idea what they are. To understand them could require a lot of remedial education and even a shift in cultural values. In some cultures, marital values and customs are very different from those in the United States. To future spouses from such countries, a prenup would seem completely antithetical to their ideal of marriage.

In the case of a premarital pregnancy, there may be a severe imbalance of power. This may lead a pregnant woman to sign almost *anything*, so that her child will be born of a marriage and not be "illegitimate." Although the term "bastard" has lately come to mean something other than a child born out of wedlock, such a birth still carries the sting of social stigma for many women, both in and outside the U.S.

When a woman is pregnant, she is usually not in a very strong bargaining position to try to improve the terms of a prenup. If she doesn't sign it, her financial situation is worse than if she signs one. Although she may be signing away some (possibly many) of her marital rights in a prenup, without a marriage she will have no marital rights at all. In either case, it's a lose-lose situation.

In addition to rushed marriages due to pregnancies, some "quickie" marriages these days are immigration marriages. Many of these are *bona fide* marriages, not marriages just to procure green cards or obtain U.S. citizenship status. But if a marriage is deemed fraudulent by the U.S. Citizenship and Immigration Services (USCIS), there is the possibility of a five-year prison term, deportation, and a fine of up to $250,000. (8 U.S.C. Section 1325.)

In every marriage-based immigration case, the Immigration Services will investigate whether the marriage is fraudulent. They will want proof that the couple married for love and not to try to get a green card for the non-citizen. They may ask for proof of commingled assets, including jointly held accounts. At the green card interview, Immigration Services may or may not question the couple about whether or not they have a prenup. If questioned about it, the couple must disclose it; otherwise the immigrant spouse could be barred from getting a green card due to misrepresentation. (See Chapter 13.)

5. The "Shaky Marriage" Syndrome.

Let's say that a couple has been cohabiting for eight years. Their relationship has always been stormy, but now they have accepted that this is its nature. They now wish to make a lifelong commitment to each other. Since they have had so much conflict in the past, however, this couple wants to determine what would happen financially if they got a divorce.

Some recent studies show that extended premarital cohabitation may be a negative screening factor toward the success of a marriage. The theory is that the legal marriage does not become "intentional" and "valuable" if a cohabitating couple simply slides into marriage. An extended period of cohabitation is a "sunk cost," as it were. Even if a relationship is not very good, a greater amount of time in one makes it harder for a partner or a couple to end it. There is also less opportunity to meet a more suitable partner if you're cohabiting. An interesting article about this phenomenon is "The 'Cohabitation Effect': The Consequences of Premarital Cohabitation," Amie Gordon, *Berkeley Science Review*, 8/12/12.

Other studies seem to find that cohabitation does not necessarily mean that marriage is more likely to fail, particularly if you take onto account the ages of couples moving in together. See "Briefing paper prepared for the Council on Contemporary Families," Arielle Kuperberg, University of North Carolina, Greensboro. Kuperberg found that the magic age is 23; if the cohabitation started at that age or older, there was no increase in the probability of divorce.

But people who have had a difficult cohabitation may have lots of questions about the future of their relationship. Such a couple may be on the right track in their desire to get a prenup signed prior to marrying. Some cohabiters have always kept their finances separate and would like to continue to do so. This can be set up in a prenup. If things change in the future and the terms of the prenup turn out to be unsustainable, they can later amend it or even abandon it by signing papers to revoke it.

6. *They are afraid of divorce, and they want to plan now for what will happen if they split up.*

This fact pattern comes up quite frequently. People hear the statistic that 50 percent of marriages end in divorce (and that 60 or 70 percent of second marriages end up in divorce) and they're scared. It appears that these statistics may be overstated. (See Chapter 5.) Perhaps each of their parents divorced. Perhaps one of the future spouses (or both of them) had a previous marriage that ended in divorce. Perhaps they felt burned by the financial terms of that divorce.

I often hear reports from both men and women clients and other people I meet that they were unfairly treated in their divorces. Generally, though, when I ask them about this, it appears that the terms of their divorces were fair in the sense that they comported with the existing law.

Perhaps he lost 50 percent of his assets, but it turns out that 100 percent of the assets was property acquired during the marriage. The court considered them marital property to be shared equally between the spouses. She complains that she didn't receive any of his retirement assets, but when I probe more deeply, I learn that she kept the family home.

Yes, divorce hurts. People feel the sting, and perhaps the engaged couple in question figures (maybe rightly so) that their chances of divorcing are significant.

There have been many studies in recent years of which factors predict a high probability of divorce. These studies have been developed by various academicians, as well as by the *National Survey of Family Growth* conducted by the U.S. Department of Health and Human Services, Centers for Disease Control and Prevention, and the National Center for Health Statistics.

Some of these contributing factors include age (older is better), levels of education (higher is better), the number of previous marriages, blended families upon remarriage, employment status, family income (again, higher is better), involvement in a religious organization, differences in ethnic or religious backgrounds, alcohol or drug abuse, a history of depression or mental illness, premarital cohabitation, and parental divorces.

A man or woman who still seethes from a previous divorce may not marry again until there is some financial certainty established for the new marriage. Previously divorced people often want to put into place financial rules that would apply if they got divorced again – whether it might happen shortly after the marriage, a "gray" divorce happening in their later years, or in years in between. They want to put into place an orderly and predictable way to divide assets and income in case the marriage ends in divorce. This is a supportable reason to have a prenup, especially since such a client is statistically more likely to divorce in a second (or subsequent) marriage than in a first marriage.

These rules can be set up in a prenup, and it can be very helpful to such a couple to alleviate the financial stress and uncertainty of getting married. In this way, a prenup can be "marriage friendly."

7. They want some certainty in the event that one future spouse has significant prior debts.

Money issues are among the leading cause of marital friction, according to many surveys. Marriage is a financial partnership (among other things) and yet people often marry without financial disclosure and a full knowledge of the spending habits and financial behavior of their future economic partner.

Every prenup requires full financial disclosure of assets, income, and debt. This disclosure must be accurate, detailed, and complete. The financial disclosures are generally included in the prenuptial agreement and are signed and acknowledged by a notary public. Anything withheld from the financial statement can be grounds for overturning the prenup.

The point here is not that a couple must have a prenup in order to provide that level of disclosure but that the prenup process will provide it. Couples can learn about each other's finances and spending habits. Certainly, they can speak directly with each other and share financial data without a prenup, and some do. But sometimes a future spouse is embarrassed to reveal a financial fact to the other.

A way to handle that is to meet with a financial advisor who can help an engaged couple analyze their assets, debts, and spending patterns and, if the couple so desires, suggest a financial plan that can then be put into place. But remember, debt is not everything. Someone may have student loan debt because their family couldn't help them with college costs. The partner who has debt may have many wonderful attributes that the other partner may not have. But it's good to get it out in the open before the marriage.

Another question that often comes up when couples are marrying is whether one future spouse will be responsible for the other's debts after the marriage. The concern may be for debts accrued before the marriage. In that case, the answer is generally no, but with some caveats. (See Chapter 7.)

It should be noted that, in general, a prenuptial agreement can't change state law with respect to a creditor's rights; state law will override what may be written in a prenup agreement. For instance, if a couple is in a community property state, both spouses are liable for debt accrued during the marriage even if it was incurred by only one of the parties. If their prenup says that the debtor spouse alone is responsible for that liability, a creditor does not have to respect that language in their "private" contract. The creditor can still collect from the couple's "community" property. A prenup, however, could require the debtor spouse to reimburse the other spouse for any such loss.

8. *One future spouse left a job and/or city, or changed a financial position, to marry the other.*

I call this one the *promissory estoppel* prenup. It happens when an individual leaves a city and/or job in order to marry someone. It happens quite frequently, and it's a very big risk for the party who has relocated. Another very common version of this pattern concerns a woman who leaves her career in order to have children and build a family in the marriage.

Promissory estoppel is a legal term. It occurs when someone makes a promise and another person reasonably relies on the promise, changes his or her position, and suffers a financial loss as a result of relying on that promise. The person who made the promise is legally "estopped" by a failure to stand by it. That's why it's called promissory estoppel.

To receive a promissory estoppel award for damages (unless voluntarily given by the promisor), there must be a lawsuit. In the case of divorce and compensation for leaving the job market to have a family, the lawsuit is the divorce action, in which divorce law essentially evaluates the loss when alimony and property division are determined.

In the case of a person relocating to marry, that person may want to have a written agreement within a prenup that provides for a non-judicial settlement of the loss, particularly if the marriage does not last a long time.

A prenup could be as simple as just providing for that: a monetary settlement for the relocating party to start over again, either in the city in which he or she lived previously or the place where that party relocated. In legal language, that's called "making the injured party whole." The settlement can vary, depending on how long after the marriage the divorce occurs.

It's hard to look into the future to determine a loss before the fact, so arbitration can be the method of choice to determine the remedy for these situations. This resolution procedure can be set into promissory estoppel prenups to create fair reimbursement for spouses who changed their positions to marry, in order to get them back on their feet, as it were, and to make them whole again.

. . .

In the next chapter, we'll look at some of the types of couples who typically seek prenups, and how these people might benefit from getting prenups before marriage.

CHAPTER 3

WHO ELSE MIGHT BENEFIT FROM A PRENUP?

Wealthy people and people from wealthy families are the usual candidates for prenups. As noted in Chapter 2, there are some other situations where prenups can be extremely helpful in creating marital peace. However, there is a caveat: a reasonable reason for a prenup can result in a toxic prenup, if the process is corrosive and the terms overreaching. (See Chapters 16 and 20.)

But with that caveat, there are some very good reasons to have a prenup, or at least explore the option.

When a new client comes to me (or an engaged couple, for prenuptial agreement mediation), I do an interview to see what issues they are facing. The typical prenup issues occur over and over again. As lawyers, we tend to call these situations (and sometimes, people themselves) "fact patterns." Usually we keep this language to ourselves, to be used among our colleagues and other attorneys. But sometimes the term slips out when we are talking with our clients. This can cause some amused reactions on the part of the clients.

But for lawyers, a fact pattern is a very important concept. In law school, we are given complex factual situations and are asked to describe how we would address the fictional client's problems as attorneys by applying the law to those specific facts. This training turns out to be very good preparation for a law career, because this is actually what we lawyers do when we practice law.

The term "practicing" law is also very significant. When lawyers get cases in a certain area of law, we see typical fact patterns and learn to devise legal solutions. The more cases we get in an area of law, the better we become at problem-solving. Our toolbox of solutions and options for our clients in that area of law becomes more substantial. So "practicing" law (similar to "practicing" medicine) is an ongoing process in which we increase our skills and ability to help people as we gain more experience.

About ten years ago, aghast at several nasty prenup agreement negotiations in which I had represented clients, I started writing about prenuptial agreements for the general public. I first wrote "Five Realties about Prenuptial Agreements – Why Having One May Be a Bad Choice for Your Marriage" and then "Ten Things I Hate about Prenuptial Agreements." (Since then I've written many articles on the topic of prenups.) I posted these articles online in several places. I think people were really impressed because an attorney had written them, and yet they criticized the brutal and insensitive way attorneys often handle prenups.

The articles went viral. Many people from all over the country are still reading them. In fact, people all over the world continue to contact me to ask my thoughts about their upcoming prenuptial agreements.

These people also share with me their experiences (mostly negative, in fact some very negative) in going through the prenup process – including the negotiation of terms, and damage to their once loving relationship. And this at a very tender time – right before the wedding. I have been contacted by people who decided to marry with a prenup they thought was very unfair. I also have been contacted by people who decided not to marry their fiancé after the other person demanded that they sign it. You might call such a person "prenup jilted."

From these contacts and the many prenup clients I work with both as counsel, consultant and mediator, my skills in the field of prenuptial agreements have greatly evolved and continue to evolve with each case I take on. This is what "practicing law" means.

There are a limited number of types of prenuptial cases patterns we see. We see them over and over again. But even within each set of "fact patterns" there are numerous variables that make the handling of each case different. Aside from the "law" and the "facts," when addressing prenups, there are many intangibles as an attorney deals with clients and opposing counsel (note that negative word, "opposing").

For instance, scratch the surface of a male attorney who is very adamant about limiting rights of a new wife, and keeping all financial control with his male client in a first marriage of relatively young people. You may find that the attorney is in his second marriage, has a "second" family, and may be paying alimony to his first wife. His view on prenups may be greatly affected by his personal experience. He may be one of those types of people who feels himself "burned" in his prior divorce because he was required to share his income after the marriage, as well as sharing the assets developed during the marriage.

Or the attorney representing the more moneyed spouse may be a female attorney who is married, or not married but has an active and well-paying professional career as a lawyer. This type of attorney may not be very sensitive or sympathetic to a woman who is a homemaker, or who has a job with low earning potential, and not a "career." That attorney might align herself with her more moneyed client, and push for restrictive economic rights for the less moneyed spouse.

Or take the attorney who is the family attorney of the wealthy parents of the future more moneyed spouse. It would be very difficult for that attorney to not follow the directions of the future more moneyed spouse's parents. If that attorney did so, that lawyer would lose an important client. That attorney essentially has a conflict of interest, because the parents' views may be contrary to the attorney's working toward the views, goals, and desires of their prenup client. These well may include the health of the marriage and the client's concern and sympathy toward the client's future spouse. (See Chapter 8.)

When I first meet a new prenuptial agreement client, I need to find out many facts in order to do my job properly. The first interview of a prenup client is very important, and it is best done by the attorney. Significant legal experience is required to tease out issues that are subtle and important in thinking about what should be in the prenup. These are best drawn out in a face-to-face verbal interview by the person who will be representing the client. This can never be adequately done by a written pre-session informational form filled out by the prospective client. That would not be adequate to permit the lawyer to do the probing that is necessary to draft a prenup that addresses a client's actual aims and situation in the most thoughtful way possible.

Some of my questions of prenup clients lead to other questions. In the prenups I draft, the aims of the prenup are clearly stated in the document, as well as the factual situations that this particular couple is dealing with. The provisions regarding the financial "rules" of the marriage organically flow from this. Each prenup is different, because each couple is different.

Prenups should not be a one-size-fits-all document. That's one of the reasons (there are many others) why online prenup forms are a mistake. The online forms will either be used when inappropriate, or will result in an inappropriate solution to a complex financial relationship that intimately affects the marriage.

Some of the financial facts that need to be brought forth and analyzed in connection with a prenup of high-income or wealthy people are quite complex. For instance, it is not enough to just know that your client (or his or her future spouse) is in a business partnership, Subchapter S corporation, or limited liability company. All the details of that business need to be revealed and analyzed. The tax returns of the business entity must be reviewed and understood. The terms of the pertinent organizational agreement must also be considered and understood. (See Chapter 9.)

There are many personal relationships that need to be teased out and understood in the first interview. Comprehending the views of the future spouses is important, particularly as they relate to finances and the economics of the upcoming marriage. But there is also a need to understand the relationships among the families of origin of each of the future spouses. The initial interview should also cover the future spouses' financial situations, their educational training and employment experience, their earnings potential, and whether or not they plan to have children.

If it's a second or subsequent marriage, then questions about the children of prior marriages become important. Also, a review of the divorce settlement agreement (sometimes called a separation agreement) from a previous marriage (and a client's obligations under it) may be essential.

Among the important questions is the inheritance potential – or "expectancy," in legal terms – of both future spouses. This is sometimes an awkward question for the clients. But it is an important one, as it often directly relates to prenups.

Some of my questions have to do with my client's financial background. Some have to do with the length of his or her relationship with the future spouse, their sources of income and earnings, and their assets. Some questions have to do with their parents, whether the parents of the future spouses remain married, and what their financial condition is.

I find out about the future spouses' business ventures and their parents' business ventures. I ask about siblings and what their financial and family situations are. If there are many divorces in the families of origin, I would like to know about it, as this may be one of the factors leading the couple to have a prenup. Having parents who divorced is a factor that may negatively affect the likelihood of longevity of the upcoming marriage. A parent's divorce may make an upcoming spouse believe his or her own marriage may not be long-lasting. On the flip side, some children of divorce report that their experiences lead them to hold onto marriage more strongly.

When it comes right down to it, lawyers are money doctors. It is certainly very true for prenup lawyers. But the special rule about prenup lawyers is that even though we deal with money and finances, we are also "marriage doctors." The document generated by our work – the prenup – has a direct and fundamental effect on this upcoming valuable personal relationship – the marriage. This is because the money terms in the prenuptial agreement resonate at the very heart of a marriage. It can have the effect of a harmonious vibration or a dissonant one.

Having said all this, what follows is a summary of the most prevalent "good" reasons for having a prenup. Although not all male clients are the more moneyed spouse, in these descriptions I have taken the liberty of using the pronouns that are most typical in the cases that come to my office.

1. Marriage in mid-thirties. He has accumulated substantial assets.

People are getting married later in life than they used to. When they marry, they are generally substantially older than their parents' ages when their parents married.

For today's millennial generation, the median age of first marriage for men is 28.7 years, and for women, 26.5 years. (*Marriage Rate Declines and*

Marriage Age Rises, D'Vera Cohn. Pew Research Center data of 2011 marriages. www.pewsocialtrends.org) This includes first marriages of the entire population, including non-college educated people. This is a big step up from 1960, when the average age for men was a little under age 23, and for women a few months older than 20. (It's possible that today the average age of first marriages is even higher than the 2011 statistic reported above.)

Delayed marriage is especially prevalent for professionals, the college educated, and people engaged in businesses. These the are people I often work with on prenups.

Some of the delay has to do with the sense that these people want to achieve financial stability and establish their careers prior to the marriage, an idea that wasn't as prevalent in the preceding generations. This is especially true of women, who in the 1960s and 1970s generally did not embark on full-blown careers. Today's world is more complex, and there are more challenges to making a living and providing for children and a household than in prior times, which may be one of the reasons for later-in-age marriages. Two-career (or two-job) families now are frequent.

Because of this delay in the age of first marriages, more of the Generation X clients (born in the mid-1960s through the early 1980s) and the Millennial clients (born in the early 1980s through the 1990s) have established careers and have accumulated assets. They are finding out about prenuptial agreements, and some of them are exploring having one prior to their marriage.

If you ask these marrying Generation X clients and millennial clients if their parents had prenups, they would almost always say no. It's very likely all four of their parents were under 25 (or in the case of millennials, under 30) when they married. It used to be that a person's career path was developed *during* marriage, not before marriage. In general, the parents had nothing at the time they were married (except each other and love), so a prenuptial agreement was not on their radar screen. In those days, marriage was viewed as a total partnership, personal and economic. Also, prenups didn't even start to be legally enforceable until the 1970s. (See Chapter 5.)

Some of the delay in marriage among my prenuptial agreement clients is due to involvement in their careers that they find enjoyable and interesting. Some may be due to the sense that marriage is not as permanent as it used to be. In actuality, the percentage of divorce has been dropping steadily since 1980, and marriage longevity may be increasing. (See Chapter 4.)

Often there is a disparity in the accumulation of assets between the future spouses. That's what may give the (more moneyed) spouse the idea that a prenup is necessary. Sometimes the spouse that accumulated the assets did it at great personal cost, by denying himself or herself disposable income in order to save part of his or her earnings.

The build-up of premarital assets by a future spouse can be significant. I have seen people in their late thirties who have accumulated $1 million dollars in assets by the time they marry without the help of family money, and working in not particularly lucrative careers. Although this is unusual, it will lead the person who has accumulated the assets to wonder about having a prenup.

This person, by his hard work, forgoing luxuries, and through diligent saving and investing, wonders if he would be required to share – perhaps equally – the premarital assets accumulated at so much personal cost if there was a divorce. (See Chapter 7.) The answer is generally no. But this is a reasonable concern that can be addressed in a prenup to put that person's mind at ease.

But there is a problem: maybe his future spouse does not want one. (This happens very often, in fact, almost invariably.) Her parents married in 1972 without a prenup, and they're doing just fine. Her parents' marriage is a true partnership. And she wonders if a prenup will change their relationship for the worse. It's certainly making their relationship much worse now while they're discussing it.

What happens when you have these two opposing views? How can they be mutually accommodated?

2. She built up an ongoing business before the marriage.

When someone is actively engaged in business that he or she created through which that person derives earnings, concerns about the business can be a trigger for wanting to have a prenup. It's different than being an employee and receiving salary or wages that are reportable on a Form W-2 for tax purposes.

Businesses (or a portion of them) that a spouse created are often considered marital assets to be divided in a divorce, especially if the spouse is actively engaged in that business during the marriage. People are concerned about several things if they divorce while engaging in a business. The first is how to quantify the non-business spouse's interest. The second is how to pay that other spouse fairly for his or her interest in the business if there is a divorce. The third is how to make sure the business-owner spouse is able to retain ownership and control of the business after a divorce. These are all valid concerns.

At the time of a prenup negotiation, that future spouse may believe that the other spouse has no rights (moral or otherwise) in the business. That future spouse's attorney needs to explain the rules about contribution to the marriage to the client. (See Chapter 4.) For purposes of the prenup, the future spouses need to figure out a way to provide fairness to the non-business spouse, and also meet the other goals of the business-owner spouse. A prenup may be a good way to do this. (See Chapter 9.)

3. He works in his parents' business.

This is a variation of the above scenario, which comes up frequently in my practice.

He works in his parents' business. That's both the good news and the bad news. The good news is that he makes a very good living in a stable family business and (hopefully) enjoys his work. He has very good job security. If everything works out, the parents will gradually let go of control of the business to him, perhaps retaining a passive income interest. After they die, he will inherit the business. Sometimes he's working with brothers or other family members in the business. The parents are probably gifting business interests to the son (or thinking of doing so in the near future) as an estate-tax saving strategy.

The bad news is that his parents are very concerned that the business stays within the bloodlines. Even though they didn't have a prenup, they are very concerned about their son's marriage. They are very afraid that if his marriage ends in divorce, the ex-spouse could have a claim on the business assets or income or worse, a claim for an ownership interest in the business. They do not want this, and want to keep claims of ex-spouses totally impossible.

His brother was going to get married, but his parents' chilled that engagement by demanding that the brother enter into a very restrictive prenup that was drafted by their business attorney. The brother's fiancé balked, and they are no longer engaged. Now they want my client (or my client's fiancé) to sign the exact same prenup for the upcoming marriage. (Another variation I've often seen is where the brother's fiancé did sign the very restrictive prenup, which puts extra pressure on the present fiancé to sign the exact same one.)

The problem in this situation is that the usual prenup "solution" by the parents' attorney (who is now their son's attorney) leaves the new spouse out in the cold financially without thinking of other ways to solve the problem of interference with the family business. After all, looking into the future, she will have contributed all her efforts to the marriage. Why will much of the future husband's efforts be off the table at the time of a divorce? The result is a very unbalanced situation.

The new non-business spouse in a first marriage is certainly worthy of developing financial security as time goes on, whether the marriage ends in divorce or death. There are other ways to think out of the box to meet both the family's goals and the new wife's and the son's goals. (See Chapter 9.)

4. The "shadow party" prenup: His parents are wealthy and want him to have a prenup to protect his inheritance and lifetime family gifts.

This is one of the most frequent prenup fact patterns I see in my practice. It's called the "shadow party" prenup. A "shadow party" in legal lingo is someone, not your client, who is influencing, or perhaps directing, the terms of the prenup. Generally, it's the parents of one of the future spouses. If their child doesn't comply, they can threaten disinheritance (which they do sometimes). Compounding this problem is that often the attorney representing the child of the wealthy parents is the parents' business or estate planning attorney.

When one of the future spouses has a family that is wealthy, often that wealth was made in the generation of the future spouse's parents. They started out with nothing and created a hugely successful business. They didn't have a prenup – a prenup was not on their radar screen and may not have been enforceable when they married. The parents' marriage may be ongoing.

But for their children, they want each child to enter marriage with a prenup. It's not just a desire — it's a demand. If a child doesn't comply, that child will go against the wishes of his parents, something the future spouse doesn't want to do. If he complies, the future wife is devastated, because she feels her fiancé is not on her side. Her feelings are hurt because of the lack of trust and the withholding of potential resources. Also, her relationship with the in-laws may be irreparably altered or damaged. The future husband is in a terrible situation – he has to either disappoint his parents or disappoint his spouse-to-be. I have not yet encountered a case where the future husband aligned with his fiancé on this.

But here is another problem imbedded in the "shadow party" situation. It has to do with the less moneyed future spouse.

She has told her parents about the prenup, because she couldn't keep something so important from them. Her parents are livid. They believe a prenup ruins the trust that a good marriage needs and makes it less than a joint venture. Her parents don't know how they will look the future husband's parents in the face at the wedding.

Often in these cases, the first draft of the prenup written by the wealthy family's business lawyer or their estate-planning attorney is overly restrictive. It may entail no sharing of assets or of income derived from the family assets whatsoever, except if the owning or earning party wishes to. Sharing would be in the complete control of the moneyed party – forever – even after death.

The entire thrust of these prenups is how the wealthier, more moneyed future spouse could minimize or eliminate the post-marriage rights of the less moneyed spouse in case of a divorce, and also ensure that the prenup would still be enforceable under that state's laws.

Every time I see one of these, I am shocked anew at its tone. The motives of the parents are not hard to see. They want to make sure a divorced ex-spouse doesn't have access to their hard-earned wealth. The difficulty is why would the son want or permit a document like this sent out to his future spouse in his name, when he loved her enough to plan a marriage to her. This is always a very hurtful moment. Tears are often shed. Hers.

And this type of prenup may be unnecessary to achieve the parents' goal, because the wealthy parents can (and usually do) get to the same result by creating an estate plan that involves passing property to their child through trusts to keep property within bloodlines. Also, a requirement to share income earned from these business assets is not such a terrible thing. In fact, it can be very healthy to a marriage. (See Chapters 8 and 17.)

5. "Gray" prenups for later-in-life marriages.

This is one of the best reasons to have a prenup. Two people are marrying. They have children from their previous marriages. The previous marriages either ended in death or divorce. They want to make sure the children from their previous marriage inherit at least some of their property, but also want to make sure their new surviving spouse is protected. They have loyalty to both their children and their new spouse. Another complicating factor is that sometimes one or more of the grown children needs financial help during their parent's lifetime, which can cause marital strain unless discussed with the future spouse and pre-planned by the new elder spouses.

Having a prenup in this situation can be a very good thing. It tends to create peace within the newly extended blended family, because inheritance and money are addressed in a way that encourages trust and respect. It often makes provisions for the children of each of the new spouses upon their parent's death. It thus takes into account the reasonable wish of a parent to provide for his or her own children at death. This often results in greater acceptance of the new step-parent. The prenup also can provide security for each of the new spouses. It balances the financial loyalty a person has to the children of a previous marriage and concern and love for the new spouse in a reasonable and rational way.

In some gray prenups, income and assets are left totally separate and under the control of the owner of the assets. Keeping everything separate can be appropriate in some situations, especially if each future spouse has independent financial security at the time of the marriage.

But it is important that the new couple take a good look at their own future financial security. This is often left out in a gray prenup. As a loving gesture, elder spouses need to ensure that the other spouse will be financially secure in case of death of one of the new spouses, and perhaps even in the event of divorce.

There are inheritance planning options that can help the elder couple meet both goals – to provide for each other, and to provide for their own children. One of the most effective in this situation is QTIP and credit shelter trusts, which allow the surviving spouse to be supported during his or her lifetime, while still providing for distributions to the children of the first marriage. (See Chapter 10.)

Anyone marrying later in life should keep in mind the possibility of an extended stay in a long-term skilled nursing facility at the end of life. Although this won't happen to every person, it is a significant financial risk. Having a prenup that says that one of the spouses will not be liable for the other's nursing home cost will not work to limit the "community" spouse's obligation. Federal and state Medicaid laws override prenups, which are essentially private contracts between spouses. (See Chapter 11 for more information on "gray" prenups.)

6. People who want to fix a bad prenup.

I see a number of clients who come to me after their marriage has taken place, perhaps several years afterward. They had a very corrosive prenuptial agreement negotiation process, generally running very close to the wedding. They each had a lawyer, and with the back and forths, they just didn't have time to get the terms of the prenup to where they wanted it, and signed it anyway.

They were both very angry about the resulting document. They both felt their lawyers didn't listen to what they had said, but went ahead and wrote up what the attorneys themselves thought was right. They both feel very bad about this, and it's been eating away at them since the marriage.

Fixing bad prenups and helping overcome corrosive experiences can be a very important job for a prenuptial agreement lawyer or prenuptial agreement mediator. Bad prenups can be fixed and good prenups created.

They now want to see me (generally as a mediator) to review the prenup with them and help them formulate changes. They want the changes to be reflected in an amendment to the prenup. They are more relaxed about the financial aspects of their relationship now that they have been married for several years and have a child, which in their minds has changed things a lot.

Depending on what state you live in, you may be amending a prenup or entering into a postnuptial agreement. Different rules of enforceability may apply to each. (See Chapter 19.) But in any event, you can revise your prenup after the marriage to reflect your current wishes and situations. If you both wish to change it, you ought to take steps to create the revision and make it a legal document.

People with prenups also have the power to terminate their prenup completely. This should be done with much thought, and with a formal written agreement, signed by both spouses and acknowledged by a notary public. It's best to consult counsel prior to embarking on this.

7. People who didn't have time to do a prenup – the "prenup-postnup."

This is another frequent fact pattern. The wedding date is looming. The prenup is complex or they just can't decide on certain issues. They have been working on it (plus doing wedding planning) for two months. The wedding is two weeks away, and the prenup is still not ready. They want to focus on the wedding now, and on their joy to be marrying each other, without thinking about the prenup. The prenup process has been a horrific experience, which keeps taking them into a bad mental state. They do not want to ruin their wedding with this.

They both agree to put it off until after the marriage. They want to give it a rest. Even though the prenup was initiated by the more moneyed spouse, he trusts his wife-to-be to continue the process after the marriage. Each relies on the cooperation and good faith of their promise to finish the prenup after their marriage.

But now the prenuptial agreement is called a "postnuptial" agreement, and it may be subject to different rules regarding enforceability than a prenup. (See Chapter 19.)

CHAPTER 4

WHAT ARE "GENEROUS" PRENUPS AND THE ROLE OF "CONTRIBUTION" TO MARRIAGE?

Generosity, contribution, and creating financial security are crucial to the health and success of a marriage. Not realizing the negative consequences, many people (especially young people) may sign prenups that distort these values and put negative pressure on their unions before the fact. A prenuptial agreement can encourage asset hoarding when unnecessary and can upset the balance of control in a marriage so that many major decisions are made by just one of the spouses, another destabilizing aspect of prenups.

Generosity in marriage.

What does *generosity* have to do with marital success? Recent studies have shown what everyone always knew – the importance of generosity in marriage. But since academics have to prove these common-sense concepts with studies, here's a summary of the recent studies on the topic.

One of the academic institutions interested in this topic is the University of Notre Dame, which established The Science of Generosity Initiative in 2009 with a $5 million grant from the John Templeton Foundation. The Initiative includes funding for scientific research on generosity as applied to marriages.

Part of this money was put to use to fund a major study of marital generosity headed by W. Bradford Wilcox, a sociology professor at the University of Virginia, who is director of the National Marriage Project (NMP) at the university. According to its mission statement, NMP is a nonpartisan, nonsectarian, and interdisciplinary initiative that conducts research and analysis on the health of marriage in America. Included in its mission is research aimed at identifying strategies to increase marital quality and stability.

An academic research study, "Generosity and the Maintenance of Marital Quality," was one of the results of this funding. (75 *Journal of Marriage and Family*, 1218–1228 (2013) hereinafter the "Wilcox/Drew Study.") Wilcox and Jeffrey Drew, a professor of family studies at Utah State University, conducted the study, which involved a survey of 1,365 married couples, ages 18 to 45, from across the U.S. The study examined whether generosity in marriage was associated with increased marital quality.

The research study defined generosity as "small acts of kindness, displays of respect and affection" and "a willingness to forgive one's spouse his or her faults and failings." The study found that generosity was positively correlated with marital satisfaction and negatively associated with marital conflict and perceived divorce likelihood. Lack of generosity was correlated to reports of thoughts of divorce, or "subjective divorce likelihood," as the study terms it.

The study concluded that both the receipt of marital generosity from one's spouse and the giving of marital generosity to one's spouse are associated with marriages that report a higher level of satisfaction. The opposite is also true: less generosity means less marital satisfaction and more marital conflict. So generosity works on both the giving and receiving levels in a marriage.

The study shows that marital quality is at its lowest when neither party behaves in a generous manner. There is also decreased satisfaction when there is an imbalance of levels of generosity.

To be fair in summarizing the results of the Wilcox/Drew Study, due to "limitations of data" noted in the study, Wilcox and Drew are not sure whether the generosity enhances the marital quality, or whether good marital quality brings about more generosity. They conclude that generosity and marital quality are related, and suggest that future researchers should examine the reasons why.

Notwithstanding the "chicken or the egg" dilemma referred to above, it is clear what Wilcox's own view is. As Wilcox later explained in the *New York*

Times, "Living that spirit of generosity in a marriage does foster a virtuous cycle that leads to both spouses on average being happier in the marriage." ("The Generous Marriage," Tara Parker-Pope, *New York Times*, December 8, 2011.)

The Wilcox/Drew study cites a number of other studies that conclude that generous behavior communicates a desire to "invest in" the relationship and thereby can lead to its success and continuance. This type of interaction is termed "relationship maintenance behavior." The receiver of generosity has an increased sense that his or her expectations for the relationships are met. This increases marital satisfaction and stability.

If giving and receiving are at roughly equal levels, partners in the relationship will report they are happy in their marriage. This is a concept that seems analogous to the concept of contribution to marriage (see below), because contribution, also, is a gift of generosity. When contribution of spouses in a marriage is in balance, the marriage generally works.

This finding directly relates to prenuptial agreements.

The driving purpose behind (most) prenups is to identify resources and assets that will be held separate from the other spouse and put beyond their reach. In fact, in its typical form, a prenup is the opposite of generosity.

There are ways to make a prenup more generous. One of them is to put into the contract planned generosity to the less moneyed spouse to lighten that spouse's financial load.

Generosity by paying premarital debt.

Paying a spouse's premarital debts is a very good example of how to build generosity into a marriage. This can be a term that is part of a prenup.

Many young people have accumulated substantial student loan debt in order to acquire their college educations and professional degrees. What is the level of the debt? What are the terms? Does the couple plan to view this as a separate debt during the marriage, or will they agree to use excess marital funds to pay it down or off during the marriage?

Another issue to think about is why is there student debt? Perhaps one of the spouses had to put themselves through college and graduate school, and the other spouse's education was paid for by their parents. Is it fair to penalize the future spouse who was not raised by an upper middle-class family? Family of origin issues need to be thought about and the meaning of these different backgrounds processed.

Often the couple will view the student loan debt as personal to the spouse who incurred the debt for that spouse's education. Or the more moneyed party simply accepts the standard form of prenup provided by their attorney that says that each party is responsible for their premarital debt. I see this presumption that debt should stay with the debtor party as flawed logic.

Consider the following scenario. What if one spouse incurred a lot of undergraduate and law school debt? Say that spouse got a law degree and is a practicing lawyer who earns a good living. What if the spouses contribute all their earnings to the household? Doesn't it make sense for the couple to view the student loan debt as a household debt, similar to a mortgage? Questions arise, of course, if the marriage ends in divorce and the student loan isn't fully paid off. These questions can be addressed either by the couple in their divorce negotiations, or in the prenup.

The problem when a party to a prenup is held responsible for his or her debts is that the party will need to use earnings to pay them off, earnings that then can't be shared with the other partner. That causes an imbalance. In an extreme reaction to a future spouse's premarital debt, the prenup may then say that all earned income is separate, and that each party pays a portion of each expense. That might be okay for friends or cohabiting partners, but it may be detrimental for the flowing togetherness and mutual generosity that supports a marriage.

In the standard prenup, student loan debt and other debts such as credit card debt is firmly put into the "separate property/separate debt" category to be paid by the person responsible for incurring it. But it doesn't have to be. Think out of the box if you are embarking on a prenup. Make thoughtful decisions about everything.

If you want to lessen the "separate debt" regimen, you can think of premarital debt as a marital debt either initially, or over a period of years. The debt payments can "vest" as marital debts according to a schedule of the couple's choosing.

There can be either mandatory or precatory (aspirational) language in the prenup talking about how and when and by whom that student loan or credit card debt will be paid. The agreement may say that income earned by the parties during the marriage *may* be used to pay down this debt (precatory), or *shall* be used (mandatory). A commitment to help one's spouse relieve a spouse's financial burden is a strong gesture of love, commitment, and generosity.

When my parents grew up during the Great Depression, both their families suffered greatly due to unemployment. One of the casualties was dental care. By the time my parents got married, my mother's teeth were in very bad shape, and many had been extracted due to lack of funds when she was growing up.

Fixing my mother's teeth became the first priority for my young parents in their marriage. It took many years and multiple expenditures when money was still tight. But they got my mother the dental care she needed in the first years of their marriage. It involved many extractions and many dental bridges. It was so important to them that I learned about it from them as a very young child, although the dental work was completed before my birth.

They were very proud of this joint venture and often spoke of it. It helped cement their marriage. It meant they cared about each other. Often prenups can interfere with loving gestures like this one.

Many couples do the same as my parents did for each other when they marry. A more wealthy spouse may pay off his or her future spouse's credit card bills, or other debt, such as a car loan. These are wedding presents that have perhaps even more meaning of commitment and love than a wedding ring with a large diamond. Also, it's good for married couples to start off with a clean financial slate, if possible. One party shouldn't be burdened by something that's easily resolvable by the other party.

Generosity can be alive and well even *within* a prenup if the parties (guided by their attorneys) can build it into their prenup. (See Chapter 17 for some drafting ideas on how to reflect and support generosity.) That's how you can start to build a Generous Prenup.

What is "Contribution to Marriage"?

"Contribution to marriage" is a legal concept that addresses the mutual efforts that make a marriage work. It is one of the touchstones of a good marriage. Marriages can fail if contributions are not balanced or appreciated.

"Contribution" is a legal concept akin to "generosity," because when a party contributes to a marriage, they are exhibiting generosity to the other spouse. Generosity and contribution are really the flip sides of one coin. Nurturing both sides of the coin is crucial to sustaining a healthy marriage.

The interpretation of "contribution to marriage" in every state includes both monetary and non-monetary contributions to the marital venture. Spouses bring different efforts to the union. The law in every state respects householding efforts as much as income-earning efforts. When one person is contributing 100 percent of their efforts to the marriage and the other person less than 100 percent, because perhaps his or her business was designated in a prenup as "separate property," the marriage can fail due to the imbalance of contributions.

Here's an example of how that can happen. I see this over and over again in the prenup cases that come to my office.

It's Thursday morning. I get an email from someone named Julie. She's to be married in three months. She is a librarian in a public library.

Her fiancé, Robert, wants a prenup. She is 31. Her fiancé is 35. Julie's conception of marriage was to share all aspects of life – including financial. That's what her parents did, and they are still married, and financially comfortable.

Robert is involved in a business he started right after college. It's grown to be quite a large business, involving many employees. It produces significant revenue, producing a healthy net income for Robert.

Robert had told Julie he wanted a prenup but was not specific about the terms.

Four months after the prenup is mentioned (and three months before the wedding), Julie gets the draft. She doesn't understand most of the legalese, but she does see in the draft that Robert wants all his interest (present and future) in this business in which he is actively engaged to be his separate property.

The draft prenup says that any proceeds from his businesses will also be separate property. During the marriage, he's willing to pool part of his income (the part designated as "salary" on his tax return) with Julie's salary to support them and their new family. But any business income earned by Robert that is not characterized as "salary" would be Robert's separate property. The amount of "business income" on his tax return dwarfs the amount of money Robert receives as "salary." Robert wants to be able to grow the business by continuing to use the part of his income designated as "business income" back into the businesses. He also wants to keep the growth of the value of the business as his separate property.

What's wrong with this picture?

This is a scenario I see over and over again. It involves a clash between a cooperative view of marriage as a financial joint venture and an autonomous view — that marriage should consist of independent activities with certain defined and limited modes of financial sharing.

But it is also understandable from Robert's point of view that he should have some credit for the 13 years prior to the marriage that he formed and grew his business. Somehow this needs to be addressed in ways that reflect his post-marital work in the business. Also, Julie's interest in having both their contributions count needs to be addressed. Robert and Julie (and their attorneys) will need to figure out what will happen if the parties divorce, especially if that happened in the later years of the marriage.

But does the draft prenup adequately reflect these goals and the sense of what the marriage will be of both Robert and Julie, and what might be fair in the future?

Julie is starting to grasp what marriage to Robert would look like. They expect to have children right away. She has not accumulated significant assets. Her income is average for a college grad of her age and geographic area. She expects to drop out of the job market for a while to raise a family.

The result would be that Julie's efforts would be devoted 100 percent to the marriage, and Robert's wouldn't.

Julie would be the primary parent and householder while Robert worked. She would continue her career as a librarian perhaps part-time after the children started school, perhaps full-time some time later. She would hear about

Robert's business success, and perhaps she would know about his additional investments of proceeds from the income of his business (which would remain separate property).

Perhaps at some point he would sell his business. Those proceeds would also be separate property. Because the prenup only counted "wage" income as marital, even if Robert also shared some of his "business" income (as he promises, in encouraging Julie to sign the draft prenup), Robert would retain almost total financial control of the couple's resources.

When she re-read the terms of the prenup she was presented with and discussed them with her attorney, her feelings toward Robert were at a low point. And this was three months before the planned marriage. Why would a person who said he loved her treat her like this?

Aside from her financial fears about the future, she found Robert's control of what he wanted to share with her intolerable. After all, she was going to share *all* her efforts with Robert. He was basically withholding much of his efforts from her and the family they were going to create. This didn't seem very much like a partnership to Julie.

What the law says about it.

People feel good about their marriages if they feel the other spouse is contributing as much as he or she is. Conversely, people are dissatisfied with their marriages if they feel the other person is not pulling his or her weight. Most of the complaints about marriage that divorce lawyers hear involve the concept of "contribution." The problem with prenups is that many of them directly lead to a significant imbalance of contributions to a marriage, which turns into marital strife.

The legal concept of "contribution to marriage" is one that is reflected in states' statutes and further developed in the case law. It applies to both property division and alimony in virtually all states. The law clearly provides that contributions to marriages can be economic and non-economic.

Often, the wife in a marriage leaves the full-time job market for a while to focus on having a family. When she returns to the job market, it is often at first part-time. Even when she returns to full-time work, her lifetime earning potential is compromised. This is true even if the woman had a professional career prior to marriage. She has left her career and relegated it to second place to concentrate on her family, home, and marriage.

This can work out just fine if the marriage lasts, but what if there is a divorce? How can a wife's contribution be fairly valued if a prenup signed years before the breakup says that it won't be fairly valued? Prenups that reward financial activity over family and home contributions do just that. In fact, that is exactly what Robert and Julie's draft prenup (described above) does. It lets him keep some of his efforts to himself, while Julie is sharing all of hers.

In many states, lost economic opportunity is embedded into the law as a factor in divorces. Massachusetts law is typical. For purposes of both alimony and property division, it takes into account the economic and *non-economic* contribution of both parties to the marriage as a factor to be considered. In Massachusetts, a court will consider occupation, amount and sources of income, vocational skills, employability, and opportunity of each for future acquisition of assets or income when determining property division. The court is also specifically permitted to take into account the contribution of a party as homemaker to the family. (Mass. Gen. Laws chapter 208, § 34.)

For purposes of alimony, under Massachusetts law, factors include "income, employment and employability of both parties, including employability through reasonable diligence and additional training, if necessary; economic and non-economic contribution of both parties to the marriage; marital lifestyle; ability of each party to maintain the marital lifestyle; lost economic opportunity as a result of the marriage; and such other factors as the court considers relevant and material." (Mass. Gen. Laws chapter 208, § 53.)

In valuing non-economic contributions for purposes of alimony and property division, Massachusetts is in alignment with virtually all the other states.

The concept of "contribution to marriage" plays out in many court cases involving division of assets in a divorce. Looking at these cases gives insight as to how courts define what "contribution" is, how it's valued, and the various types of contributions people make in their marriages. The upshot of these cases (and state statutes) is that a party's contributions as a homemaker is an important factor to be considered in distributing financial assets after a divorce.

For instance, a New York court articulated a wife's contributions as homemaker as follows:

> Marriage is an economic partnership . . . with a significant noneconomic component. The nonremunerated efforts of raising children, making a home, performing a myriad of personal services and providing physical and emotional support are, among other noneconomic ingredients of the marital relationship, at least as essential to its nature and maintenance as are the economic factors, and their worth is consequently entitled to substantial recognition. *Capasso v. Capasso*, 506 N.Y.S.2d 686 (1986).

As an Illinois Court put it:

> Like a commercial partnership, the parties in a marriage function by sharing duties and by dividing their labor, without which the relationship could not succeed. It is conceded that the relationship cannot successfully operate without the acquisition of some capital. The accumulation of that capital, however, will not occur, especially if children are present, unless the homemaker-spouse contributes a significant part of her energies to the marriage. The services of both are necessary for the continuance of the relationship. *In re Marriage of Haffey*, 206 Ill. App.3d 859 (1990).

The result is that marriage is viewed as a shared enterprise akin to a financial partnership, in which the parties are equal partners and should share equally in all the results of the marriage, including the financial results. The laws in all states start with the presumption that all property developed during the marriage is marital.

There are some proponents for valuing the wager earner's efforts as more valuable than the homemaker's efforts. But these views generally do not succeed in court actions. These proponents attempt to argue that that all of a wife and mother's duties should be valued on an hourly basis in a divorce.

For instance, some of her services could be valued on an hourly basis as an employee working as a nanny, personal shopper, cook, or housekeeper. But you cannot adequately value making a home for the family in monetary terms. There is a meaningful and profound contribution made by a homemaker and mother that is not present when the duties are done by hired help. (This is not meant to disparage dual-party working spouses. That is simply another valid choice spouses can make as a couple.)

One could say that by giving a married couple the ability to have children and raise them is a form of "capital" that our social culture assesses as equal to the monetary capital that can be earned by a husband who is freed up to earn income and amass property during the marriage. The courts merely reflect and affirm these cultural values. What happens to the marriage with a prenup that does not affirm these cultural values? These values have arisen for a reason. What happens when they're taken away?

It reminds me of an old joke I heard in my childhood that was going around in my parents' generation. Its goes like this:

A boy was born with a hexagonal nut in his navel. It caused him much embarrassment as he grew up. He couldn't remove it no matter how hard he tried. Finally, after he became a young man, he traveled to Tibet because he heard that there was a wise man there who might help him remove the hexagonal nut. After climbing up the mountain he was told to sit down. The wise man told him to remove the hexagonal nut in his navel. He began to unscrew it. He turned the screw for many hours. Finally, the screw came off. Very excited, the young man stood up, and his butt fell off.

Why did I bring up this joke here? What possible relevance does the joke about the hexagonal nut in the navel have to prenuptial agreements?

Jokes, as we all know, often have an element of seriousness. At their core, they are not funny at all. The "hexagonal-nut-in-the-navel joke" is an example of this.

It teaches us that we may not know the reason for something, but if we monkey around with it, we can destroy something very essential and precious. Removing the "nut in the navel" in a prenup by creating terms regulating a marriage that are different than what has developed in our laws and culture can have severe repercussions to a marriage. That's because you are monkeying around with the very basis (the "boilerplate," if you will) of what a marriage is. Figuratively speaking, when you enter into a prenup, make sure that you have not disturbed the basic balance of a marriage. Otherwise, when you stand up – well, now you know the rest of the joke.

• • •

Getting back to Robert and Julie, it is now 30 years after the marriage. Robert's "separate" business is now worth $10 million, rather than the $300,000 it was valued at when the marriage began. Will Julie be fairly compensated if she put her career on the back burner to take care of children, household, and family? Not if she signed the "usual" prenup that says the value of Robert's business as well as any increase in its value belongs to Robert.

Think about how this inequality may reverberate through the marriage. Perhaps Julie didn't really think about what might happen in the future when she signed it. But as time went by, she started realizing that she was contributing 100 percent of her efforts toward the marriage and Robert was not. He may have been contributing his salary toward the marriage, but not the build-up in value in his business, or the "business income" that was not characterized as salary.

She knew how much the value of the business was increasing during the years by seeing various financial reports of the business. She also saw that Robert had lots of investments in his own name that were purchased by the business income he was allowed to keep under the prenup. Julie started to feel cut out and hurt. It was now 30 years into the marriage, and obviously she could not, at that point, start a major career. Bad feelings ensued. Robert felt badly, too, but he was a businessman. He thought "a contract is a contract." He didn't want to relinquish the benefits he had under the prenup contract.

What if the marriage ends in divorce? This prenup had predetermined a grossly unbalanced "contribution to marriage" regime. It may have been the major culprit in the breakdown of this marriage. The prenup became a self-fulfilling prophecy leading to divorce. That's the problem couples marrying who want a prenup face – how to structure a prenup that does not weaken the marriage and make divorce more likely.

(See Chapter 9 for ways to address this potential imbalance and still have control and ownership of the business remain with active spouse after a divorce, while giving the other spouse a fair shake for his or her contributions to the marriage.)

How prenups set up a control problem.

The distinction between "separate property" and "marital property" (which all prenups set up) has a direct effect on the behavior of the spouse owning the separate property, and on the sensitivities of the non-owning spouse. This distinction is bound to impact the undercurrents of the marriage, unless both parties are similarly situated in terms of assets and income.

People with separate assets will tend to think about them, looking at the monthly reports of the securities company holding the assets. They will work to better the results in any separate real estate and other separate assets owned. What if the marital funds are inadequate to take a financial step that the couple wishes to take? The non-moneyed spouse will wonder why a contribution of separate assets or income can't be made to help the marital unit proceed with their financial aims. Most prenups track contributions of separate property into joint property and require that this property be returned to the spouse owning the separate property. Most also divide any upside gain between the two investments. The temporary contribution of separate property may have a negative emotional impact on the less moneyed spouse.

Yes, the more moneyed spouse can decide to freely contribute separate property to the marital estate. That's in all prenups. But the element of control held by only one party can upset the balance of control in a marriage. When many major decisions are made by just one of the spouses, this can upset a marriage, and it is another destabilizing aspect of prenups. (See Chapter 17, "Is There a Way to Make Both Parties Happy?")

. . .

In this chapter, I've described the importance of generosity in marriage, the problems prenups pose, and how non-financial contributions are very important to acknowledge and appreciate in a long-term successful marriage. In the other chapters of this book, you will find much detail on techniques to build in generosity into a prenup, and how to balance this with the understandable goals of the more moneyed spouse. In all prenups, a balance needs to be struck between providing fairness, marital protection, and security for both parties, and an economic structure that reflects the parties' contributions of their time, attention, and work toward the success of the marriage.

CHAPTER 5

HOW DID PRENUPS ORIGINATE AND HOW POPULAR ARE THEY?

In the not-so-distant past, courts and lawmakers rejected the validity of prenuptial agreements. The rejection was based on cultural values; it was the common and deep-seated belief that prenups encouraged and promoted divorce. Marriage was thought of as a permanent relationship. As a result, prenups were believed to be contrary to the public policy of supporting and maintaining marriages, since they included contractual divorce provisions.

Public policy is a legal concept through which the amalgam of custom, culture, protection, and moral values combine to synthesize the laws and court decisions that regulate the social order of people. Public policy is one of the permissible grounds on which courts can make findings and support decisions in cases. As a matter of "public policy," the maintenance of the institution of marriage was (and is, to this day) protected.

In the 1970s, things began to change. Laws were enacted giving validity to prenuptial agreements and courts began enforcing them. Now, prenuptial agreements are enforceable (with safeguards) in all 50 states. Prenups are now either allowed by statute in many states, or by cases that have been decided by state courts (termed "case law"). In jurisdictions where there are prenuptial agreement statutes, court cases fill out the details of the statutory laws.

The divorce rate statistics, as well as the frequency of couples seeking prenups in the media, will also be discussed later in this chapter.

A short history of prenups – why they were deemed unenforceable before 1970.

When people married in the 1970s or even in the 1980s, prenuptial agreements were extremely rare – almost nonexistent. State courts generally refused to honor them by finding them unenforceable. Why? Because courts, reflecting social values of the day, believed that prenuptial agreements "contemplated" divorce in that they facilitated or encouraged divorce and therefore led to marital instability.

As the Virginia Supreme Court put it, "[a] contract which incites the hope of financial profit from the separation of married people should not be enforced." *Cumming v. Cumming*, 102 S.E. 572 (Va. 1920).

A 1931 article in a well-respected legal research series articulated the dangers of prenups in these words:

> An antenuptial contract limiting the husband's liability to a certain sum in case of separation invites disagreement, encourages separation, and incites divorce proceedings, thereby tending to overthrow and destroy those principles of the law of marriage requiring that the husband and wife live together during their natural life, and that the husband, within his financial ability, shall support his wife; and because of the interest that the public has in such causes, the question of alimony is a matter for the court, and the action of the court will not be controlled by an antenuptial agreement of the parties on this subject. 70 *American Law Reports* 826 (1931).

This quote emphasizes the historical responsibility of a husband to support his wife. This obligation was an integral part of the marriage contract, because wives in general did not work outside the home. As a result, the public policy aimed at protecting wives would not permit the support obligation to be modified by a contract between the parties. Similar protections still apply today with respect to children – parents cannot contract away or settle children's rights in a divorce or in a prenup.

An exception to this rule was prenups that settled property rights of spouses that would come into effect upon the death of one of the spouses.

The thought was that this made sense due to the estate-planning needs of spouses in second marriages with blended families. This type of prenup was enforceable in many states, either by case law or by statute. See, e.g., *Del Vecchio v. Del Vecchio*, 143 So 2d 17 (Fla. 1962).

The invalidity of prenups with respect to divorce prior to the 1970s was also related to the nature of property rights of spouses under prior law. At that time, most property developed during a marriage (and before the marriage) was titled in the husband's name. In a divorce, whoever held title to property owned it. This made support rights for women crucial in divorces. Since there were limited or no property rights for a wife in a divorce, there was very firm public policy against prenups, because prenups could limit support rights for women. Laws providing for equitable distribution of property between spouses at divorce changed this "title" concept. These laws started coming into effect in the 1970s. (See Chapter 7.)

In addition, courts and legislators believed that by limiting a husband's financial obligations for spousal support upon divorce, prenups provided a ready-made exit plan. (This is still a well-founded objection to prenups.) As a result, the stability of marriages would be weakened and "wife dumping" would be encouraged, because the husband would have no or limited financial repercussions. (See Chapter 15 and Texas alimony laws.)

The Tennessee Appeals Court articulated this assumption with a somewhat brutal hypothetical:

> Such contract [prenuptial agreement] could induce a mercenary husband to inflict on his wife any wrong he might desire with the knowledge his pecuniary liability would be limited. In other words, a husband could through abuse and ill treatment of his wife force her to bring an action for divorce and thereby buy a divorce for a sum far less than he would otherwise have to pay. *Crouch v. Crouch*, 53 Tenn. App. 594 (1964).

Courts also viewed that a marriage was not just between the two spouses, but between the spouses and the state (through its judicial system).

The state was viewed as a third party to the marriage. (This view still holds true in every state.) In a Florida case, the court stated as follows:

> The law is well settled that contracts intended to facilitate or promote the procurement of a divorce will be declared illegal as contrary to public policy. The reason for the rule as defined by the law writers is that a suit for divorce is in realty a triangular proceeding in which the husband, the wife and the state are all parties. The marital relation, unlike ordinary relations, is regarded by the law and the state as the basis of the social organization. The preservation of that relation is deemed essential to the public welfare. *Gallemore v. Gallemore*, 94 Fla. 516 (1927).

There were also religious concerns involving the sanctity of marriage and the promotion of private morality that required oversight by the court system. The upshot was that the relationship between spouses should not be determined by private contract.

Here's how the Florida Supreme Court put it in *Potter v. Potter*:

> Our civilization and moral standards rest largely upon the existence of homes and the family relation. The existence of the family relation is based upon the sanctity of the marriage relation and for that reason the State is a party interest in every marriage contract and so zealously does it regard and guard this interest for the promotion of public welfare and of private morals as to hold itself to be a party to every marriage contract which is entered into or recognized by the parties within its jurisdiction. *Potter v. Potter*, 101 Fla. 1199 (1931).

Why did the courts and society change their views about prenups?

As we have seen, prenups were previously viewed by courts and society as altering the essential elements of marriage and also marital rights upon divorce or separation. Why and how did courts start changing their views about prenups around 1970?

Divorce was starting to become more easily obtainable. California was the first to adopt "no-fault" divorce in its Family Law Act of 1969, which became effective on January 1, 1970. Under this new law, there was no longer a need for a "guilty" party in the divorce action. It provided for dissolution of marriage on the basis of "irreconcilable differences." One party alone could obtain a divorce on these grounds without the assent of the other.

The new California law was a momentous change in the law. Prior to that, there had to be specific "fault" grounds for a divorce, such as adultery, mental cruelty, habitual intoxication, or abandonment. The new "irreconcilable differences" grounds eliminated the need for couples to have or fabricate "fault" grounds for divorce, the latter which had been a common practice. By 1977, nine states had adopted no-fault divorce laws. The last laggard state to allow no-fault divorce was New York, which finally allowed it in 2010.

The first seminal prenup case was the famous *Posner* case from the Florida Supreme Court.

The *Posner* court began by discussing the "sanctity" of marriage. Marriage – once thought to be practically indissoluble once entered into – had started to change. Even without universal recognition of no-fault divorce, in *Posner*, the court took judicial notice that the ratio of marriages to divorces had reached a "disturbing rate" in many states. It further noted that many groups were advocating no-fault divorce laws. *Posner v. Posner*, 233 So.2d 381 (1970).

Among the groups at that time advocating for no-fault divorce were the American Bar Association's Family Law Section and the National Conference of Commissioners of Uniform State Laws, which had drafted a no-fault provision into the Uniform Marriage and Divorce Act.

On the other side of the philosophical divide, some people remained against the no-fault divorce laws. When California's no-fault statute was passed, Ronald Reagan was governor of California. He later confessed to his son, Michael, that signing the law one the "greatest regrets" of his political career, believing it led the country to increased divorces and marital instability.

Notes on reasons for the increased divorce rate.

From 1960 through 1980, the divorce rate more than doubled from 9.2 divorces per 1,000 married women to 22.6 divorces per 1,000 married women. (*The Evolution of Divorce*, W. Bradford Wilcox (2009), 34 *National Affairs*, Winter 2018.) Part of this reflected the change in divorce laws, which lent moral legitimacy to divorce. But factors other than changes in the divorce law were at play in the increase of the divorce rate in the 1970s and 1980s.

The women's movement started to question the acceptance of the "male head of household" paradigm and the assumption that women's roles were confined to the home. Women began to have different and increased expectations of marriage.

The sexual revolution of the 1960s and 1970s added to the destabilization of marriage. Extramarital partners became more common, and expectations for fulfillment in marriage (sexual and otherwise) increased. People left their marriages much more readily than ever before. There was also an anti-institutional and anti-church view that became prevalent that reduced the perception of the permanence and "sanctity" of marriage.

The rate of young adults graduating from college doubled between 1950 and 1970. Laws changed. Women were becoming creditworthy without the signature of their husbands. Women were entering the job force in greater numbers. Women were now becoming capable of providing their own support and did not have to rely on the historical protection of men. They were free to leave marriages. This was a great change for women who would have been economically forced to stay in an unhappy marriage. Divorces were beginning to be a commonplace fact of life, rather than an exception.

Posner and its progeny.

Ultimately, the Florida Supreme Court in *Posner* concluded that with "divorce such a commonplace fact of life," it was reasonable to want to settle the financial terms of a marriage prior to the wedding by a prenup.

The solution in the *Posner* case was for courts to allow prenuptial agreements if they had certain protections both at the signing and when the agreement came into effect. One of these is that the prenup was not initially intended to procure a divorce. Prenups would no longer be void *ab initio* as "contrary to public policy" but would be allowed or disallowed on a case-by-case basis. There would be other protections, such as full disclosure and knowing waiver of marital rights in order for a prenup to be allowed. (See Chapter 18 on enforceability.)

Other courts soon followed *Posner*. Some of them started saying that prenups might actually *promote* the stability of a marriage. The argument was that if a couple could have a marital contract more suited to their needs and values, their marriage could have a better chance of surviving.

As the Supreme Court of California put it:

> Neither the reordering of property rights to fit the needs and desires of the couple, nor realistic planning that takes account of the possibility of dissolution, offends the public policy favoring and protecting marriage. It is only when the terms of an agreement go further – when they promote and encourage dissolution, and thereby threaten to induce the destruction of a marriage that might otherwise endure – that such terms offend public policy. *Marriage of Dawley*, 17 Cal.3d 342 (1976).

The ongoing challenge of prenups – then and now – is to distinguish between prenups that make equitable property and financial planning agreements that support and encourage marriages, and those prenups that have financial terms that promote and encourage divorce. This is a slippery slope, indeed. This is, in essence, the subject of this book.

Because of the prevalence of divorces, there were more second and third marriages of older people who had accumulated substantial assets and had children from previous marriages. Thus, as the Supreme Court of Alaska said, prenups could reduce conflicts "that naturally inhere in these later marriages." The court also noted that prenups can encourage marriages, because without "the ability to order their own affairs as they wish, many people may simply forgo marriage for more 'informal' relationships such as cohabitation." *Brooks v. Brooks*, 733 P.2d 1044 (Alaska 1987).

Prenups can encourage and support marriage, particularly of mature people in second and third marriages. But what about younger people in first marriages? Does settling one's financial affairs at the start of a first marriage cause the marriage to weaken? And what can be done about it, to soften the blow and provide equity for the less moneyed spouse and provide fairness for both spouses?

How many people sign prenups?

A quick look at the internet reveals thousands of attorney websites that would have you believe that prenups are common, and as important to have prior to a marriage as a marriage license. My Google search today of "prenuptial agreement attorney" revealed 534,000 results and "prenuptial agreement lawyer" garnered 664,000 results.

Here's a sales pitch from one law firm:

> Many couples are reluctant to discuss prenuptial agreements. They say to themselves, "Why should we think about the possibility of divorce when we are not even married yet and we are in love?" Unfortunately, one in two marriages in the United States end in divorce. You may think that such an outcome is impossible in your case, but many couples have thought the same thing and suffered severe financial consequences.

Even in light of the present enforceability of prenups and the marketing push by attorneys and financial planners, the media tends to overestimate the percentage of married couples who sign prenuptial agreements prior to their marriage. As of this writing, there has been no statistical research project to determine the number of people entering into prenups.

In my law practice, during the past 25 years I have seen just two cases where clients had existing prenups when I met with them: an estate-planning case, and a case where the clients wanted to modify their prenup. The would make the overall percentage of clients entering into a prenup in my practice far less than one-tenth of 1 percent. My practice generally consists of middle-income to wealthy clients, the type of clients who fit the profile of people seeking prenuptial agreements. If you add lower income clients to these statistics, the overall percentage would be even less.

The prevalence of prenups among wealthy clients is assumed to be greater, but actual statistics are difficult to obtain. The percentage may still be relatively low even in these cases. There are many in the news – mostly celebrity prenups. Other people with high incomes and accumulated assets (particularly those entering second or subsequent marriages) may sometimes have prenups as well.

It's impossible to find statistics in public records. Prenuptial agreements are generally not registered in state or public records – they are private contracts. They often include a confidentiality agreement, which makes finding out about them even more difficult. If the marriage is ongoing, there would be no way to track them. If a divorce occurs, the prenuptial agreement itself is generally not filed with the divorce case. It may (or may not) be referred to in the separation agreement filed with the court. But finding a divorce case in court archives that even mentioned a prenup would be like finding a needle in the haystack.

There is a "meme" out there citing a 5 percent rate for prenups entered into by couples marrying. This seems to be based on an unsupported statistic cited in a 1996 magazine article, which was referenced in a 1997 law review article written by a third-year law student. This statistic has bounced around the internet ever since and is clearly "fake news," not in accordance with the actual facts on the ground. This is how the urban myth of the 5 percent prevalence of prenups was born.

Arlene Dubin, a matrimonial lawyer practicing in a large New York City law firm, author of *Prenups for Lovers: A Romantic Guide to Prenuptial Agreements* (Villard 2001), also conjectured on the prevalence of prenups. In her book, she says that statistics are scarce, but "anecdotal" evidence suggests that "5 to 10 percent of couples and 20 percent of remarried couples now enter into prenups." She predicted that by 2020 more than 50 percent of couples would have prenups before marrying.

Dubin's statistics are not supported and her predictions have not come true. It is 2017 now and very few people are getting prenups. Any percentage nearing the 5 to 10 percent level might possibly pertain to a very wealthy class of individuals who are marrying. But even most of these people don't marry with prenups, particularly if it is a first marriage. Dubin's prediction in 2001 that 50 percent of newlyweds would have prenups by 2020 is simply way off base.

Adding to the misconception of the frequency of prenups are recent surveys undertaken by the American Academy of Matrimonial Lawyers (AAML), which have attracted much media attention. In a 2016 press release, the organization said it had conducted a recent survey of its own members. It found that that 51 percent of the members *who responded* to the survey had experienced an increase in number of millennials *"requesting"* prenuptial agreements. It further found that 62 percent of the respondents saw an increase in the total number of clients *seeking* prenups in the past three years. (Press Release, American Academy of Matrimonial Lawyers, October 28, 2016.)

When interpreting these results, it is important to take into account that the AAML is a select organization of divorce attorneys representing, in general, the moneyed class of individuals, including the fabled "one percent." (OK, maybe the "two percent.") Its membership consists of approximately 1,600 divorce lawyers with significant divorce litigation experience. This is a miniscule percentage of attorneys – there are over 1.3 million licensed lawyers in the United States.

In order to join AAML, an applicant must have trial experience in handling complex matrimonial law litigation as lead counsel. Litigation attorneys, in my experience, tend to be strong proponents of prenups. The survey indicates that when polled, many AAML members have noted an increase in clients *seeking* prenups. It does not reach the percentage of completed prenups. It does not tabulate how many of these clients took the step of beginning negotiations or drafting prenups and how many completed and signed prenups. The survey also does not reflect the general population of attorneys (even attorneys who specialize in prenups), as the membership of AAML is so small.

Given that that the typical AAML client is very prosperous, any statistic applicable to the practices of the members of this professional group would not be representative of marrying couples in general, or even for couples in higher income or asset brackets. Maybe wealthier people are getting prenups more frequently, but there still is no way to verify the premise. The overall percentage including the higher income/asset class population is likely well below 5 percent, and could possibly be below 1 percent, although somewhat higher for second marriages for people who have significant assets.

Is it true that 50 percent of all marriages fail?

Many people seeking prenups are concerned about the high divorce rate. The statistic that 50 percent of all marriages end in divorce that has been bandied about in the media may not be accurate. Interestingly, the types of people who generally are interested in prenups fit the demographic profiles of people whose marriages have a better chance of lasting. They have more education, higher incomes, and in general, are older than the average first time marriage partners, if they are marrying for the first time.

The 50 percent divorce rate may be simply another urban myth. The divorce rate for first marriages is likely to be somewhat lower – somewhat higher than 40 percent, but less than 50 percent. See "What Is the Divorce Rate, Really?" Bella DePaulo, PsychologyToday.com. Researchers have started to debunk the 50 percent statistic, which may have been based on a conceptual error.

The report of a 50 percent divorce rate apparently arose from a 1981 National Center for Health Statistics (NCHS) study that found that in 1980 there were 2.4 million marriages and 1.2 million divorces. The study included people entering into first marriages, as well as men and women who had married before. Many studies indicate that second and subsequent marriages have a greater probability of failing than first marriages, thus skewing this statistic.

In addition, the statistic for 1980 that there were 1.2 million divorces and 2.4 million marriages failed to take into account the 54 million marriages that already existed at that time, many, if not most, of which were "weathered," and may not have been as likely to see a divorce. As a result, the reported divorce rate was likely less than 50 percent once you took into account that huge backlog of married people in 1980 who did not get divorced in that year.

Another factor that affected the divorce statistics was that the 1980 NCHS study dated from a period in which the divorce rate in the U.S. was close to the very highest it's ever been.

The divorce rate began to rise in the 1960 and 1970s, and peaked at 5.3 divorces per thousand in 1981. It has been declining ever since, dropping gradually to 4.7 in 1990 and to 3.6 per thousand in 2011. (These statistics are based on *all* people, including children and unmarried people.) When you look at statistics for the "at risk" population, i.e., people who are currently married, the statistics also show a decline in the women's divorce rate (that's what the NCHS survey tracks), falling from a peak of 22.6 divorces per 1,000 married women in 1980 to 16.9 divorces in 2015. (National Center for Health Statistics, U.S. Census Bureau, American Community Survey.) This is a significant reduction.

The current divorce rate is about two times that of 1960, but has been declining since reaching its highest point in the early 1980s, when the 50 percent divorce rate statistic was promulgated. The divorce rate has actually declined by 25 percent from 1980 to 2015, having reached a 40-year low in 2015.

Many commentators now estimate the lifetime probability of divorce to be somewhere between 40 and 50 percent. (*Divorce Rate in the U.S.*, Lydia R. Anderson, National Center for Family & Marriage Research, Bowling Green State University.)

The statistics of a high divorce rate in the 1970s and 1980s may have been affected by the size of the baby-boom population – the 75 million Americans who were born between 1946 and 1964. When this group reached marrying age and young adulthood, the divorce statistics were the highest. Likely this demographic group was affected by the increasing availability of "no-fault" divorce and the women's movement. The baby boomers may be especially divorce-prone and may be skewing the statistics. The trend is clearly toward fewer divorces, according to data from many commentators and researchers.

But the 50 percent divorce rate statistic has been widely perpetuated by the media, is now deeply imbedded in the public's imagination, and has become an "urban myth."

What are the risk factors for divorce?

The backgrounds of marrying couples have a direct correlation to the risk of divorce. For instance, if you have an annual income over $50,000, have a college education or more, and are over 25 years old when you marry, your risk of divorce is substantially less than that of the general public. (*Social Indicators of Marital Health & Well-Being*, Theodora Ooms, and Alan J. Hawkins, *The State of our Unions, Marriage in America 2012*, The National Marriage Project, pages 74–75.)

These factors are almost always present in the demographics of people seeking prenups. People seeking prenups in first marriages are generally highly educated, employed at professional or highly compensated jobs, and are older than the median age at the study. As a result, the fabled 50 percent divorce rate may not apply to them.

On the other side, factors that lead to a higher chance of divorce include the following: your parents were divorced, your parents married others after divorcing, either or both of you have been married before, there is a significant age difference between you, and the prospective wife is two or more years older than the prospective husband. ("Divorce Stats That Can Predict Your Marriage's Success," Anneli Rufus, *The Daily Beast*, posted 5/19/10.)

The step-child, step-parent relationships can be difficult, and people bringing children to a second or subsequent marriage experience a natural conflict between loyalty to their children and their new spouse. As a result, the divorce rate tends to be higher if either party has children from previous marriages or relationships.

But even if the 50 percent statistic were true, given the challenges of living and of being married, the percentage of marriages that last for a lifetime is surprisingly high. The drawbacks to prenups are legion (see Chapter 16 and discussions throughout this book), including setting up a negative interaction between you and your loved one at the outset of your marriage.

Taking into account the way prenups are generally written, you may be swapping equitable state laws with contractual provisions that often end up being unfair. And why not give your spouse a fair result even if the marriage *does* end in divorce? And as you will see in Chapter 6, there are many civilized ways to get a divorce if it turns out that you need one.

HOW DO PEOPLE GET A DIVORCE? LET ME COUNT THE WAYS

We frequently see headlines about nasty litigated divorces, usually about divorcing couples who are celebrities or public figures. People are drawn to articles about other people's marital travails. There is a sense of relief or *schadenfreude* for married readers – thank God it's not us going through a divorce – at least not yet! (The word *schadenfreude* comes from the German, literally "harm" and "joy," the joy that comes from hearing about someone else's troubles.)

Litigation is indeed horrifying. If you have to endure a litigated divorce, you will be under an ongoing personal attack that can take over your life. You will think of almost nothing else. It can be prolonged, often taking two years or more to get resolved in a court judgment. It takes a lot of time for your lawyer to prepare and respond to all the discovery requests, depositions, and hearings. Every fact presented in the trial itself must be meticulously supported and presented with due attention to the rules of evidence. Because this entails a lot of legal work, the cost can be quite substantial. It will cost many times more than you expected when you entered into the process of litigation.

It causes you to re-live, over and over, the circumstances that brought you to divorce court in the first place. You will have to testify as to every horrible thing your spouse did to you, if it is a "fault" divorce. Even if it is a "no fault" divorce, the outcome as to property division and support will be buttressed by detailed facts that your attorney must seek to present or admit in the case evidence and testimony. Financial records will be presented and analyzed in detail. There may be competing valuations of real estate and businesses. There may be conduct issues that affect the calculus of who gets what in the divorce. It's a very cumbersome process that is presented to a very overburdened court system.

In most states, there is no right to a jury in a divorce case, so the decision comes from a single judge. The judge will have his or her own opinions of the facts of the case and whether or not to give more credence to the wife's or the husband's evidence. The judge is in total control as to how to divide assets and income, and also about decisions having to do with children.

Trials are very public. Anyone can come into the courtroom and listen to the testimony. Occasionally for "good cause," a record or part of it may be "sealed," which means it will not be obtainable by the public. But sealing a record is rare and at the discretion of the court. The presumption is that all court records are public, so there must be a compelling reason to argue in front of the judge that the case records should be sealed. Your embarrassment at having the details of your marriage and court arguments made public is not a good enough reason. Allegations of adultery, cruel and abusive treatment, drug and alcohol addiction, and domestic violence may be in the court record available to all to see (including your children, friends, and relatives) at any time in the future.

If there was any goodwill between you and your former spouse, it will be gone, probably forever. There is no way that you will be able to shield your children from the litigation and the feelings it engenders in you, whether they are very young or young adults. This process can be very hurtful to them, no matter what age they are when you divorce.

Having said all this, sometimes divorce litigation is the only way for a spouse to get an equitable settlement in the divorce. Litigation does have a positive attribute (aside from all its drawbacks) in sometimes creating a "level playing field." Sometimes a judge will order a moneyed spouse to advance money to the other spouse, so that the less moneyed spouse will be able to pay legal fees. It requires each of the spouses to disclose all their assets and liabilities. The judge will apply the law to the facts of the case. This often helps a less powerful spouse to get needed information in order to assess what is a fair settlement.

The fear of litigation is one of the major reasons people seek prenuptial agreements. This is a reasonable aim. People want to avoid the cost, uncertainty, and stress of litigation. But it is important to bear in mind that most prenups also change the basic economic and financial aspects of a marriage. These marital terms have been built up and formulated through the culture and are reflected in the state laws that have developed over many generations. You and your future spouse may be giving up or distorting marital values to address the fear of an event that may never happen.

So if litigation is your fear, before you jump into getting a prenup, you need to be aware of all the methods and processes that couples can use to get a divorce. There are many ways to get a divorce short of litigation, as well as different types of litigation. Many divorces are not very contentious, and ugly litigated divorces are quite rare.

Most prospective clients think there are only two ways to get a divorce — through mediation or litigation. In reality, these are only two of the many kinds of divorce processes available. I'll briefly describe all the processes, from the simplest to the most complex and difficult.

1. The parties represent themselves and don't have attorneys.

This is called a *pro se* divorce. (*Pro se* means "for oneself" in Latin.)

You probably know the joke about the person who represents himself — that person has a fool for a client. Actually, *pro se* filings are fairly frequent in divorce courts. When you look at the demographics of divorcing people, many are low income and cannot afford attorneys. Free legal services generally don't offer divorce services. Usually (and understandably) *pro se* divorces are motivated by a person's lack of funds to engage a professional, or a wish to save money. *Pro se* divorces can work adequately for very simple cases — short marriages where there are no (or few) assets and no children.

Courts are generally very protective of *pro se* litigants. Although courts and court employees cannot give legal advice, in my experience, judges give *pro se* divorce litigants extra attention and assistance in understanding what they are about to do. I've seen judges raise an issue not considered by the couple in court, and ask them to consider it and change their divorce agreement accordingly.

People in longer marriages who have children and have accumulated assets may be in a riskier position when trying to do the divorce *pro se*. Power imbalances and unfairness between the spouses in their negotiations can be present. For anyone with children or assets such as retirement assets or owning a home, going it alone may be unwise.

Important issues involving rights to retirement assets (generally considered marital assets to be divided) may be missed. Possibilities of contractual obligations that may come later, such as a later sale of marital home, may not be envisioned. I've seen many instances where the parties have to go to court at a future date (with attorneys) to unwind and construe the incomplete and ambiguous drafting of important provisions in their self-drafted separation agreement. In these cases, a "do-it-yourself" divorce may end up being more costly in the long run.

A variation on this is "unbundled" services, in which the parties (or one of them) engages an attorney to professionally draft the separation agreement (also called a "divorce agreement" or "divorce settlement agreement). The attorney can give guidance to that party (not the other party) as to issues to be decided in the divorce. The other party may (or may not) engage a lawyer to review the documents. The client may decide that his or her lawyer not be lawyer of record in the case, and not be present at the divorce hearing in court. These "unbundled" services are becoming more common. In some states, court-mandated disclosure of the off-site attorney's services and participation is required. As a result, sometimes court documents need to say that they were prepared with "assistance of counsel."

2. The "surgical divorce."

This is a term I've originated for a fairly simple divorce, where one party has engaged an attorney and the other is *pro se*. I'm asked this question a lot: "Why can't you represent both of us?" It is considered a conflict of interest and therefore unethical for one attorney to be the attorney for both parties to the divorce. Attorneys are bound to represent the interests of their client. And as much as you might think there are no disputes between you and your spouse as you head toward divorce, one (or more) conflict may raise its ugly head. That's why one lawyer can't represent both of you. (An alternative below is to use an attorney functioning as a mediator, not as a lawyer.)

In a "surgical divorce," the attorney for a party gets all the facts from the client and drafts a separation agreement and the other filings needed for the divorce. The aim of the separation agreement is to comport with the terms the court would likely approve under the applicable statutes and case law, which means it's intended to be fair to both spouses.

If the other party is not represented, the attorney (as well as the spouse) can communicate directly with that other spouse and address questions and issues. If the other party is represented, then the attorney must deal with the opposing attorney (again, an ethical rule to be followed).

By working with an attorney, you may find legal or practical issues that you and your spouse did not address. You also may find that something you and your spouse thought was "fair" perhaps isn't, in light of what you are learning about your mutual rights and obligations under the divorce laws of your state. You might find some better ways of doing things as a result of suggestions by your lawyer, who hopefully has a lot of experience in divorces. Your attorney can provide a helpful reality check for you (and, indirectly, your spouse) as you work through the process.

The court papers and separation agreement will be drafted professionally. The terms are set for the period of marital disengagement and also (very importantly) provide a roadmap for the future. If the other spouse has not already done so, he or she may (and often should) consult with an attorney before all the papers are signed. That attorney will provide helpful feedback, which should aid the process.

If there are any unresolved disagreements along the way, hopefully both spouses can resolve them readily now that you have been advised of what the rules of divorce are. Or if an issue proves intractable, you can seek resolution of that particular issue through mediation or marital counseling. Through all this, you're on the path to a civil divorce (in both senses), and will probably easily come to a settlement on all of the issues.

Sometimes, in a "surgical" divorce, the spouses do not bring the attorneys to court for the hearing. Your attorney will let you know whether there are special issues that may make it prudent to bring one (or both) of the attorneys to the hearing on the divorce, which is required in most states. Sometimes having an attorney (or both attorneys) at the hearing can help an uneasy judge feel more inclined to approve an unusual argument or provision in a separation agreement.

If you have decided that your attorney will not be at the divorce hearing, your attorney can prepare you for the judge's questioning and appropriate responses. If you run into problems, you can ask for a short "continuance" and telephone your attorney, who can be on call during the hearing date to assist if needed.

You would be surprised at how many divorce cases fall into the category of "surgical" divorces: two nice people, who, for whatever reasons, can't stay married. They want to move forward fairly and expeditiously toward divorce. The process is client-driven. It reduces the escalation of acrimony during the divorce. As you can imagine, this type of divorce is generally one of the least expensive of the professionally prepared divorces. As a professionally prepared divorce, it is drafted carefully and soundly, with practical and workable provisions. The spouses benefit from the experience of divorce counsel. This all bodes well for the client and the other spouse as they transition into post-divorce life.

3. The mediated divorce.

Mediation and related fields have been called ADR, which stands for Alternative Dispute Resolution. ADR is becoming very common and often the first step toward resolving a divorce – so much so that many practitioners are dropping the word "alternative" and calling these out-of-court techniques simply "Dispute Resolution." The idea is that clients should view the ADR techniques as the *primary* way of getting a divorce, and litigation the secondary and alternative dispute resolution technique.

In a mediated divorce, a neutral mediator (either a lawyer or non-lawyer) helps the spouses come to an agreement about the divorce. The mediator should be well-versed in divorce law. Mediators cannot advocate for either party and cannot provide legal advice. However, mediators can provide legal "information," and some of this can be about the laws in your jurisdiction, and what terms people generally adopt (in the mediator's experience) to reach a settlement.

Each of the parties can consult with their own individual counsel during the course of the mediation and prior to signing the divorce agreement. The cost of mediation (even including the cost of the reviewing attorneys) can be a cost-effective way to get a divorce. Mediation may not be suitable if there are difficult issues such as spousal support, disputes about property division, very unbalanced power between the spouses, or a lack of knowledge or financial sophistication on the part of one of the spouses. In very high asset cases, the resolution may be more suitable to a collaborative divorce. (See below.)

There are several "styles" of mediation: facilitative, evaluative, and transformative.

Some mediators blend these approaches. Describing them in detail is beyond the scope of this book. But very briefly, here are the distinctions:

Facilitative mediators use standard mediation practices such as finding the interests behind the parties' positions, reframing, active listening, validating points of view, defusing "hot" speech, and helping clarify communication misunderstandings.

The clients make their own decisions, with the mediator "facilitating." The mediator structures the process and leads (sometimes very subtly) the parties toward resolving their disputes. The facilitative mediator does not give advice, nor does the mediator intersperse the mediator's own views or goals into the mediation. Some facilitative mediators may let the clients make their own "deals" with very little information about what most divorcing people do, or what the law (cases and statutes and courts) might find to be a fair settlement. Some mediators (including myself) believe it is important for mediation clients to know what rule of law is, what the range of settlement is on various issues, and what courts generally approve as consistent with divorce law.

The role of *evaluative mediators* is to evaluate the dispute presented to him or her through the lens of existing law. For this reason, this type of mediator is almost always a lawyer. This mediator sifts through the "facts" of the dispute and seeks to predict how the dispute (here, the terms of the divorce) would be decided by a judge if brought to court. The evaluative mediator basically functions as a judge in that he or she gives the mediation clients a preview of what the mediator thinks the judge's rulings will be. Evaluative mediation is similar to conciliation. (See below.)

Evaluative mediation is often entered into after a court case is in progress. Attorneys are frequently present at the mediation sessions. Caucuses in which the mediator might meet separately with one or the other party are frequent. In fact, in some evaluative mediations, the parties rarely (or never) meet face to face, and the mediator goes from room to room, practicing what is called "shuttle diplomacy." The goal is to get the litigating parties to come to agreements using the mediator's evaluation of the relative strengths or weaknesses of a party's lawsuit to encourage parties to come to a settlement.

The final theoretical type of mediation is *transformative mediation*. The goal with this mediation process is to get the parties to come to an agreement by effecting changes in the thought process of the mediation clients, not just aiming for a resolution of specific disputes. It has the ability to transform not only the relationship between the parties, but even the character of the individuals involved.

The process is open-ended, unlike facilitative and evaluative mediation. The goal is not necessarily toward "settlement" – settlement is presented as one possible outcome.

Mediated prenups. Aside from its use in divorces, mediation is also an excellent way to begin the process of getting a prenup. Often when negotiating a prenup, there is an imbalance of power in favor of the more moneyed spouse. The mediator needs to be very mindful of this, and be skilled enough to be able to make sure that the less moneyed spouse's goals and concerns are heard, acknowledged, and reflected in the process and in the resulting agreement. (See Chapter 20 for more on mediated prenups.)

4. The conciliation process.

Conciliation is a type of mediation, bearing most similarity to evaluative mediation. It is often practiced by an individual who has significant firsthand knowledge of results in litigated divorce cases, often a retired judge. To be clear, "retired" judges aren't necessarily judges who have reached retirement age. Often, they are judges who have transitioned their careers into arbitration, mediation, case evaluation, and consulting and conciliation, before reaching retirement age.

A conciliator may use all methods of mediation, including interest-based facilitative mediation, taking into account the parties' personal and financial interests, aside from the legal strengths of their positions. But the main difference between mediation and conciliation is that the conciliator will often present settlement proposals to the parties, based on the conciliator's knowledge of rulings in litigated cases. The proposals are non-binding (as opposed to arbitration, which can result in binding settlements if the parties agree to that format). Conciliation can be a very powerful tool in settling complex divorce cases.

5. Arbitration.

Arbitration can be an excellent process in resolving divorces. In addition, many prenuptial agreements require that the parties arbitrate any disputes arising from the prenup, rather than file a court case. Having said that, there are limits to what is capable of being arbitrated in the divorce context. (See below.)

Arbitration is essentially a private out-of-court trial. The arbitrator, like a judge, makes decisions about what should happen to resolve the dispute. It may be very similar to a trial, requiring the parties to adhere to the strict laws of evidence (hearsay evidence inadmissible, etc.). But often by agreement of the parties, the evidentiary rules are relaxed and not strictly adhered to.

One useful technique used in arbitration (and sometime in mediation) is *Baseball or Final Offer Arbitration*. In this method, each party submits to the arbitrator their last and best offers. The arbitrator would be limited to selecting only one of the two figures submitted, not anything in between. A party may choose to modify his or her demands down in order for that person's figure to be the one chosen by the arbitrator. Or a party may make the highest offer possible in order for the arbitrator to choose that offer. This technique allows parties to reduce their potential losses and encourages reasonableness in offers.

The arbitrators are generally lawyers experienced in litigation in the matter to be decided, and often are "retired" judges. (See conciliation above.) The parties choose the arbitrator. If they can't decide on the arbitrator, they may each choose an arbitrator, and the two arbitrators may choose the arbitrator who will then serve. The aim is to obtain a fair resolution of the matter in an expeditious and cost-effective manner. The time line is much shorter than for a litigated divorce – several months as opposed to up to two or three years for the court action. The cost is generally much less, even though each party is almost always represented by an attorney, and the parties have to also pay the arbitrator's fee.

Arbitration can be binding or non-binding, depending on the choice by the parties prior to commencing the arbitration. Non-binding arbitration means a party who does not accept the arbitrator's "award" (which would be termed a "judgment" in a court of law) can go to court to litigate the matter. Having said this, many (if not most) cases do settle after non-binding arbitration, especially if the arbitrator is a retired judge or a litigation lawyer very experienced in the area of the dispute, in this case, in divorce law.

With binding arbitration, the award is permanent and binding. The winning party can take the arbitration award to a court of law and enforce it if the losing party does not comply with it.

Certain issues may not be subject to arbitration, or if arbitrated, the result is not binding. One of these is matters dealing with the unemancipated children of the marriage.

Courts in all states retain jurisdiction over the interests of minor and unemancipated children. It is public policy that parents cannot contract away the rights of children. Another issue that may or may not be subject to arbitration is spousal support, depending on the state in which the parties reside and what the facts of the case are. Again, here there may be a statewide public policy exception in which the state's interest in protecting a divorced spouse may overrule the private contract (the separation agreement or the prenup).

In some states, as long as the arbitrator applies the relevant state standards, the arbitrator's award on alimony can be binding.

Arbitration can be an excellent way to address and resolve valuation issues (mainly pertaining to businesses), which cause the run-up of costs and time spent in litigated divorces. Parties can decide to arbitrate some but not all issues in connection with the divorce to facilitate it and break an impasse on certain subjects. A prenup can be as simple as requiring a divorce to be subject to binding arbitration rather than a court process with the caveats above about what issues are subject to arbitration.

6. Med-Arb – an emerging method of dispute resolution.

Med-Arb stands for Mediation/Arbitration. This is a new area of dispute resolution in which the mediator is also the arbitrator. The parties agree to embark on mediation. The parties have also agreed that if the mediation process does not result in agreement (or to the extent it does not), then the mediator switches roles and becomes the arbitrator, and issues an award (i.e., a decision).

However, there is a risk in the Med-Arb process. The person serving as a mediator may have gained information in confidence, and also may have offered information to steer the parties toward settlement. There is a risk that this may taint the arbitrator's decision because the arbitrator may no longer be seen as (or be) impartial.

There is also concern that has been expressed within the Arbitration bar. Arbitrators, like judges, are supposed to maintain public confidence in the integrity and fairness of the arbitration. Switching roles from mediator to arbitrator may muddy the waters and contaminate the arbitration process.

To prevent these potential problems, the parties could be allowed to opt out of having the same person serve as the arbitrator if they wish. Or they could also have a written agreement at the outset that the mediator should not serve as arbitrator if they do not come to terms. Before embarking on Med-Arb, it is important to check the applicable laws (case law and statutes) in your jurisdiction.

7. Collaborative divorce.

Collaborative divorce is a relatively new divorce process that involves two clients, each represented by a collaboratively-trained attorney. The parties in a collaborative divorce agree to have a fifth person at all the group meetings – a neutral process coach (NPC), sometimes called a neutral process facilitator or divorce coach. It's a team process.

Collaborative divorce is a very effective method to resolve complex cases in medium- to long-term marriages. The parties meet face-to-face in a series of meetings with their own collaboratively-trained counsel and the NPC. At the outset, the parties and their attorneys sign a contract not to litigate while the parties are working within the collaborative process to resolve their divorce. The contract includes a provision that the parties must keep all income and assets "as is," and spending is limited to that which is in the ordinary course of their marriage. This provides the same financial protection (see below) as a divorce litigation filing does.

Most importantly, the collaborative contract provides that if one of the parties opts out and decides to litigate, neither of the parties can use the services of their collaborative attorneys for the litigation, or anyone in their law firms. This provides a safe haven for the collaborative process (often called a "safe container") and provides maximum motivation for a settlement as they all work through the practical issues relating to the divorce. I call this a "marriage to the divorce," because the parties have committed themselves to work out their divorce in this setting and pursuant to this process. You might call it a positive final act of their ongoing marriage.

The fifth person – the NPC – is generally a trained therapist or a psychologist. The NPC attends all the meetings to make sure that emotions, negative language, and unproductive conduct don't disrupt the process. The NPC is concerned with the process and interactions of all four participants (the two clients and two attorneys), as well as the behavior of the clients *vis á vis* each other. The NPC can help one or both of the clients with the emotional difficulties of the divorce, although they are not acting as a therapist for either of them. The NPC addresses attorney behavior as well, because we attorneys can begin to act aggressively, which may not be productive for the collaborative process.

Collaborative counsel advocates for their own collaborative clients. Generally, the advocacy is not very apparent in the five-way meetings, which tend to have the flavor of co-mediation sessions. Your collaborative lawyer will provide strategy, legal advice, and education about the law in private sessions with you. In the group sessions, attorneys (and clients) generally back off from direct vocal advocacy, and there is a sense of interest-based negotiations, as in mediation. Very often the attorney for one client will form a respectful bond with the other spouse during the sessions.

Financial analyses can be presented by neutral experts retained during the process and are reviewed by everyone. Disclosure is full, transparent, and accurate. There is an attempt to have communications be positive, not blaming, and constructive rather than limited and angry. People are in a better position to think outside of the box and be creative.

There is a culture of "truth saying" in collaborative divorce that is tremendously helpful to solving problems in a respectful way. This is the diametric opposite of conventional divorces, where the truth is withheld and documents are not provided freely. In litigation, the parties function generally from positions articulated solely by their lawyers, who sometimes misrepresent what a client may really want. The "real-time" aspect of the collaborative divorce five-way meetings has its dangers, but can be a refreshing way to cut through positions and get to what is really important for divorcing couples, which sometimes turns out to be mutual.

Collaborative divorce is an excellent way to get through complex divorces, many of which would have been litigated had the parties not agreed to try this method.

8. Divorce negotiation with no divorce filing until all terms are agreed upon.

This can be similar to the surgical divorce and can be very simple, depending on the issues and the level of differences in views between the parties and their lawyers. Sometimes if there is a great deal of conflict, the lawyer-to-lawyer negotiation might be prolonged (and therefore, expensive). In some of these cases, the negotiations might not result in a conclusion – a signed separation agreement. But often divorce negotiations do work.

This is actually the most common type of divorce I see in my law practice. I call this a "garden variety" negotiated divorce. The lawyers should check in with their clients often, so as not to negotiate without reflecting their clients' wishes and aims. Lawyers sometimes forget this important guideline. The client spouses are also free to communicate with each other directly and try to resolve some of the issues between themselves. This happens a lot and is very helpful to the process.

Since there is no "current" litigation, the parties do not feel threatened by the thought of "going to court" during the negotiations. It works best when both lawyers are experienced in divorce law. If they are, the parties can fairly easily reach an agreement that is consistent with what the law would indicate or what a judge would rule if the case were to go to trial.

This method is not recommended if a balky spouse wants to delay the process, or if a divorce filing is needed at the outset (see below). For this procedure to work, there has to be a high level of financial trust and expectation of fair dealing between the clients. It's not recommended when there has been a history of financial malfeasance or financial dishonesty, because without the court filing, a spouse could transfer or hide assets. (See below.)

9. Divorce negotiation starting with a divorce filing at the beginning.

Many attorneys still prefer to start a divorce with a court filing, rather than negotiation. There are some good reasons for this. One is to stop the running of "length of marriage" that may affect alimony and child support obligations, as well as property division. For some attorneys, it's almost a knee-jerk reaction. It does have some negative implications, though, and the processes described above are generally preferable.

The filing of a divorce in many states creates an automatic restraining order against dissipation of assets, although assets and income can be used in the ordinary course. The automatic restraining order can be put into effect by the parties or by the court in other states after the filing. Another reason for filing at the outset is psychological. Filing creates shock value, and you are broadcasting to your spouse that you are serious about the divorce, and, perhaps, that you intend to play "hardball."

The divorce filing-first procedure carries a lot of negatives. It is usually an unpleasant surprise when the non-filing spouse receives the first letter from the other spouse's attorney. People are very sensitive to attorney letters and react strongly. The non-filing spouse must be served by a sheriff or process server, unless he or she voluntarily signs the papers. One may be understandably dismayed and alarmed (or embarrassed) when a constable shows up at that spouse's home or workplace.

Filing for divorce does address the potential problem of misappropriating assets on the eve of divorce in states that have automatic restraining orders. (In my practice, I find financial malfeasance extremely rare among my divorce clients.) Filing right away is also helpful if a support order or parenting plan is needed immediately and the parties can't come to agreement. Filing does put pressure on the parties to come to a decision before the judge decides the issues in the divorce for them.

10. Litigation ending with settlement before trial.

Sometimes it is clear that there will be no useful negotiation between the spouses. It is a high-conflict case that needs the help of the court to resolve it. The case is already adversarial and will be ugly. It will produce a supply of horrible memories for a lifetime and detrimentally affect the children of the marriage. These cases can be very extreme and litigation is time-consuming, nasty, and stressful for the parents. There's no way to keep the upheaval from the children no matter how much the parents try.

There is a filing, perhaps many subsequent court hearings, and decisions are made by the court. There is formal discovery (depositions, production of documents, interrogatories). Litigation requires much attorney time and is therefore quite expensive. That adds more stress on the parties.

There is generally some negotiation by the parties through their attorneys. Sometimes the case is resolved at the "pretrial conference," and the terms reflected in a separation agreement resolving the case may be signed at that time.

If the case proceeds to trial, much additional legal expense ensues. Notably, a very high proportion of those cases end in settlement on the first day of trial. The problem with going this far is that virtually all the time-consuming legal work to prepare for trial (and hence expense for the client) must be completed by the day of trial.

Litigation is a very expensive way to get a divorce, although at times necessary. Ask an attorney to give you a ballpark figure on the costs you may incur. Quadruple that and you'll get an idea of what it might actually cost. Unless you have lots of money to spend on this and lots of money at stake, and you do not want your spouse to have what they are asking for, try to use one of the methods previously described.

11. Full-blown litigation ending with trial.

This is the worst of all possible worlds and the rarest. It's the ugliest and the most public of divorces. It ruins the post-marriage relationship between you and your spouse forever, because you have gone "to war." It will likely affect your children detrimentally during their lives and in their own marriages. Think carefully before deciding to litigate, especially if it looks like it will end with a trial.

The number of cases where a full trial occurs and the judge makes the decisions on the divorce are very rare. Although there are no statistics available, most attorneys believe the percentages are in the 1 to 5 percent range.

Another problem in litigating to the end is that the judge has to make an order, and often some issues aren't covered in the order, which means the former spouses may end up in court again. That's because a judge's order is not a lengthy document. It may not cover all issues and does not provide the detail that a complete and well-drafted separation agreement contains.

An actual trial adds great expenses to the divorce bill and creates a lifetime of bad memories. The parties are not in control over their own destiny, but have put the decision in the hands of a judge, whose decision may be unreasonable (not usually the case) or very unfavorable to one side or the other. This can leave one party very happy and the other party devastated.

But most often, the judge takes the middle road, leaving neither party satisfied after all the expense and trouble of litigation.

* * *

In the case where one of the upcoming spouses to a marriage is very wealthy (or his or her parents are), a prenuptial agreement may be a good way to set up the legal process that would apply if the marriage breaks up. That is not to say that the terms of the divorce as set in the prenup need to be extremely one-sided. In general, they should not be.

It should be noted that in the 30 years I have been practicing law, there has been a sea-change as to how lawyers deal with each other in cases – both litigated and non-litigated. When I started practicing, lawyers were expected to take a vigorously adversarial position on pretty much every issue on behalf of their client. Now, lawyers are more cooperative and tend to view a divorce as a "problem" that needs to be mutually solved. Divorce litigation is becoming much rarer, and cooperation between attorneys in finding reasonable solutions much more frequent. This bodes well for divorcing couples, no matter what process they choose for their divorce.

CHAPTER 7

WHAT HAPPENS IF YOU MARRY WITHOUT A PRENUP?

A little-known fact is that *everyone* who gets married in this country already has signed up for a prenup. That's because when you marry, your state has a cohesive system of laws pertaining to the economic rights and obligations of married people who divorce. It also has laws that address property distribution upon the death of one of the spouses. The moment you marry, these laws (whatever they are in your state) apply in full force.

Divorce laws are flexible, depending on the circumstances. They can adjust to the particular situation of the spouses, unlike the provisions contained in most prenups, which are inflexible and determine the financial results in a divorce before the marriage even takes place.

Divorce laws are intended to be fair and have developed to protect spouses' rights in case of divorce. In the past, the protected spouse was almost always the woman. In the old common law system imported from England, the person whose name was stated as the owner of an asset controlled that property and had all the rights to it. So whoever owned the property (usually the husband) kept all rights to it after the divorce.

It wasn't until the mid-twentieth century when most common law states changed their laws so that married women would have the right to share in the assets accumulated during marriage, no matter which spouse earned them and no matter in whose name they were titled. This is called "equitable distribution" and applies in the original common law states. (At present, the original common law states are termed "equitable distribution" or "equitable property" states.) Community property states categorize property acquired during the marriage as marital property, no matter whose name the property is in. (See below.)

One of the wonderful things about marriage versus just living together is the protection of spouses under all states' laws if there is a marital breakup. This lack of fairness and protection was felt keenly by the same-sex couples in the past who were unable to legally marry. In all states, upon divorce there is an orderly and fair distribution of assets, and if needed, a sharing of income. A prenup is a private contract. It overrides the state laws that protect spouses. Because of this, it is important to fully understand the state laws before embarking on a prenup.

What are the "laws" and where do they come from?

There are several places to find the laws pertaining to divorce and death of spouses. The first and primary one is in the statutes regarding divorce and inheritance enacted by state legislatures. But these laws are simply templates that need to be fleshed out to cover various factual situations. This is done by court cases in which the facts of a particular case are presented to a judge who applies the law to the facts of that particular situation. Lawyers call this "case law."

The cases are published if they are "higher court" cases, such as state appeals court or state supreme court cases. Lawyers and divorcing spouses can look at them for guidance. But appeals are rare and judges' opinions are not published in lower court cases. These unpublished opinions are also informative, as these lower courts (termed "trial courts") are the venue in which most of the divorce litigation happens. Lawyers that are members of the divorce bar share information on these unreported cases with colleagues and with clients. Lawyers write articles about their experiences and present them at legal seminars. This is one way in which lawyers become informed about divorce law in their particular state.

The result of this practice in the context of divorce law (and also inheritance law) is that there are very few issues in a given state that haven't been clearly addressed. The law has been developed by very knowledgeable people (legislators, lawyers, and judges) applying their knowledge of the human condition thoughtfully to real-life experiences and situations. At essence, this is really what "the law" is.

In fact, throughout the U.S., these laws are surprisingly consistent from state to state, even between the two systems (equitable distribution and community property). This supports the idea that there is something uniform about the human condition itself – people's life experiences, conflicts, and ideals. Perhaps this is one of the reasons why in law school, we are told by our professors that "the law is a seamless web."

If you assume (as I do) that the law, as it has been developed, intends to be equitable, fair, and flexible to the facts at hand, applying this state law rather than a private contract written prior to a marriage makes sense. State laws pertaining to divorce and inheritance are aimed at encouraging positive social values such as the promotion of the marital relationship and financial security for ex-spouses, children, widows, and widowers.

Another result of this robust development of the law is that divorce cases are among the most susceptible to negotiating to a settlement. That's because there are so many divorce case law precedents in each state. As a result, lawyers can advise their clients what would happen on virtually every issue in a litigated divorce. This helps divorcing couples settle in "the shadow of the law," which is where lawyers generally suggest that the settlement should be.

Having said this, I will briefly describe the two systems of laws states have in the U.S., and how each of them deals with termination of a marriage by divorce. This will be followed by a description of the basic laws of inheritance in the various states.

Equitable distribution states.

Most states in the U.S. are so-called equitable distribution states. These are also known as equitable property states. Property division in these states is grounded on an "equitable" determination, based on a number of factors. These factors generally include length of the marriage, age of the parties, health of the parties, the parties' income, employability, economic and non-economic contribution to the marriage, ability of each party to maintain standard of living established during the marriage, lost economic opportunity as a result of the marriage, contribution to the acquisition, preservation or appreciation in value of assets, and contribution of a party as a homemaker to the family unit.

The presumption is that the property developed during a marriage is divided equally, even if one of the parties was the primary income earner and the other party was focused on providing a home life and care of the children. Different rules often apply to inherited property and premarital property.

The theory is that each of the parties may have different roles in a marriage, but that marriage functions as a partnership, with each spouse's efforts deemed commensurate to the other's. Each of their efforts is termed "contribution" to the marriage and is generally legally found to be equal. (See Chapter 4 on contribution to marriage.)

However, there may be other factors that may at times change the calculus away from an equal division. For instance, if there has been some sort of economic malfeasance such as gambling, money spent on affairs, or other types of "dissipation" of assets, the property division might be affected accordingly. In an equitable property state, it doesn't matter whose name (or title) the property is in for the division of assets.

When making the asset division at divorce, some states look at all property, including property accumulated before the marriage, as well as property received by gift or inheritance before or during the marriage. The law would then consider it all "marital property" subject to division. Then some of that premarital and gifted or inherited property may be taken out of the marital "pot." This would be under the applicable equitable doctrine based on the facts of the particular case. Massachusetts takes this approach.

In short marriages, premarital property is generally not included as part of the marital property estate. In those cases, often people take back the marbles they came into the marriage with. Sometimes adjustments needed to be made to put a spouse in a short marriage back on their feet. In legal terms, this is called "making a party whole."

In longer marriages, depending on the extent of premarital property, its use or need in supporting the family or the other spouse, and the amount of other marital property, some or all of it may be included as marital property.

Inheritance is another issue that is often highly dependent on the facts of a case. In general, if not needed by the other spouse, it may stay with the recipient spouse. If it has been blended into the fabric of the marriage by use in supporting the marital enterprise, it might be included as marital property.

Sometimes an inheritance was expected and counted on and affected the couple's mutual decisions about how to earn their livelihoods during the marriage. For instance, the spouses may have decided to work in nonprofits, or as artists or writers. They may not have saved for retirement, counting on an inheritance from the parents of one of the spouses to provide for them after they stopped working.

In this case, an inheritance may be divided between the spouses as marital property upon divorce, but not necessarily equally. It depends on the needs of the parties, and also their ages. The court is concerned in "gray" divorces of older spouses that each spouse is adequately protected for the future. At times, even expectations of future inheritances may become relevant, as in the case of the 65-year-old divorcing couple, where one spouse will receive a huge inheritance from aged parent fairly soon.

In summary, in equitable distribution states, there is an aim to have an *equitable* distribution of property if a marriage breaks up. Relying on the laws is intended to provide a fair result in all cases.

Equitable distribution states with prenup-like provisions.

In some equitable distribution states, protective elements of prenups are specifically included in the divorce law by statute or case law.

For instance, in New York, divorce laws protect premarital property and gifted and inherited property (as well as appreciation of that property) from being considered "marital" property by defining it as separate property. There is an exception to the extent appreciation is due in part by the contributions or efforts of the other spouse. (N.Y. Dom. Rel. §§ 236(B)(1)(d)(1) and (d)(3).)

If you have an inherited securities account in your name, and your spouse actively worked with you in deciding the investment strategy, the increase of that account may be deemed marital property upon a divorce in New York. If so, the sharing of that account will be decided under equitable principles. The same might apply if a spouse has a separate property business in which the other spouse works.

Other property in New York is divided equitably when a couple divorces, based on the usual factors set forth above.

Virginia is also an equitable distribution state with some "prenup-like" protections. Marital property is property acquired during the marriage and is divided under equitable principles. Property acquired before the marriage, as well as gifted or inherited property is separate property and stays with the spouse who owns it. (Va. Code Ann. § 20-107.3.)

As with New York law, if a spouse makes an active contribution to the separate property of the other spouse, the increase in value of the property (or part of it) may be considered marital property.

In all states, commingling of marital property and separate property can cause difficulties in divorces. Generally, if the separate property component can be traced back to its inception, and if the intent was not to make a gift to the marital estate, it may maintain its separate nature. Obviously, this can cause problems in a divorce where the parties fail to reach an agreement on the distribution of separate and commingled property.

Community property states.

A small number of states have imported laws from Spain rather than from England, as occurred in the common law (equitable distribution) states. In one state (Louisiana), the law was imported from France via the Napoleonic code. These are the so-called community property states. They are Arizona, California, Idaho, Louisiana, New Mexico, Nevada, Texas, and Washington. The U.S. territory of Puerto Rico is also a community property jurisdiction. Alaska has adopted an "elective" community property system for Alaska residents. In that state, a resident can opt into community property treatment.

The basic principle of community property law is that the acquisition of property by labor during marriage by either spouse is seen as a contribution to the marriage and therefore marital property. The presumption is that the relative value of the contribution made by each spouse is equal, no matter what form their contribution to the marriage takes. One party's labor can be in the workplace; the other party's labor can be at home.

In community property states, marital property is equally divided, without considering equitable factors. Title to property acquired during the marriage (i.e., whose name the property is titled in) may not be relevant to characterization. If an asset is deemed community property, it belongs to the community and is considered marital property, regardless of whose name is on the title.

This title/ownership issue was an important distinction between community property states and the common law states before the 1970s. In the common law states, title to property controlled which spouse kept the property in a divorce. Before equitable distribution laws began to be enacted in the common law states during the 1970s, the community property system was much more protective of spouses who didn't work outside of the home.

In the non-community property states, the question of who held title (usually the breadwinner) was the major determinant of property division in connection with divorce. Starting in the mid-twentieth century, non-community property states began to update their laws so that property division became an equitable system in which legal title to property became less relevant and equitable principles started to prevail.

Community property states distinguish separate property from community property. Separate property consists of assets a spouse had before the marriage, earnings after separation, and property gifted to or inherited by a spouse before and during the marriage. Community property consists of all property acquired by the efforts of both spouses after the marriage. In this sense, the community property states have imposed by law the typical major provisions regarding classification of premarital property and inheritances that are found in many prenuptial agreements. In fact, settling these two issues is the driving force for most prenups.

The laws pertaining to income from separate property may be different in certain community property states. For example, in most of these states, income generated by separate property such as rent, dividends or interest remains separate property during marriage. But in other states, income from separate property becomes community property during the same marital period. Choices pertaining to merging income from separate property into marital property can be made in prenups. (See Chapter 17.)

Generally, appreciation of separate property remains separate, unless a party is entitled to "reimbursement" or the community acquires some interest in the separate property. This happens if the appreciation is the result of a spouse's work, labor, or efforts during the marriage. A common example would be if after marriage one spouse worked in a business owned by that spouse as separate property, and that work resulted in an increase in the value of the business.

Can a court take equitable factors into account when making property division in a community property state?

In most community property states, community property is divided equally upon divorce, and separate property stays with the original owner. However, that may not always be the case.

For instance, in Texas, community property is divided by what is "just and right" in each particular divorce case. Some of the factors used by a Texas court, such as disparity of earning capacity, ages and health of spouses, and anticipated inheritance, are very similar to what might be applied in an equitable distribution under "equitable" distribution. (Tex. Fam. Code § 7.001 et seq.) Other factors that can be weighed in Texas include the amount of separate property of each spouse and amount of community property available to divide between the spouses.

Washington State is another community property state that applies a "just and equitable" standard to property division, after considering a number of factors. These include the extent of community property and marital property, the length of the marriage, and the economic circumstances of the parties at the time of divorce. (Wash. Rev. Code § 26.09.080.) This means that a spouse can be awarded more than half of community property, and separate property can be divided under equitable factors.

Similarly, in Nevada, the court has the authority to divide community property unequally if the court finds that there is a "compelling reason" to do so. (Nev. Rev. Stat. § 125.150(1)(b).)

Wisconsin is a community property state with a presumptive equal division of marital property. But a court in Wisconsin can deviate from the equal distribution based on a number of factors, including how much separate property each of them has that is not subject to division. (Wis. Stat. § 767.61(3).)

In California, if the community estate is underwater, meaning the community debts exceed the community assets, the court has the ability to allocate debt equitably based on factors such as relative ability to pay. (Cal. Fam. Code § 2622(b).)

Alimony in equitable distribution and community property jurisdictions.

Alimony is still important in some cases, even though women are now more active in the workforce. Alimony is now gender neutral in all states. There is no appreciable distinction in the laws of spousal support as between the equitable distribution states and the community property states.

Alimony is generally considered separately from property division. Spouses accrue rights to property during a marriage, and also accrue rights to support, if needed and if appropriate under the support laws of the state. As a result, in general, alimony is not supposed to come from assets (or income from assets) that have been divided in a divorce. It's a sharing of income based on equitable factors that existed during a marriage, with state variations as to amount and duration. In a court case, an analysis by the judge would be expected, based on the applicable case law and statutes.

(For a more detailed discussion of alimony laws, see Chapter 15.)

Retirement benefits in divorce.

There are two basic types of retirement plans: "defined contribution" plans such as 401(k)s, IRAs, and 403(b)s, and "real" or "defined benefit" pensions, such as company pensions (very rare now), teacher pensions, and federal pensions. Social security is similar to a defined benefit pension, in that a person receives a certain determined benefit periodically.

Defined contribution plans are funds of assets created by an employee's contributions (and sometimes an employer's). Defined benefit plans are different. With a defined benefit pension, employee contributions will be taken out of paychecks, but the plan benefit itself is based on years of employment and is often affected by the level of the last several years of salary. The actual appraised value of a defined benefit pension is generally much greater than the lump-sum amount the employee (and the employer) has put into the fund.

Retirement benefits are generally divided into premarital and postmarital elements by an apportionment approach in both community property and equitable distribution states. Since it is difficult to trace the final value between pre- and postmarital contributions and appreciation on each portion, this generally takes the form of a "coverture" formula.

The "coverture" formula is a fraction in which the numerator is the months of the marriage, and the denominator is the months from the start of the account to the end of the marriage. That formula determines the marital portion of the retirement account, which is community property (or marital property in an equitable distribution state). This value is generally divided by two to determine each spouse's portion in this "partnership" asset.

In defined benefit pensions, decisions about electing survivor's benefits to the non-employee spouse if the employee spouse dies are very important issues to be resolved in a divorce. In some states, rights of new spouses of the employee (participant) spouse can negate the rights of ex-spouses to future pension benefits.

A social security benefit is subject to federal law. It is not contractual interest such as a company pension or a defined contribution account. As a result, you can't ask a state court to divide a social security benefit. However, a social security benefit can be actuarially valued and be taken into account when making the overall property division. Also, if one spouse gets a much greater social security check than the other, a compensating support payment to the other spouse could be agreed to in the divorce settlement agreement. Or more of a spouse's pension can be distributed to the spouse with a lower social security payment to compensate for the difference. Ex-spouses may obtain derivative social security benefits if the marriage lasts ten years or longer; these derivative benefits are independent, not the result of a "division" of the other spouse's benefits, and do not affect the benefits to which the working spouse is entitled.

How is a closely held business treated in divorce?

What if a spouse works actively in a business and has an ownership interest in it? How is this treated in divorce? With this issue, also, there are no appreciable differences between community property and equitable distribution states.

Division of businesses is one of the thorniest and most contentious issues in divorces. This is because when a party is engaged in a business, he or she is spending marital efforts in earning money, and also is potentially increasing the value of the underlying asset. That underlying interest may a sole proprietorship, a C corporation, an S corporation, or an interest in a partnership or limited liability company. To further complicate things, the business might have been bought or invested in with separate property of the working spouse. It may also have been partly capitalized by marital money or money from outside investors.

There is a "community efforts" doctrine articulated in community property states. Under this, the law recognizes that time, toil, and efforts of both of the spouses during the marriage belong to the community estate, i.e., the efforts produce "marital property" in the language of equitable distribution states.

Sometimes a spouse's earned salary from the business entity is set at an artificially low level. That spouse might receive the salary plus a stream of non-wage "business income." This raises a conflict as to whether the non-salary part of the business earnings is "separate" or "marital." Additionally, the business income may be plowed back into the business to help it grow. Thus, figuring out the marital portion of the increased value of a business during a marriage might be difficult, expensive, and subject to dispute.

When a spouse uses his or her efforts in a business bought with separate property, how does that relate to efforts of the at-home spouse? A New York appeals court said that the stay-at-home spouse had indirectly contributed efforts to the business. *Price v. Price*, 69 N.Y.2d 8 (1986). This is the same result that would occur in an equitable property state, even if the business started as premarital property. However, an opposite result may occur if it's a premarital business in which the owning spouse's efforts are passive and not active. See, e.g., *Hartog v. Hartog*, 95 N.Y.2d 36 (1995).

If alimony and/or child support are payable in a divorce, issues of "double counting" may arise in valuing a closely held business for property division. In general, the value of a business will depend on what someone will pay for it. Often the value is based on the income that a business earns. If a spouse is deriving income from the business, the active spouse's reasonable earned income should be subtracted from business income in assessing the fair market value of the business. See, e.g., *Sampson v. Sampson*, 62 Mass. App. Ct. 366 (2004). In that way, the income subject to the support payments is not, in essence, double counted by being part of the property division, too.

In paying out the non-active spouse, parties can agree on a payout during a time period with interest, similar to a mortgage. Closely held businesses are a good topic to address in a prenup, and can lead to predictable and fair results. (See Chapter 9.)

What happens when you change your domicile?

When you move from a community property state to an equitable distribution state (or vice versa), there may be some confusion and uncertainty in terms of which marital laws will apply. In general, if property is community property, it will remain so when moving to an equitable distribution law state. But separate property may be in question in the new jurisdiction. Without a prenup, newly acquired property after the change of residence (whether marital, inherited, or gifted) will fall under the rules of the state in which you now live.

These issues can be addressed and resolved in prenups by the choice of law provision. This provision designates which state's laws will apply to the contract at signing, and even if the parties move out of state. However, it is important to have an existing prenup reviewed by an attorney practicing in the new state when you move, especially if you move from an equitable distribution state to a community property state, and vice versa. There may be requirements of the new jurisdiction that need to be met, and couples can mutually agree to amend the prenup as may be needed.

What happens if you die without a prenup?

I am always surprised that many prenup drafts I receive from attorneys for the more moneyed spouse leave the issue of inheritance completely open. Why not assure a minimum distribution if the marriage ends with the death of a spouse? An oral promise by a spouse to sign an estate plan later does not guarantee any minimum distribution to the other spouse. A general requirement specifying a minimum ("floor") percentage of an estate to be transferred to the surviving spouse can be written into a prenup. I incorporate this in all the prenups I draft.

There are potential problems if you save the decision until later. A spouse may decide to disinherit their spouse, and the disinherited spouse may not even know about it. Or the spouse may be engaged in another relationship at the end of their life. Or the other spouse may start to become "eccentric" in a way that doesn't rise to the level of legal incompetence, but can cause disinheritance.

Also, provisions in the prenups can help regulate and determine estate provisions when there are children from previous marriages. (See Chapter 10.)

It should be noted that provisions in prenups override state inheritance laws. The material below explains what those inheritance rights are.

Intestacy (dying without a last will) and "Taking Against the Will."

Widows and widowers have rights to inherit in all states, even if there is no last will (intestacy), if they are not named in the last will, or if they are beneficiary of an unreasonably small inheritance. These spousal inheritance rights can be enforced under state law. (Note that prenups almost always have provisions that take away these state law rights.)

Probate and non-probate property: "Probate" assets are assets in the deceased spouse's name. These flow through the will to the beneficiaries named in the will. The deceased spouse may also have "non-probate" assets that do not flow through the will. These include life insurance policies, annuities, and retirement assets with beneficiary designations, as well as property held in trusts. Non-probate assets also include property held in joint names or accounts designated as "payable on death" (POD) or "transfer upon death" (TOD). It is possible that all of a deceased's property is non-probate. If so, the last will (if he or she had one) would be a nullity and would not need to be probated.

Intestacy: Intestacy laws are intended to protect the spouses and children of people who die without wills, and reach only probate property. The laws were designed during the times when women often died in childbirth, lives in general were of shorter duration, and many couples had previous spouses who were deceased. As a result, there were often children from previous marriages to consider. The intent of the laws was to provide distributions to the surviving spouse, and also to children of the deceased, some of whom might not be the children of the surviving spouse.

In most states, there are still vestiges of this old law encapsulated in the intestacy statutes, even though people now have a much greater life expectancy. There are variations, but the surviving spouse receives a certain proportion of the deceased spouse's estate (30 to 50 percent). The rest of the property is distributed to the children of the deceased.

The problem with the law is that it is "blind" – it doesn't take into account the needs of the surviving spouse, or whether that spouse has received other (non-probate) assets, such as life insurance policy proceeds or retirement accounts. In addition, it sometimes is applied even if all the children were the children of the marriage, with children receiving their share outright at age 18. You could have a circumstance where a widowed mother of underage children has half of the estate of her deceased husband, and the children the other half. That's why it's so important for people to write wills.

Uniform Probate Code (UPC) (1969), drafted by the National Conference of Commissioners on Uniform State Laws, sought to remedy this problem. The UPC either in its entirety or with variations has at this time been adopted by 17 states, including community property states and equitable distribution states. The details vary from state to state, but the basic template remains the same.

The UPC provisions relating to people dying without wills have been designed to create a fairer system for what gets transferred to the surviving spouse and what is transferred to children and other relatives. Under the UPC, there is a major distinction between situations where all the children are from the current marriage or a previous marriage. If all the children are the children of the decedent and the surviving spouse, the surviving spouse would then receive the entire probate estate of the decedent.

This is consistent with the usual result when couples intentionally draft estate plans – first to the surviving spouse, and then to the children of that couple. If it is a blended family, then the result is similar to the "old" intestacy laws – the surviving spouse will receive part of the estate, and the children (including the children from the present marriage) would receive the other part. (UPC Sections 2-102 and 2-103.)

Taking Against the Will: But what if the decedent spouse left a will that disinherited the spouse or left the spouse with an unreasonably small legacy? The legal proceeding that deals with this situation is called "taking against the will," "taking an elective share," or "taking a forced share." It is a court proceeding in which the widow or widower elects to take a statutory amount instead of what was (or what was not) left to that spouse under the will.

In the states that have not adopted the UPC, the forced share amount is similar to what a spouse would have received if the other spouse had died intestate. Sometimes property subject to the elective share is transferred outright to the surviving spouse. In some states (including Massachusetts), the amount transferred to the surviving spouse is required to be held in an income-only trust, with the remainder at that spouse's death to go to the children of the deceased spouse or the other beneficiaries in that spouse's last will. (Mass. Gen. Laws chapter 191, § 15.)

In many of these states, only assets in the probate estate can be reached by this process. In some states (including Massachusetts, by case law), the spouse's election can reach property held in a revocable trust (a non-probate asset) established by the decedent spouse. *Sullivan v. Burkin*, 390 Mass. 864 (1984).

The problem, of course, is that enlarging the scope of the forced share in a state might entail litigation, as in the *Sullivan v. Burkin* case, which had to be appealed to the highest state court. A surviving spouse has enough on his or her mind aside from meeting deadlines, including the deadline for making the forced share claim and filing a lawsuit, especially when the disinheritance may have been a very devastating surprise after the death.

The Uniform Probate Code and the "augmented" estate.

To the rescue comes the Uniform Probate Code. For spousal elections to take against the will, the UPC takes a nuanced view of assets that are in the "base" for a claim of a spousal elective share of a decedent's estate. In addition, it takes the modern position, viewing the marriage as a shared economic partnership.

In order to figure out what the surviving spouse's elective share is, the first step is to determine the "augmented" estate. There are variations among the adopting states as to the exact formula involved in making this determination, but the basics are as follows:

The augmented estate includes the decedent's net probate estate, non-probate transfers to others, such as life insurance proceeds, retirement assets, property placed in revocable trusts, and the decedent's interest in joint tenancy property, as well as certain transfers made by the decedent within two years before the death. It also includes the surviving spouse's assets, including transfers made to the surviving spouse by the decedent during the decedent's life, and what is transferred to that spouse upon the decedent's death, as well as transfers the surviving spouse or the deceased spouse may have made to others. It provides a very good picture of what the surviving spouse already has, or will receive, from the decedent's probate and non-probate estate.

If the surviving spouse already owns (or will own) more of that spouse's share of the augmented estate as calculated under the statute, that spouse would not elect to take against the will.

There is a great deal of variation among the states that have adopted the UPC-based elective share provisions. Some states have adopted UPC type statutes for their elective shares laws, without adopting the entire UPC. Massachusetts has adopted the entire UPC, but has omitted the elective share provisions and still uses its old "forced share" laws for this election.

In some states, property owned by the decedent before the marriage, and all income and gains derived from that property, and inheritances and gifts received by the decedent are not included in the "augmented" estate. Inclusion of life insurance policies paid to others and retirement assets paid to others varies among the states adopting the UPC.

Under the 2008 amendments to the UPC, the marital portion of the augmented estate increases with the length of the marriage, reflecting the increase in the marital economic partnership, similar to that which is reflected in divorce laws. The augmented estate is multiplied by a percentage that starts at 3 percent for marriages of less than one year, and caps at 50 percent for marriages lasting 15 years or more.

As a result, the surviving spouse would receive half of the marital portion of the augmented estate as a forced share if the marriage is of 15 years duration or more. (In some states, the figure under the UPC as adopted would be a lesser percentage if it is a "blended" family.) The UPC law, then, is similar to the "old" elective share laws, but provides a more nuanced result based on actual financial realities and brings elective-share law into the modern view of marriage as an economic partnership.

It is important to note that virtually all prenups completely eliminate the right to receive an intestate share of a spouse's estate, as well as the right to take a forced share. That's why it's so important to think about and include inheritance provisions in the prenup if the marriage ends due to one of the spouse's death.

Are spouses responsible for each other's debts?

A huge concern for some couples who are intending to marry is whether they will be responsible for each other's debts. Sometimes this concern is a precipitating factor for people considering a prenup before marriage.

The general rule in both equitable distribution and community property states is that premarital debts incurred by a spouse are that spouse's responsibility alone. As for debts incurred after marriage, in equitable distribution jurisdictions, debts incurred by one spouse for "family necessities" may be considered a joint responsibility. These are generally limited to expenses for food, shelter, basic medical care, and the like. So theoretically, other than this narrow exception, the debts of one spouse cannot be levied (i.e., collected) on assets owned by the other spouse in equitable distribution states.

But a problem can arise after marriage with respect to collection of pre-marital or postmarital debts if there is joint property. A debt collector can attempt to collect the separate debt by attaching a debtor spouse's interest in property – even in jointly held property. Technically, the creditor cannot take the other spouse's interest in that property, but defending against the legal action can be costly to resolve.

In community property states, postmarital debts of either party can be attached and collected from the post-marriage community property, even if the property is titled in the non-debtor's name. Premarital debts can be collected from spouse's share of community property.

As a result, in either an equitable distribution or a community property state, if there is a premarital (or postmarital) debt problem, it is important to assess possible claims on postmarital property, and whether such property should be held jointly or separately.

It should be noted that a prenuptial agreement cannot change state law with respect to debt collection. State law will override what you may have written in your agreement. Thus, if you are in a community property state that holds both spouses liable for post-marriage debt incurred by one of the parties, and your prenup says that you alone are responsible for that debt, a creditor will not have to respect that language in your "private" contact.

What you can do in a prenup is have the other spouse indemnify you and hold you harmless for that debt your spouse incurred. That means, as between you and your spouse, by contract (the prenup) your spouse would be required to pay the debt, or reimburse you if you paid the debt for your spouse. But this only works if that spouse has assets or income to make good on his or her promise.

Chapter 8:

PRENUPS FOR WEALTHY PEOPLE AND FOR PEOPLE FROM WEALTHY FAMILIES

Protecting a wealthy spouse from loss of control and possession over his or her wealth in a marriage is one of the most common and understandable reasons for having a prenup. The wealthy spouse may have an interest maintaining control over his or her assets during marriage, and also upon divorce or death. This needs to be balanced with what's important for a marriage – love expressed by generosity and caring about someone's future security – whether the marriage lasts forever or not.

Prenups in the news.

Wealthy spouses are especially apprehensive about what happens if there is a divorce after a short- or medium-length marriage. Prenups that are drafted to meet these issues commonly go far beyond what may be needed to address these concerns.

Another concern of the wealthy party might be to avoid litigation if the marriage ends in divorce. The publicity surrounding contested divorces of the rich and famous is uncomfortably exposing. We all remember the Paul McCartney and Heather Mills divorce of 2008, which was fodder for the tabloids for two years. The couple did not have a prenup. The judge's 58-page judgment containing all the details of the divorce was released to the public. It is interesting to note that Paul McCartney has since remarried – again without a prenup. A reason for this may be his new spouse's own wealth.

Fallout from the McCartney divorce included a satirical mockumentary of Heather Mills's life story. The British tabloids printed false, hurtful, and allegedly defamatory stories about her, for which they later apologized. She had become a target for misogynistic sentiments. A journalist wrote in the *Guardian* that "She has somehow become the vessel through which it is acceptable for both pundits and the public to express their very worst feelings about women." Headlines about the case included one referring to her as "Lady Liar."

The problem faced by McCartney and Mills is that in England, prenuptial agreements had not been deemed enforceable in courts of law. This has changed since the McCartney and Mills case with a 2010 British Supreme Court decision, *Radmacher v. Granatino*,UKSC 42, in which a prenup was upheld.

In the U.S., prenups are upheld in every state with various protections based upon the facts of a case. (See Chapter 18.) Yet some of the wealthy and famous do not opt for this protection.

The Kelsey and Camille Grammer divorce after 13 years of marriage was in the news for several years. They married in 1996 after he had earned a great deal from his appearances on "Cheers" and "Frasier." But apparently, his net worth was zero at the time of the marriage. Applying normal California community property law, the two agreed to divide the assets accumulated during the marriage in half.

Before Donald Trump married Ivana in 1977, the parties entered into a prenuptial agreement. Trump's attorney was Roy M. Cohn. During the marriage, there were three additional (postnuptial) agreements. As Trump said at the time of the first postnuptial agreement, it was he who suggested it. "I thought it was appropriate," he said. "I was upwardly mobile."

In the end, the couple settled, apparently under the terms of the final postnuptial agreement. Ivana reportedly received a lump sum, the family mansion in Connecticut, an apartment in Trump Plaza, and use of the Palm Beach mansion. She also received a housing allowance and alimony. Ivana reportedly received much less than half of the assets accumulated during the marriage, however.

Marla Maples was not so lucky. After a five-year marriage to Donald Trump, she reportedly received a $2 million settlement, at a time when Trump reportedly had an estimated net worth of $5 billion. The marriage ended just months short of a milestone in the parties' prenup that would have increased her settlement upon divorce. (See below for discussion of the possible negative effects of milestone triggers in prenups.)

According to a Charlie Rose *60 Minutes* interview in 1998, Bill Gates said that there is no prenuptial agreement between him and his wife, Melinda. They reside in the state of Washington, a community property jurisdiction, under which laws they would equally divide assets accumulated during their marriage if there were a divorce. Bill and Melinda may feel this would be a fair result if they divorced.

When Mark Zuckerberg married Priscilla Chan, everyone wondered whether there would be a prenup. The marriage was in California, a community property state. Zuckerberg had previously signed a "relationship contract" with her, but this was a "lifestyle" contract that set a minimum of quality time they would spend together. It seems Zuckerberg may be something of a workaholic.

Celebrity divorce lawyer Raoul Felder said of the Zuckerberg and Chan marriage, "You can bet your last dollar – actually you can bet his last dollar – that he has a prenup. If he doesn't, he ought to go to a psychiatrist and not a lawyer." Notwithstanding Zuckerberg's possible mental state and Felder's biting comment, it is possible that Zuckerberg may have skipped the prenup. Perhaps he felt that he should have "skin in the game." Perhaps he thought it fair to share post-marriage accumulation of wealth with Priscilla in accordance with California community property laws.

It is interesting to note that the marriage took place the day after the IPO of Facebook. That IPO established a value for Zuckerberg's interest in stock at the date of the marriage. Whether or not there was a prenup, it will be crystal clear what the post-marriage increase of Zuckerberg's Facebook holdings will be, which might be community property under California law. It may be that there is a prenup, and that it addresses the characteristic of the post-marital gain on Facebook stock. Perhaps the prenup deems it marital property to be equally shared under California's community property laws.

If it is true that Bill Gates and Mark Zuckerberg opted out of a prenup or specified in a prenup that post-marriage wealth (even that which is derived from "separate property") would be shared, it shows their appreciation of valuing each spouse's contributions to the marital venture.

How the issue of prenups arises for people of wealth.

For wealthy people who do opt for a prenup, its terms can provide predictable and easy-to-administer financial results when the marriage ends. But when a person is wealthy, he or she can afford to be generous in the terms of a divorce. This is often forgotten and not encouraged by the more moneyed spouse's lawyer. Having that generosity memorialized in a prenup can serve to make divorce less likely and the marriage happier.

In my practice, I see four basic situations in which prenups for wealthy people arise.

The future spouse may have created wealth through his or her own activities and work efforts. Perhaps the future spouse has created a business or is a high-level executive in a business. Perhaps the person is an accomplished actor or athlete. Generally, this type of person who has self-made wealth is older than the typical person marrying for the first time. That person might be entering into a second (or third) marriage.

The second situation arises when the future spouse's parents have already died, and he or she received an inheritance through direct transfers by will or has an interest in property held in trust. Sometimes the future spouse's own earnings are modest, and sometimes they are substantial.

A third instance may be where the future spouse's parents are wealthy and still living. They amassed their wealth either by themselves or through inheritance. The parents almost never had a prenup, but they have heard horror stories of divorces. They want to make sure that in a divorce their son or daughter gets to keep their property. Perhaps they have given lifetime gifts to their child, but the bulk of the inheritance will come later, upon the parents' deaths.

The fourth scenario is where the parents have a very profitable ongoing business in which their child, the future spouse, is employed. That business will eventually be solely owned by their child or owned by a family group that includes their child.

All these situations have their unique challenges in figuring out how to balance the origins of the money, control by the wealthy spouse (or the one with a substantial expectancy of wealth), with provisions in a prenup that will support the marriage and provide equity to both spouses that reflects their efforts during the marriage.

One of the problems in these situations is the dynamics of the negotiation process, which may be quite challenging and distressing. Without some clear thought as to how to proceed both as to the substance of the prenup and the process, the "wealthy party" prenup can cause irreparable harm to the upcoming marriage.

A typical client scenario.

Here is how a conversation about a prenup usually begins.

I get a call from a woman. Let's call her Alicia. She is to marry Elliot in several months. A big wedding has been planned and paid for. Alicia and Elliot have been dating for four years and engaged for one. They are living together. Alicia is 28 and Elliot is 31. They plan to have children soon. They are both teachers, working in different school systems.

Elliot's parents have accumulated a great deal of assets, from a combination of his father's work as an executive in several Fortune 500 companies and his mother's inheritance from her parents, who in turn received it from the maternal grandmother's father, who had railroad interests in the early twentieth century.

Elliot's parents are retired, and Elliot has an older sister who recently married. The parent's estate-planning lawyer (who they call their "family" attorney) prepared a prenup for Elliot's sister, which was quite restrictive in terms of wealth sharing. The sister's fiancé, not wanting to be seen as a weak male partner, signed it without comment. Now they want Elliot and Alicia to sign the same prenuptial agreement.

Alicia has met Elliot's parents, and so far has had a warm relationship with them. But discussion about a prenup has had a very negative effect on her and on her feelings toward Elliot's parents. The first draft was created by their family lawyer. Alicia's lawyer has not been able to negotiate any significant changes to its terms. It is presented as a "take it or leave it" document. Elliot feels Alicia should sign it, because his sister did, and he assures Alicia that he'll treat her fairly during their marriage, no matter what is in the prenup.

Furthermore, he can't even imagine any situation in which they would get divorced. They are quite compatible, and very much in love.

Yet Alicia and her attorney are concerned about the prenup draft. What the prenup says is that all gifted and inherited property received by Elliot and all the income generated by it will be solely his forever. This would be true even if the marriage lasts for many years, and even if it ends with his death. When he dies, the prenup is silent about what happens to the inherited and gifted property in Elliot's name, and all other property acquired during their marriage. That means, even if the marriage has lasted 40 or 50 years, when Elliot dies, he has the power to give his property to anyone he chooses, and leave nothing to Alicia outright.

While Elliot assures Alicia that she will be his beneficiary when he dies, his estate plan could be changed at will during his lifetime. What if, at age 75, Elliot becomes enraptured with another woman and changes his will? What if Elliot becomes angry with Alicia, doesn't divorce, but changes his will so that others receive his property upon his death?

If they married with no prenup, the spousal "elective share" state law protection for a disinherited spouse would be available. (See Chapter 7.) But the prenup says (as do virtually all prenups) that Alicia would be precluded from exercising those rights. It's very different from the typical estate plan for a first marriage, in which the entire estate goes to the surviving spouse. The prenup seems like the worst of all possible worlds, and leaves all control in Elliot's hands. It's really affecting Alicia's feelings toward him, especially given his attorney's intransigence, which she is starting to attribute to Elliot.

Alicia starts thinking about these dynamics. She and Elliot are committed to their professions. They both have modest incomes as teachers. The money coming from Elliot's family, if shared, can help them improve their living standards. It can provide financial security for the family beyond what they are able to attain themselves, and both of them would like Alicia to leave the job market for a while to raise their children.

But Alicia starts wondering about her future security. She's starting to wonder what exactly will be shared. Elliot wants her to sign the prenup as is, and she is starting to wonder if she should really marry Elliot.

If she had married someone without family wealth, she and her future husband might be thinking of ways to maximize their earnings. In all states, earnings during marriage, no matter who is the earner, are marital property. If Alicia had married someone who wasn't wealthy or from a wealthy family, her prospects for security and accumulating wealth might be greater. Perhaps they would both be attempting to maximize their income and wealth during the marriage.

She's now thinking that it might in fact be better to marry someone from a modest background who has more of a reason to be a go-getter. This is the ironic situation many future spouses face when they marry someone from a wealthy family.

Here's a somewhat similar yet different scenario. Let's assume the future wife's family has the wealth. The future husband expends all his earnings during the marriage to support the family. The wife from the wealthy family may not work outside the home. The couple is counting on the wife's family wealth to provide for their retirement and to supplement their lifestyle. But when there's a divorce after a long marriage, the husband can be left without adequate financial security.

This can happen whether or not there is a prenup. In a Massachusetts case, there was a 48-year-long marriage without a prenup. The husband was 76 years old at the time of the divorce. The parties had relied on the wife's trust fund for their future financial security. The husband had contributed all his earnings to the upkeep of the household during the marriage. When the couple divorced, there was insufficient marital property, if shared equally, to provide for the husband in his old age. *Comins v. Comins*, 33 Mass. App. Ct. 28 (1992).

In *Comins*, the Court decided that the wife's interest in the trust was a marital asset. The judgment provided 44 percent of the marital estate to the husband and 56 percent to the wife. This, in spite of the admissions by the husband that he slapped his wife in the face on six to eight occasions "to stop [her] raving which was unbearable." The husband had to litigate in the lower court and defend an appeal by the wife to a higher court to receive this judgment.

If the Cominses had entered into a prenuptial agreement (not available when they married in 1940), the husband would have not been able to receive the additional distributions that the Court required from the trust assets. They would not have been included in the calculation of marital property. He simply would have been out of luck.

A similar case in Maryland involved a situation in which there was a prenup signed prior to the marriage. Again, in that case, the wife was the more moneyed spouse. In the prenup, the husband relinquished all rights to property the wife had prior to their marriage, and those that might be acquired during the marriage. He also relinquished all rights to her estate if she died first. After the wife's death, pursuant to the terms of the prenup, the husband was disinherited. During their 44-year marriage, the husband had been steadily employed as an electrician and had turned over all his paychecks to the wife. She had repeatedly assured him that she "would take care of him." *Martin v. Farber*, 68 Md. App. 137 (1986).

The husband in that case did not prevail in his lawsuit seeking to invalidate the prenup as being unconscionable. The appeals court affirmed the validity of the prenup, only providing the husband a claim to his wife's estate to the extent he was able to trace his own earnings into her separate estate.

So, if you are thinking of signing a prenup, you should assume that the terms of the prenup will prevail, despite the assurances made to you by your future spouse. (See Chapter 18 on enforceability.)

How to solve the problem posed by family wealth.

It's ironic that family wealth poses problems to a marriage. But, if you think outside the box, you'll find that it is possible to create provisions that can foster mutual parity during a marriage. Putting these terms (or some of them) into the prenup will benefit both parties, as it will create goodwill between the spouses and strengthen the financial venture component of the marital bond.

Here are some ideas you might consider.

Sharing income from gifted or inherited assets.

The prenup could state that inherited and gifted property continues to be separate property. But to the extent income is generated from the separate property it becomes marital property upon receipt.

For example, let's say the daughter of wealthy parents receives a gift of stock in a corporation. The dividends paid on the shares of stock could be deemed marital property. If paid out, the dividends could be put into a joint account of the couple. Alternatively, if the parties prefer, the dividends could remain as separate property and kept in the separate account of the receiving party.

If the asset is a mutual fund, the spouses can choose not to have the dividends reinvested but rather distributed to the marital couple. Or if reinvested, the amount of the dividends (plus growth on the dividends) could be calculated in a reasonable manner and become martial property.

Under this scenario, the value of the principal (the stock itself) could grow, and the stock holdings would remain separate property.

The parties to the prenup have these possible choices to make – if they are able to act freely. (See below for "shadow party" problem.)

Sharing investment gain or appreciation attributable to gifted or inherited assets.

Let's take the same example as above. The wealthy parents of one of the spouses gives their daughter shares of a corporation worth $500,000, either before or during the marriage. The prenup could provide that gain in the value of the shares during the marriage becomes marital property to be shared during the marriage. Or, alternatively, in the event of divorce, a certain percentage of the gain in the value could become marital property during the marriage.

There can also be a schedule for the vesting of gains so that, say, after five years of marriage, 10 percent of the stock has vested into marital property, with the vesting to continue ratably according to a schedule based on the number of years of marriage, with 100 percent of the gain (or a lesser percentage, if desired) vested into marital property at some point in the future to be divided in the event of a divorce.

The philosophical question is how much wealth is enough? A person getting married with the prospect of wealth in the future (or present wealth) could and should think about his or her own security. But, also, a person can be realistic about what is needed in the future. Maybe that wealthy spouse doesn't have to keep everything. When you're married, the question is how much do you want to put into your marriage and how much do you want to keep for yourself.

Vesting of the principal of inherited or gifted property.

The same techniques discussed above regarding sharing and vesting income and gains can be considered to provide some sharing of the original asset value ("principal") of a separate property asset. This can be applied to both gifts and inheritances, those received before and during the marriage. The principal of the gifted and/or inherited property can gradually be vested as marital property, partially or in their entirety; a portion could remain inviolate as the recipient party's separate property. Which part (if any) shall vest and what the vesting schedule is, is totally up to the future spouses, who can decide this in their prenup.

Premarital property.

Premarital property is generally identified as separate property in prenups. But these various options (sharing income, gain, appreciation, or principal, or part of these) can also apply to premarital property that is not gifted or inherited.

Mixing and matching of the various techniques.

Future spouses can decide which of the above methods (if any) will be incorporated into their prenup. They can vest income from assets, gains on assets, and principal value of assets. This mix-and-match process can be drafted into the prenup. The vesting process can accelerate in speed as the marriage proves itself by years of duration and as the spouses mature.

Vesting by months, or years, or groups of years.

A prenup can stipulate that separate assets will be vested on a schedule that changes every five years. For instance, say in year 5 of the marriage, 10 percent of separate property vests into marital property, and in year 10 of the marriage, 20 percent of separate property will have vested, and so on.

There is another possibility to consider. This same vesting schedule can happen ratably each year (at 2 percent a year) or monthly at 1/6 percent each month.

There is an advantage to having increases in vesting on a monthly schedule.

Say in the tenth year of the marriage, a certain portion of separate property vests all at once. That anniversary date is coming, and there is no way the parties are not going to focus on what happens financially on that tenth anniversary. In fact, they may start focusing on it a year or two before. This can actually cause marital problems. People may start to second-guess the strength of their marriage as the target date approaches. The more moneyed spouse may start thinking that perhaps the marriage should be terminated before that trigger date. These types of deadlines can put a lot of strain on a basically solid marriage and can cause a weakening of a marriage that is undergoing some problems.

What if a spouse inherits after the end of the marriage?

Sometimes both parties to a prenup expect to inherit from their parents. What if one party has already inherited, or his or her parents are older than the other future spouse's parents, so that the prospect of an expectancy is closer at hand?

If there is vesting of separate property in the prenup, the spouses could run into a situation that could be inequitable. Let's say the husband has inherited in year 15 of the marriage and there is a vesting process that has begun, so that by year 20, a significant portion of his inheritance has vested into marital property. Imagine a divorce in year 22 of the marriage. Then imagine the ex-wife will receive a significant inheritance after the divorce from her parents in the future.

One of the ways to address this problem is to have vesting of post-marriage inheritances after all four parents of the couple are deceased. Another way to address this timing issue is to require equalizing paybacks after the marriage ends. This would be as additional property division when a post-marriage inheritance is received by the other spouse.

Property divisions are generally made at the time of divorce. The party receiving the property gets "carryover" basis. Further, no gain or loss will be recognized upon the transfer. In order for a marital transfer to qualify for this treatment, the transfer must be "incident" to the divorce. It is defined as such if it either occurs within one year after the date of the divorce or the transfer is "related to the cessation of the marriage." (Internal Revenue Code Section 1041.)

However, the presumption that the transfer is related to the cessation of the marriage may only last six years after the divorce. An argument may be able to be made that the later inheritance subject to equalizing payment pursuant to a divorce agreement (embodying the terms of a prenup) is related to the cessation of the marriage. But even without the favorable tax attributes, equalizing transfers can be made.

If you are considering a post-divorce equalization of inheritance provision, a consult with a tax lawyer familiar with Section 1041 and the gift tax laws would be highly recommended.

Sharing "annual exclusion" gifts and educational gifts.

Often parents who have the wherewithal of some extra wealth beyond their basic needs provide lifetime gifts to their children and grandchildren. These are termed "annual exclusion" gifts, which are permitted to be made without being in the parents' estates for calculating estate taxes due upon their deaths. (Internal Revenue Code Section 2503(b).)

The donors can make these gifts every year to an unlimited number of recipients. The amount of these gifts was initially $10,000 a year, and has increased by a cost-of-living adjustment, essentially inflation. The amount of these tax-free transfers (as of 2018) has risen to $15,000 a year. A donor spousal couple can make a total of $30,000 of gifts to each recipient each year, even if the funds given are titled in only one of the spouse's names. This is called "gift splitting" and is permitted by Section 2513 of the Internal Revenue Code.

Spouses of children and grandchildren are sometimes (but not always) included in this gifting regimen. A term to consider in a prenup is to have all these annual exclusion gifts made by any of the parents to the spousal couple deemed marital property upon receipt, no matter which spouse has received the gift and which parent made it. If the gift is greater than the $15,000 (or $30,000) level, the prenup can provide a rule as to how to treat these gift in excess of the annual exclusion amount.

A wealthy or well-off family also has the opportunity to significantly divest their future estates of unneeded assets and direct them toward their grandchildren by making gifts that can be used for their education. If made properly, these are not limited to the $15,000 annual gift tax exclusion, and can be made in addition to that exclusion. In order to fall under the educational gift tax exemption, the gift must be made as a payment directly to the educational institution. If the gift is made to the parents or the child directly, the exemption is lost. Payments under this provision are not limited to tuition for higher education. They can be made to primary or secondary schools, or colleges and universities. These exclusion payments can even fund graduate studies. (Internal Revenue Code Section 2503(e).)

Wealthy grandparents can set up Internal Revenue Code Section 529 college savings plans to fund their grandchildren's higher educations. For the gift to be excluded from gift tax, these need to be funded with annual exclusion gifts (although some front-loading of gifts is available). Allowable expenses include tuition, fees, books, and supplies, including computer purchases, as well as room and board. The institutions that can receive funding from the Section 529 plans are post-secondary educational institutions, including colleges, universities, and vocational schools.

The "shadow party" problem.

Often the wealthy parents of a prospective spouse are calling the shots. They might require a prenup, and specify the terms to be included in it. The future spouse, their son or daughter, is usually powerless to change the parents' minds. If that future spouse does not abide by their parents' wishes, he or she is put in the situation of disobeying the parents. But if the future spouse complies, he or she may be offending and causing harm to their future spouse. In legal lingo, third parties who are in control of one of the parties to a transaction are known as "shadow parties." In the prenup context, shadow parties are almost always the parents of the wealthier future spouse.

Often the option of getting a prenup is a requirement and not simply a suggestion. Parents may tell their child explicitly or by inference that they will disinherit him or her unless there is a prenup. They likely believe that the inherited wealth should stay within the bloodlines and not be shared with a spouse, no matter how long the marriage may last. The parents also usually pick and hire the prenup attorney for their child, who is often their own business lawyer or estate-planning lawyer.

The family lawyer bows down to the wishes of the parents, because he or she does not want to lose this important client. In doing so, the interests and wishes of the marrying child may not be adequately taken into account. The representation of the child may be adversely affected by the lawyer's allegiance to the parents. (See Uniform Rules of Professional Conduct Rule 1.7.)

To represent both the party to the upcoming marriage and his or her wealthy parents can create a conflict of interest according to the ethical rules that apply to attorneys. It is foreseeable that the interests of the marrying client may not be the same as the interests of his parents. Because of this inherent conflict, the "family" attorney of the future spouse may accept very little negotiation to the original terms set forth in the draft of the prenup that is sent to the fiancé for review. This is generally felt by both of the upcoming spouses as extremely hurtful. It's a painful way to begin a marriage.

However, when the prenup is required by the wealthy parents, their child and the other future spouse often accept this as the cost of creating peace in the family. It does come with costs to the future spouses, however, unless the legitimate interest of the parents as well as both of the future spouses are respected and adequately accommodated.

What do wealthy parents actually do?

I receive many telephone calls from thoughtful wealthy parents of a child who is engaged to be married. They are agonizing about whether to advise (or request, or require) that their child get a prenup before marriage. They have reservations about it, understanding that a prenup could be harmful to the child, to that child's future spouse, and to the marriage itself.

These concerned calls are invariably about first marriages of relatively younger people. Generally, but not always, the parents are "self-made" people having accumulated their wealth during their marriage. Naturally, they didn't have a prenup when they got married.

I provide a number of suggestions and share my thoughts with the parents. These are thoughts and techniques that I am sharing with you in this book. I describe various state laws that deal with inherited property at divorce, the dynamics set up by prenups, and remind them about the role of generosity in the marriage. They know full well the importance of having a joint venture in the marriage, and are struggling with the concept of a prenup. Everyone is telling them their son or daughter should have one – relatives, business associates, their financial planner, and their attorney. Many of them believe it would be unethical to insist on one or even to raise the topic with their child.

I remind them that they are relatively young now (in their late 50s or early 60s) and there is probably plenty of time to see how the marriage works out. They can do some estate planning preparation at some later point in time if their child's marriage is not on solid ground. They should be aware that in many cases, state laws do not include expectancies (future inheritances) in divorce settlements. I encourage them to think about the future – what if the marriage is intact when they die? Would they want some sort of independent security for the mother or father of their grandchildren who they've grown to love as a family member?

Since the parents are my clients, I also need to advise them of estate planning that they can do to control assets that will go to the married child upon their deaths. (See below.) But I also remind them of the negative effect that these trust-planning devices may have on the goodwill between them and their future son-in-law or daughter-in-law if their participation comes to light, which is likely.

What wealthy parents can do outside of requiring a son or daughter to get a prenup.

Wealthy parents have options to control money distributed to their children by their own estate planning and business succession planning aside from requiring that their child have a prenup. (For business succession planning, see Chapter 9.) They often do this to make sure assets stay within bloodlines.

Below are some of the estate planning techniques that operate "outside" a prenup that can be used to limit a less-wealthy spouse's access to funds of the wealthy spouse's parents.

Income-Only Trusts.

Trusts are contractual agreements in which funds are held for benefici-aries by a trustee or trustees. The trust agreement establishes the terms of the trust. Sometimes, all income earned by the trust assets is distributed to the trust beneficiary periodically. This is a standard provision because trust income tax rates are quite high and the highest bracket starts at a very low threshold of income. The beneficiary pays the income tax at his or her rates on the income distributed, which are often at a lower tax rate. Whatever income is retained in the trust is taxable at the trust rates.

The Tax Cuts and Jobs Act of 2017 (TCJA) reduced the income tax rates and extended the rate brackets. The highest income tax rate for all taxpayers (including trusts and estates) is now 37 percent. This is a reduction from the prior top tax rate of 39.6 percent. For trusts and estates, the top rate of 37 percent starts when taxable income exceeds $12,500.

Compare this with when the highest rate for individuals and couples (also 37 percent) is reached under the TCJA. The top rate for single filers is reached when taxable income exceeds $500,000 (under prior law, $418,400), and for a married couple filing jointly, when the taxable income exceeds $600,000 (for-merly $470,700).

Because trusts and estates reach the highest tax rates at only $12,500 of taxable income, most trusts require a mandatory distribution of income to the beneficiaries. But there is a downside to this. Income coming out of a trust can negatively affect a beneficiary's desire to build a career. However, the income can be helpful, especially for beneficiaries who are more mature and have started to find their way toward careers and responsible family life.

The problem with these trusts as generally written is that the income always stays within the bloodlines. A prenup can alter this effect. Income gen-erated from a trust and distributed to one of the spouses can easily become marital property if the couple so desires. It can be written as a term in the prenup. Another way to handle this issue is if the trust acknowledges and respects the child's marriage and provides the distributed income be considered joint, at least during their child's marriage. This can send a very strong positive message to the child's spouse. These trusts are generally revocable and amendable, so that a parent can monitor the marriage and make changes as needed. (The problem is that they become irrevocable at death.)

In a divorce, mandatory payment of all income coming out of a trust may be considered a stream of income for purposes of computing child support and/or alimony. It is less likely that a court would consider the present value of the stream of income valuing it like an annuity. If present-valued, the income stream could be deemed a marital asset to be divided in a divorce. The argument against that is that the trust is not a marital asset, as it is not developed by the partners to the marriage. The trust assets and income can come into play when dividing marital property, as this gifted and/or inherited income and wealth can provide security and opportunity to accumulate assets for one of the spouses. In some states, a court could take this into account and designate more than 50 percent of the marital assets to the other party.

Many trusts have "trigger" dates when beneficiaries can receive assets outright. A beneficiary may have a right to receive 50 percent of the trust assets outright and the balance of the trust at age 35. Those funds that a beneficiary has a right to receive outright would be deemed to belong to the beneficiary even if the person voluntarily leaves the money in the trust. Thus it may become property available to divide in a divorce.

Discretionary Trusts and the HEMS Standard.

Trusts may also be discretionary, both as to income and principal. In a discretionary trust, the trustee can decide when and how much of the trust funds to give a beneficiary. Typical language in a trust may allow for the trustee to have "complete and unfettered discretion" or "sole and uncontrolled discretion" in determining whether and to what extent a trust's income or principal should be distributed to a beneficiary.

Some trusts require that the trustee consider the "needs" or "comfort" of a beneficiary when making distributions. Some require the trustee to look into other resources available to the beneficiary before making discretionary distributions. In some trusts, the trustee is directed to use money for educational purposes. There may also be a group of beneficiaries of one trust fund, all of whom can receive discretionary distributions, which may be unequal and sporadic. There may be a trigger event (a beneficiary attaining a certain age, or the death of the person who created the trust) to divide what's left among the group of beneficiaries.

Many trusts adopt the health, education, maintenance, and support (HEMS) standard to apply distributions of income and principal to a beneficiary. Where trust distributions of income or principal are subject to the HEMS standard (or another specifically articulated standard), there is a greater chance that an ex-spouse may have an indirect right to trust assets because the beneficiary-spouse would have a right to compel payments by the trustee.

When distributions from a trust are totally discretionary, it is very difficult for the beneficiary to compel payments from the trust unless the trustees have abused their discretion. Abuse of discretion is very hard to prove. As a result, an ex-spouse in a divorce case may find it difficult or impossible to lay claim to the trust assets (or income if not automatically distributed). That's why discretionary trusts established by third parties (such as parents) can provide some protection to a divorcing spouse in many states. This holds especially true if the trustee is an "independent" trustee.

However, if there is a pattern of trustee support of a spouse, a court could infer that the same support might be available in the future. Or if the trustee might be a "yes man" or "yes woman" for the beneficiary. If so, the trust arrangement could be attacked and it could be asserted that a beneficiary had de facto control of the trust distributions.

In a Massachusetts case on point, extremely generous distributions under a discretionary HEMS standard to a husband stopped cold on the eve of his divorce filing. As a result, the Court held the part of the trust assets it attributed to the husband as marital property. *Pfannenstiehl v. Pfannenstiehl*, 88 Mass. App. Ct. 121 (2015).

The Massachusetts Supreme Judicial Court overruled this decision, but only on the basis that the trust was a "spray" trust that had 11 current beneficiaries, not just the husband. Therefore, the trustees could have provided any one of them differing amounts of distribution, or no distribution at all. As a result, the court found that the husband was not vested in one-eleventh of the trust, his interest was mere expectancy and could not be valued for purposes of divorce property division. *Pfannenstiehl v. Pfannenstiehl*, 475 Mass. 105 (2016).

Because of their relevance in divorces, a spouse's interest in a trust needs to be disclosed. It is important for the attorney for the less moneyed spouse to review the trust instrument, as well as the assets held in the trust.

Some wealthy parents may want create a lockbox estate plan that ties up outright distribution of funds to their children for their children's entire lifetimes. This is generally the standard trust plan that comes out of many law firms these days under the rubric of "asset protection."

There is, however, a huge downside to tying up your child's entire inheritance in a lifetime trust. The child (now a grown man or woman embarking on a marriage, or even a middle-aged son or daughter) will not have the experience of truly handling his or her own money and deciding his or her financial future.

Yes, with a lifetime discretionary trust, there will always be a level of protection. But that arrangement may infantilize the future spouse and distort that child's life and marriage decisions. It is sometimes good for a person to be in charge of his or her own life and finances, even if that person makes mistakes and has some financial reversals. That's life. Let the child live it.

And what if the wealthy beneficiary dies and the marriage is intact? Might it not make sense for a trust to benefit the spouse also? After all, he or she is the parent of your grandchildren. Wouldn't that person still be the parent of your grandchildren even if they eventually divorced? And yet, very rarely is the spouse named as beneficiary of these trusts, even by making a more modest bequest than that provided to the blood child.

If your child's marriage ends in divorce rather than death, one must consider what the effect of the asset protection trust may have been on the health of the marriage. Also, one might wonder whether gifts that have been given to a spouse and kept as separate property may have affected the marriage.

With respect to the married couple, an agreement in the prenup to share distributions of trust income during the marriage and a rational plan with regard to principal and income distributions from a family trust can go far in providing reasonable stability for the less wealthy spouse. It is an expression of generosity and caring on the part of the wealthy spouse, which bodes well for a marriage.

CHAPTER 9:

DO I NEED A PRENUP TO PROTECT MY BUSINESS?

One of the most frequent reasons people decide to have prenups is that they own, or have an interest in, a closely-held ongoing business in which they actively participate in order to earn their livelihood. Sometimes this is a participation in a family business, owned by their parents or other relatives. Sometimes it's the future spouse's business that he or she developed before the marriage. Some of these have other active partners or co-owners. People understandably do not want the claims of an ex-spouse to affect the control or operations of their business.

Here's an example of how some of these business prenup situations come about.

Sara and Charles's situation.

I get a call from a potential client, who is not the business-owning spouse. I'll call her Sara. She is going to marry Charles in several months.

Charles is a college graduate with a computer science degree who works in a family-owned computer services business. Charles's father and brother are quite active in the business. The father has a controlling interest of greater than 50 percent. The business is a Subchapter S corporation, and Charles has a 15 percent interest in it. He is not an officer of the corporation, but he works in the business – quite hard – usually 50 hours a week.

The company provides a wide range of computer-related services, including computer system design, software development, and business support. Within the company there are also employees who are not shareholders, some of whom are "professional" employees like Charles and some of whom are support staff. Charles is also a part owner of the limited liability company (LLC) that owns the building housing the business, owning a 15 percent interest, with his father having a controlling interest.

Eventually, Charles's father will retire, and Charles and his brother will take over the business. Charles has been working in the business for ten years – ever since his college graduation. The father has a business succession plan in which he will gift his interests in the business and in the LLC to Charles and his brother during his lifetime, with the remainder to be transferred upon his death.

As part of the prenuptial agreement disclosure process, Charles has shared several years of his tax returns and several years of the company's and the LLC's tax returns with Sara. He has also provided to her lawyer the company's most recent financial statement prepared in connection with applying for a commercial loan.

Sara is a public school teacher. She's been working for eight years and earns $75,000 a year. Her state pension is not yet vested. It's a first marriage for both Sara and Charles, and they are planning to start a family right away. Their intention is for Sara to take some time off from her teaching career while the children are young. She and Charles both think Sara may change career paths after the children reach school age. Because of Charles's intense work schedule, she and Charles expect that most of the homemaking work will fall on her.

Charles's tax return shows his salary as $50,000. Information technology experts at Charles's level of experience and in his geographic location earn an average of $155,000 per year working for a typical information technology company. Charles has two additional streams of income derived from the family business: his share of business profits (recorded on his Schedule E), which was $200,000 for the most recent tax year and income from the LLC that holds the real estate used by the company. His interest in the LLC produced $26,000 of income last year. As a result, his total income derived from the family business was $276,000 last year.

The prenup draft provided to Sara said that Charles would share his salary with her (i.e., the $50,000 income from the S corporation). None of the other income that he derives from the business would be considered marital money. It would be his separate property. (This is very typical in the first draft of family business prenups.) Whether or not to share the rest of the income ($226,000) would be under Charles's sole and complete control.

Charles, his father, and his brother want to continue growing the business. From time to time, the father requests that Charles and his brother reinvest some of the business's profits (less income taxes payable on the profits) back into the company for future growth. The amount of the business profits reinvested in the business each year varies widely. When Charles announced his engagement, his parents demanded that all his business profits be contributed back to the corporation.

The salary paid to the son is artificially low in order to limit the amount the son (and the company) are required to pay for social security and Medicare taxes. After all, it is assumed that the son, with the increasing value of the business, will not be dependent on social security old-age benefits for his retirement. But as his salary is set artificially low, it minimizes the amount of "marital" income he may be required to share with his new spouse under the prenup. The son's prenup attorney (who is also the family's business lawyer) wants Charles to be able to control how much money he contributes the marriage, under the rubric of "asset protection."

At the present time, Sara is working, and her income for marital purposes is even higher than Charles's. When she stops working to have a family, their baseline income will be so low that it will be impossible to save marital money for their future if Charles doesn't share some of his additional "separate" income. The prenup "generously" says all marital property is to be divided in half in case of a divorce.

The path sketched out in this prenup leaves the decision of sharing business income totally to the spouse (and his parents). If the marriage ends in divorce, Charles gets the business (which may have grown quite a bit during the marriage), and he and his wife equally share what could be a very little amount of marital property.

What's wrong with this picture?

The Problem.

Keeping a divorced spouse away from control of a family business or claims that could impair the business's economic vitality are certainly reasonable motives for a prenup. The problem in this situation is that it is usually done in an extreme way and may leave the new spouse out in the cold financially, even after a long marriage. It's obviously unfair in terms of the balance of contributions to the new family unit and the marriage. There are other ways to solve the problem of control and payment of a fair share of a spouse's earnings and gain from a spouse's active participation in the family business if the marriage ends in divorce.

The non-business-owning spouse in a first marriage is making his or her own contributions to the marriage. That spouse is certainly worthy of developing financial security as time goes on, whether the marriage ends in divorce or in the death of the other party. There are ways to find a path to meet both the family's goals in keeping ownership and control interest of the business within the family-of-origin unit and to address the new non-business spouse's reasonable goals for financial security and fair treatment.

People contribute different things to a marriage, and all their efforts are part of the marriage venture. This is why in all states, when a spouse spends time and efforts in a business that produces livelihood, his or her efforts are considered "marital" efforts. The financial fruits of those efforts are to be taken into account if the marriage ends in divorce. This comes from a sense of equity and the doctrine of marriage as a partnership, each spouse contributing his or her particular efforts.

The spouse who does not work in the family business also contributes to the marital enterprise, by supporting the working spouse, taking care of the household and children, and/or working outside the home. This is reflected in the laws of various states regarding how to divide business interests after divorce.

But if business income and the value of the business become separate property without any sharing between the spouses, an adversarial relationship may be in the making. One spouse is contributing all their efforts to the marriage (work, family, children). The other spouse is putting in most of their efforts into the business, of which the other spouse only has a small part. It starts to feel like the business spouse is having an "affair" – an affair with the business. This upsets the feelings of generosity and mutual contribution that sustain a marriage.

A prenup can be a valuable tool in this situation by providing predictability, clarity, and fairness. A business interest can be protected (as well as the interest of other stakeholders) while still providing an equitable result to the non-business-participating spouse.

Business interests in court cases can cause the most costly and protracted divorce litigation cases. Many of these cases involve valuation of ongoing businesses and division of those assets between spouses. For instance, the seminal Massachusetts case, *Bernier v. Bernier*, took 12 years to resolve from the initial court filing to the final decision. The case went from the Trial Court to the Appeals Court to the Supreme Judicial Court and back to the Appeals Court. The final case was *Bernier v. Bernier*, 82 Mass. App. Ct. 81 (2012).

In *Bernier*, there were dueling valuations of the business by the parties' experts, and differing opinions on whether "key person" and "marketability" valuation discounts were appropriate. The effect of the entity being taxed as an S corporation rather than a C corporation raised other thorny valuation issues.

The Berniers' grocery business was started almost 20 years after the marriage, and there had been no prenup. The parties' financial circumstances at the time of the start of the marriage were quite modest. It was the supermarkets that changed their financial life. Often in a first marriage, like the Berniers', the couple builds up their financial wealth together and views their marriage and its fruits as a joint venture.

In the *Bernier* case, the entire value of the business was marital property because it started after the marriage. When the business is a premarital business that increases in value after the marriage, the analysis gets more complex because there may be a separate property component.

In community property states (such as Texas and California), active business efforts of a spouse working after the marriage in a premarital business may be framed as requiring reimbursement to the other spouse for his community efforts in working at the business. This reimbursement may go beyond business salary and profits and extend to increased value of the business. See e.g., *Vallone v. Vallone*, 644 S.W.2d 455 (Tex. 1982) and *Jensen v. Jensen*, 665 S.W.2nd 107 (Tex. 1984).

In California, the "Pereira" accounting rule grants to the business spouse the initial separate property investment of a business plus a "reasonable" interest rate on the separate property investment. After that, the appreciation of business due to the skills, efforts, and talents of the spouse who is working in the business (and not to outside market forces) is treated as community property. The "Pereira" rule is still used to value the community property interest in single-person professions and small businesses such as sole proprietorships. *Pereira v. Pereira*, 156 Cal. 1 (1909).

The "Van Camp" accounting method is another method used in California. This method is used where contributions to the growth of a business are more complex, involving other people and outside market forces. *Van Camp v. Van Camp*, 53 Cal. App. 17 (1921).

In New York (an equitable distribution state), the indirect contributions or efforts of the other spouse as homemaker and parent can be considered as a compensating contribution to a business. As a result, if there is an increase of the value of separate property (such as a premarital business) during the marriage, some percentage of that increase may be considered marital property.

A New York court specifically cited the importance of the "wide range of unremunerated services to the joint enterprise, such as homemaking, raising children and providing the emotional and moral support necessary to sustain the other spouse in coping with the vicissitudes of life outside the home." *Price v. Price*, 69 N.Y.2d 8 (1986).

It is clear in the Sara and Charles scenario above that Charles's compensation is being kept artificially low. To the extent his salary is not commensurate with the true value of his time, if this were a marriage without a prenup, the marital estate would have an equitable right of reimbursement to the marital estate.

But what about the business income (as opposed to the salary) that is plowed back into the growth of the business? And what about the growth of the business itself? What's fair if the business was started before the marriage?

What's fair if the business is started after the marriage? Standard prenups can lead to pretty extreme results on this issue.

There might be a long first marriage that ends in divorce. The business-owner spouse could have a business worth $500,000 at the time of the marriage that is now worth $10 million. There could be $1 million of saved marital assets to be divided equally. As the business's value grew during the years, the non-business spouse's knowledge of this disparity may have had a negative effect on the marriage. Is there a way to change this calculus that feels fair to both sides when they are embarking on marriage?

Working profits that are not characterized as "salary" are also part of the business spouse's efforts. The question to address in a prenup is what rules to impose on business earnings – whether they are distributed to the business spouse or not. Also, what rules should the prenup impose on the growth of that spouse's interest in the business over time. In other words, if there is a divorce, what is the other spouse's marital interest in the business?

There are cases that analyze whether money put back into a business as "retained earnings" is available to determine child support and/or alimony. These cases can provide theoretical insight as to how to analyze the marital portion of these investments retained in a separate property business.

For instance, in one case, the Massachusetts Supreme Judicial Court looked at whether the retained earnings of the father reinvested in an S corporation (of which he was CEO and 65 percent owner) were available to determine child support. The amount reinvested into the corporation was significant.

The Court looked at two major factors to see if this income was "available" – whether there was a legitimate business reason justifying retaining corporate earnings and whether the father/shareholder was able to control corporate distributions to himself. By examining the motives behind the reinvesting, a possible intent to shield income from child support by means of retained earnings can be determined.

For this, the corporation's history of retained earnings and distributions is relevant. Also, a shareholder/CEO with a controlling interest has a fiduciary duty to the business, its employees, and other shareholders when making distributions or retaining earnings. *J.S. v. C.C.*, 454 Mass. 652 (2009).

You can see how complex this analysis can be.

How to address business income and gain of value during a marriage.

The first step in representing a client when business assets are involved is to seek full disclosure regarding the business assets. If you are the future spouse who is an owner and works in the business, you should expect to be asked to disclose everything that is relevant to the ownership, value, and operation of the business.

Parties intending to enter into prenups should, among other things, give and receive full and complete financial disclosure. This is generally required for the agreement to be binding and enforceable. (Some states have limited exceptions.) It's good practice to over-disclose rather than under-disclose when negotiating a prenup. If there is a family business (or if the future spouse has a business), knowing everything about the business prior to signing the prenup or formulating its terms is of highest importance.

That means the parties and their lawyers need to review the financial statements, loan applications, buy-sell and other shareholder and voting agreements, certificates of incorporation and bylaws, options, records of third-party investments in the business, tax returns of the entity for several recent years, tax returns of the spouse who owns and works in the business, and other relevant financial records. If the entity is an LLC or partnership, the operating or partnership agreement should be reviewed as well.

It's important to understand the business in detail. If a spouse is waiving his or her interests in the business or in the business income or gain in its value, that spouse needs to know what he or she is waiving. Another reason to see what's going on in the business is to try to determine an equitable way to treat the income of the business and the growth of the business during the marriage in the prenup. The two parties to the upcoming marriage can and should do this collaboratively so there is understanding on both sides.

Sometimes the spouse working in the business does not fully understand the structure and economics of the business before the prenup discussion starts, especially if it is a family business and the parents are running the business. Going through this process can be a good opportunity for the future spouses to discuss their future and their future financial plans and how they will both contribute to the marriage. This can help them decide the financial issues relating to the existing business to be determined in the prenup.

For instance, the spouses can set a rule about income derived from the business entity. They can decide that all salary is shared as marital property. They can also decide that other income is or isn't shared or is partially shared. For instance, the business profits can be deemed shared in whole or in part. If contributed back to the business, the non-business spouse could develop an interest or "phantom interest" in the business. If the business increases in value during the marriage, the couple can also decide how to share that gain if there is a divorce. (See below for payout methods.) In Charles and Sara's prenup, they can decide to share (or not to share) Charles's LLC income from the rental of the building. Also, it is important to track payment of taxes on income from separate assets so that that tax is paid by separate income.

How to determine the gain in the value of the business.

Addressing the gain in value of the business interests over time can be done in a prenup.

The parties could value the spouse's interest in the business at the time of the marriage as a baseline. This information may be available from the business if there has been a valuation for stock option purposes or for recent equity investments, or valuations for estate purposes of recently deceased shareholders. Then, if there is a divorce, the value of the business (or the spouse's interest in the business) can be re-determined. The increase would be measured by the difference between the baseline and current valuation. The parties can decide in the prenup whether the increase in value is marital property to be divided equally or divided in some other way.

If the business was started before the marriage and the parties do not wish to have it appraised at the time of the marriage (due to cost, difficulty, or timing), sometimes a "coverture" formula is used to determine the marital portion. Under this method, a fraction is used where the numerator is the duration of the marriage and the denominator is the entire time the business has been operating, from inception to the time of the divorce. That fraction determines the marital portion of the business. It can be divided equally or in some other proportion as decided by the parties. Parties need to remember that they should be deciding the terms of the prenup – not their parents, advisors, or business associates.

In family businesses, generally stock is privately held. Otherwise, the stock price could determine the value of the interest. But there are other standard methods used in business valuation cases. In a prenup, the parties can agree on a valuation method and set specific parameters to make an assessment of the value of the business at the time of the marriage and at the time of divorce (or death) easier.

For instance, some businesses are generally valued as a multiple of gross or net sales. Some businesses (such as real estate holdings) can be valued on the basis of fair market value of the assets. Each type of business has a preferred method of calculating its fair market value. Parameters to put the chosen method into effect can be written in the prenup to remove areas of possible argument later on. Often it is worth obtaining expert advice when drafting the prenup as to which particular method or formula reflects reality better in order to accurately value the particular type of business the party (or the party's parents) are engaged in.

If there are multiple owners, the parties to the prenup could decide if a "minority interest" discount for lack of control should apply to valuation and how much the discount should be. If so, the fair market value of the business would be reduced by this calculation. There may be other business factors affecting market value of the business in question. The parties can decide what they are and how to apply them.

The business might be in an industry that has marketability issues. Or lack of liquidity of the business assets could result in discounts in market value. If a spouse is a "key man" or "key woman" whose absence in the business would decrease the value of the business, this circumstance should be taken into account. In a service business, such as technology consulting or a physician's practice, it would be important not to double count the income from the spouse's services that would be devoted to child or spousal support after a divorce when valuing the business.

Payout methods and maintaining control of the business.

It is important for the business owner (and other owners in the company) that the payment of the spouse's interest at divorce or death not interfere with the operation and financial health of the business. Often there are existing shareholder or operating agreements that address this issue.

The business spouse will reasonably want to retain control of the business after the divorce and not have the ex-spouse as a business partner. There are some exceptions, but this is generally the case. Therefore, the payment of the marital interest to the non-business spouse will not be made as an interest in the business. These are legitimate concerns that can be addressed in the prenup. The payment terms need to be feasible for the spouse business-owner as reflected in the prenup negotiations.

The prenup can provide payment to the non-business spouse from assets other than the business, such as a lump sum in other assets. If there are not adequate liquid assets, the prenup can give an option to structure the payment with a down payment and a promise to make periodic payments or pay the balance at some future date. There can be language that the deferred payment can only be made if there is a lack of reasonable liquidity. There can be security on the obligation, such as a mortgage on real estate. The interest rate on the note and term of the payment can be set in the prenup.

Often the interest rate corresponds to an outside index, such as the three-month Treasury bill rate set by the U.S. Treasury, the LIBOR index, or the 30-year mortgage interest rate either set at the outset, or recalibrated during the years in which the note will be paid off. The loan can be an amortizing loan or an interest-only loan with a balloon payment at a certain date.

The prenup should have the standard provision that if a party breaches the obligation, the breaching party pays the other party's attorney's fees. That provides further assurance that the non-business spouse will be paid out over time. The ongoing obligations could also be assured by life insurance to provide quick payment if the obligor spouse dies before full payment.

Use of arbitration for decision-making in a prenup involving a business.

Having an arbitration clause in the prenup – especially where there might be questions of business valuation – can be very useful.

There are many ways to handle arbitration. The parties may mutually choose an arbitrator, whose decision on value shall be binding. Or, if they wish, the decision of the arbitrator would not be binding to the parties, and they could proceed to court if either is dissatisfied with the arbitrator's award. Often, even if non-binding, couples will not take the matter to court due to the time and expense involved.

The parties may agree on an arbitrator. If they cannot agree, each party can choose an arbitrator, and the two arbitrators can select a third arbitrator who will be retained by the parties to make the determination of the value of the business. Or all three assessments of values by all three arbitrators could be averaged to find the value of the business.

One method of arbitration might be especially helpful to speed up the arbitration of a defined issue. It is called "Baseball Arbitration" (also called "Final Offer Arbitration"). Its name derives from its frequent use in major league baseball salary disputes. It's a method that helps parties quickly come to a reasonable position in arbitration after the arguments of each side have been heard by the arbitrator.

In Baseball Arbitration, each party privately submits to the arbitrator his or her best possible offer. One party will give the maximum price they are willing to pay the other spouse for the business interest. The other party submits the lowest price they are willing to receive for the interest.

The arbitrator can choose only one of these two best offers. This provides a great impetus to settle – and to settle quickly, and within a reasonable range. Knowing that your prenup requires Baseball Arbitration if there is an impasse helps to eliminate diverging or extreme positions and can lead to negotiated settlements.

What can parents do to keep business succession within a family?

This section really goes to the question of "Do we really need a prenup?" As discussed in Chapter 8 regarding trusts, there are many things that families can do to keep family assets (including family businesses) within the family of origin. Below are a number of techniques that are typically used.

Restrictions on Transfer and Buy-Sell Agreements.

Business entities (corporations, LLCs, partnerships) are often "close" corporations founded by one or a few controlling parties. They are not publicly traded. Close corporations can protect themselves against unwanted shareholders by enacting restrictions on transfers of stock or other ownership interests in the entity. These would be set forth in the partnership, shareholder, or operating agreements. Some of these can protect the interests of a spouse-owner, and also the other owners if one of the owners gets divorced. Many of these shareholder agreements or operating agreements have provisions dealing with the interests of divorced spouses, having them revert into nonvoting rights to receive distributions.

Although unusual, there can be a requirement in one of these company agreements that unmarried shareholders provide the company with a prenuptial agreement prior to marrying. A written waiver by the owner's spouse-to-be of his or her future interest in the business may be required. I have never actually run across this in my practice, and it does not include any protections *vis-à-vis* the shareholders who are already married before the restriction was enacted.

The more usual restriction that appears in many corporate bylaws and shareholder agreements is a generic prohibition against the transfer of shares without the approval of the other partners or shareholders. These are often contained in buy-sell agreements and cross-purchase agreements.

In these types of agreements, the substitute shareholder would have no right of control but would retain the right to receive corporate distributions. Or, instead, an involuntary transfer to an ex-spouse may trigger a right, but not the obligation on the entity or the other shareholders or the spouse-shareholder to purchase the shares or interest that would have been transferred to the non-business ex-spouse. The price is normally a fair market valuation price determined under a formula or methodology set forth in the shareholder agreement. This can be a very difficult and uncertain process if the company is a start-up.

Having said this, having a close corporation or other entity put restrictions on transfer shortly before the divorce can cause problems and could start a whole new level of inquiry and litigation in a divorce action. The argument could be made that the spouse-owner had a level of control in enacting the new provision, and that it would essentially be avoidable under the "fraudulent conveyance" laws existing in every state. This could lead to a dispute that could be very lengthy and expensive to resolve in court.

Estate freezing techniques.

Parents with taxable estates often give away property irrevocably during their lifetimes in order to reduce their estate tax. To do that, they must file federal gift tax returns and use some of their unified gift and estate tax exclusion. In 2018, as a result of the doubling of the estate and gift tax exclusion under the Tax Cuts and Jobs Act of 2017 (TCJA), this is $11.2 million per person, and $22.4 million per couple. It increases every year by an inflation adjustment.

As a result, if a parent has an asset worth $11 million and transfers it to their children, the property is out of their estate for estate tax purposes and most of the parent's unified credit is used. The tax benefit is that all subsequent gains would be included in the younger generation's estate, with the estate tax (if any) to be paid in the far distant future.

But the TCJA includes a sunset of the increased exemption. On January 1, 2026, the exemption amounts will automatically revert to their pre-TCJA levels, indexed for inflation unless there is further legislation that continues the expanded exclusion or that eliminates the estate tax in its entirety.

Family Limited Partnerships.

One of the ways this estate freeze is accomplished with respect to a business is by setting up family limited partnerships (FLPs). The parent business owner might be the controlling owner, or general partner, and hold only 1 percent of the interest in the family business. The other 99 percent of the business would be held in limited partnership interests owned by the children. At the time of the formation of the FLP, the founder could make gifts of the interests to the limited partners, using some of the founder's unified gift and estate tax credit. It's one of the "estate freeze" techniques that wealthy people use.

One of the benefits of FLPs is that the valuation of the gifted interests can be reduced substantially because of lack of control discount and lack of marketability discount. Valuation reductions of 25 to 40 percent are often asserted when reporting on the gift tax return, but the higher levels of discount are often a flag for an audit by the Internal Revenue Service. Also, there have been recent attempts by the IRS to limit the benefit of FLPs, and Congress may act to close this loophole at some point.

The general partner would manage and control the business, and be responsible for the debts and liabilities of the entity. The general partner is at risk. So generally, the general partner interest is held by a limited liability entity, such as a corporation or an LLC. As a result, the parent who controls it has no personal liability. The children's interests would be non-controlling and would have asset protection aspects, because limited partners have limited liability. The children would be passive recipients of income from the operation of the business.

If the limited partner is sued by a creditor or soon-to-be-ex-spouse, only the income stream would be at possible risk, and not the asset itself. The creditor (such as the ex-spouse) could only get a "charging order" to receive distributions from the FLP, but only if the distributions are made. As another asset protection feature of FLPs, at times a limited partner may recognize income for tax purposes, but no actual distribution of income will be made. It might be held within the partnership entity, similar to reinvesting corporate profits described above.

Installment Sale of Interest in Business to an Intentionally Defective Grantor Trust.

An Intentionally Defective Grantor Trust (IDGT) is another estate freezing method. It starts out with an irrevocable trust that is funded with assets, either given by the grantor or that are sold to the trust in exchange for a promissory note. The assets may be FLP or another business. To the extent assets are given to the IDGT, a gift tax return will be filed.

It is designed as a so-called grantor trust for income tax purposes due to certain language in the trust agreement. Because it's a grantor trust, income earned by the investment is taxable to the grantor, generally a wealthy parent. That reduces the parent's estate by the tax payments.

To make the trust a grantor trust, certain powers are drafted into the trust agreement. A typical trigger that will make the trust a grantor trust is the power to swap trust assets with other assets of equivalent value. But for estate and gift tax purposes, an IDGT is a completed gift. As a result, all appreciation is excluded from the grantor's estate and will eventually be in the children's estate. That's why it's called an estate "freezing" technique.

In the right circumstances, IDGTs are the best of all possible worlds. Asset appreciation is out of the grantor's estate, and income tax is paid by the grantor. As you may remember from Chapter 8, if the income was earned by the trust, it would be subject to the high tax rates and compressed tax brackets of trusts, or paid by the beneficiaries of the trust, who are in the next generation. Because the wealthy grantor is paying the tax on the IDGT, it helps get more money out of the grantor's very large taxable estate, thus reducing his or her estate tax obligation.

For estate tax purposes, the trust assets are not part of the grantor's estate. An exception is to the extent that a promissory note remains unpaid at the time of the grantor's death; it is an estate asset to that extent. If the transfer was a sale to the children (rather than a gift), they will pay full value for it over time. As a result, their basis will be the purchase price of the asset. The appraised price of the asset may be reduced due to a valuation discount, such as lack of liquidity or lack of control. But beware – the IRS is starting to crack down on these valuation discounts per a recently issued Treasury regulation.

Because the IDGT is a grantor trust, the grantor can sell appreciated assets to the trust without recognizing capital gain on the sale. The grantor is essentially selling the asset to himself – that's why there is no gain. A business held in a protective entity, such as an LLC, an FLP, or a corporation, could be sold to an IDGT.

Use of IDGTs and SCINs.

Another twist on this sale to IDGT scenario involves a Self-Canceling Installment Note (SCIN). This is a promissory note for the sale that provides that upon the grantor's death, the remaining principal is forgiven.

Normally, the unpaid amount of a promissory note is included in the holder's estate. But a SCIN seeks to change that rule; a SCIN cancels the installment note upon the holder's death. Remember, in this case, the grantor sold his business to the IDGT and took back a promissory note. With a SCIN, the promissory note states that if he dies, all unpaid principal will be forgiven. Understandably, the IRS does not like this arrangement without imposing tax consequences.

In order for this arrangement to be blessed by the IRS, there would need to be a premium in the interest rate charged or in the total amount of principal to be repaid. The interest rate would need to be higher than the market rate and/or the amount to be repaid needs to be above the face value (i.e., the borrowed amount). This technique can be considered by people late in life who may not live until the note's maturity.

In both the sale and the gift scenario, increases in the value of the business asset will accrue to the next generation – the generation of the children holding interests in the business.

Sound complicated? You bet it is. And laws keep changing. Uncle Sam continues to devise new ways to put the screws on taxpayers (and the creative imaginations of their tax lawyers). At some point the IRS may completely prohibit the SCIN tax treatment. It is important to see a tax attorney if you seek to reduce or eliminate income or estate tax exposure by SCINs, valuation discounts, and other sophisticated tax planning methods.

CHAPTER 10

HOW A PRENUP CAN HELP WITH ESTATE PLANNING

It used to be (and still is in many instances) that the typical prenup had terms for a financial settlement if the marriage ended in divorce. But it was completely silent on inheritance provisions if the marriage ended with the death of a spouse. Actually, it's not silent, but worse than silent. In the typical prenup, the less moneyed spouse (nominally both spouses, but really aimed at the less advantaged spouse) has waived all rights to the estate of the other spouse, even if the marriage is intact at the moneyed spouse's death.

This is simply an unwritten custom in prenups written by lawyers. There is really no rational basis for this. If not required in the prenup, writing a will in favor of a spouse is just a "handshake" deal. The lack of an inheritance provision just gives more control to the moneyed spouse and has the potential to greatly harm the other spouse.

A prenup is usually much less generous than the typical template in an estate plan for a surviving spouse if there is no prenup. That's because the typical prenup gives essentially zero assets to the surviving spouse. It totally lacks reasonableness if it's a first marriage of people who intend to have children together. This waiver of estate rights is what I call a "knee-jerk" prenup provision. It has been a legal custom but should really be thought about and carefully considered.

No, you shouldn't leave inheritance for later.

Take the typical 30-year-olds entering into a first marriage. Prenups often have provisions under which inheritance rights and obligations are not addressed. That means that either party can disinherit the other at his or her sole discretion if a death occurs *while the marriage is ongoing*. The disinherited spouse has no recourse.

If that surviving spouse contests the prenup, he or she will be breaking the "breach of contract" clause. This means that the contesting spouse would have to pay the legal fees of the estate of the wealthy dead spouse in defending against the claim. The richer spouse's estate that seeks to enforce the "no inheritance" provision of the prenup will probably win in court, because in all likelihood the provision will turn out to be enforceable.

The inheritance rights of spouses upon the death of the other spouse are important. A disinherited spouse has the state law right to a share of an intestate estate, which is an estate where the decedent failed to write a will. That spouse also has state rights to "take against a will" and get a reasonable part of the deceased spouse's estate if the spouse is disinherited by the will or receives only a very small legacy. These are two major inheritance rights that a spouse almost always waives in a prenup. (See Chapter 7.)

Often I receive a first draft with no inheritance provision. When I question a client about this lack of an inheritance requirement, she or he says, "Don't worry. We intend to plan for the inheritance by preparing our wills *after* the marriage." But I *do* worry. When I ask the other side's attorney why there isn't any inheritance provision that at least provides a floor of benefits for the survivor, he or she says, "The clients can work this out after the marriage through an estate plan." But is that a safe place to put a less moneyed spouse?

There are many problems in omitting the topic of inheritance in a prenup. This omission can have a very cruel impact when the more moneyed spouse forgets to draft a last will and testament providing for his or her spouse, or revokes one after a temporary marital spat. Here's another way in which the omission can arise in a potentially tragic manner.

An actual horror story.

Here's a scenario that can happen when inheritance is left out of the prenup for the parties to deal with later.

It's 8 a.m. on a Tuesday. It's my fourth day of vacation. I've just woken up. I'm in China on my dream vacation trip with a tour group. It's my first two-week vacation in six years. That's the life of a lawyer. Leaving the job for two weeks is a big deal for us. Clients' problems don't disappear. And although my law partners are very capable, they don't know the background and details of each of my cases. I'm hoping nothing major will happen while I'm away.

It's 7 p.m. on Monday in Boston (there's a 13-hour time difference), and I've checked my work emails while I'm here in China. I do this every day a number of times – even when I'm on vacation. That's also the life of a lawyer. We're pretty much always on call for our clients.

I see ten emails from my client Jane. She has just informed me that her husband, Ronald, has died suddenly in a car accident. Ronald was 54, about Jane's age. They each have children from their previous marriages. It was a totally unexpected death.

A few years back, when she married Ronald, Jane and he entered into a prenup. (Another attorney was her prenup counsel.) The prenup had the typical (but dangerous) language about waiving all marital rights upon termination of marriage by death. So unless Ronald executed a new last will after the prenup was signed, Jane would be out of luck with no recourse.

Jane told me in an email that shortly after their marriage, Ronald said he would re-write his will. He also said he would change the beneficiary designations on his retirement assets and life insurance to split his estate between Jane and his children from his previous marriage. But Jane never followed up on it with him. She doesn't know whether or not he completed the changes or wrote the new will. She is panicky, because, aside from losing her life partner, she depends on him for support. She is very scared (understandably so) about her financial future.

In this instance, eventually, Jane made inquiries with every attorney with whom Ronald had any contact in the years before his death. She also looked for a will all over the house. After several nerve-wracking days of searching, she found a copy of a post-prenup last will and the name of the attorney who had drafted it. That attorney had the original document. Ronald did come through with his intent to change his estate plan. He did write a new last will, and he also changed the beneficiaries of his retirement accounts and life insurance as he had promised. Jane had been added as a beneficiary along with his children.

But that's not always the case. Not all of these situations have happy endings. Our law practices abound with situations involving children or spouses of people that have passed away who put off basic estate planning until it was too late. Yes, it's too late to do estate planning after you die. You can't redo your estate plan then, and neither can your loved ones. That's why it's called a "will" (i.e., it's *your* intent, not someone else's).

Also note the word "last" in "last testament." You can't write another one because you're dead. That's why it's called the "last" one. Whatever legal documents exist at your death contain your last wishes. They must be followed by the court probate process and by trustees under their fiduciary obligations after your death.

There are other situations in which this circumstance arises in a dangerous way when the prenup has no requirement for inheritance.

At the end of a long marriage, perhaps Mr. or Mrs. has contracted either dementia (severe or slight), or maybe has contracted a case of simple extreme orneriness (beyond the usual marital bickering). Or there could be a big marital blowout (spat) resulting in the spouse, in fit of pique, removing the other spouse from their estate plan and as beneficiary of other assets.

Here's another nightmare. They sign a prenup with the typical lack of inheritance protection. They are married for 30 years, maybe 40. At the end, one of the spouses has a new love interest. It's just an affair and the marriage is not legally ending, but the spouse wants to leave his or her estate to the new lover. There is nothing to stop this from happening if there is no inheritance requirement in the prenup. The surviving spouse is simply in an irretrievably unfortunate position and has no legal rights.

What does "consideration" have to do with it?

When you think about it, in virtually all prenups, the less moneyed spouse is giving up rights. Is that person getting something in exchange?

It seems logical that she or he should be trading those forgone marital rights for other rights. That's the legal concept of "consideration" in contracts. As law students, we learned that to have a valid contract, there must be an exchange of consideration given and received on both sides, and that the exchange should be roughly equal, or in legal terms "sufficient."

The less moneyed spouse always gives up marital rights in a prenup. Otherwise, there would be no reason for it. But what rights does the less moneyed spouse receive in exchange? The right to marry? The more moneyed spouse is also getting the right to marry the new spouse. Presumably, those rights to marry and to be with each other in an intimate relationship and institution called "marriage" are equal. It doesn't make sense for them to be part of the prenup consideration calculation.

But surprisingly, the notion of consideration in the law of prenuptial agreements is highly limited. In fact, consideration may not be needed at all for a prenup. This is inconsistent with normal contract law, where consideration is necessary for a valid contract.

For instance, the Uniform Premarital and Marital Agreements Act (UPMAA) (2012) provides in Section 6 that prenuptial and postnuptial agreements are enforceable without consideration. The same rule is articulated in Section 2 of the prior uniform act, the Uniform Premarital Agreement Act (UPAA) (1983). In the comments to Section 2 of the UPAA, the drafters state specifically that a premarital agreement is enforceable without consideration, and that they are restating the "almost universal" rule that the marriage itself is the consideration for the agreement.

By the time of the 2012 UPMAA, no-fault divorce laws had been adopted throughout the country. Under these laws, either party could leave the marriage without cause. If you can't force someone to stay married to you, one could view that the marriage itself as providing no consideration. Perhaps that's why the UPMAA eliminates the notion of consideration in its entirety in Section 6. The drafters of the UPMAA rationalize the lack of a consideration requirement by stating that other controls in the act, such as procedural requirements and tests of unconscionability, address indirectly the concerns that would be raised through lack of consideration.

But do they really? It's very difficult to prove unconscionability (see Chapter 18), and it is very difficult to provide adequate proof that the procedural requirements have been violated. As a result, prenuptial agreements are generally lopsided, taking away from one side without giving anything in return. That doesn't have to be the case. A rule of reasonableness (and generosity) can apply when formulating the terms of a prenup.

Ways to provide consideration.

If a spouse is giving up certain marital rights upon divorce, why not provide consideration for the waiver? That spouse could be given greater inheritance rights than the laws would provide if the marriage ends in the death of his or her spouse. That would be a rational quid pro quo. Or at least that spouse could receive the same inheritance rights that would apply through intestacy or under the "forced share" rules. They could be written into the prenup as a minimum inheritance provision. (See Chapter 7.)

Reasonably protecting a less moneyed spouse even if the marriage ends in divorce is a logical way to write a prenup with mutual consideration in the personal sense. Remember what the word "consideration" really means. Its basic meaning is caring about someone. That's how people feel about each other when they marry. (See Chapter 17 for more on the topic of consideration.) That's why having no consideration in a prenup at the time of the marriage can be so jarring.

Many states, even some equitable property states, provide quasi-prenup provisions in which inherited and gifted money, as well as premarital property, are not subject to equitable distribution upon divorce. (See, for instance, divorce laws of New Jersey, New York, and Pennsylvania.)

A *quid pro quo* for giving up some marital rights could be to *add* a right upon marrying. One of these could be that any income received from premarital property becomes marital upon receipt. Or the prenup can include a provision that says that the income generated by gifted or inherited property becomes marital. (See other techniques in Chapters 8 and 17.) In other words, people can confer rights in the prenup that are actually above and beyond the marital rights conferred by the laws of the state controlling the prenup. Providing that extra benefit would be consideration, when some rights are being withdrawn.

As stated, I strongly recommend having an inheritance provision in a prenup as a safeguard if the marriage ends in the death of one party. It can be articulated as a minimum "floor" for inheritance from each other if the marriage ends in death. This "floor" can vary, depending on whether it's a first marriage of relatively young people, or a second (or subsequent) marriage of middle-aged or older people. It can also vary by whether or not there are children of previous marriages.

When I draft prenups, the minimum "floor" amounts on inheritance from either spouse can be exceeded voluntarily. In other words, the prenup doesn't say, "The parties shall leave each other 80 percent of their estates," but rather, "The parties shall leave each other *no less than* 80 percent of their estates." There can also be provisions that change the minimum percentage depending on how long the marriage is. Thought should be put into this provision, including thinking about increasing the floor over time as the marriage proves itself. It can be very different, depending on whether it's a first marriage or if there are children of prior marriages.

Marriage is the best tax shelter around.

Formulating a prenup can generate thought as to how your estate plan can create value for you as a new couple. You can set up a plan for the future estate tax savings within the prenup. My prenups require a trip to an estate-planning attorney within three months after the wedding. The prenup establishes the basic estate plan requirements within its terms.

Getting back to the consideration question, what if you sign a prenup relinquishing marital rights that turn out to be in the $3 million range? And let's say that you are the less moneyed spouse with very little in the asset department, and your new spouse is very wealthy, with assets over $22 million.

You may not realize this, but if you die before your spouse (or even after your spouse – see below regarding portability), you have given your spouse $7.48 million. How can that be?

Marriage is still the best estate tax shelter out there (but certainly not the only reason to get married). As of 2018, the exemption for gift and estate tax for each spouse as a result of the Tax Cuts and Jobs Act of 2017 (TCJA) is $11.2 million, and the current federal estate tax rate is 40 percent. For the couple, the estate tax exemption totals $22.4 million.

The wealthy spouse can save estate taxes because the less moneyed spouse is bringing something financially valuable to the marriage – his or her federal estate and gift tax exemption, also called the credit shelter. Your spouse can save more than $4.48 million (40 percent times $11.2 million) in federal estate taxes due to your being the deceased spouse and providing your credit shelter to the wealthy spouse and you've given up another $3 million in marital rights.

That produces a total of $7.48 million estate savings available upon death due to the exemption provided by the less moneyed spouse. This is actual cash –it's a real dollar contribution by the less moneyed spouse. (You'd need to subtract that spouse's assets from the total to get the real number.)

The use of the less moneyed spouse's exemption is available, no matter which spouse is the first to die. (See below on portability, the QTIP, and credit shelter trust planning.) But it is important for the less moneyed spouse to understand what he or she is giving up and possibly be compensated for it.

Beware of a gift-splitting Trojan horse.

Take the situation of John, who is wealthy, and Susan, who does not have a great deal of assets. They are marrying, both of them for the third time. They believe that the third time's the charm and that their marriage will last for a lifetime. As Oscar Wilde famously said, "Marriage is the triumph of imagination over intelligence. Second marriage is the triumph of hope over experience." She is about to sign a prenuptial agreement with the following language:

> In the event that John chooses to make a gift in any year from his separate property to someone other than Susan, Susan, at John's request, shall "split gifts" with him for gift tax purposes and execute any documents reasonably required to accomplish the same.

A reasonable assumption in reading this provision is that John wishes Susan to join him in giving annual exclusion gifts under Internal Revenue Code (IRC) Section 2503(b) to his children from his previous marriages. (See Chapter 8.) The annual exclusion for gifts is now set at $15,000 per year to each recipient. If you give gifts of this amount or under, they do not count as part of your non-taxable $11.2 million estate.

If Susan joins John in making the gift (called "gift splitting," sanctioned by IRC Section 2513), John can make gifts of $30,000 per year to each of his children and grandchildren and can reduce his taxable estate accordingly.

But what if 15 years after the marriage, John presents Susan with a gift-splitting tax return in which he wants to give $22.4 million to his children tax-free? That means he intends to use his entire $11.2 million exclusion and also Susan's entire $11.2 million exclusion.

John is very wealthy — he wants to make the pre-death gift so that the increased value of these assets will be taxed in his children's generation. The provision Susan signed in the prenup can be interpreted to require Susan to join in the gift splitting of any amount, not just the $15,000 annual gift tax exclusion. As a result, under the terms of the prenup, Susan must relinquish her own credit shelter in its entirety.

That language in the prenup had a broader meaning was lost on her (and her attorney) when she signed the prenup years earlier. What it means is that anything she is able to give her own children will be taxed at the 40 percent estate tax rate starting with the first dollar.

She has essentially given John a gift of $4.48 million (40 percent times $11.2 million), plus the $3 million in marital rights she waived in the prenup. That totals over $7.48 million. Not a good result for Susan, unless she has been adequately compensated for her "gift" to John. Note that the usage of Susan's federal exclusion could (and did) occur as a lifetime gift by the more moneyed spouse before either of them died. The gift and use of her credit shelter could happen, followed by a divorce. Susan would have no recourse to change this result.

If you are the less moneyed spouse signing a prenup, make sure that any gifts are limited to annual exclusion gifts under IRC Section 2503(b), unless you believe you are adequately compensated.

Estate tax planning that benefits married couples can be contemplated in a prenup.

Tax policy is put into effect in the Internal Revenue Code. This policy reflects an interest in encouraging marriage and supporting marriages and child raising by financially benefitting married couples. A single tax filer pays a lot more income tax than if he or she was married to an at-home spouse. A joint tax return gives great benefit to married people who have disparate incomes. The tax code abounds with deductions and credits for families and children.

Not many people pay federal estate tax, especially after the exemption limits were doubled by the TCJA. But many people who are considering prenups are very wealthy people who will be liable for federal estate tax upon their deaths (unless the law pertaining to taxable estates changes). Many states also have an estate tax. Many of these states have lower thresholds than the $11.2 million currently applicable for the federal estate tax. (Massachusetts is one of several states where estate tax is triggered by estates of more than $1 million in assets.)

There are two components to the tax savings produced by marriages that end with the death of a spouse: the portability of the federal estate tax exemption available to a surviving spouse, and the ability for a wealthy deceased spouse, through tax planning, to utilize both spouses' federal tax exemption amounts. This is done by using the portability laws and also by creating credit shelter trusts and/or QTIP trusts. Here's how these techniques work.

What is portability and how to use it.

Congress introduced the concept informally known as "portability" as part of the 2010 Tax Relief Act, made permanent by the American Taxpayer Relief Act of 2012. It allows a surviving spouse to use the unused federal estate tax exemption of a deceased spouse when the survivor eventually dies. The fancy name for this is the DSUE, which stands for "deceased spouse unused exclusion." The DSUE amount (i.e., the portability amount) can be claimed by the timely filing of Form 706 Estate Tax return after the death of a spouse. The election will be lost if not made within that time period, which is generally nine months after the death.

The federal exemption from estate tax (in 2018) is $11.2 million. That means if you die with $11.2 million in assets or less, you do not have to pay federal estate tax.

Let's assume that the first deceased spouse died first with $200,000 in assets that she gave to the children of her previous marriage. That left a $11 million unused tax exclusion at her death that can be claimed by the surviving spouse when he dies. If the surviving spouse has $22.2 million in his or her own assets, no federal estate tax will need to be paid upon that spouse's death. (Calculation: $22.2 million less the husband's $11.2 million estate tax exclusion, less the first deceased spouse's $11 million portability DSUE equals zero.) At the current estate tax rate of 40 percent, the less moneyed deceased spouse has saved the other spouse $4.4 million in estate tax ($11 million times 40 percent estate tax rate).

Portability law is a taxpayer-friendly law. It allows a surviving spouse to utilize the unused exemption of the deceased spouse just by filing a claim for it. Prior to this enactment, the unused exemption could be only claimed if the survivor had done sophisticated tax planning involving QTIP trusts or credit shelter trusts. (Note that there are still good reasons to use trust tax planning to capture the exemption – see below.) As a result, portability is a post-death "fix" for people who didn't do the sophisticated estate planning necessary to fully utilize both spouse's estate tax exclusions.

Portability does have its limitations. It does not apply to the Generation Skipping Tax (GST) exemption that permits a skip of assets to the grandchildren's generation without an extra layer of tax. It generally is not applicable in the various states' separate estate tax regimes. If the survivor is not a U.S. citizen, portability will not be available, unless his or her country has a tax treaty provision with the U.S. allowing it.

A good (and bad) result of portability is that the gain on the assets that have been "ported" to the survivor's estate will be part of his or her estate upon that second death. This could create a taxable estate upon the death of the second spouse. But a benefit will be that the tax basis of the survivor's assets will be a "step-up" of basis for tax purposes to the date-of-death value of both the survivor's assets and the decedent's assets that were ported to the estate of the last to die of the spouses.

If the assets had been placed in a QTIP trust, there would be a step-up in basis to fair market value upon the death of the first spouse. Upon the survivor's death, the portion that was ultimately taxable to the survivor's estate would receive a second step-up in basis. But the part that funded the credit shelter amount at the first death would retain date-of-death basis value set at the time of the first death, with no step-up when the surviving spouse dies.

Another advantage to portability is that the surviving spouse has complete access to the inherited funds without any restrictions. If a surviving spouse receives the assets without a trust, that spouse has total control over income and principal of the amount received.

Often this is what the spouses wish – but sometimes not. If there are children from prior marriages, the preference may not be for the survivor to have total control of the deceased spouse's assets but for there to be some control over usage by the surviving spouse. This way assets not used by the surviving spouse can eventually get to the children, who may be children of a prior marriage. Setting up trusts is a good way to do this.

QTIP trusts and credit shelter trusts can create estate tax savings and provide for control of distributions.

Setting up estate-planning trusts can save money, and it can also address spouses' concerns to provide for each other and ultimately to leave property to their children of a previous marriage.

The tax code provides for an estate tax deduction of all amounts given outright to a spouse upon a death. This is called the "marital deduction" and is sanctioned in IRC Section 2056. Once this deduction is made, the estate tax is assessed on the remaining assets of the deceased spouse. By this tax provision, a more moneyed spouse can give property to the surviving spouse tax-free at his or her death and can often reduce his or her remaining assets to a non-taxable amount.

The estate tax on the money given to the surviving spouse is deferred until the surviving spouse's death. That second-to-die spouse will also have the benefit of the estate tax exclusion. For many estates, this can provide full estate tax protection for spouses, when the combined estates are below the current $22.4 million exclusion. If all the funds are transferred to the surviving spouse at the first death, the surviving spouse could end up with a taxable estate, because only one $11.2 million exemption is available. This situation can be addressed by the portability provision exercised at the first death, but only if the portability election was timely made at the time of the first death. (See above.)

There are some planning advantages to forgoing the portability election and actually creating estate-tax sensitive trusts to take advantage of the two $11.2 million exemptions.

Let's say the more moneyed spouse wants his surviving spouse to have use of the money, but wants whatever is left over to go to the children of his or her prior marriage. The couple can use QTIP trusts and credit shelter (or "bypass") trusts to achieve that result.

You've probably seen the term QTIP trust in news articles from time to time. QTIP stands for "Qualified Terminable Interest Property." If you give assets outright to your spouse upon your death, there is a martial deduction from your total assets when you compute the estate tax. There is no "terminable interest" when you give the property to your spouse outright. But what if you want to give property to your wife in trust for her life, and then what's left goes to your children from a previous marriage? Your wife's interest will eventually end, so, in tax language, it is "terminable." Normally the marital deduction would not be available for that terminable interest under IRC Section 2056. Because it would not qualify for a marital deduction, it would be taxable in the first to die's estate.

Enter Internal Revenue Code Section 2056(b)(7). It provides that a trust for the benefit of a spouse with others receiving the trust asset after her death can be considered marital deduction property if certain specified provisions are contained in the trust document. If trust complies with the QTIP rules, it will be considered a "qualified" terminable interest trust, that is, a QTIP trust.

For QTIP treatment, the surviving spouse must have the right to receive all the income generated by the trust property, paid at least annually during his or her lifetime. There must be no other beneficiaries of the trust during the surviving spouse's lifetime. There are several other requirements in order to achieve QTIP treatment. The executor of the estate of the decedent must make a timely QTIP election in order to have QTIP property pass to the surviving spouse under the marital deduction.

When the QTIP election is made, the executor will decide how much of the QTIP property will be taxable in the first to die's estate and how much will be taxable in the surviving spouse's estate. The elected QTIP assets in the trust for the surviving spouse are taxable at the time of the second spouse's death. They will be part of that spouse's assets subject to estate tax.

Whatever remains of the QTIP trust after the death of the lifetime beneficiary can go to other beneficiaries named in the trust as remainder persons. These can be the children of the marriage or children of previous marriages. The bequests can be set in any distribution amounts or percentages desired. Property for these beneficiaries can (but do not have to) continue to be held in trust.

When you are formulating a prenup, depending on the financial situation, some of your property can go into a QTIP trust and some can go to your children outright immediately after your death. The template for these issues can be set in a prenup.

In a QTIP trust, the surviving spouse can even have greater rights than merely receiving the income from the property. The trust instrument can provide that he or she can also receive principal payments at the discretion of an independent trustee. Or the trustee (even if the surviving spouse is trustee) can provide principal to the spouse-beneficiary under the HEMS standard of support, which stands for "health, education, medical, and support."

Another possible distribution option for both the QTIP trust (and also the credit shelter/marital trust arrangement described below) is to increase the support options and control by the surviving spouse to give that spouse a "5 by 5" power. This allows the surviving spouse to have the right to receive up to the greater of $5,000 or 5 percent of the trust principal in any year. The spouse can exercise this noncumulative annual power without the approval of an independent trustee.

The surviving spouse can also have a "special power of appointment" to have a say in where some of the trust property in the first spouse to die's trust might go after the surviving spouse's death.

One of the advantages of a QTIP trust (over the credit shelter/marital trust arrangement described below) involves the decision of how much of the QTIP property will be put in the marital deduction part of the trust. In the case of a QTIP trust, this decision is made at the time of the first death, and not by a pre-set formula. That way, the current circumstances of the surviving spouse and the children of the first marriage can be taken into account as well as the amount of overall assets at the time of the first death.

A related estate-planning technique is called a credit shelter trust (sometimes called a bypass trust or a family trust). It is set up in conjunction with a marital trust. It achieves a similar result as a QTIP trust arrangement. The credit shelter trust uses all or part of the credit shelter (the estate tax exclusion), currently $11.2 million. It will not be subject to federal estate tax.

One difference is that the credit shelter trust can be set up as a "spray" trust. This means it can provide for income and principal distributions to the surviving spouse, and also to others, such as children or grandchildren. With a QTIP trust, all income and principal must be paid to the surviving spouse. In a credit shelter trust, the trustee can control these distributions of income and principal based on what the terms of the trust instrument are.

The credit shelter trust may have grown in value substantially between the first death and the death of the surviving spouse. But even so, it won't be taxed again for estate tax purposes until the assets are distributed to the eventual beneficiaries, and then only after these beneficiaries die. However, its tax basis will be the fair market value at the first spouse's death, so if the trust or eventual beneficiaries sell the assets, there will be a recognition of capital gains, with tax to be paid if the assets have appreciated in value.

In order for the credit shelter trust assets not to be taxable as part of the estate of the surviving spouse, there need to be some restrictions on control. Basically, the surviving spouse's discretionary control on the property she provides herself must be limited. However, an independent trustee may make discretionary distributions to that spouse. The spouse as trustee can also make distributions to him- or herself, under the HEMS standard.

After setting up the credit shelter trust, the rest of the assets would be transferred to a marital trust for the use of the surviving spouse. This would provide a deduction from the taxable estate of the first to die, with the assets in the marital trust being taxable at the surviving spouse's death.

In order to get the marital deduction for the surviving spouse, similar provisions as are in the QTIP trust are required in the marital trust. The surviving spouse must be the only beneficiary during his or her lifetime. The children of the grantor spouse (or the surviving spouse) can be the beneficiaries after the surviving spouse's death.

In the overall estate plan, not all property must go into trusts. Some of the grantor's property could be given to the surviving spouse outright at the time of the first death, and some also outright to the children of a prior marriage. Some property can be held in trust to permit lifetime support of a spouse with remainder to the children.

There are significant non-tax reasons to opt for estate-planning trusts rather than relying on portability to make full use of your estate tax shelters. Aside from preserving property for the children of the prior marriage, assets held in trust provide creditor protection and can provide professional management of the funds. An independent trustee can be the neutral "middle person" between the interests of the surviving spouse and the children of the prior marriage. The trustee can preserve assets for the children of a prior marriage while still reasonably supporting the surviving spouse.

The Total Return Unitrust (TRU) is a new kind of trust that is being used more these days. It is used to reconcile the differing investment strategies that benefit the lifetime income beneficiary with the interests of the ultimate beneficiaries. The surviving spouse may want to maximize income, whereas the children who receive the property later may want to maximize capital appreciation. The TRU is able to accommodate the interests of both and can help the trustee maintain peaceful interactions between surviving spouse and the children of a deceased spouse.

It is important to consult with an experienced estate-planning attorney to discuss all these options. It may make sense to do the consult at the time you are formulating the terms of a prenup, so that one (or more) of these estate-planning techniques can become embedded as terms in the prenup's inheritance provisions.

. . .

A prenup can provide an opportunity for a couple to think about future estate planning and how to provide security for a surviving spouse. It can also initiate a discussion of how most efficiently to use the tax laws. In this way, the prenup discussion can be a time to plan for estate tax savings that can provide more overall inheritance for each other, as well as the spouses' children or other heirs. (For additional information about estate-planning techniques and other issues relevant to older couples marrying, see Chapter 11.)

By balancing and determining what will happen after the death of a spouse and putting terms to create that in the prenup, the parties to the marriage (especially older couples with children from previous marriages) can ensure fairness to each other and their children. Knowing that such an arrangement is in place can create peace within the extended family at the beginning of this new marriage.

CHAPTER 11

THE "GRAY PRENUP": SHOULD SENIOR NEWLYWEDS GET PRENUPS, TOO?

P eople are now calling divorce of an older couple a "gray divorce." Similarly, I call a prenup between seniors planning to marry a "gray prenup." Similar to a gray divorce, a gray prenup has its own particular issues and challenges.

What is a gray marriage and what are the challenges of a gray prenup?

When older people (in their 50s, 60s, 70s, and beyond) get married, they often have children from previous marriages. Their financial loyalty is divided between their children and their new spouse. They generally wish to give and secure a financial legacy for their children. Hence the need for a prenup.

If their first spouse has died, the person considering a prenup may think of part of the premarital assets they inherited from their deceased spouse as coming from the children's deceased parent. They may feel they morally owe it to the children of that marriage. They may want to help their children establish themselves in life, including helping them with buying a first home or setting up a business. They may want to provide financial assistance and support for their children's children.

The senior who is remarrying also wants to make sure their new spouse is both secure in their life together and protected if the elder spouse dies before the new spouse. Some seniors are financially secure, and some are not. Sometimes they have a fairly equal level of assets, and sometimes they do not.

In order to meet the interests of loyalty to each other and loyalty to the children from their previous marriages, a balance needs to be struck. Balancing these competing interests is a frequent challenge in later-in-life marriages. These may be the primary objectives in formulating a gray prenup.

Good prenups should handle this balance in a sensible and coherent way. This can be done by formulating and memorializing the basic terms of a mutually conceived estate plan in a prenup. There are many horror stories about seniors that remarry who disinherit their children in favor of their new spouse. Creating a reasonable balance of inheritance upon death goes a long way to creating goodwill between the children of one spouse and the new spouse. In this way, prenups can create peace among and with the grown children of senior newlyweds. This peace within the blended families can further support, protect, and help sustain the upcoming marriage.

But sometimes the financial needs of seniors themselves must be the primary aim in a gray marriage because of lack of assets or income of one or both of the spouses. It is important for spouses (even gray spouses) to take care of each other during their lives together. After all, one of the purposes of marriage is to support, sustain, and protect each other. This chapter describes some of the options that can be established in a prenup (or outside of a prenup) that can help provide security and mutual support for the gray spouses and also meet their aims with regard to their children from their previous marriages in an orderly and thoughtful way.

The Cinderella syndrome.

Remember Cinderella? It's a very famous story that goes to the root of the problem. It takes place in a faraway, long-ago kingdom. Cinderella is living contentedly with her mother and father, who love her dearly. Then her mother dies, and her father marries a wicked stepmother, who favors her own daughters while treating Cinderella as a virtual slave in her father's house. She's not even permitted to go to the king's ball to have a chance to meet the prince and possibly be chosen as his bride.

Fast-forward several hundred years to today. A mother dies, and the father remarries. The new spouse also has children from her first marriage.

The father doesn't think about estate planning, and he wills his entire estate to the new spouse upon his death. The security and needs of his first family are forgotten and disregarded.

It's very hurtful for a child whose parents' lifelong marriage ended in the death of one of them to find that the remaining parent has remarried and the wealth accumulated during the first marriage will fall into the hands of the new spouse, and from there, perhaps to the new spouse's children from a previous marriage. I've heard this story many times during my years practicing law. Not being careful to plan fairly between the sets of adult children from the blended family can cause heartache for the children, as well as for the parents. Families can get torn apart over this. Parents can lose the respect of their children.

Another wrinkle in this situation may be the differences in the needs of the grown children. Some children are quite self-sufficient and don't really need much (or any) financial help. Some children are not established or may have chronic livelihood or health problems. These issues also need to be addressed during the life of the parents (the new gray couple) and after their deaths. It's complicated but important to tackle these problems.

So part of the prenup project for people in this circumstance is to think about the current financial plan and envision the future when one and then both spouses have died. For this type of planning, accountants and financial planners can be very helpful, as can seeking counsel from an attorney. People need to be aware of the estate-planning options available to them. (See Chapter 10.)

A typical gray prenup scenario.

Gray prenups come in as many flavors as the factual situations behind gray marriages. One of the new spouses may be somewhat wealthier than the other. If there is a new gray spouse who needs financial security, terms for financial security of the less-wealthy spouse if that spouse outlives the other should be thought about carefully. If both spouses are wealthy, perhaps they do not need to transfer their wealth to each other after their deaths. The prenup can state that their financial lives during marriage and after death will be kept totally separate.

Here's one version of the various gray marriage scenarios I've often seen in my prenup practice. I receive an email from Bill. He is in his early 50s. He is marrying Mary next month. It's a second marriage for both of them, after divorces from their first spouses. They each have teenage children and children in college. Mary strongly believes they need a prenup. She believes they should each waive all their marital rights in the prenup. Both she and Bill are working. They are not wealthy, but they have similar earnings from work, and they also have similar amounts saved up in retirement and other assets. They plan to buy a house together.

Mary feels that her entire "estate" if she dies first should go to the children of her previous marriage, and she wants to memorialize that in a prenup. Bill sees that he and Mary could be married for a very long time – possibly 30 or 40 years. He feels that they both may have a need to support each other as a unit as they go through life together. He feels that their joint financial needs should come first, and if Mary dies, he should inherit at least most of her assets. Is it advisable to have a prenup in this situation? Are there other possibilities? If there is a prenup, what should it say?

They are in this very typical "middle" situation where allegiance to children of the first marriage needs to be somehow blended and balanced with economic allegiance to each other. This balance needs to be flexible enough to change in time to assess their needs first as a couple and then after the death of one spouse. They need to figure out what is possible to provide to their children later on. What they will give in financial support and gifts to their children during their lifetime as a couple should also be considered.

State law provides for surviving spouses to receive part of their spouse's estate at death if the marriage is ongoing. For instance, there are spousal share elective rights to take against wills in every state. These laws will create a minimum of what would be provided to the surviving spouse and a maximum of what could be provided to the children of a deceased spouse. These rules apply if a spouse is unhappy with what is provided to him or her in the deceased spouse's will.

In most states, that roughly translates into 30 to 50 percent of a person's assets going to the surviving spouse, and the rest to the children of the prior marriage, although the calculation is more complicated in states that have adopted the Uniform Probate Code elective share rules. (See Chapter 7.)

If that arrangement works financially for the couple and the children, then there may be no reason to get a prenup. They can simply write wills that express the same elective share percentage (or a more generous percentage to the surviving spouse, if desired). The surviving spouse would not elect the spousal share, because that spouse will have received it (or more) in the estate plan of the decedent spouse.

If there is not enough wealth to transfer assets outright to their children upon the first spouse's death, assets can go into a trust, with distributions going to the surviving spouse during his or her lifetime, with the remainder going to the children of the prior marriage. (See Chapter 10 for descriptions of QTIP trusts and credit shelter trusts.)

If in reasonably good health and not elderly, the spouses could obtain life insurance to secure an inheritance for their children while protecting the new spouse with their assets, some of which could go to their own children upon their death or be added to a trust where the children would eventually receive what is left after the death of the other spouse.

Typical wills of spouses in intact first marriages have all assets going to the surviving spouse. When the surviving spouse dies, all that's remaining goes to the children of that marriage. But what if the surviving spouse remarries? Some of the assets from the first marriage could end up with the family of the new husband or wife.

Often people don't really worry about this because they want their surviving spouse to be remarried, happy, and secure in their new life. They also trust their surviving spouse to be fair to the children of the first marriage. But some people very strongly want their assets to stay within the bloodlines. If so, an estate plan can be set up to reflect this aim.

There is a legal concept in many states termed a "contract to make a will." With this arrangement, the parties sign a contract, formally executed in accordance with that state's laws. It might state, "If we are married at my death, I agree not to provide more than 40 percent of my entire estate (including life insurance and retirement assets) to Jon, Joanna, and Erika, my children from my first marriage, with the remainder to be distributed to my dear wife, Ellen." Ellen would make a parallel contract. That would ensure an inheritance for both parties in states that permit a contract to make a will. It may lessen the need for a full-blown prenup.

What if Ellen transfers some of her property to her children before her death? Can that be added to the contract to make a will so that her children's percentage reflects pre-death gifts made by her? Maybe, but now it is starting to look more like a prenup would be needed in which there can be restrictions on lifetime transfers of assets. The prenup can set the basic terms, and a spouse can set up a trust reflecting the terms. This would be a better alternative than a contract to make a will. Upon the first death (if there are enough assets), there could be an outright transfer or a transfer in trust to the children of the first marriage, in addition to making provisions for the surviving spouse, perhaps by means of a QTIP trust. (See Chapter 10.)

Needs of children of the prior marriage.

Spouses in a gray marriage are sometimes faced with needs and expectations of grown children for financial support from their parents. If it is a second marriage, the new spouses can make decisions collectively about how this support would be made.

Perhaps there could be an asset pool available for gifts and assistance to children each year. It could be in an amount that the spouses agree upon, and the amounts could change by mutual decision. There could be a separate pool for gifts for each of the spouses. Unused gifts could be rolled over to the next year. If there is one child of one of the spouses that requires extra assistance, that can be discussed by the spouses to see if they can be aligned in the help they want to provide that child.

The spouses may decide that gifts and assistance from a parent to a child of a previous marriage could be made from separate assets of that spouse to his or her children. The spouses can discuss overall limitations in gifting. These "rules" could (or could not) be in a prenup.

Should you tell your children you have a prenup?

Sometimes it is appropriate to let the grown children know that their parent is considering a prenup or has entered into one with the new spouse in the gray marriage. Details of what is in the prenup can be withheld from the children or can be articulated in a very general manner.

A parent might frame the discussion by saying, "We have set the terms of our prenup so that we will support each other during our lifetimes, and after we both die, all of you (all the children) will share in what's left of our estate." Or, "When I die, you will receive part of your inheritance. After Selma dies, you will receive the rest of your inheritance. I have put property in trust for Selma to support her after I die, but I expect there to be money left over for you three children after Selma dies."

Letting the children know that you have considered them will be helpful for creating peace within the newly extended family.

How to handle decisions on retirement plan distributions.

Sometimes in a gray prenup in a second marriage a spouse will wish to provide for a surviving spouse by naming him or her as beneficiary of all or part of the spouse's retirement assets. That's an understandable way to provide for a surviving spouse in the event of death. In some cases, the children of the previous marriage can be benefited with other assets.

A typical provision in prenups in a late-in-life marriage may state that retirement assets are separate property, and that a spouse is not required to name the other (surviving) spouse as beneficiary of his or her retirement assets. Another provision generally says that the spouse can name the other as beneficiary (in any amount or percentage of the assets) if he or she so desires. The language used might say, "Notwithstanding the provisions of this Agreement, each spouse has the right to transfer property to the other during his/her lifetime, or at death, through last will, or otherwise."

But what happens when the spouses agree in the prenup *not* to name each other as beneficiary of a retirement asset and they intend that this waiver be put into effect upon death? Will the waiver in the prenup work to waive spousal rights? The answer is no, at least in the case of ERISA-qualified retirement assets.

Many types of retirement assets are ERISA-qualified. ERISA stands for the Employee Retirement Income Security Act, which was enacted in 1974. ERISA-qualified plans are private sector retirement plans that include 401(k)s, SIMPLE IRAs, SEP IRAs, Keogh plans, ESOPs, and profit-sharing plans, as well as 403(b) plans used by private tax-exempt organizations.

Retirement protections in ERISA were further strengthened by the Retirement Equity Act of 1984. At the time of the 1984 enactment, President Reagan declared that "each person in a marriage has a right to benefit from the other's pension. No longer will one member of a married couple be able to sign away survivor benefits for the other. A spouse's written consent will now be required on any decision not to provide survivors' protection."

The law provides that if the retirement asset offers benefits in the form of annuities (whether a "defined contribution" or a "defined benefit" plan), that pension must be paid as a joint and survivor annuity with the surviving spouse receiving at least 50 percent of the participant's annuity payment if a joint and survivor annuity. The surviving spouse must receive 50 percent of the actuarial value of the retirement asset if it is to be paid as a pre-retirement death benefit. The participant's spouse can waive this right and receive a lesser amount of payment (or no payment at all) by giving consent in writing.

If the ERISA-qualified plan is a "defined contribution" account in which the employee and sometimes the employer contribute money to create a retirement fund (such as a 401(k) if a lump-sum payment is available), then the surviving spouse must be left with not less than 50 percent of the ERISA-qualified retirement account balance or a survivor annuity with that value. If that spouse waives his or her rights, the waiver must be in a notarized writing.

Some defined contribution plans, such as 401(k) plans, do not offer any annuity benefits. These require that the surviving spouse is the 100 percent death beneficiary (unless that spouse waives his or her rights).

The ERISA protection is so strong that it overrides other named beneficiaries or any contractual obligation, such as those that may be found in a prenup. A signed and notarized prenup might say that a spouse has waived his or her rights in the future spouse's retirement account, but the prenup will not supersede federal law, which provides for these spousal protections. The waiver for ERISA purposes cannot be executed until *after* the marriage, because a person must be a "spouse" to waive rights. In addition, the participant spouse must be at least 35 years old at the time of the waiver.

It is important to note that even if your children are 100 percent beneficiaries of your ERISA-qualified retirement assets and you do not change the beneficiaries after marriage, your surviving spouse will have a claim for 50 percent (or 100 percent, depending on the type of plan) of the account balances.

Accordingly, if there is to be a waiver established in the prenup, it is good to have the time that the spouse must sign the waiver be a term in the prenup. For instance, the prenup could specify that within 60 days of the marriage, the waiver or waivers will be executed by the non-participant spouse and the prenup could specify the terms of the waiver. Or do it before the honeymoon if you're traveling to a dangerous place by airplane.

The surviving spouse could be provided with something less than 100 percent (or 50 percent depending on the plan), or any percentage of the retirement plan if there is a waiver. The ERISA rights waiver is so significant that the waiving spouse's signature must be acknowledged by a notary public and/or witnessed by a plan representative.

Note that Traditional IRAs, Rollover IRAs, and Roth IRAs are not ERISA-qualified. A spouse can disinherit his or her surviving spouse in an IRA beneficiary designation without spousal recourse under federal law.

Let's say that a spouse has ended working at a company in which he or she had accumulated a great deal of retirement savings in the 401(k) plan. That spouse could roll over the 401(k) assets into a Rollover IRA with spousal consent. At a later time (but still during the marriage), that spouse could change the beneficiary designation to someone else, *without* his spouse's consent, because the IRA is not ERISA protected. This has been done to many a surviving spouse's surprise and dismay when that spouse discovered she or he was not the beneficiary of the IRA after the death of the IRA-owner spouse.

How to handle divorce in a gray prenup.

In any divorce, even one with a prenup, there will be issues of property division and support to resolve, as well as support of children, medical insurance, and life insurance. When there is no prenup, these are addressed by the couple generally "in the shadow of the law." The state laws and case law on these topics are assessed by the parties' attorneys, who will generally apply these rules without having to litigate the matter.

In a divorce with a prenup, the parties are seeking to define what will happen upon a divorce, which may take place many years after the marriage begins. It is difficult, and even at times impossible, to guess what financial situations will exist in the future. But that's what people signing prenups with divorce provisions must do.

Chapters 7 and 15 describe the basic rules regarding property division and alimony applicable in most states. There may be public policy in a state that applies if, at the time of a divorce, a dependent spouse cannot support him- or herself. These public policies may override the terms of a prenup.

Spouses marrying later in life need to consider providing a reasonable amount of protection for the other spouse, even if the marriage ends in divorce. In many late-in-life marriages there is not enough time to build up "marital property" through working and careers prior to the time of the divorce. The marriage might occur after the retirements of the parties, or close to it.

Parties need to think about how to replace the marital property that develops during a long marriage of younger people. This marital property protects both spouses. But in a gray marriage, the parties may have already stopped working and creating marital property by earnings, investments of the excess earnings, and adding to their retirement accounts. There might be a more wealthy spouse and a less wealthy one.

But the parties can decide how to provide financial protection for each party. These protections can be written into a prenup. One way this can be done is by vesting a reasonable amount of separate property into marital property during the marriage or providing for reasonable asset division and/or spousal support if the marriage ends in divorce (or death).

Spousal support can be quantified and described in the gray prenup, as well as what sources it might come from. Having a blanket waiver in alimony may not be enforceable, again on public policy grounds, if the less moneyed spouse is unable to support him- or herself. (See Chapter 15.) It might be better rather than running the risk of invalidation to define reasonable terms in the prenup. It is also a good way of showing a future gray spouse that you care about your new partner's well-being, even if the marriage were to end in divorce.

Change in the income tax treatment of alimony in the TCJA.

Most people who have prenups are wealthy or at least have some significant resources. A wealthy person who is entering into marriage with a financially dependent spouse can make provisions for supporting the former spouse if the marriage ends in divorce. Use of alimony trusts was a way to combine security for a divorced dependent spouse in conjunction with estate planning for the more wealthy spouse.

Under the Tax Cuts and Jobs Act of 2017 (TCJA), the deduction for alimony payments under Internal Revenue Code Section 215 and the inclusion of the payments in the receiving spouse's income under Section 71 have been eliminated. The effective date of this change is for separation agreements entered into after December 31, 2018, and for court decrees rendered after that date. But that doesn't change the use of alimony in some divorces.

One of the ways a paying spouse was able to set up structured alimony payments under prior law was by means of an alimony trust. This was a technique that could benefit a dependent spouse and could also provide tax benefits and a return of capital to the more moneyed spouse. After the death of the supported spouse, the spouse setting up the alimony trust could either reacquire the trust assets, or transfer it to other beneficiaries, such as the children of a prior marriage.

A paying spouse would transfer a fund of income-producing assets transferred into a trust. Internal Revenue Code Section 682 permitted the support income paid out to the less moneyed former spouse to be reported in the recipient's taxable income (similar to alimony) rather than being included in the payor ex-spouse's taxable income under the grantor trust rules. Because the paying spouse was discharging an obligation of support, the income earned by the trust would have been taxable to him or her under the grantor trust rules, but for the exception provided by Section 682.

This tax advantaged treatment was no longer available as of January 1, 2018, as Section 682 was repealed in its entirety under the TCJA.

The nursing home cost risk in gray marriages.

One of the worries about getting older is the chance that one of you will become mentally or physically disabled to the extent that you can no longer be taken care of in your own home by your spouse. Anyone marrying later in life runs the risk of ending up in a nursing home – sometimes for an extended stay.

Although this won't happen to everyone, when it does, it is a significant financial drain. Skilled nursing facilities are very expensive, and Medicare pays only up to 20 days per illness fully, and up to another 80 days with a co-payment. The 80-day co-payment is currently $164.50 per day, and can be covered by a Medigap insurance policy, provided the you have one. If not, the co-payment is paid by the resident on a "private pay" basis. After the 100 days have expired, the "private pay" cost of staying in a skilled nursing facility can range from $10,000 a month to $17,000 a month, depending on the facility and its geographical location.

The statistics for length of stays and chances of ending up in skilled nursing facilities are found in a number of places. The statistics vary, but here is what I have been able to glean from various sources.

About 5 percent of those 65 years and older are currently in skilled nursing care facilities at any given time. Of these, 50 percent of nursing home residents are 85 years and older. Of the "oldest old" (those over 85), 24.5 percent are in nursing homes and almost 50 percent of people 95 and older live in nursing homes. Statistics from 2015 show that 62 percent of men and 71 percent of women live to age 80, and 22 percent of men and 34 percent of women live to age 90. This confirms what they say – many people live into their 80s, but much fewer live past their 80s. It's like the old "Roach Motel" ad from 1978: "Roaches check in, but they don't check out."

One trade group source says that of people who have bought long-term care insurance at age 60, 35 percent of them will use their policy benefits after a 90-day elimination period. (*What Is the Probability You'll Need Long-Term Care?* American Association for Long-Term Care Insurance, www.aaltci.org.)

According to the various statistics that I have been able to find (which vary somewhat), 44 percent of residents who enter a skilled nursing facility stay less than one year (either because they don't survive, or they leave the facility). The mortality rate upon entrance into skilled nursing is very high. Within the first 12 months, as many as 50 percent of the new residents will die, with many of these dying in the first six months. However, the average length of a stay is longer – about two years and four months – due to some residents who have very long stays.

A long-term insurance trade group states that of the people who need long-term care in nursing homes, 44 percent of nursing home residents stay less than a year, 30 percent stay between one and three years, and 24 percent spend more than three years. (*What Is the Probability You'll Need Long-Term Care?* American Association for Long-Term Care Insurance.)

The average time spent in a nursing home is significant because nursing home care is so expensive. A long stay can deplete the financial assets of any couple, including a couple in a gray marriage. It appears that nursing home stays might be getting shorter, due to advances in receiving care at home and the prevalence of assisted living facilities.

It is the "more than two or three years" in a nursing home that poses a financial danger to many elder couples. After Medicare coverage, you're on your own and you will be "private pay." A long stay in a nursing home can wipe out a lifetime of savings.

The question is how long the stay will be. The cost of nursing homes stays is currently upward of $100,000 a year in rural areas, and upward of $200,000 a year in some urban areas. With these costs, for most elder couples you have a recipe for financial disaster.

Who is responsible for these costs?

As discussed above, Medicare will typically only cover up to 100 days of short-term rehabilitation in a nursing facility (with a patient co-pay for days 21 to 100). Medicare does not pay for long-term custodial care in a nursing home.

Individuals must pay privately for nursing home care out of their current income and savings. In many states, once an individual has less than $2,000 in assets, either by having spent assets down, or by having engaged in advance planning to position assets so as to make them non-countable, Medicaid, which is a joint federal-state program, can cover the cost of the individual's nursing home care.

The bad news is that spouses are responsible for each other's nursing home costs. And worse news is that you can't avoid financial responsibility to pay for your spouse's stay in a nursing home by stating that you're not responsible for it in a prenup. For Medicaid purposes, the gray spouses are viewed as one entity. State and federal laws supersede the private contract provisions you make in a prenup.

There are a few possibilities that can mitigate this rule. Elders who are in a second or later marriage who have kept their assets largely segregated may be able to employ a strategy called "Spousal Refusal" at the time the ill spouse wishes to apply for Medicaid to cover nursing home care. On the Medicaid application, the ill spouse would indicate that the well spouse (also called the "community" spouse) is refusing to cooperate in the Medicaid application process. The Medicaid agency might then consider only the assets of the Medicaid applicant spouse. The Medicaid agency will, however, require the applicant spouse to assign all of his or her support rights to the Medicaid agency, which would then have the option of suing the well spouse for the cost of the nursing home care paid by the agency.

Results of this strategy vary by state or even by county of residence. Using a strategy of Spousal Refusal may insulate the assets of the community spouse (the spouse who is not in the nursing home) from the cost of the ill spouse's nursing home care, but it is not guaranteed.

As stated above, the separate assets of the spouse in the nursing home in many states will have to be spent down to $2,000 to qualify for Medicaid. And worse, the community spouse has to spend down his or her assets to leaving only about $120,900 in assets under current laws (and somewhat less in some states). That doesn't leave the community spouse much in the way of security for his or her old age. In some states, the well spouse can protect assets over that amount by purchasing Medicaid-compliant Single Premium

Immediate Annuities (SPIAs) with the excess assets. But that technique makes the assets retained by the community spouse illiquid.

The Medicaid eligibility laws depend on federal law and the laws of the state in which you reside, not the "choice of law" selected in your prenup. That means the spouse at home may have to use most of his or her assets to support the spouse in the nursing home.

The community spouse's income (as opposed to assets) can stay with that spouse. The nursing home spouse's income will be used as a part payment to the nursing home for the costs of staying there. The community spouse may get to keep some or all of the nursing home spouse's income if the community spouse has income under about $3,000 per month and needs it for his or her support.

The house you and your spouse live in may be treated as a "non-countable" exempt asset at the time of a Medicaid application as long as the community spouse lives there. If Medicaid planning is done, title to the primary residence may typically be transferred to the community spouse if it is not already in a Medicaid asset protection trust in order to avoid the Medicaid agency placing a lien on the house.

The community spouse may then want to write a new estate plan to place the house into a testamentary supplemental needs trust for benefit of the Medicaid recipient spouse in order to protect the house in case the community spouse pre-deceases the Medicaid recipient spouse. Note that some people choose to transfer real estate and other assets into Medicaid asset protection trusts at least five years before needing to apply for Medicaid in order to preserve real estate and those other assets for their heirs. There are advantages and disadvantages to such planning, and also ethical considerations that people often address when thinking about transferring assets. A visit to an elder law attorney is important if you want to assess any of these planning tools.

So it doesn't matter what the prenup says about the payment of nursing home expenses. Federal and state Medicaid eligibility rules require consideration of the assets of the community spouse, and these laws will override what's in the prenup.

What to do about the nursing home cost risk.

Late-in-life partners who are considering marriage may want to make an appointment with an elder law attorney who is an expert in planning for nursing home costs. And unless one or both partners are extremely wealthy and can easily absorb the potential cost and financial risk of a long stay in a nursing home, they might consider purchasing long-term care insurance as part of their marital obligations. This obligation to buy nursing home insurance can be put into a prenup. Or instead of long-term care insurance, the parties can seek to address the potential loss by buying life insurance.

People wonder if they should get a divorce to prevent the community spouse's assets from being depleted for nursing home costs. Attorneys and financial planners sometimes suggest this. This is called a "Medicaid divorce."

State laws and practice in various state courts vary greatly on the effectiveness of divorcing your nursing home spouse (who may or may not be competent), not to mention the ethical implications for the spouses (and their attorneys). Is it really a *bona fide* divorce? Will the state court approve it? Has the nursing home spouse given up assets without consideration to the other spouse in the marital settlement in order to qualify for Medicaid? Is this considered a fraudulent transfer for Medicaid purposes, and can the nursing home spouse have their eligibility for Medicaid coverage refused because of it?

A prenup could require the couple to get divorced if one is permanently institutionalized or in a nursing home for greater than a certain number of years. But the question is whether or not the divorce judge will consider the marriage to be legitimately ended under the laws of your state. So a divorce may or may not help the community spouse overcome the Medicaid requirement of using the community spouse's assets to support the other spouse's nursing home costs.

What if we have decided to not get married? Can we have a contract anyway?

Some elders opt not to marry each other, for a number of reasons. One of these is the nursing home cost risk that applies to married couples. Others opt to forgo legal marriage for a host of personal reasons. Some do not want to share assets and income and simply do not want to enter into a prenuptial agreement.

Many elder unmarried couples do wish to share living expenses and cohabitate. A couple may consider entering into a "Relationship Agreement" or "Living Together Agreement." (Younger cohabitants can enter into these as well.)

These agreements vary greatly and have many potential terms. Some of them focus on the practicalities of running a household – who will wash the dishes, go food shopping, etc. Others focus on how the couple will pay for their living expenses. For instance, the agreement can define how the daily cost of living (including housing, utilities, food, and cost of car and other transportation) will be shared.

If the couple intends to reside together, whether in a house, rental apartment, or an assisted living facility, the agreement can set terms as to what will happen if one of them gets sick or dies. Who will continue to pay the costs of the residence? Will the sick party who needs to move into a nursing home have any liability? Will the estate of the deceased partner have any liability to continue sharing costs? Will a more wealthy elder cohabitant pay personal expenses of the other? Will it be clear that these payments will not be recouped by that person's heirs?

If the parties are buying a home together, the provisions get more complex.

A full-blown section and specific provision about what happens during the co-ownership is very important to define their respective rights and obligations. What will happen if they break up and one of them moves out? How will the equity be valued? How will it be paid to the person leaving the house, and how will the other person refinance the mortgage so that the departing person's liability to pay the mortgage is terminated? Will they continue to co-own? What will be the rules if the remaining partner gets a housemate to share rent? How will the ongoing financial commitments to share expenses be dealt with?

What if the cohabitation ends with the death of one of the parties? Issues that can be addressed are distribution of tangible property and payment of debts arising from the relationship. An agreement can include mechanics for the children of a deceased cohabitant to access the tangible personal property of their parent in the house or apartment the parent lived in. Ownership of tangible property such as household furnishings bought jointly or accumulated during the relationship can also be addressed. The agreement can contain a dispute resolution clause in case any issues are unresolved at the time the relationship ends.

More rarely there are provisions involving financial support of one of the parties by the other after a breakup. But if they are there, they are likely to be enforced in a court of law. However, they will not have the income tax attributes of alimony under Internal Revenue Code Sections 71 and 215 (i.e., deductible to the payor, includible into the payee's income). Note that this beneficial tax treatment has been eliminated effective January 1, 2019 in the recently enacted Tax Cuts and Jobs Act of 2017.

Some cohabitation agreements require maintenance of health insurance or Medigap insurance. Some have requirements that health care proxies, powers of attorney, last wills, and other documents be created to be applicable during the time of the cohabitation, and that they specify who will be the agents and personal representatives in those documents.

It is important to note that relationship contracts do not rise to the level of enforceable prenuptial agreements that are valid if the cohabitants marry each other. It is very important to seek the advice of a lawyer if you have an existing cohabitation contract and you intend to legally marry your partner. You will need to review the cohabitation agreement and redraft an entirely new agreement as a prenuptial agreement, in accordance with the laws of your state. (See Chapter 18 on enforceability.)

Another issue to be aware of is the potential that cohabitation leads to a "common law" marriage. In some states, a couple will legally be considered married without having formally wed if they have been living together as a married couple. There are nine states plus the District of Columbia that still have common law marriages, either by statute or case law.

The requirements differ from state to state, and there is no mythical "seven-year rule" as to the length of cohabitation required. Most common law marriage states require the couple to hold themselves out as married and conduct themselves such as to lead a belief in the community that they were married. This conduct might include referring to each other as "husband," "wife," or "spouse" when in public.

If you have a common law marriage, the rules in your state regarding property division and spousal support in a divorce will apply. But a disclaimer in a "living together" agreement stating that no legal or common law marriage is intended by the parties will go a long way in rebutting any presumptions that may exist.

ARE LGBT PRENUPS DIFFERENT FROM OTHER TYPES?

When same-sex marriage first became legal in Massachusetts in 2004, a *New Yorker* cartoon by Michael Shaw pictured a middle-age heterosexual couple watching the news on TV. The husband says to the wife, "Gays and lesbians getting married – haven't they suffered enough?"

Notwithstanding the trials and tribulations (and joys) of marriage, it has been said by many LGBT people that one of the best things about the legalization of same-sex marriage is same-sex divorce. With the rights, privileges, and duties that come with legal marriage, access to courts and the body of laws that relate to divorce are very helpful to LGBT couples who are disengaging their relationships.

Same-sex marriage became federal law across the entire U.S. in 2015 with the U.S. Supreme Court decision in *Obergefell v. Hodges*, 135 S. Ct. 2071; 576 U.S. ___ (2015). Prior to *Obergefell*, people in same-sex relationships relied on a patchwork of contracts and estate-planning documents to provide protections for themselves and their children. Many people did not do the requisite planning. A multitude of state laws, cases, and theories were drawn upon to deal with the fallout when a same-sex union disintegrates. Many people suffered disastrous consequences. The equitable and useful remedies pertaining to legal divorce were simply not available.

What used to happen to lesbians and gay men when relationships broke up.

The horror stories abound of lifelong partners not being able to visit their dying spouse in a hospital. In many cases, assets jointly saved after a lifelong union were legally taken by blood relatives of the deceased partner instead of the surviving partner. There were (and sadly, still are) many struggles involving custody of children. The rights of a biological parent of the children frequently trumped those of a non-biological parent. In some cases, parenting rights of a partner who had formed strong bonds with a child were cut off.

Before *Obergefell*, the lack of available law led to chaotic breakups and gross injustices to people in gay and lesbian relationships. Because the law was not settled, legal recourse was very expensive. Partners could not rely on anything provided by divorce law. It was a big loss, since divorce laws are created to ensure a fair split of all marital assets, taking into consideration the non-monetary contributions of a stay-at-home spouse.

There were virtually no statutes pertaining to a division of property for unmarried couples. Virtually no state permitted unmarried cohabitants to receive alimony at the end of a relationship. Couples did not get the income tax benefits of any support paid by agreement of the parties.

Unless agreement was reached by the former partners, a complicated and expensive lawsuit was the only way to force a property division or support when a same-sex partnership ended. These pre-*Obergefell* cases relied on equitable theories such as unjust enrichment, constructive trust, common law partnership, promissory estoppel, implied contract, and breach of fiduciary duty. Such cases were expensive (and thus unavailable to many) and often unsuccessful.

Because the law was so unclear, the less moneyed partners in these breakups were especially victimized. Often, they could not feasibly proceed in court to try to obtain financial value for their many years of contributions to the relationship. This put the wealthier person who could afford litigation in the driver's seat and could force an unfavorable settlement for the other party, or no settlement at all. This one-sided result was the norm and occurred repeatedly.

Divorce law is really important. By evaluating each case on its own merits in the context of the statutes and case law, the courts provide fairness and finality to divorcing couples. With *Obergefell*, same-sex couples now have the benefit of this experience and plethora of laws.

Prenups come with a healthy body of prenuptial agreement laws. These provide protections for the contracting future spouses. One of them is an element of fairness, oftentimes voiced as the absence of unconscionability. These protections vary from state to state but are present in all states when assessing the enforceability of prenups. (See Chapter 18.)

But contracts between cohabiting, unmarried couples did not necessarily provide such fairness. Same-sex couples, even if they were in very long-term relationships, were not legally married and therefore not protected by the laws governing prenups. Their contracts, even if obviously unfair, would likely be enforced.

For instance, in one Massachusetts case, a court said that a contract between unmarried heterosexual cohabitants who had been in a 25-year relationship did not have to meet the heightened public policy requirements of a contract between spouses or a prenuptial agreement. The court upheld a contract leaving the house, titled in the male partner's name, to him, even though the female partner had made the typical "womanly" contributions to the household as well as having earned income that she contributed to the household. At the time of the trial, the woman partner did not have any savings and only a small pension. *Wilcox v. Trautz*, 427 Mass. 326 (1998).

In another case involving a heterosexual couple, a court found no right to an equitable distribution of property for an unmarried couple, as would occur in a divorce. In that case, both parties had contributed to a farm property used as a "pick-your-own" raspberry business. The court stated that there is no recognition of marital rights in cohabitation and that the man failed to make a case for equitable relief. It was a very harsh result for the male partner. *Collins v. Guggenheim*, 417 Mass. 615 (1994).

With same-sex marriage, LGBT people now have the opportunity to formalize their relationships by legally marrying. Consequently, all the laws of divorce apply to them. Divorce laws are a very well-developed body of laws that can aid in simplifying struggles if the marriage ends in divorce. For LGBT people, knowing how these laws now protect them provides a greater sense of security, which serves to preserve and nourish their marriages. There is no longer a festering of contemplation of the unknowable (and perhaps inequitable) results if there is a breakup. Legal marriage sustains the commitment of all couples – including LGBT couples.

The process of affording legal protections to same-sex couples began in Vermont in 2000 by legislation. Vermont was the first state to legalize civil unions, a "marital-type" relationship for gays and lesbians. Then came Massachusetts, with full-fledged marriage though the *Goodridge* court decision in 2003. This case set the start date for gay and lesbian marriages as May 17, 2004. *Goodridge v. Department of Public Health*, 440 Mass. 309 (2003).

I was in the street in front of City Hall in Cambridge, Massachusetts, at midnight on that night when the law was put into effect. City Hall was kept opened at midnight so that people could start getting their marriage licenses at the moment marriage became legal. Joyous crowds singing patriotic songs watched the stream of couples as they lined up to get their marriage licenses.

After that, through court cases and legislation, same-sex marriage began to be allowed across the country. By 2015, over half the population of the United States could enter into same-sex marriages where they lived.

Full federal recognition of same-sex marriages across all 50 U.S. states came with the *Obergefell v. Hodges* decision in 2015. This case finally afforded same-sex couples the same protections under the federal law in their unions as heterosexual couples have always enjoyed. *Obergefell* also ensured that all state laws regarding divorce and inheritance would apply to same-sex married couples. These laws are hugely important for same-sex couples who wish to enter into prenups.

It was a welcome relief to same-sex couples to be able to rely on state laws to provide equity and security if the marriage ended in divorce or death rather than the patchwork of difficult court cases and "workarounds" that often produced grossly unfair results.

Different attitudes toward prenups among gay and lesbian couples.

When given the right to marry, many gay and lesbian couples already had years of cohabitation behind them. In many cases, they had raised children together or were in the process of doing so. For many of these couples, the idea of having a prenup was not acceptable, as they had already worked out the financial terms of their marriages to their satisfaction and had time-tested their relationships to be durable. Their financial lives had often already been intertwined over the course of many years. Many LGBT couples in long-term relationships opted to get married without a prenup.

For newer couples, gay men tend to gravitate toward prenups more readily than lesbian couples. Gay men with successful careers and high incomes often have a history of financial independence. Many have developed substantial assets during their years of earning, even if they are relatively young. Many (but not all) gay men do not plan to have children after they marry.

Gay men have often been financially independent from each other during cohabitation, perhaps sharing expenses according to a formula. This formula is often a 50-50 sharing of expenses, even if their incomes are disparate. Many of the gay men I've met and worked with don't want to share assets in the future except on a purely voluntary basis. Because they often do not have children, they may name their own heirs (friends or blood relatives) if the marriage ends in death, but they also may want to benefit their spouse.

In general, my gay male prenup clients don't see any value in sharing increases of value of separate assets or income derived from separate assets. They are also not usually interested in vesting separate property into marital property during the marriage. They have operated independently in the past and wish to continue doing so.

Where each of them can survive financially without the other, there is no need for mutual financial protection. But this independence may actually have some negative implications to the durability of their marriage. When people don't need each other, they can more readily walk away from marriage. Financial need is part of the connection that keeps marriages together through good times and bad. The result of "not needing" each other is evidenced by the prevalence of divorce among celebrities and wealthy people.

Gay men have strong feelings about what would happen if they divorce, generally wanting to retain their financial independence and not have to support the other spouse. Alimony is not an appealing concept for most of them.

Therefore, the prenups gay men want are generally very strict ones, where each party keeps his assets and income after divorce, and alimony is bilaterally waived. There are, of course, instances where the financial security of the two future spouses varies widely. In such a circumstance, the usual challenges as to how to structure a prenup when there is a wealthier spouse and a financially dependent spouse should be considered as a loving option.

Can a prenup exist where a party or both parties essentially waive all their marital rights? There is case law in Massachusetts that says no. In a Massachusetts case, a court held that a prenup that strips away substantially all marital rights at the time of execution is not enforceable. *DeMatteo v. DeMatteo*, 436 Mass. 18 (2002).

In *DeMatteo*, the court noted that Massachusetts had an interest in protecting the financial interests of spouses when they divorce. The court opined that marriage is not a mere contract between two parties but a legal status from which certain rights and obligations arise. It concluded that as a result, the freedom to limit or waive legal rights in the event of divorce is not appropriately left unrestricted. The court ultimately held that if all other requirements are met, a prenup will be valid "unless its terms essentially vitiate the very status of marriage" by stripping a spouse of his or her marital rights at the time of execution.

Does this *DeMatteo* holding not apply to marriages where waiver of marital rights would not put a party in danger of not being adequately secure after a divorce? What does this mean with respect to a gay or lesbian couple (or an elder couple) who intentionally have decided to keep all their income and assets separate?

There are no published Massachusetts cases addressing this issue. This lack of case law may be due to the fact that parties in this situation are likely to be independent and financially strong. Neither party would litigate because there would be no reason to test their prenup by a lawsuit. A prenup that strips each spouse of marital rights may be deemed enforceable, assuming both parties were reasonably financially secure at the time of the signing. Marital protections in prenups and through the courts are for those who need them, not for those who do not.

But a similar agreement waving all marital rights for a young straight (or gay) couple embarking on their first marriage could be invalidated in Massachusetts and in some jurisdictions. Massachusetts law would say that the prenup is not enforceable because it strips a spouse of virtually all marital rights that would normally develop in a marriage, at the time of the signing. In other states, the prenup could fail on the unconscionability standard at signing, or as not being "fair and reasonable" at the time of its execution. (See Chapter 18 on enforceability.)

For lesbian couples, the situation is often different. Lesbian couples are, after all, women. They statistically earn less money and often have less financial stability and secure employment. Like many heterosexual couples, lesbian couples often need each other as financial partners to support themselves and their family unit. They often have finances that are more intertwined than gay male couples. Lesbian couples are more likely to be raising children together.

Like heterosexual couples, young lesbian couples very rarely opt to have a prenup. If one of them wants a prenup, it's generally because of a high level of personal or family wealth on the part of one of the partners or a great disparity in earned income. If there is to be a prenup, it needs to be done with care and a view toward the future to protect the less moneyed spouse as the relationship matures. In this way, the prenup will be similar to the prenup of heterosexuals who marry, particularly those who plan to have a family.

Complicating the situation for lesbian couples is that they more frequently than gay men have children from prior marriages or relationships. Some of these children may be grown or young adults. This sets up blended family and step-parent issues. The couple needs to balance attention and care to each other's financial situation with allegiance and care to the children of their prior relationships, as in a "gray" prenup. This balancing effort sometimes results in the need for a prenup.

Does marriage always entail a sharing of property?

American culture assumes spouses will become one financial unit, developing rights and responsibilities as the marriage lengthens in time. Prenups are very unusual in America, because they are contrary to the American cultural ideal of marriage. (See Chapter 5.)

Interestingly, in most Europe Union countries and some other countries around the globe, different views of marriage are permissible by their laws when the marriage is initiated.

In some European Union countries, couples have the choice of selecting among several marital property "regimes" when they decide to marry. These are essentially marital contracts with similar consequences as prenups. The marriage contract is prepared by a notary, and one simply chooses the matrimonial regime by checking off a box in the application to marry. Such a contract addresses property rights but does not address spousal support and child support. Even though which regime one chooses has significant implications, the marriage contract is often signed without the input of an advising lawyer.

Generally, these rules are similar in the various European countries. If no marital contract is entered into, the default option is "matrimonial property." This default entails a complete separation of premarital, inherited, and gifted assets. These remain the separate property of the spouses. All property acquired after the marriage is considered marital property. Does this sound familiar? Yes, it does. This application of law is very similar to marital property laws in the U.S. community property states.

A couple can also choose other regimes when marrying. Typically, there are two: a "separation of property" regime and a "universal community property" regime. In the "separation of property" regime, everything remains the sole property of each spouse and there is no community property. Jointly titled property would be divided in accordance with the laws of the country under co-ownership principles. With the "universal community property regime," all property is considered marital property no matter when and how the property was acquired. In the case of divorce, this type of property would generally be divided equally.

A couple could also vary these regimes in many (but not all) foreign countries by entering into an actual, full-blown prenuptial agreement.

These regimes are for property division. There are statutes in other countries that define rights upon death.

In many European countries and also elsewhere, such as Brazil and other South American countries, heirs-at-law have rights that cannot be lessened by estate plans and last wills and testament of decedents. These rights are similar to the U.S. intestacy laws (see Chapter 7), but they override what the decedent may have wanted. In order for a different allocation of an estate, the omitted heirs-at-law would need to waive their statutory rights. It doesn't matter what the last will said. The heirs' rights apply and, to that extent, negate what's in the decedent's last will.

Some millennials and other younger Americans in heterosexual relationships envision an economically independent marriage. Many (both men and women) buttress their notion on an egalitarian marriage or on feminist principles. For some, especially well-educated professionals, this might work out for them in the future. However, separate finances can also cause problems when people have different life trajectories, such as investing in parenting and a family versus investing in a business venture or a career. In addition, lopsided results (some of which may result from luck) can cause dismay and disturbance in a marriage if there is not sharing in the results of the marital venture.

"Tacking" issues can be addressed in prenups.

Among the divorce issues facing same-sex couples is the concept of "tacking." Tacking is adding (or not adding) the years of cohabitation to the length of the actual legal marriage. Some same-sex marriages had decades of cohabitation before the legal marriage.

Tacking is important because length of marriage affects rights and obligations when divorce occurs. The length of the marriage is one of the equitable factors in determining divorce rights. A long marriage leads to heightened financial responsibility when a marriage ends. It is an important factor when assessing the division of assets upon divorce. Longer marriages are strongly correlated to the obligation to provide spousal support, both as to amount and duration.

When gay and lesbian people began to legally marry under *Obergefell* and prior state laws, the tacking issue became very important. Would the duration of periods of cohabitation before same-sex marriage be allowed to be "tacked on to" the duration of the marriage, or not? Sometimes that period would consist of many years. Would it matter whether the couple had a marriage ceremony earlier, before same-sex marriage was legalized? Does it matter if the couple entered into a state-authorized civil union (such as Vermont's) or state or local "domestic partnership" prior to their legal marriage? What if they had married in Canada and resided in a non-same-sex marriage jurisdiction at the time of their marriage?

Tacking is considered on a state-by-state basis. There are a multitude of factual issues needed for the assessment of whether or not a prior period should be tacked on to the marriage. Adding to this confusion, different judges might reach different conclusions on the same facts, even within one state. As a result, this issue is rife for full-blown litigation in a divorce action, which makes the issue an appropriate one to be settled in a prenup.

For same-sex couples who had a period of cohabitation or non-legal marriage, they can mutually decide in a prenup when to consider their marriage to have begun. The prenup memorializes this date if needed for a divorce. In doing so, they can think about what their understanding of the start date means for their marital obligations toward each other. (This same process can apply to heterosexual couples who marry after a long period of cohabitation.) Because judges vary so much in deciding tacking issues, the parties to a prenup can essentially make this decision prior to their marriage.

The effect of prior cohabitation agreements after legal marriage.

Some gay and lesbian couples had entered into cohabitation, partnership, or "living together" agreements at some point during their cohabitation, prior to the legalization of same-sex marriage.

Many questions arise with respect to these after the couple enters into a legal marriage. Will the terms of the cohabitation agreement regarding property rights, support, and issues regarding children be in effect after the marriage? Very likely not.

Entering into a legal marriage is entering into a new assemblage of laws. Since most states view the "state" as a party to marriages, private contracts such as cohabitation agreements may not be respected in a divorce court.

In general, the vast majority of cohabitation agreements do not rise to the level of a prenuptial agreement. For example, they almost universally lack the full financial disclosure required between parties to a prenup. Prenuptial agreements need to be entered into before a marriage, in *contemplation* of marriage. Cohabitation agreements are executed at a time when marriage is not contemplated or imminent. In addition, to be enforceable, prenuptial agreements require that the signers must know what marital rights they are waiving under the laws of their state in order to be valid. The waiver should be in the body of the prenup so that people explicitly give their assent of what they are waiving. (See Chapter 11 for more information on cohabitation agreements.)

Before the advent of same-sex marriage, when a same-sex couple signed a cohabitation agreement, they *had* no marital rights. In most cases, they didn't expect to ever be able to legally marry. As a result, they were not waiving marital rights but rather conferring rights and creating an understanding with each other. For these reasons, a couple that signed one should assume that it will not be enforced as a prenup if they divorce or if one of them dies.

Same-sex couples who signed cohabitation agreements or "living together" agreements should think about whether they wish to have a formal prenuptial agreement prior to their legal marriage. If they have gotten married prior to reading this book, they can think about whether they wish to enter into a postnuptial agreement. (See Chapter 19.)

Are gay male couples changing the concept of marriage?

A bedrock principle or at least aspiration for most heterosexual marriages is sexual fidelity. Among the gay male population there is a significant culture of non-monogamy. Some of this non-monogamy is consensual and open. This value is included in many legal marriages of gay men.

A San Francisco State University study from 2010 followed more than 500 gay couples over many years and found that about half of all couples had sex with someone other than their partner, with their partner's knowledge. This study, however, may be flawed as it was aimed at assessing relationships and sexual patterns of behavior posing a risk of HIV infection. As a result, the sample population may not have been representative of the gay male population.

Some gay men (and also some gay women) have objected to the concept of same-sex marriage – at least for themselves – in finding the aspirations and culture of heterosexual marriage repressive. For some, marriage entails assimilation into "straight" culture, and accordingly their own "queer" culture and identity is perceived to be devalued and lost.

As Catherine Stimpson, former dean at New York University, said, part of the delight of being a lesbian was "sometimes feeling like a quasi-outlaw." By getting married, she believed she would undermine her "edgy nonconformist streak." ("Gay Couples, Choosing to Say 'I Don't,'" Cara Buckley, *New York Times* (10/25/13).) Another commentator, Esther Perel, an expert on infidelity and monogamy, terms queer and polyamorous people "monogamy's dissidents."

The term "queer" has undergone a transformation in meaning over the past 30 years. Early on it was a term of disparagement. Gays were called "queer" as a pejorative, similar to the prior derogatory term "fag" or "faggot." In recent years, LGBT people (often now called LGBTQ – the "Q" being added for the word "queer") and others have embraced the term "queer" as representing a positive value. The term can even subsume straight allies, who may call themselves "queer" because of their liberationist values. It's transformational, much like "Obamacare," which at the outset of the Affordable Care Act was a highly pejorative term and now is just the familiar name of the legislative act.

Part of this queer sensibility – especially for gay men – is a "liberationist" culture that appreciates and values sexual freedom and honesty on the subject of sex. This includes a desire to reduce the American cultural stigma around sexual freedom. For some others, particularly some lesbian women, there are feminist-based critiques of marriage, objecting to it on the basis of its patriarchal history and restrictive laws and its history of oppression of women. There are also criticisms that gay marriage is for the privileged class and that more attention should be paid to social causes such as gay bullying and gay youth homelessness. Some object to marriage on the basis that they believe it stigmatizes single people, giving married couples special privileges.

As one journalist said, "Nor could I add up the hours my partner and I spent eyeing marriage as if it were a fat slug on the carpet that we needed to deal with but didn't really want to touch." ("What Does Gay Marriage Mean?" J. Bryan Lowder, Slate.com, 10/28/2013.) For some LGBT people, getting married is as abhorrent as signing a prenuptial agreement.

Dan Savage, an LGBT media journalist, is one of the pundits of the new gay non-monogamy camp. He is married to his long-term (male) partner, but criticizes an American excessive esteem of strict monogamy in marriage, considering it an "obsession." Savage suggests a "monogamish" model for some marriages, which may involve occasional extramarital sex or frequent extramarital sex, but always coming back to the "home base," the marriage partner. His view, as he puts it, is that "the marriage is more important than fidelity." Savage believes that in some marriages more honest discourse about sexuality and our sexual urges is needed, even if this might lead to an affair. He also believes that for some couples, monogamy might be the best choice.

Would this "monogamish" model work in some same-sex (or heterosexual) marriages? And can a couple's ideals concerning their sexual life, with protocols involving affairs and disclosure, find their way into a prenup? (See Chapter 14, "Lifestyle Clauses.")

Some same-sex couples do not want to enter into the mainstream, choosing to value their "differentness." Being gay is as much a cultural identity as a sexual orientation. It's an identity, similar to being African-American or Jewish or deaf. Some refer to this as having a "queer sensibility." Straight children of gay and lesbian parents and straight parents of gay men and lesbians often have this "queer sensibility."

When same-sex marriage rights were passed state by state and with the *Obergefell* decision, same-sex couples found there was much social pressure to marry – even if they didn't want to. They may have had reservations about the institution of marriage or about the flaws in their own relationships.

The *Obergefell* ruling has given the freedom to marry, but it does not create an obligation to marry. Marriage is purely an individual decision that needs to be carefully considered. Planning for marriage may include a prenuptial agreement, should it be appropriate for a particular couple.

When entering into marriage, same-sex couples sometimes feel that they are inventing ways of interacting with respect to raising children, taking care of livelihoods, and addressing the practicalities of living together. They are explorers in a brave new world of heteronormative assumptions.

There are theories that same-sex marriage might influence heterosexual marriage to become more egalitarian and less reflexive to traditional gender roles, a process that seems already ongoing in heterosexual marriages. Also, the great joy and appreciation of many (if not most) gay men and lesbians of the opportunity to marry may well give heterosexuals a greater appreciation of the institution. It is clear by now that gay and lesbian marriage has not destroyed the institution of marriage. It may improve it, with new models of partnership, equality, and, possibly, sexual freedom.

Financial benefits of same-sex marriage.

There are many financial benefits that come with marriage.

Married couples have the right to receive the higher of their social security benefit or their deceased spouse's when one of them dies. Under current law, if you have been married for at least ten years and you divorce, you can opt for your social security benefit, or half your former spouse's if it is higher.

Now that same-sex marriage has arrived, many companies no longer permit domestic partners to be included in their employer-sponsored health insurance. Married partners can be included and can have medical insurance coverage even upon divorce in most cases.

As described in Chapter 10, getting married is the greatest estate and gift tax shelter around. The federal tax laws greatly benefit married couples in this way. Inheritance rights for married people are also very important. (See Chapter 7.)

A major detriment to being married is responsibility for nursing home costs. Married couples are responsible to use each other's assets to support a long, skilled nursing home stay for one of the spouses. (See Chapter 11 for explanation of this financial exposure.)

Cohabitation agreements for those LGBT people who decide not to marry.

For reasons described above, a small but significant number of gay men and lesbians in relationships have made the intentional choice not to legally marry. This is also true about a segment of the partnered heterosexual community. If people opt to not marry, they do have the option of having a cohabitation agreement. (See above for effect of cohabitation agreements after legally marrying.)

Cohabitation agreements have been around for a long time. The particulars and enforceability is a question of state law and the facts of each situation. In some states, surprisingly, laws prohibiting cohabitation by opposite-sex couples are still on the books, but rarely enforced. (See Mississippi, Michigan, Florida, and Virginia.) This is in spite of the statistics that nearly 60 percent of married U.S. adults cohabited with their spouse prior to their marriage. (Data from the 2006–2010 National Survey of Family Growth.)

Another issue facing cohabitants is their exposure to "common law marriage." Common law marriage is recognized in only a small number of states, perhaps a dozen or so at current count, and diminishing every year. If you reside in one of those states and intentionally hold yourself out as being "married," you can be drawn into the common law marriage net. If you are in one of those states and you have a serious intent of not being married, you can express that intent in a cohabitation agreement.

When children are involved.

For couples who have or are contemplating having children, agreements about supporting and raising children may find their way into prenups. As to unemancipated children, however, the courts will always retain jurisdiction and can overrule any agreement made by the parents in order to protect the children.

The standard that courts apply is what is "in the best interests" of the children. Parents can set standards for child support and custody in prenups, but these are provisional and can be overturned or modified by a court if the court believes the terms are not in the children's best interests.

In some states, if a child is born after the marriage of same-sex parents, the child is deemed to be the child of the same-sex couple. In a 2015 Massachusetts case, a lesbian couple had a son through in vitro fertilization using a known sperm donor. The couple's names were on the birth certificate. The couple filed a petition for second parent adoption of their child by the non-biological parent. They were concerned about her parenting rights if they traveled outside the commonwealth or relocated to a state where either same-sex marriage was not recognized or where the presumption of parentage did not apply to same-sex married couples. They had not notified the biological father of the proceeding.

The Court held that they did not have to give notice of the proceeding to the known sperm donor under M.G.L. Chapter 210, § 2, because he was not a "lawful parent." In Massachusetts, the law states that a child born to a married woman through artificial insemination with the consent of her spouse is the legal child of the woman and her spouse. (Mass. Gen. Laws chapter 46, § 4B.) The donor, whether known or unknown, was not deemed to be a lawful parent entitled to notice under the statute. *Adoption of a Minor*, 471 Mass. 373 (2015).

The outcome of this case could be different in another state depending on its laws about assisted reproduction. One additional lesson to be learned from *Adoption of a Minor* is that the artificial insemination statute only applies to *married* couples (including LGBT couples), emphasizing the importance for unmarried same-sex couples to enter into written agreements with a known sperm donor. Such agreements have not been litigated in Massachusetts but are considered essential by practitioners. You will find many published court cases in other states online that describe the various issues that may be litigated.

Second parent adoptions of biological children of one same-sex spouse are still very important. A second parent adoption is the legal procedure in which a non-biological parent becomes a legal parent of a child without terminating the biological parent's parental rights. Although all states now recognize same-sex marriage, some may not recognize parentage of the non-biological parent as a matter of law if the child is born during the marriage. Also, many children of a spouse that were born before the marriage are being raised by two LBGT married partners. In some cases, partners may consider an adoption process for these children also.

Another important reason for a second parent adoption is to establish rights of the non-biological parent in the event of divorce. The commitment to pursue this can be put into a prenup, but the adoption must take place before a divorce (or death) for the rights and obligations to flow from the new legal parentage.

A second parent adoption is essential to ensure that a non-biological parent's rights are fully protected in another state. In a recent *per curiam* decision, the U.S. Supreme Court affirmed that adoptions in one state must be respected by other states. *V.L. v. E.L.*, 136 S. Ct. 1017; 577 U.S. ___ (2016).

After *Obergefell*, one would expect that the non-biological spouse of a child born during the same-sex marriage would be treated as a parent. However, this could, in some states, be disrupted by a biological father or an uncooperative judge. Prenuptial agreements can include a commitment to pursue a second parent adoption upon the birth of a child of the marriage.

If there is a known sperm donor, it is highly advisable to have a signed agreement between the sperm donor and the marital couple prior to the insemination. This can determine the rights and obligations for each of them. Some same-sex couples want the sperm donor to have involvement with the child; some do not. Although the enforceability of such agreements may be in question, it is important for all parties to have absolute clarity about their expectations in such arrangements.

Gay men and surrogacy laws.

Many gay couples choose to adopt children. A growing number, however, choose to have children through surrogacy. This involves contracting with a female gestational carrier to conceive through in vitro fertilization (IVF), carry the child through pregnancy, and ultimately relinquish custody of the resulting child at birth.

Most gay couples find a surrogate through an IVF clinic or surrogacy agency. The clinic or agency will match the gay male father or couple with a woman who will bear the child. Sometimes the surrogate is a person known to the intended parents. For all of these situations, contracts are extremely important, and a specialist attorney is needed to draft the contract.

Although traditional surrogacy (where the surrogate is the egg donor and therefore the biological mother of the child) does sometimes occur, it is more likely that the IVF procedure will involve donor eggs. The gestational carrier is therefore not the biological mother. This makes it easier to establish the legal parentage for the intended parents.

It is legal in some states to provide for expenses and fees of the surrogate. It is not legal to "pay for the baby," such as providing a large sum for the woman who bears the child. Surrogacy is not meant to be a way for women of child-bearing age to earn money.

However, there are significant fees that can be paid to the carrier in some states. The contract can reimburse the gestational carrier's expenses, including medical insurance, uninsured medical expenses, maternity clothing, house-keeping, post-birth recovery, and sometimes lost wages. The cost of surrogacy also involves payment of fees to the surrogacy agency, social workers, and attorneys, as well as for the cost of the IVF procedure itself.

There are many ads on the internet soliciting "gestational carriers." There are screening factors for the gestational carriers — that they be financially sta-ble, enjoy being pregnant, and have a desire to help others create a family. Other requirements aim to provide a thorough genetic background for the child. An agency will also investigate the background of a carrier.

Some gestational carriers have ongoing relationships with the "forever grateful" intended parents, as one ad for a surrogacy agency optimistically puts it. This continued relationship (and its limitations) should be clearly delineated in the contract between the intended parents and the gestational carrier.

A number of states have laws permitting surrogacy and are favorable to the process. Some states have no laws regarding surrogacy. Of these, some have published court decisions, and some have no court guidance on the topic. Surrogacy is banned or heavily restricted by statute in a number of states. In many states, traditional surrogacy is banned, but gestational surrogacy arrangements are permitted.

The danger for prospective intended parents in connection with enforce-ment of the surrogacy agreement generally occurs in two situations. One of these is when the gestational or traditional surrogate refuses to relinquish cus-tody to the intended parents. The other is when the baby is born with birth defects or a race that is different than the one expected, and the intended parents refuse to accept the baby. In many states, such as California and Massachusetts, the intended parents can obtain a judgment of parentage prior to the child's birth in order to avoid the first situation, in which the surrogate refuses to relinquish custody of the baby to the intended parents.

Some gay men choose to memorialize their wishes with respect to creating a family in their prenup; many do not. In any event, state statutes regulating surrogacy will override any provisions regarding the process and the custody of resulting children that might be set forth in a prenup. But having the discussion regarding the future spouses' goals in family building can be helpful in settling an issue before the marriage. This may be an important discussion, whether or not it ends up as a term in a prenup. As a term, it might be written in "aspirational" or "precatory" language, rather than being a legally binding requirement.

Gestational contracts also raise interstate legal issues when the law of the state of the surrogate conflicts with the law of the intended parents. Additional complications may arise when the "choice of law" provision in the gestational contract names the laws of still another state that applies to the contract.

Can a prenup resolve parenting issues after a relationship ends?

There are many situations where a child is the legal (biological or adoptive) child of only one of the spouses, and the other spouse has helped raise the child. When the relationship ends, a legal parent may try to prevent the other parent from continuing the parent-child relationship. Unless the parties agree, litigation is likely.

These situations arise when the couple (LGBT or heterosexual) has not petitioned for a second-parent adoption. With a second-parent adoption, the non-biological parent becomes a legal parent of the child. The laws that apply the presumption of parentage to married couples do not apply to children born or adopted prior to a marriage.

The litigation can be quite complex. One legal theory raised by the non-biological parent is that he or she has become a *de facto* (or "psychological") parent of the child. A de facto parent is one who does not have a biological relationship with the child but has participated intimately in the child's life. This parent has resided with the child and the biological parent and has shared caretaking functions, as well as other parental functions, such as discipline, providing for education and medical care, and serving as a moral guide.

Sometimes serious harm can result to a child when contact between the child and the de facto parent is terminated. These cases are very difficult for the non-biological parent to prove and win in court. A recent Massachusetts case, however, gives hope to non-biological parents in this situation. In that case, the court ruled that a non-biological mother who, with her former partner, "received the child into their home and openly held out the child as their child" was a full legal parent of the child. *Partanen v. Gallagher*, 475 Mass. 632 (2016); see also Mass. Gen. Laws chapter 209C, § 6(a)(4).

Couples who have decided to enter into a prenuptial agreement can resolve some of these potential problems within the terms of a prenup. They can set a second-parent adoption plan in effect in the prenup or can deem a party a de facto parent. This will go far in solving disputes that could develop later, with the caveat that any parenting decision may be reviewed by the court under the "best interests of the child" public policy doctrine. A court does not have to accept the parents' plans about the child or children. However, the statements of the parents as to what they believed to be in the best interests of the child or children at the time they signed the contract may be influential in court.

In prenups, other issues such as a commitment to nominate the non-biological parent as guardian of the child or children or including estate-planning provisions that benefit the children could be set forth in a prenup.

CHAPTER 13

SHE'S COMING FROM ANOTHER COUNTRY TO MARRY ME. WHAT ABOUT IMMIGRANT SPOUSE PRENUPS?

Bruce is in love. His beloved is a Thai woman named Janjira. They met on an online international dating site five months ago and formed a bond. Even though they are from different countries, they have much in common and have fallen in love. They have visited with each other both here and in her country of origin, and they have decided to marry. She will be coming from her county on a fiancé visa, and they will soon wed.

Janjira is 32. She is a high school graduate. Janjira has a good clerical job in Bangkok in a local business. She is just now working on improving her English language skills, which are currently, quite weak. She does know how to say, "I love you" and "I look forward to living with you."

Bruce is 65. He is a retired businessman, well established financially, with ample assets for his retirement. Bruce has two children, one from each of his previous marriages. Both of them are older than Janjira, have families and children, and are financially secure. They live in other states, and he doesn't have much contact with them. Why not have a young spouse to provide comfort to him in his elder years?

Janjira loves Bruce also, and is looking forward to a more secure financial life than exists in Thailand, a developing country currently in a chaotic political state. There are questions about Thailand's long-term stability. It is now under strict military rule. She's always wanted to live in the U.S. She loves Bruce Springsteen.

Bruce has been receiving advice from his attorney and his financial planner. They both have told him that he should make sure he has a prenup in place before marrying Janjira.

He agrees it's a good idea. But what are his obligations if he sponsors Janjira through the immigration process? And what are the risks? And how will any potential protection created for his benefit affect his beloved Janjira? And how will Janjira respond to the idea of a prenup? He would like to know the answers to these questions before taking this very big step toward his future happiness.

Getting a green card by marrying.

Marriage to an American citizen or resident is the most common path to getting a green card. A green card, originally named for the special pale green paper it was printed on, permits a foreigner to obtain legal U.S. residency.

Immigrant marriages to U.S. citizens or to lawful permanent residents and other family-based applications account for about a quarter of all green card applications. These family-based green cards are about double the number of green cards that are issued for employment-based immigration categories. ("Persons Obtaining Legal Permanent Resident Status by Broad Class of Admission, Fiscal Year 2016," Department of Homeland Security.)

There are many methods for getting foreign spouse or future spouse residency status. Some couples marry overseas. Some marry while the immigrant spouse is in the U.S., either legally or illegally if the spouse has overstayed his or her visa. An immigration lawyer should be consulted once a marriage is contemplated to find the best way to gain residency for a foreign spouse.

To qualify for marriage-based immigration, the marriage must be a *bona fide* marriage. It must not be a fraudulent marriage that was entered into merely to obtain citizenship. United States Citizenship and Immigration Services (USCIS) officials investigate each application to see if there is reason to suspect fraud. (All forms cited in this chapter relate to the official USCIS forms.)

Will Bruce and Janjira's marriage be deemed fraudulent? Probably not. There are good and loving feelings on both sides. Janjira may have a secondary reason for marrying Bruce, but is that grounds for fraud? Probably not. Bruce also has a lot to gain from marrying a lovely woman 33 years his junior. Who's to say that's not a *bona fide* marriage?

Getting a fiancé visa and a green card.

In this chapter, for simplicity's sake, I will only address the procedure for immigration using a fiancé visa and its implications for prenuptial agreements.

The aim in obtaining this visa is to get "adjustment of status" so that the immigrant spouse-to-be can eventually become a resident under U.S. immigration law and obtain a green card. After that, the green card holder can become a U.S. citizen.

The first step is to get a fiancé visa if your fiancé is outside of the U.S. and you plan to marry here. That's called a K-1 visa, and it entitles the visa applicant to enter the U.S. to marry an American citizen. This involves the filing of a "Petition for Alien Fiancé" by the U.S. future spouse. (Form I-129F.) This form includes questions that aim to determine whether the marriage is *bona fide*.

These inquiries include questions such as whether you and your fiancé met in person during the two years immediately preceding the filing of the petition, and will ask you to describe the circumstances of your in-person meeting. If you have not personally met each other, you will need to ask for a waiver based on "extreme hardship" or that a personal meeting violated "strict and long-established customs" of your fiancé's foreign culture or social practice. (Instructions to Form I-129F.)

There is also a personal interview of the foreign fiancé at a U.S. consulate in his or her home country. If the foreign future spouse is in the U.S. unlawfully, there is a waiver process where he or she may be able to leave the U.S. to have the visa consular interview in the home country and return to the U.S. without facing the three- to ten-year ban on re-entry for those who are here illegally. ("Application for Provisional Unlawful Presence Waiver," Form I-601A.)

The U.S. future spouse will need to file an affidavit of support to show that they can financially support their fiancé during his or her "visit" to the U.S. to marry.

Once the petition has been approved, it is valid for six months. Your fiancé can come to the U.S. at any time during that period. However, once they are in the U.S, you must marry each other within 90 days of their date of entry in order to comply with the K-1 visa. If you're thinking of entering into a prenup, that may be a very short time period between their entrance and the time of marriage, especially for a foreign spouse with poor English language skills and no familiarity with what a prenuptial agreement is. (See enforceability issues below.)

Once you have married, the "adjustment of status" process takes place. The U.S. spouse who is the citizen or legal permanent resident (LPR) files a "Petition for Alien Relative" with the USCIS for his or her new spouse. (Form I-130.) You may be able to file the "Application to Register Permanent Residence or Adjust Status" (Form I-485) at the same time. There will be a required interview with the USCIS, and documentation such as passports and official travel documents will need to be provided. You will receive your final decision by mail.

If successful, your immigrant spouse will have earned conditional permanent residence status by means of a temporary green card. The conditional green card is valid for two years. When it expires, the immigrant spouse becomes an unlawful resident, unless he or she has gained an "adjustment of status" to remove the condition during the 90 days before the card expires. A conditional card cannot be renewed. The U.S. spouse and the immigrant spouse will need to file a "Petition to Remove Conditions on Residence" to remove the condition. (Form I-751.)

If the immigrant spouse overstays the conditional green card (or visa), the penalties are severe. If the unlawful presence is in excess of 180 days, but less than one year, the immigrant spouse is subject to a three-year bar to re-entry. If the unlawful presence is one year or more, he or she is ineligible to re-enter the U.S. for ten years.

What if we divorce within the two-year period while we're waiting for the permanent green card?

The immigrant spouse may apply to remove the conditions on permanent residence even if there is a divorce and the marriage ended within the two-year period of the conditional green card. Whether the marriage is intact or you have divorced, when the immigrant spouse appears at the USCIS interview to remove the condition, he or she will need to satisfy the officials that the marriage is a *bona fide* marriage. (See below.) The U.S. spouse (or former spouse) may appear at the interview but is not required to do so.

After the spouse has received a permanent green card with the conditions removed, as a spouse of a U.S. citizen or as the spouse of a legal permanent resident, he or she can apply for U.S. citizenship after holding the green card (including the conditional green card) for a period of three years. Once that spouse has become a citizen, the sponsor spouse's financial obligation is ended. (See below for terms that might be considered for an immigrant prenup.)

As noted above, the green card is valid for two years. If the parties divorce within two years of the foreign spouse's entry into to the U.S., there is a presumption that the marriage was entered into fraudulently. The statute states that the presumption can be overcome if you establish ". . . to the satisfaction of the Attorney General that such marriage was not contracted for the purpose of evading any provision of the immigration laws." (8 U.S.C. Section 1227(a)(1)(G)(i).)

If the immigrant's U.S. spouse refuses to jointly file the "Petition to Remove Conditions on Residence," the immigrant can file for a waiver stating that the marriage was entered into in good faith or that removal from the U.S. would result in "extreme hardship." (Form I-751.) During the USCIS interview to remove the conditions on the green card, they will need to convince the examiner that the marriage had been *bona fide* but ended for the same reasons marriages sometimes end in divorce.

The sponsor spouse has ongoing financial obligations.

What are the requirements of the U.S. citizen or sponsor spouse? And what happens to that commitment if the legitimate marriage of Bruce and Janjira hits the rocks? Are there ways to protect both of them?

The sponsorship obligation is quite significant. If you're thinking of marrying someone from another country and want to have a prenup, be careful and get legal advice. A visit to both an immigration lawyer and a prenup attorney is certainly in order.

The "Affidavit of Support" – what does it entail?

When applying for adjustment of status to become a legal permanent resident, the sponsoring U.S. citizen or sponsoring U.S. permanent resident must sign the "Affidavit of Support" (Form I-864), promising to financially support the immigrant. This is to ensure that the sponsor has sufficient financial means to support the immigrant. The purpose is so that the immigrant spouse will not have to rely on government funds for support. The public policy objective is for the immigrant spouse not to become a public charge and use public funds for their support.

The sponsor must prove that family income equals or exceeds at least 125 percent of the U.S. poverty level for the family unit of the size of the sponsor's new family. In fiscal year 2017, 125 percent of poverty level for a family of two was $20,300 in most states. Part of this support can be met by the U.S. spouse providing "in-kind" benefits, such as food and housing.

If the U.S. sponsor fails to provide this support, the immigrant spouse can sue the sponsor to enforce the support obligations. But it may be difficult for the immigrant spouse to obtain means-tested benefits, as the U.S. spouse's income and assets will be considered available to the immigrant.

If the immigrant receives means-tested public benefits, such as food stamps, Medicaid, and Supplemental Security Income (SSI), prior to the time the sponsor's obligation ends, the sponsor spouse is responsible for repaying the government or agency that provided the benefits. The U.S. spouse can be sued in court if they don't repay these debts.

It is important to know that this sponsorship obligation persists even after a divorce.

A prenup purporting to eliminate or shifting the sponsor spouse's liability will not be effective as to the federal (or state) government's claim. (See below.)

When is the sponsor's financial obligation terminated?

The sponsor spouse's obligation terminates at the earlier of the following:

1. The sponsored immigrant becomes a U.S. citizen.
2. The sponsored immigrant worked and obtained 40 quarters of qualifying coverage under the Social Security Act. As of 2017, this means that the immigrant's earnings during a quarter must be at least $1,300 for it to count as qualifying. Quarters in which the sponsored immigrant receives any federal means-tested public benefits are not counted as qualifying. Forty quarters of qualifying coverage are required. This process takes at least ten years.
3. The sponsored immigrant permanently leaves the U.S. and abandons legal permanent resident status.
4. The sponsored immigrant obtains a new sponsor after a removal proceeding and a new grant of adjustment of status.
5. The sponsored immigrant dies. If the immigrant dies, the sponsor will nonetheless be obligated for past unpaid support obligations.

(8 C.F.R. Sections 213a.2(e)(2)(i)(A)-(E) and 213a.2(e)(2)(ii).)

Effect of a prenup on the federal support obligation.

What if an immigrant marriage breaks up and there is a divorce or separation before the green card is issued or before the conditions on the green card are removed? What if the marriage ends before the immigrant spouse becomes a citizen or before the immigrant has 40 quarters of qualifying social security earnings? What if the prenup had a provision that waived spousal support? Will this relieve the sponsoring U.S. spouse from his or her obligations under federal law? What if the marriage is intact, but the immigrant spouse is not working and seeks federal, state, or local means-tested benefits such as food stamps, Medicaid, or SSI?

The answer is clear. Nothing in a prenup will prevent the sponsor spouse from being held responsible for his or her obligation under the federal support rules. That spouse will have to provide the minimum support for the immigrant and will need to pay back governmental benefits that the immigrant spouse might have received during the period of sponsorship. Note that if an immigrant spouse is not working, the period of sponsorship could last indefinitely if the immigrant does not become a citizen, because the spouse would not be accumulating qualifying quarters earnings for purposes of social security.

From the federal government's point of view, there are essentially three parties to the sponsorship contract: the federal (or state or local) government, the person applying for the green card, and the U.S. sponsoring spouse. Immigration law provides that a divorce does not terminate the sponsor spouse's obligations. So even if you have a prenup that waives the right to alimony or support, it will not prevail. (See below for what you can do in a prenup.)

What does immigration marriage fraud consist of?

People who enter into a marriage fraudulently for immigration purposes can pay a heavy price. The law states that the perpetrators (each of the spouses) can face prison, fines, or both. The prison term can be up to five years. The fine can be up to $250,000. (8 U.S. Code Section 1325(c).) Both a prison term and a fine can be ordered. Most likely the immigrants themselves will not be prosecuted criminally. Rather, they will in all likelihood be deported and never allowed to return. The sponsoring spouse may face the penalties and prison.

How does the USCIS detect marriage fraud? Mainly this takes place within the various interviews involved in the process, from obtaining the K-1 fiancé visa, through the citizenship interview. The USCIS will look for "indicia" of fraud.

Maybe the couple had no preexisting relationship or had never personally met each other prior to the immigration process. (See Questions on USCIS Form I-129F "Petition for Alien Fiancé.") Or the immigrant might pay the U.S. citizen to marry him or her or offer services to the sponsoring spouse, sometimes even sexual services.

Sometimes the plan is more complex. An immigrant may divorce their spouse in the home country intending to marry an American to get their green card. After that, they might divorce their U.S. spouse, remarry their original spouse, and petition as a U.S. legal permanent resident to bring the original spouse to the U.S.

For immigration purposes, it is important to prove to the satisfaction of the USCIS hearing officer that the marriage was entered into for love and/or the other benefits that people sometimes marry for, and not solely to obtain U.S. citizenship. The hearing officer can subpoena witnesses and request evidence in addition to obtaining oral and written testimony from the applicant. The hearing officer generally interviews the U.S. spouse of the applicant.

Facts that may trigger suspicion of fraud include the spouses being of different races or nationalities, not speaking the same language, large age difference, differences in cultural and religious backgrounds, or differences in levels of education. In a good number of immigrant marriages, such as that between Bruce and Janjira, there is a great disparity in incomes, assets, and education that could give rise to suspicions. But most probably in Bruce and Janjira's case, the examiner will be satisfied that this is true love or that at least the love is as great as the convenience aspects of the marriage.

At the time of the green card interview, the USCIS examiners want to make sure the spouses know each other well and live together. A question might be, "Who woke up first this morning?" or "Which side of the bed do you sleep on?" or "What kind of toothpaste does he use?"

The USCIS examiner also likes to see evidence of commingled assets, which it views as "typical" for married couples. These would be evidenced by jointly held assets, actively used bank accounts, jointly held securities accounts, CDs and mortgages, houses held in joint tenancy, etc. Joint apartment leases and driver's licenses with the same address can provide support for the existence of a "real" marriage. Shared utility payments even if the bill is in only one name can also be helpful. Evidence of trips together, boarding passes, photos of the couple at various locations, and taxes filed as married will also help prove the marriage is *bona fide*.

The USCIS appears to take a very traditional view of marriage and is not very open to modern views of marriage as two financially independent people forming a marriage bond. A couple that have signed a prenup to separate their finances and are following this plan may have a tougher case to make with the USCIS that they have a *bona fide* marriage.

The applicants do not have to disclose the existence of a prenuptial agreement, if not asked by the USCIS examiner. But if asked, they must disclose it and may have to provide a copy. If they don't and its existence is discovered later, the immigrant's application could be denied on the basis of misrepresentation.

Some immigration field officers view prenups negatively. They may see a prenup as an indication that there may be fraud involved in the application. The applicant can rebut this presumption. For instance, if it is a second marriage and there are children of a first marriage, or if both spouses have assets, the USCIS may be more inclined to understand that a couple might want to keep their assets separate. However, it may be good policy nonetheless to have some commingling of assets and income in the prenup to show the USCIS examiner that this is a "real" marriage.

Enforceability issues can abound in immigrant prenups.

When there is a fiancé K-1 visa, time is of the essence. You and your fiancé must marry each other within 90 days from the date of his or her entry into the U.S. This can pose an enforceability problem.

Even under the best of circumstances, prenups generally take several months to consider, negotiate, draft, revise, and sign. In the case of an immigrant prenup, one of the contracting parties is a person from a different culture. The person is in the process of relocating to another country and marrying, two life-changing events.

Often the incoming spouse's command of English language may be weak (or almost non-existent), or the future spouse might not be well-educated. For that person, a bilingual attorney or a translator may be needed. There may be a need for a certified translation of the prenup into his or her own language. This takes time.

There are also cultural factors that can impair the immigrant spouse's ability to evaluate and understand a prenup. In many countries, prenups don't exist. If the concept is explained to the immigrant spouse, there might be shock and distaste for the idea because the concept is so foreign to him or her.

The immigrant spouse may start to think their fiancé is ungenerous or is using them. In the immigrant's culture, marriage may mean sharing everything. By asking for a prenup, you risk making your new spouse and his or her family quite upset, and they may become suspicious. Not a good way to start a marriage.

Prenups require an informed waiver of marital rights that would accrue in the jurisdiction of the marriage. Federal and state laws regarding marriage and inheritance need to be revealed and understood prior to signing. Due to the restrictive 90-day time frame within which the marriage must take place, the immigrant's language skills, education, and unfamiliarity with prenups may raise questions of enforceability, which would arise at the time the prenup went into effect.

A serious ground for unenforceability is duress or coercion. Duress is defined as an action to pressure someone to do something against their will or against their better judgment. If there are only 90 days to marry once the immigrant spouse is in the U.S., and the idea of a prenup is sprung on that future spouse after they have arrived in the U.S., will it rise to the level of duress? It would certainly help if the prenup was discussed prior to the time he or she arrived in the U.S., or even before the couple got engaged.

What if the immigrant spouse did not have access to a lawyer to represent them and did not have sufficient time to consider the prenup with their lawyer? Would that be indicia of duress? What if the agreement was given only to the future spouse a couple of days before the wedding? What if he or she was strongly encouraged to sign it "or else"? (The "or else" would meaning voluntarily leaving the U.S. or deportation.) Would that be proof of duress? On the other hand, the concept of duress may be somewhat offset by the immigrant spouse's strong desire to become a U.S. resident.

To gain more time to consider a marital agreement, the immigrant spouse and the sponsor spouse may consider the idea of entering into a postnuptial agreement – one that is drawn up and entered into *after* the marriage. Possibly, the agreement can be entered into after the entire immigration process (including the granting of citizenship) is completed. (See Chapter 19 for more information on postnups.) There are, however, a number of issues with respect to postnups involving an immigrant spouse. Will the immigrant follow through with his or her promise to sign one? Will the two parties be able to come to terms in the postnup?

In general, postnups tend to be more like divorce agreements because you've already married. In other words, the postnup has to be more "generous" than the prenup to be enforceable.

What a prenup can do for an immigrant marriage situation.

As discussed above, the existence of a prenup itself can pose some risk in the form of suspicion of fraud on the part of the USCIS examiners. But this suspicion can be overcome if the marriage is a *bona fide* marriage.

In addition, the obligations to support the immigrant spouse and pay back means-tested benefits received cannot be nullified by a prenup, which is essentially a private contract between two individuals. Similarly, there are some cases in the context of immigration that do not allow the sponsor to waive the state law obligation of a married person to support their spouse. There are also some other significant enforceability issues as described above.

So if there is to be an immigrant prenup, what can be in it, what aims can it address, and what good can it do?

Factual representations to counteract fraud attacks.

In all the marital agreements I draft for clients, I have a very robust "Statement of Facts" section. In this section I recite what the parties' situations (personal and financial) are and their reasons for wanting a prenup or a postnup.

I believe the Statement of Facts section is important for a number of reasons. It defines the parties' goals in the agreement, and by doing so, helps them articulate and clarify them. The Statement of Facts underlines the notion that the prenup is indeed a mutually negotiated agreement that is agreeable to both parties, and that both of them are signing it freely and voluntarily.

In an immigrant prenup, this section is even more important, because it can lay out the facts for the USCIS examiner (if the prenup is requested as part of the immigration process) as to why the marriage is real and not fraudulent. Facts pertaining to how the parties met each other and what contacts they had prior to the marriage are helpful. Any other facts that show the existence of a genuine relationship, and not just a pretext for immigration, would also be considered helpful. Existence of concerns for children of previous marriages can be stated in this section as well.

It could also be important to make other representations in the prenup that buttress the genuineness of the marriage for USCIS purposes. If assets are to be held separately (at first, or always), reasons for this could be stated in the prenup. If income is to be separated, this would be the vehicle to plainly state how and why.

Have some generous terms in the prenup.

The USCIS will want to see that when you are marrying, you intend to share at least some of the benefits of marriage. If the immigrant spouse is less moneyed, you may want to have some financial terms in the prenup that benefit him or her. There can be provisions relating to sharing current income that would go into a joint account or sharing assets on a vesting basis, that is, in which a defined percentage of separate assets could become marital assets as the marriage increases in length. (See Chapter 17 for possibilities.)

This is similar to what a court would consider in a divorce without a prenup – length of marriage is a strong indicator of how to determine what marital property is and how it's divided. If there is an alimony provision in the prenup, so much the better. It shows your concern to treat your spouse fairly and if it is a real marriage, to benefit your spouse as the marriage goes on in years, as in a "normal" marriage.

There can be a provision that addresses what will happen if the marriage breaks up and the immigrant wishes to return home. The U.S. spouse can make the immigrant "whole" by making the transition easy and funding his or her resettlement in their country of origin. Divorce provisions to resettle the immigrant spouse who wishes to remain in the U.S. are also possible.

Alimony is a dirty word.

No one likes alimony. Payors don't like to pay it, and recipients (believe it or not) don't like to receive it. But sometimes it's necessary to put someone back on his or her feet.

Anyway, if you are the U.S. sponsor, you've signed up for support until the immigrant spouse becomes a citizen or has 40 quarters (at least ten years) of qualifying earnings for purposes of social security.

Accordingly, if the prenup has language waiving spousal support, it might raise questions by a USCIS interviewer. It might give the appearance that the waiver of spousal support was a *quid pro quo* for the cooperation in the sponsor signing the "Affidavit of Support." Any waiver of support in a prenup should be carefully drafted. The sponsor spouse could seek to limit support during the period of sponsorship to the federal requirements (125 percent of poverty family income level) during the immigration process. The other choices are alimony waiver, partial waiver, alimony subject to state law standards, or a variation on state law standards.

Requirement to follow through on the immigration process.

This is important for *both* spouses. It's important for the sponsor spouse to cooperate with the immigration process if there is a divorce before the permanent green card is issued or before citizenship is achieved. This benefits both parties, because the sponsor's obligation ends when the spouse becomes a U.S. citizen. And it's only fair for the sponsor spouse to cooperate and help the immigrant spouse achieve at least part of the mutual expectation they had when they were married.

The sponsor spouse can promise in the prenup that he or she will cooperate in the joint filing of the "Petition to Remove Conditions on Residence" to remove the conditions on the initial green card. The prenup can provide that the sponsor spouse will furnish whatever copies of financial documentation are needed in the future to substantiate the *bona fide* nature of the parties' marriage. The prenup may provide also that the U.S. spouse will accompany the immigrant spouse to a hearing or interview before immigration personnel, if required, regardless of the parties' marital status at the time of the hearing or interview.

The prenup should enjoin the sponsor spouse from taking any action that would cause the immigrant spouse's immigration process to be derailed or to encourage USCIS to deport the spouse.

After the immigration process is completed, and perhaps after the sponsorship obligation is fulfilled, the prenup can function as any other prenup would. For possible provisions, considerations, and evaluations of terms and decisions to be made in the prenup, refer to other chapters of this book.

CHAPTER 14:

WHAT ABOUT PRENUPS WITH INFIDELITY CLAUSES OR OTHER "LIFESTYLE" PROVISIONS?

Prenups with "lifestyle" provisions intended to control or define behavior during a marriage are the newest "flavor du jour" of prenups. They appear frequently in the celebrity news cycle. There is often a financial punishment for the transgressor of these provisions, so it can be very costly for a spouse to violate these. The terms in these prenups can range from financial behavior in the marriage to how often the husband can watch football.

Here are some of the types of lifestyle clauses attorneys see in their prenup practices.

Friends and family:
- How many times a year the in-laws may visit.
- How many times a year the mother-in-law may stay overnight.
- How often spouse may visit his or her parents.
- Penalty (say $300) each time he or she is rude to the other spouse's parents.
- How much time each spouse can spend with friends.
- How much "quality time" the spouses will spend with each other, and when.

Personal care:

- A "marital fat" clause applying penalties for wives or husbands who gain weight.
- How much weight gain would put someone in violation of the prenup.
- Penalties for smoking, drinking, or drug use.

Householding:

- Who will walk the dog.
- Who gets the dog if they divorce.
- Who will do the housework.
- How clean the house must be kept.
- Who will do the yardwork.
- Who will take care of the cars.
- How many times a year the executive's spouse must host parties.

Finances:

- Who will balance the checkbook.
- How much money a spouse can spend without notifying or getting approval from the other spouse.
- How much income shall be shared between the spouses.
- What types of income will be shared.
- How much a spouse's "allowance" will be.
- Who will make decisions on investments.
- What the goals will be for saving money.
- How premarital debts will be paid off or paid down.
- Who will provide health insurance.

Children:

- A "no diaper" or "no children" clause.
- How many children the couple will have.
- Rules for naming of newborns. Name after a parent or grandparent? What last names will be used.

- What schools the children will attend.
- What the religious upbringing of the children will be.

Should lifestyle clauses be Included in a prenup?

The possibilities for lifestyle clauses are endless. But should lifestyle clauses such as the ones listed above be included in a prenup? And are they enforceable?

Prenups usually contain important *financial* arrangements that come into play at divorce and at death. They are quite specific, clearly articulated, and, in general, easy to understand and to put into effect. The aim is for the parties to have a clear understanding of what their obligations are. In addition, a further aim is for a judge (in a later divorce action) not to need to exercise discretion in construing the terms of the prenup and implementing them.

Often in a divorce, the prenup terms are incorporated by reference into the divorce agreement. Alternatively, the terms can be written as terms of the divorce agreement. In most states, a judge still has to approve the terms of the divorce, as the court oversees the institution of marriage during a divorce as a matter of public policy.

When a prenup deals solely with purely economic rights and obligations, there are ways to draft it so that it is extremely likely to be enforced by a court when it comes into effect at divorce or at death. The terms in a typical prenup relate to support and property division and are typically straightforward.

Lifestyle terms are on another footing entirely.

During a marriage, spouses organically develop hundreds of lifestyle terms. The choices a couple makes as to these lifestyle choices are personal to the couple and can change over time. Setting rules in a prenup may actually stifle this part of the marital venture.

Marriage is fluid with respect to many issues as it progresses through the years. How a person envisioned his or her marriage at the outset may not come to be as the years go by. Life is always presenting us with surprises, and we (and our marriages) must often make adjustments in our expectations and behavior. That's why putting lifestyle provisions in a prenup may be a mistake and should be entered into with trepidation.

Lawyers use the words "precatory" for wishes that are made in contracts that don't rise to the level of something that is "mandatory" and must be put into effect. Lifestyle terms fall more within the precatory framework than terms that a court will deem as required and enforceable.

Lifestyle provisions may actually be more suitable for postnuptial agreements, and they are often put in them. Postnuptial agreements can be entered into when a couple is running into a specific serious problem that is derailing a marriage. A postnuptial agreement with lifestyle provisions addressing the problem can be helpful. (See Chapter 19 on postnuptial agreements.)

Another reason not to put lifestyle provisions in a prenup is that they are easy to violate, and once violated, the taboo against violation of these commitments in the prenup is breached. As a result, there is a sense that other prenuptial agreement provisions can now be violated. This can spread into other promises made by spouses to each other, even if they are not in written agreements. That's how lifestyle provisions can actually make a marriage worse.

Some "light" lifestyle provisions may have a place in a prenup, such as questions regarding what types of accounts into which the parties' income (earned and unearned) shall be placed and how much individual control the parties will have over their own incomes. It's also very helpful to have plans for the paying down or paying off of debt of a future spouse, bearing in mind that generosity in sharing the burden will make the marriage more likely to thrive.

Regulating sexual behavior in prenups.

Here's a joke I recently found on the internet. A couple in their 70s is negotiating a prenup. The future wife says, "If we divorce I want to keep the house." He says, "That's OK with me." She says, "I want to keep the Rolls Royce." He says, "That's OK with me." Then she says, "And while we are married, I want to have sexual relations six times a week." And he says, "Put me down for Fridays." This is obviously a (very funny) joke, but similarly silly provisions have made it into the annals of prenups.

In one famous 16-page prenup from 1995, Rex and Teresa LeGalley agreed to engage in "healthy sex" three to five times per week." This New Mexico prenup was required to be filed in the Bernalillo County Clerk's Office in Albuquerque, New Mexico, Document No. 95-065775. That's why we know about it. The existence of this prenup was picked up by many newspapers all over the country.

Although they were fairly young at the time of their marriage (Rex was 39, Teresa 31), it was Rex's third marriage and Teresa's second. In their prenup, in addition to the healthy sex requirement, they agreed to retire at night at 11:30 p.m. and wake up at 6:30 a.m. Rex was assigned full responsibility for "family leadership and decision-making" and neither spouse could leave anything on the floor overnight, unless packing for a trip.

In addition to many other "lifestyle" provisions, the LeGalley prenup stated that neither spouse was allowed to drive any closer to another car than "one car length per 10 mph," and never allow their fuel gauges to drop below the half-tank mark. That one-car length resonates in many marriages. See my article "Driving Your Spouse Crazy – Literally" on huffpost.com and the PowerPoint on maritalmediation.com.

Since the LeGalleys appear to still have joint property as of a few years ago (found via an online search), I assume they are still married and a court did not have to parse the meaning of "healthy sex" in a litigated action. That would have been an interesting court case to read.

In another situation, a boyfriend refused to marry his future wife unless she signed an agreement to have sex with him at least twice a week.

Requirements to have sex a certain number of times a week may run into the prohibition of soliciting sex – at least for unmarried couples. Contracts between unmarried persons that involve paying for sex are unenforceable as against public policy. For instance, in a famous California palimony case, the California Supreme Court held that a contract between unmarried persons was held invalid if the sexual acts form an "inseparable part of the consideration for the agreement." *Marvin v. Marvin*, 18 Cal.3d 660 (1976).

Using sexual services as consideration for a contract for unmarried people is not permitted on public policy grounds. Contracts involving sex are deemed, in the words of some cases, as so far beyond the pale as to be "meretricious." This word, which now means tawdrily and falsely attractive, has etymological roots in *meretrix*, which is Latin for "to earn" or "a prostitute."

But what about contracts between married people specifying sexual contacts. In a marriage? In the institution of marriage, sexual acts are considered to be one of the roots of the marital relationship. Will these "sex" clauses be enforceable in a court of law? Aside from a judge having to ascertain what "healthy sex" might be, are there other problems in writing sexual activity clauses in a prenup?

"Bad Boy" and "Bad Girl" clauses in prenups – what's a court to do?

Joking aside, some prenups (a very small number) include provisions relating to sexual behavior. Most of these address what happens if a spouse "strays" from the marriage and has an affair, or has more than one. It is very rare that these provisions are put into prenups, but it does happen, and we hear about it in the news, especially when the prenup is that of a serially married celebrity or public figure. In modern lingo, these provisions are called "bad boy" or "bad girl" clauses.

Aside from regulating how often the couple will have sex as with the Rex and Teresa LeGalley prenup, marital behavior prenup clauses might include:

- Whether attractions to other people will be revealed and discussed during the marriage.
- What happens if a spouse is "unfaithful" and has an affair?
- How will "unfaithfulness" be defined?
- How will an "affair" be defined?
- Will there be an economic punishment or penalty?
- Will the marriage end if there is an affair?
- What will be the terms of the divorce?

One might view these provisions as a prophylactic measure to ensure faithful conduct in a marriage. But like the other non-sexual "lifestyle" clauses discussed above, violation of these breaks down the taboo against such behavior, especially if the marriage continues. Once the levee is breached, the water flows through fast and faster, and the breach may get bigger and bigger. Most celebrity prenups have confidentiality provisions, so the "bad boy" and "bad girl" clauses are rumored, but not confirmed.

Many of these "bad boy" "bad girl" prenups have financial penalties for straying. There might be a provision that if the wife has an adulterous relationship, she will forgo alimony. Whether this is enforceable is highly questionable. Another such provision might be that if the husband strays, the wife would get double alimony if the marriage ends, or the victim-spouse might get a "bonus" paid out in cash or property. The cash penalty could be paid either at the time of the affair, or afterward at the end of the marriage.

In general, state divorce laws do not provide a financial penalty for adultery, unless the adultery results in spending on the paramour, which is considered "dissipation" of marital assets. In that sense, like gambling losses and other examples of wasting marital assets, the innocent spouse's share of marital property would be returned to him or her in a divorce action. The real loss in the current no-fault divorce environment is the actual money loss, which is generally half (i.e., the marital portion) of the illicit spending.

Although in many states adultery remains a ground for divorce, it is rarely used these days and it carries little or no weight in a no-fault divorce with respect to property division or alimony. Black-robed judges just don't want to get into the sexual relationships (or any of the emotional relationships) within a marriage that has broken down. They believe they are in no position to make judgments on the intimate nature of a marriage, and they don't want to assess fault or penalties.

But in a prenup, parties can put in provisions that regulate and punish adulterous behavior. While the public policy against straying as evidenced in the no fault divorce laws has gotten weaker over the past few decades, the commercial contract provisions that are put into prenups can put financial teeth into the prohibition against having dalliances. Thus the "bad boy" "bad girl" provision against cheating can express the future spouses' values and standards.

Often the "no cheating" clause comes in the context of a postnuptial agreement rather than a prenuptial agreement, where an incident (or incidents) of infidelity has already occurred. Or these clauses might find their way into the prenups where one of the future spouses has already had a marriage that failed due to an extramarital affair. Serial adulterers are statistically more likely to stray again.

But how much of a money penalty will it take for that person to say "Ouch! I won't do it again!"? Probably a lot. And if the taboo against extramarital affairs has been violated once, it may be likely to be violated again in the present marriage.

Some (rare) prenups contemplate open relationships and polyamory. These might outline the conditions – including revealing (or not revealing) outside relationships to the other spouse, or how often a spouse can have them. There are other rules applicable to "outside" relationships that could be memorialized in a prenup.

For instance, the paramour could be required to be with someone that the other spouse doesn't know. Perhaps the possibility of infidelity in the marriage would only be allowed to arise when both parties have decided that sex is no longer a part of the marriage, but they want to remain married.

Dan Savage (see Chapter 12) sees value in open relationships for many couples. A prenup for interested couples could afford the desire to have sex with someone outside the relationship to fulfill a spouse's needs without incurring the pain and marital instability that results in betrayal and secrecy.

How do you define what "infidelity" is?

If you have an infidelity clause, how should "infidelity" be defined? The devil is in the details. Should it be defined as "sexual relations"? What does that mean? Would it mean sexual intercourse? Should it require penetration? What if this is a prenup of a lesbian couple?

Is it any "intimate" relationship? How would that be defined? Does infidelity include flirting? Does it include kissing and petting, but not penetration? Does it include oral sex? (Can't get that picture of President Clinton out of my head!)

Does infidelity include phone calls, emails, and text messaging? What needs to be the content of an instance of infidelity that violates the prenup?

Does it include contacting an old boyfriend or girlfriend on social media? Does it include having lunch with an old boyfriend or girlfriend or having email contact? Does it include holding hands?

Does an "affair" include an "emotional affair" where there is romantic intimacy but no overt sexual contact or consummation? Emotional affairs result in a deep emotional bond that can have an extremely detrimental effect on an ongoing marriage. Whatever an emotional affair is for the contracting future spouses, they will need to spell it out in the prenup and write a term for how they will address it. Will they address it by requiring that it be revealed to the other spouse? Or requiring that it end with no further contact? Or will they take a more expansive view and leave it out of the prenup, and let the emotional affair run its course?

Enforceability of infidelity clauses.

Some courts find that infidelity clauses in a prenup are unenforceable when a state has a public policy supporting no-fault divorce. See, for instance, *Diosdado v. Diosdado*, 97 Cal. App. 4th 471 (2002). The *Diosdado* agreement was actually a "marital settlement agreement" entered into after five years of marriage, precipitated by an instance of infidelity by the husband.

The agreement provided as follows:

> Section 2. Obligation of Fidelity: It is further acknowledged that the parties' marriage is intended to be an exclusive relationship between Husband and Wife that is premised upon the values of emotional and sexual fidelity, and mutual trust. The parties hereto are subject to a legal obligation of emotional and sexual fidelity to the other. It shall be considered a breach of such obligation of fidelity to volitionally engage in any act of kissing on the mouth or touching in any sexual manner of any person outside of said marital relationship, as determined by a trier of fact. The parties acknowledge their mutual understanding that any such breach of fidelity by one party hereto may cause serious emotional, physical and financial injury to the other.

The husband had an affair with another woman, and the wife had independent proof of the husband kissing the woman. The prenup could have awarded $50,000 in liquidated damages to the wife for the violation.

The *Diosdado* Court refused to enforce it, saying:

> The family law court may not look to fault in dissolving the marriage, dividing property, or ordering support. Yet this agreement attempts to penalize the party who is at fault for having breached the obligation of sexual fidelity, and whose breach provided the basis for terminating the marriage. This penalty is in direct contravention of the public policy underlying no-fault divorce.

It is important to note that in California, adultery is not a ground for divorce. The only grounds for divorce in California are irreconcilable differences that have caused the irremediable breakdown of the marriage or permanent legal incapacity to make decisions. (Cal. Fam. Code § 2310.)

Courts in some states, however, may enforce infidelity provisions if proven. But what will proof consist of, and what will be the legal standard of proof that must be met in the lawsuit? "A preponderance of the evidence" as in most civil lawsuits? That means chance of being supported by the evidence must be over 50 percent. "Beyond a reasonable doubt" as in a criminal case? That's almost 100 percent proof. Or by "clear and convincing evidence," which is an intermediate level?

The required level of proof could also be put into the prenup. The level of proof set forth in the *Diosdado* agreement – a "preponderance of evidence" – is a very light standard. But nonetheless, it was not enforced by the Court. How do you prove what's behind someone's heart and emotions? Courts simply don't like to get into this.

As you may suspect from the above discussion, one of the downsides of cheating clauses is that they can make divorces more expensive and protracted because of the litigation that might be required. Prenups generally aim to make divorces easier, less expensive, and quicker. A possibility is to place the lifestyle provisions in a separate document stating each other's wishes and intentions. Although not legally binding, these precatory statements could help clarify issues and express the couple's mutual intent as to what fidelity means for their marriage.

Another roadblock to enforcing infidelity clauses are the confidentiality or "gag" clauses in many prenups. Confidentiality clauses are routinely broken when litigation is required, but in the case of infidelity, many couples may wish to retain their privacy and not have their intimate lives revealed in a public forum. For this reason, the "cheater" is likely not to contest the contractual punishment for straying.

The confidentiality clause can impose indemnification against losses that result in making the contents of the prenup, or even its existence, public. It also can set a fine or penalty for breach. The penalty provision can be quite severe. For instance, a spouse's divorce award of $5 million under the prenup could be cut in half if the terms of the prenup are revealed. The penalty could be assessed if there is a breach of the provision years after the marriage ends.

An important part of a confidentiality clause in a prenup can be a prohibition against revealing photos or writing a "tell-all" book about the marriage, whether or not the marriage breaks up after a steamy affair. I sometimes have seen that type of clause in separation agreements (which is the agreement pertaining to the divorce terms) in cases in which there had been no prenup.

The Uniform Laws on enforceability of lifestyle provisions.

For a modern "uniform" word on enforceability of lifestyle clauses, we can take a look at the Uniform Premarital and Marital Agreements Act (2012) (the UPMAA). Section 10 addresses "Unenforceable Terms" but is silent on infidelity clauses and lifestyle clauses. The drafting committee's comments to Section 10 note that there is "a general consensus in the case law that courts will not enforce premarital agreement provisions relating to topics beyond the parties' financial obligations [as between each other]." It cites the California *Diosdado* case.

Comments to Section 10 of the UPMAA do go on to say that a few courts have chosen to enforce certain lifestyle provisions. The case cited is not an infidelity lifestyle provision, but rather a prenup term that required a party to cooperate in obtaining a Jewish religious divorce (a *"get"*). *Avitzur v. Avitzur,*

58 N.Y.2d 108 (1983). Prenups that relate to what religion children will be brought up may be unenforceable as to children born of the marriage, under the "best interests of the child" analysis. These court decisions are made at the time of a divorce in the separation or divorce agreement. The focus is on the "here and now," not what the parties contracted at the time of their prenup.

A provision in a prenup that binds the parties not to have any children is likely not enforceable. There is a fundamental constitutional right to have children. See *Cleveland Board of Education v. LaFleur*, 414 U.S. 632 (1974), which holds pregnancy as a fundamental civil right, and *Skinner v. Oklahoma*, 316 U.S. 535 (1942), which held that a statute that mandated sterilization for habitual criminals infringed upon fundamental rights. These U.S. Supreme Court precedents would likely control a dispute related to an agreement not to have children contained in a prenup and deem the provision unenforceable.

An influential modern treatise on family law is the *Principles of the Law of Family Dissolution* (2002), promulgated by the American Law Institute (ALI Principles). It also sheds some light on how lifestyle or infidelity clauses might be construed in prenuptial agreements.

Chapter 7 of the ALI Principles deals with "Agreements," including prenuptial, postnuptial, and divorce agreements. Section 7.08(1) of the ALI Principles provides that a term in a prenup is unenforceable if it "limits or enlarges the grounds for divorce otherwise available under state law." Section 7.08(2) provides that a term that "would require or forbid a court to evaluate marital conduct in allocating marital property or awarding compensatory payments" is unenforceable, unless and to the extent it incorporates principles of state law "that so provide." This language could bring lifestyle and infidelity clauses into the enforceable or unenforceable column, depending on state laws.

As the drafters' comments to Section 7.08 of the ALI Principles note, many but not all states do take marital misconduct into account when allocating marital property or setting the terms of alimony, but that about half the states bar the consideration of fault entirely. The aim of Section 7.08 is to honor the public policy of the state in this regard, whatever it is.

As the Comment states, "Spouses may not by their agreement require courts to hear evidence and make determinations concerning the spouse's relative marital misconduct, when state law provides otherwise." Note b. to Section 7.08. Query as to the effect of selecting a jurisdiction in the "choice of law" section of the prenup that is a state that *would be required* to evaluate marital misconduct in determining property division and spousal support.

When evaluating lifestyle provision penalties in a prenup, a facts and circumstances analysis will be important, both as to current facts and circumstances and those that are reasonably foreseeable in the future. A court will tend not to impose penalties that are excessive in comparison to the marital property the breaching party is supposed to receive under applicable law as a settlement. Courts tend to not enforce agreements that leave parties in financially precarious positions.

On the other hand, a lifestyle provision with a penalty will need to have an "ouch" factor to work as a deterrent. Balancing the "ouch" factor with possible court disallowance will be the challenge in drafting the lifestyle provision desired to control or curb non-financial behavior.

Lifestyle provisions also come into play when a marriage continues after an incident of infidelity and a couple enters into a postnuptial agreement. One of the keys here to enforceability is that the postnuptial agreement should not *promote* divorce, but rather should help sustain the ongoing marriage. Getting this balance just right on this slippery slope can be a challenge. Courts could find a penalty clause agreement to be so financially tempting that it could create an incentive for terminating a marriage.

A North Carolina court enforced a reconciliation (postnuptial) agreement that involved an infidelity clause. Shortly before the time the husband's affair came to light, pursuant to that agreement, he transferred two houses, the furniture in them, and the couple's cars to the wife. The court enforced the agreement. One of the reasons for the court's ruling enforcing the agreement was that the couple remained married for nine years after the transfer took place. Therefore, according to the court, it did not create an incentive for the wife to leave the marriage. That would have been against the public policy of the state. *Dawbarn v. Dawbarn*, 175 N.C. App. 712 (2006).

But the *Dawbarn* situation has a flip side. According to the husband, he stayed married to the wife for those nine years because the reconciliation agreement terms would have left him with so little. In his words, he said that as a result of the agreement, "I felt that I had no choice but to remain married to Linda Kay Dawbarn, even though our marriage has been less than happy for quite some time in the recent past."

A court might have found the terms of the *Dawbarn* agreement to be unconscionable. Or a court could have decided to invalidate the contract on the basis of the lack of proportion between the property transferred and the consequence of the infidelity. But this Court did not, also rejecting argument of duress. (The wife had threatened to sue the person with whom the husband had the extramarital affair to pressure him to sign the agreement.) The Court threw out the duress claim of the husband on the basis that the three-year statute of limitations on the claim of duress had expired.

Can prenups include "covenant marriage" provisions?

Some people want to know whether they can enter into a prenup that completely eliminates "no-fault" as a ground for divorce. Some question whether their separation agreement can be required to be adjudicated by an agreed-upon third party who would be named in the agreement. Perhaps that adjudicator can be chosen by the leader of an organization the spouse is connected with, trusts, or admires, such as the president of a fraternal organization like the Loyal Order of Moose or the pastor of a church or the rabbi of a synagogue.

What drives these questions are some people's wish to have a more durable marriage contract than the typical no-fault marriage, which, these days, some people might believe "is really written on toilet paper when you think about it."

This describes an established and existing concept known as "covenant marriage."

Covenant marriage is a special form of marriage, legal in only three states: Arkansas, Arizona, and Louisiana. It is a marriage option in which the couple accepts more limited grounds than "no fault" in case they divorce. The couple also agrees to obtain premarital counseling before marriage, and may be required to enter into counseling before a divorce.

In a covenant marriage, grounds for divorce are generally limited to one or more of the following: adultery, commission of a felony, and substance, physical, or sexual abuse. In some cases, divorce is permitted only if the spouses have been living separately for a period of time, one or two years depending on the state. In Arkansas, people who are already married can opt into covenant marriage after the marriage has taken place. (Ark. Code Ann. § 9-11-804.) The Arizona law and the Louisiana law have templates similar to the Arkansas law. (Ariz. Rev. Stat. § 24-901 et seq.; La. Civ. Code Rev. Stat. § 9:307.)

Arkansas adds a ground for divorce of offering "such indignities to the person of the other as shall render his or her condition intolerable." (Ark. Code Ann. § 9-11-808(b)(5)(C).) Louisiana adds as a ground for divorce "outrages of the other spouse, if such habitual intemperance, or such ill-treatment is of such a nature as to render their living together insupportable." (La. Civ. Code Rev. Stat. § 9:307-B(6).)

The aim of covenant marriage is to promote and strengthen marriages and reduce the divorce rate. Some language used by supporters suggests that covenant marriage can foster an environment for "traditional family values" that are established by the "faith community."

It should be noted that Section 10(b)(4) of the UPMAA provides that a term in a premarital or postmarital agreement that penalizes a party for initiating a legal proceeding leading to a divorce is unenforceable. (Section 10(b)(4).) What if a couple sought to enter into a covenant marriage in a state that does not have a covenant marriage statute but which has adopted this UPMAA provision? The covenant marriage provision in the prenup would likely fail.

There *are* cases in which courts have enforced prenups that specified adultery or fault-based grounds would *not* be used as a ground for divorce. See, for example, *Massar v. Massar*, 279 N.J. Super. 89 (1995) and *Eason v. Eason*, 384 S.C. 473 (2009). However, other than the covenant marriage states with their specific statutes, there may be no existing case law requiring parties to *avoid* no-fault grounds as the basis for a divorce as a requirement in a prenup.

This is consistent with ALI Principles Section 7.08(1), which states that a term in a prenup or postnup is not enforceable if, by its terms, it limits or enlarges grounds for divorce beyond those that state law permits. State laws reflect a state's public policy. Therefore, if there is no covenant marriage statute in a state, it is unlikely that that state's courts would permit a party to forgo his or her rights to file a no-fault divorce.

What happens to the rest of the agreement if a lifestyle provision or a filing grounds restriction set forth in a prenup or postnup is invalidated by a court when the parties divorce? Most agreements have a savings clause, which says something like, "If any part of this Agreement shall be illegal, void or otherwise unenforceable, the remainder thereof shall continue in full force and effect." But that doesn't always happen if a portion is invalidated. Sometimes the missing part affects other parts of the prenup.

This reminds me of that old joke that I included in Chapter 4, about the awkward result of the hexagonal nut being removed from a boy's navel. (His butt fell off.)

The severability clause is one of the "boilerplate" clauses in a prenup, but not all boilerplate clauses are necessarily enforced.

What if a lifestyle provision said that a husband or wife who strayed would lose all marital property if there were a divorce? A court might well determine that the penalty would be against public policy, especially in divorces of older people. That court might be understandably be concerned that the parties to the marriage had adequate security as they aged. But there would be concern under other fact patterns, too. The penalty may be viewed as disproportionate.

Would a court reduce the penalty? Or would a divorce judge throw that provision out and try to keep the rest of the prenup intact? Or would the judge throw out the entire prenuptial agreement? That would depend on the facts and circumstances of a particular case.

This strongly encourages the drafter to make sure any lifestyle penalty clauses are reasonable in all the financial circumstances of a marriage – whether present or foreseeable future circumstances.

CHAPTER 15

WHAT'S ALIMONY HAVE TO DO WITH IT?

A limony" is a highly charged word. Even when we lawyers and media-tors try to tamp down emotions by calling it "spousal support," it raises strong negative reactions on both sides of the alimony divide. It is indeed a hot-button issue.

Men (usually the payors) are generally outraged that after a marriage is over, they still have to pay support to their former wives. This result even can occur if the marriage ends with a wife's unfaithfulness with another. A man might well complain, why should I pay alimony when I no longer have the serv-ices of my wife? It just doesn't make sense to him.

Women, too, dislike the idea of alimony, because it represents an unwanted tie with a husband that they would prefer were out of their lives. It also smacks of uncomfortable dependency. It has become a derogatory word for women, too. Young women often believe alimony is an antiquated vestige of the past. They are often eager to sign prenups that include a waiver of alimony to prove their *bona fides* as independent, modern women.

But sometimes, even these days, spousal support may be a financial necessity after a marriage ends.

Because alimony is sometimes needed, there are laws in every state that provide for alimony to an ex-spouse under certain factual situations. There are variations in the law, as to when alimony is triggered and how to calculate its amount and duration. But no jurisdiction to date has barred a soon-to-be divorced former spouse from making a claim for alimony and causing it to be provided, under appropriate circumstances.

A brief history of alimony.

In earlier times and lingering well into the twentieth century in some states, a husband in a marriage had control of virtually all property, including the property that a woman brought into the marriage, such as an inheritance. He also had control of property accumulated during the marriage. This historical relationship in marriage came primarily from English common law. It is termed "coverture," because when a man married, he essentially "covered" the woman, and she became a *femme couvert* under the protection of her husband. In other words, when married, the husband and wife became one person, "and that person was the husband," as the common saying of the time articulated it.

As William Blackstone put it in his in his *Commentaries on the Laws of England* (1756), "coverture" had the following meaning:

> By marriage, the husband and wife are one person in law: that is, the very being or legal existence of the woman is suspended during the marriage, or at least is incorporated and consolidated into that of the husband: under whose wing, protection, and cover, she performs every thing. [sic]

The coverture concept was aimed at protecting women who, in those times, had little access to independent economic wherewithal. Power over money and support remained with the husband until his death, and then it was handed over to the sons of the marriage to continue taking care of their mother until her death.

The wife basically gave up her legal existence when she married. She had no right to own property on her own or to make contracts. Her husband had the right to control any income generated from her real estate during his lifetime. Anything she earned or inherited during the marriage legally belonged to the husband. She could not sign a contract nor incur debt without her husband's permission. She could not sue in court or be sued in court.

Women had limited means to survive economically outside of marriage. The laws made divorce next to impossible. Marriage was universally viewed as a religious sacrament and was indissoluble except under extreme grounds. Sometimes it took a legislative act to get a divorce.

Vestiges of coverture in the United States still lingered into the 1970s. Married women were not usually able to get credit or obtain a mortgage without the consent of their husband. With the enactment of the Equal Credit Opportunity Act of 1974, a woman could finally apply for credit on her own.

Under this backdrop of women's extreme dependence on the financial decisions and control of men, husbands had the legal duty to support their wives during marriage and upon separation or divorce. As part of the marital contract as it was understood, the wife had a duty to provide domestic services to the husband and provide childcare for her family. Part of the unspoken duties of wives was the duty to share a bed and fulfill the sexual desires of their husbands.

Since wives were so dependent on their husbands, if a marriage ended, alimony would continue until the woman remarried and was under the care and protection of another husband. This concept of alimony ending at the remarriage of an ex-wife has survived to this day, either by state statute or by legal custom.

There are strong modern arguments that the right to alimony is a contractual right to a share of the other spouse's income derived from the economic partnership of marriage. For example, in many marriages, alimony could be seen as compensation for loss of earning capacity due to having and raising children and performing most of the household duties.

The influential modern treatise on family Law, the *Principles of the Law of Family Dissolution* (2002) promulgated by the American Law Institute (ALI Principles), takes the view that alimony awards are compensatory and that their purpose is to address financial earning capacity losses that occurred during marriage. See ALI Principles, Chapter 5, "Compensatory Spousal Payments."

Chapter 5 of the ALI Principles provides that alimony should be based on equitable principles of loss allocation. These include loss of earning capacity due to caretaking responsibilities. (Section 5.02(3)(a).) It also compensates for losses that occur from the "changes in life opportunities and expectations caused by the adjustments individuals ordinarily make over the course of a long marital relationship." (Section 5.02(3)(b).) In addition, the ALI Principles note that the income earner's claim to benefit from the fruits of his or her own labor should be *primary* to the claims of the former spouse. [emphasis added]. (Section 5.02(3)(c).)

In most states, alimony is based on the "needs" of the divorce ex-spouse. The need is consistent with the "station of life" that the recipient had during the marriage (if financially possible). Spousal support is not currently based on the partnership concept, although many arguments have been made for that interpretation. When a subsequent husband (or cohabitant) comes along, he will presumably fulfill the wife's financial "need," and the obligation of the former husband would be eliminated. In this way, the early concept of coverture seems to persist in our divorce laws even today.

Oddly, in alimony situations, there is a disconnect that is keenly felt by the paying spouse. The paying spouse still has the duty to support, but he or she no longer gets the "services" of the divorced spouse, including housework or having a sexual relationship. Sometimes, a paying spouse is fully employed and working hard, and the non-working spouse might not be working up to his or her economic capacity. Perhaps the children are grown and out of the home. This raises the issue of unfairness, resolved in part by the possible imposition of *imputed* income. Imputed income is earnings a dependent ex-spouse might reasonably be expected to be able to obtain in the workplace. It can be imputed to him or her in a divorce case to assess the amount of spousal support to be paid.

Does marital guilt play into awarding of alimony? It certainly did in the past, when only an "innocent" wife had the right to receive alimony. If she left her husband for no "just cause" or had an affair, she would be barred from receiving alimony.

Nowadays, fault-based divorce has been mostly phased out. Judges do not want to investigate the reasons for the dissolution of a marriage. They don't want to analyze why affairs happen and assign fault. Of course, this is understandably very difficult to accept by a spouse who feels wronged by a spouse who strayed during a marriage, if that spouse is now required to pay alimony to the spouse who left the marriage.

Leaving a household or having an affair (or affairs) generally has little or no impact in a divorce case or the ordering of an alimony award. In a New

Jersey case, a court indicated that perhaps an egregious infidelity case (not an ordinary marital straying) could affect an alimony award. This type of "egregious" fault would be one that goes beyond marital indiscretion, such as deliberately infecting a spouse with a loathsome disease. *Mani v. Mani*, 183 N.J. 70 (2005). But in general, only economic fault may be considered in an infidelity, such as money spent on a paramour that depleted family resources.

It's important to understand the alimony laws.

When thinking about a prenuptial agreement, it is important to think about and consider the possible need for alimony in the future by a spouse. At the time of entering into the marriage, both spouses may be gainfully employed. That's particularly true of first marriages, so it's hard to envision this happening.

But what if a spouse becomes disabled, or leaves the job market for a long period of time to raise children, or has a financial setback? What if the parties decide to each concentrate on one major function of the marriage, such as earning money for one spouse and householding and child-rearing for the other? It's really impossible to predict the future, but that is exactly what you need to do to address the alimony issue attentively.

When thinking about this, it's very important for you to understand the alimony laws in your state if those laws will control your prenup. If you decide to incorporate the alimony laws of a different state in the "choice of law" provision in your prenup, you'll need to understand those other laws. In general, knowing about the range of alimony laws in various states will benefit you, so that you can be as fully informed as possible when you decide what will be in your prenup regarding spousal support.

Alimony laws in various states.

What follows is some general information on alimony laws and alimony reforms that exist in various U.S. states.

There is not an appreciable difference in alimony between common law (equitable distribution) states and community property states. In all states, alimony entails a case-by-case analysis by a judge. Nowadays, alimony may be awarded to the husband or the wife. Each state has a separate set of statutory and case law, but they are all actually quite similar in effect.

Most states provide a checklist of factors to be considered when a judge makes an alimony award. These factors generally determine whether alimony should be awarded, how much the alimony payments should be, and the duration of the alimony award.

Here's a typical checklist of factors, taken from New Jersey divorce laws:

- Actual need of a party.
- Ability of a party to pay alimony.
- Length of the marriage.
- Age of the parties.
- Health of the parties (physical and emotional).
- Standard of living established during the marriage union and the likelihood that each party can maintain a reasonably comparable standard of living. (The new 2014 New Jersey law adds, ". . . with neither party having a greater entitlement to that standard of living than the other.")
- Earning capacities, educational levels, vocational skills, and employability of the parties.
- Length of absence from the job market of the party seeking alimony.
- Parental responsibilities for the children.
- Time and expense necessary to acquire sufficient education or training to enable the party seeking maintenance to find appropriate employment, the availability of the training and employment.
- History of the financial or non-financial contributions to the marriage by each party including contributions to the care and education of the children and interruption of personal careers or educational opportunities.
- The equitable distribution of property ordered and any pay-

outs on equitable distribution, directly or indirectly, out of current income, to the extent this consideration is reasonable, just, and fair.

- The income available to either party through investment of any assets held by that party. (Most states include this income into the calculation of alimony, especially as to assets that were not previously divided as marital property. Many separation agreements solely focus on current earned income when setting alimony terms.)
- The tax treatment and consequences to both parties of any alimony award, including the designation of all or a portion of the payment as a non-taxable payment.
- Any other factors that the court may deem relevant.

N.J. Rev. Stat. § 2A:34-23 (2014).

But the exact amount of alimony and its duration are left unaddressed in most statutes and are subject to a judge's discretion.

The discretion of a judge to weigh these factors has been a source of criticism by litigants (especially men and men's rights groups) as conveying too much decisional power to judges. And it is true that judges' lower court decisions on alimony, even within a single state system on cases that seem to present the same facts, often vary significantly.

There are relatively few published cases at the trial court (as distinguished from appeals court) level on amount and duration of alimony. Only those rare cases that have been appealed are published and available to the public. Also, most of the state statutes do not specifically address the amount of alimony or length of an alimony award, leaving this to the discretion of judges.

Divorce attorneys gain knowledge as to the parameters of alimony awards by their direct experiences in trial court, sharing experiences with other attorneys, and attending legal seminars, in which other attorneys publicly present the lower court rulings they have encountered on the range of alimony awards under various fact patterns. This gives lawyers good knowledge of the existing parameters, so that clients can be advised as to what to expect and what to accept. This knowledge usually leads to settlement rather than litigation on alimony issues.

Alimony laws are changing in some states.

There have been a number of changes in some states' alimony statutes to provide more certainty as to an alimony award.

For instance, in Massachusetts in 2011, the Alimony Reform Act became law. It provides guidelines for length of alimony based on length of marriage. For instance, if the marriage was 16 years long, alimony would continue for "not more" than 80 percent of the number of months of the marriage. For a marriage of more than 20 years (a long-term marriage), the alimony could be ordered for an "indefinite" length of time.

The amount of alimony was also defined. The law stated that alimony should "generally" not exceed the recipient's "need," or between 30 and 35 percent of the difference between the parties' gross incomes. This language has caused some uncertainty in the state as to whether the alimony is triggered by "need," or whether the guideline percentages of 30 to 35 percent should apply even if the "need" is less. (Mass. Gen. Laws, chapter 208, § 53.)

This is an ongoing question in Massachusetts, especially when the payor is a very highly compensated business executive.

The argument that an alimony award reflects partnership income interest would tend toward supporting the 30 to 35 percent calculation even if it is more than the "need" of the dependent spouse. If totally based on need, in essence, the old coverture laws would still be in effect. It is to be noted that "need" is determined by "station in life," so the dependent spouse's need if she was the spouse of a highly compensated business executive would be greater than that of a dependent spouse of a public high school teacher.

The Massachusetts Alimony Reform Act also provides that when a payor reaches full retirement age for purposes of social security retirement benefits, he or she is presumptively relieved of paying alimony, unless there are good reasons to continue the payments to the dependent spouse. But baby boomer spouses are working much longer than their parents, and age 65 or 66 is no longer a typical retirement age for baby boomers. What if the earner works longer than this age? Would alimony still be payable? In Massachusetts, this depends on the facts and circumstances of a particular case. An older person may be ordered to pay alimony for "good cause shown." (Mass. Gen. Laws, chapter 208, § 49(f)(1).)

New York enacted a very specific alimony reform law in 2015 providing for amounts and duration of alimony. It is more restrictive than the Massachusetts laws and the laws of many other states. For instance, for a 16-year marriage, alimony may continue for only between 30 and 40 percent of the length of the marriage. That's much shorter than the current Massachusetts law. The annual income from the payor spouse is limited to earnings of $178,000 when calculating alimony. What if the earner party's income is $400,000? Is it fair to limit that spouse's earning when doing the alimony calculation? There is a possibility for applying a higher earned income base and duration (including lifetime) at a judge's discretion if the result of the formula is "unjust" or "inappropriate." (N.Y. Dom. Rel. § 236B(6)5.)

In Florida, a "First Husbands Advocacy Group" is pressing for changes in Florida's alimony law. The group's motto is "Fair is fair, we want our share, we want our welfare. We are entitled to it. We earned it. We sacrificed."

The group wants to eliminate "lifetime" alimony. Actually, in Florida, there is no "lifetime" alimony. But there is a possibility of an alimony award that is "indefinite in duration," so that a payor spouse would need to go back to court to change it. In that sense only, it is permanent. The men's group also wishes to have the amount and duration of alimony calculated by a formula. So far, the bills (which had been passed by the legislature) have been vetoed by Governor Rick Scott, mainly due to the inclusion of the premise that children will split their time equally between both parents.

New Jersey enacted an alimony reform act in 2014 that does away with "permanent" alimony. Now the length of the payments cannot exceed the length of the marriage, unless the judge finds "exceptional" circumstances. The exceptional circumstances can include the dependency of a spouse, and also whether or not a spouse has given up a career or a career opportunity. As a result, these exceptions may swallow up the rule.

When looking at the retirement of an earner in New Jersey, the payor's motives in retirement and his or her ability to maintain support payments will be analyzed. There are specific guidelines to prevent people from receiving alimony when they are in another relationship, even if they are not married to their new partner. The new law specifically provides that even if the couple is not living together, the relationship may be considered cohabitation. If cohabitation is found, a court may suspend or terminate alimony, but not "reduce it" as the new law in Massachusetts permits.

In California, as well as in most community property states, alimony is based on a facts and circumstances analysis, with consideration of the usual list of factors, similar to that of New Jersey. In short-term marriages (i.e., a marriage of less than ten years), support is generally not ordered for longer than half the length of the marriage. For marriages "of long duration" (longer than ten years), a court will generally retain jurisdiction indefinitely pending agreement of the parties or future court order. (Cal. Fam. Code, § 4336.) That means a party would have to go to court to ask for a termination date for an alimony payment obligation.

For purposes of temporary (pre-judgment) spousal support, different California counties have devised formulas for calculating support amounts. Courts may, but do not have to, employ these formulas. Spousal support ordered at the completion of a divorce action cannot be based on any formula and must be based on a big-picture analysis of the enumerated factors in the statute. (Cal. Fam. Code § 4320.) Because there is tremendous judicial discretion in the spousal support area and results are highly unpredictable, private ordering via a premarital agreement may be the only way couples can achieve predictability and certainty and retain control − but only if the alimony provision in the prenup is enforceable. (See below.)

In 2015, there was a push by a men's advocacy group headed by Steve Clark to modify California's spousal support laws. Clark was unhappy that he had been ordered to pay alimony to his former spouse for the rest of her life, unless she remarried. Clark's proposal would have eliminated the court's ability to award or enforce spousal support. Prior existing orders for less than ten years would be terminated. For prior existing orders in excess of ten years, the support would have been phased out over a five-year period and then terminated. The proposed measure failed to obtain the requisite number of signatures and never appeared on the ballot.

Texas is another community property state. Texas has such stingy alimony laws such that it has been known as the "wife-dumping" state. It gives new meaning to the lyrics of the Tammy Wynette hit song "Stand By Your Man" for those wives who live in Texas. In fact, prior to 1967, the Texas Constitution prohibited alimony.

In 1995, Texas became the last state to provide for permanent, court-ordered alimony (called "spousal maintenance" in Texas). The maximum amount allowed was $2,500 a month (or 20 percent of the payor's gross income, if less), with a maximum duration of three years, unless the recipient party was disabled. That was the most stingy and extreme alimony regime in the United States. Then in 2011, Texas laws were amended, and they now provide an alimony cap of the lesser of $5,000 per month or 20 percent of the payor's income. (Tex. Fam. Code § 8.055.) But this alimony law is still quite restrictive when compared with those of the other states.

In Texas, a spouse can only qualify to receive alimony if he or she cannot earn sufficient income to provide for his or her "minimum reasonable needs." Community property received in the divorce and the dependent spouse's separate property will be considered sources of income for the dependent spouse.

There are durational limits in the 2011 Texas statute.

If the marriage is less than ten years in length, there is no alimony with some exceptions, such as incapacitating mental or physical disability. If the marriage is ten years in length and up to 20 years, the maximum duration is up to five years. If the marriage is at least 20 years but not more than 30 years, the alimony can last for seven years, and if married for 30 years or more, it can last for up to ten years. (Tex. Fam. Code § 8.054.)

However, the duration will be the shortest reasonable period that allows the spouse seeking alimony to earn sufficient income to provide for that spouse's "minimum reasonable needs." There is nothing in the Texas law about "station in life." It appears that this concept is not part of the analysis for purposes of Texas alimony law. The usual list of factors will be analyzed when determining the amount and duration of alimony. (Tex. Fam. Code § 8.052.)

As a result, Texas law still penalizes the unemployed homemaker spouse who does not pursue a career, even if the other spouse had developed a high-earning career during the marriage.

To give the complete picture, property division in Texas divorce is sometimes a mitigating factor to the harsh alimony laws. In most community property states, marital property is divided equally. Texas has a different rule. The judge must properly weigh all the facts of the case and make a property division that is a "just and right." (Tex. Fam. Code § 7.002.) Disparity of earning capacities is one of many factors that a judge can assess, as well as the size of the community estate and the amount of separate property of each of the spouses. Fault, such as adultery, is also a factor in Texas property division. As a result, property division is not always equal in Texas, and an unequal division can mitigate a harsh alimony award.

Note that under The Tax Cuts and Jobs Act of 2017 (the TCJA), the deduction for alimony payments under Internal Revenue Code Section 215 and the inclusion of the payments in the receiving spouse's income under Section 71 have been eliminated. Accordingly, the amounts received under a prior alimony order by a former spouse will be overstated, as that recipient spouse will no longer be required to pay income tax on the support payments. As a result, the alimony formulas of the various states will need to be reviewed and likely modified. The TCJA changes go into effect for separation agreements entered into after December 31, 2018, and court decrees rendered after that date, so there is a one-year reprieve on this reversal of former income tax treatment.

Can alimony be waived in a prenup?

Because of the difficulty of foreseeing the future, courts have tended to be wary of absolute waivers of alimony in prenups, especially in prenups of younger people in first marriages. When you marry at 30, you simply don't know what your situation will be at 55 or 60 or 70.

On the face of it, it seems that alimony would be an excellent candidate to be settled in a prenuptial agreement. It's what many people seeking prenups want to do the most. However, some state courts and judges will not enforce alimony waivers based on public policy concerns about the support of former spouses. These concerns are similar to the policy concerns when the terms of a prenup are written to decide issues of child support and child custody. (See discussion about child-related issues below.) States do not readily relinquish their oversight role in protecting dependent spouses or children.

Having said that, alimony waivers in prenups are allowed in many states, with certain controls. In others, they may be permitted depending on the factual issues that pertain at the time of the execution of the prenup and/or at the time of divorce. In other words, in those states an alimony waiver might not be void *per se*, but voidable under certain circumstances.

The basic rule is that an alimony waiver may be enforced if the prenup leaves the dependent ex-spouse with sufficient property and or appropriate income or employment to support him- or herself. Almost all states have a provision that an alimony waiver will be unenforceable if it leaves the dependent ex-spouse relying on public assistance for support.

But aside from this extreme of a total alimony waiver, there are many variations of what kind of waiver, and its extent, that can be written into the terms of a prenup. The possibilities are a complete waiver or a partial waiver, with various trigger points and possible methods of calculation that people can write into a prenup. Whether or not they are allowed by a court is a question for your prenup attorney to (try to) determine.

The alimony provisions of the influential 1983 Uniform Premarital Agreement Act (UPAA), which has been adopted with variations in a number of states, provides in Section 3(a)(4) that parties may modify or eliminate spousal support. It provides that parties can contract in a premarital agreement "with respect to any matter . . . not in violation of public policy . . . " (Section 3(a)(8).) The drafters' comments note that there is a split of authority in the states as to whether a prenup can control the issue of alimony. Another trigger in the UPAA unenforceability of an alimony provision is if the alimony provision is "unconscionable" when executed and if the party contesting the prenup was not provided with fair and reasonable financial disclosure. (Section 6(a).) Financial disclosure standards and the question of what is an "unconscionable" agreement are to be determined by state law standards. (Section 6(c).)

The modernized version of the Uniform Premarital and Marital Agreement Act (UPMAA) was promulgated in 2012. It has no provision directly bearing on an alimony waiver, except if a modification or elimination of alimony causes a party to be eligible for public assistance. (Section 9(e).)

The UPMAA, however, provides an optional drafting choice for states that wish to provide protection to a dependent spouse at the time of enforcement. It provides that a court may refuse to enforce a term of a premarital agreement if the term was unconscionable at the time of signing, or if enforcement of the term would result in "undue hardship" for a party because of a "substantial change" in circumstances arising since the time the agreement was signed. (Section 9(c).) This provision, if adopted, could provide a "second look" at an alimony waiver in a prenup as it allows for a substantive fairness review at the at the time of a divorce. Some states have adopted this provision.

Burden of proof is a concept in law that requires a litigant to prove his or her case. Otherwise, the case is thrown out. In most prenup laws, the burden of proof is on the person contesting the prenup.

Consistent with this, UPMAA Section 9(a) places the burden of proof on the party challenging the prenup. But it has optional language to shift the burden of proof to the party who seeks to enforce the terms. The burden of proof is something people can determine and set as a term in their prenuptial agreements – it's an issue subject to negotiation.

The influential ALI Principles (see above) address enforceability of terms of a prenup (including waiver of alimony) in Chapter 7. It seems to present a more expansive view of under what circumstances an economically dependent spouse might be protected. It says that a court should not enforce a term that works a "substantial injustice." (Section 7.05(1).) This includes a change in circumstances, and also, most interestingly, what the magnitude of disparity might be between the outcome under the prenup and the outcome "under otherwise prevailing legal principles." (Section 7.05(3)(a).) The person claiming that the agreement would work a substantial injustice has the burden of proof as to that question.

What do state courts say about waivers of alimony in prenups?

State courts have been changing their views toward enforceability of alimony waivers. As you might expect, there are differences in approach among the various states. In states with flexibility on alimony waiver, the trend seems to be that the longer the marriage and the greater the support needs of a spouse at the time of divorce, the more inclined a court might be in viewing a premarital waiver of alimony as unenforceable. Another factor might be how much other property exists to provide security for a dependent spouse.

However, it should be noted, that many states have adopted the "unconscionability" standard to be applied only at the signing of the agreement. Under that standard, the terms must rise to a high level of egregiousness at the time of the signing in order for an alimony waiver to be unenforceable. That's a very difficult standard to meet for a contesting spouse.

In California, until 2000, parties could not waive spousal support in a prenup. This was changed by a case in which the California Supreme Court held that waivers of alimony were not in and of themselves invalid. *In re Marriage of Pendleton and Fireman*, 24 Cal. 4th 39 (2000). That case held that public policy was not violated by permitting enforcement of a waiver of spousal support executed by intelligent, well-educated, self-sufficient persons with advice of counsel.

In *Pendleton*, both parties had post-graduate degrees, and at the time the divorce was filed each had a net worth of approximately $2.5 million. In adopting the UPAA, the California version had eliminated UPAA Section 3(a)(4), which stated that one of the matters that can be dealt with in a prenup is the "modification or elimination" of spousal support, so enforceability of alimony waivers was an open issue to be decided by the courts.

Two years after the *Pendleton* case, California law was amended to provide that a spousal support waiver is enforceable, but only if the party waiving the support was represented by independent counsel at the time he or she signed the agreement or if the agreement was not unconscionable at the time of enforcement. (Cal. Fam. Code § 1612(c).) This means that a person who is represented by counsel and waives alimony might still be able to challenge the waiver at the time of the divorce based on unconscionability, as determined under state law standards. (Cal. Fam. Code § 1615(b).)

But what is "unconscionable" in the context of an alimony waiver?

In a 2013 California case, an alimony waiver was held unconscionable in a 16-year marriage. At the time of the marriage, the wife was a high school graduate who had a part-time job at as a shoe salesperson at Nordstrom's.

The husband was a Harvard Law School graduate with $3 million of separate property assets and an income of roughly a half million from his law practice.

At the time of the separation, the husband had separate property valued at more than $10 million and earnings of roughly a million dollars per year; the wife had no separate property and no income. Under the prenup, the wife was entitled to furniture, a Jaguar automobile, half the net proceeds from the sale of the marital home, and $200,000, payable over five years. The court concluded that these assets, compared to what she was likely to receive in court-ordered alimony, were "manifestly inadequate." The facts of the case met the unconscionability standard. *In re Marriage of Facter*, 212 Cal. App. 4th 967 (2012).

But where does a court draw the line between an unconscionable waiver of alimony and an enforceable waiver? That's a question for the courts to address, and the answers vary greatly. But it's clear that the level of egregiousness must be very high in order to satisfy the high standard of unconscionability to lead to unenforceability of an alimony waiver.

A Virginia court addressed the issue as to when a prenup is unconscionable. The wife was a recent immigrant from Morocco with limited English language skills. The husband brought the wife to his attorney's office and told her that she had to sign "a marriage paper." She thought she was signing something like a marriage license. There had been no financial disclosure. At the time of the divorce ten years later, the husband's net worth was approximately $20 million. He had told her prior to her signing the prenup that he was a "poor man" and didn't have much money. The alimony waiver was found to be unconscionable. *Chaplain v. Chaplain*, 54 Va. Ct. App. 762 (2009).

In Wisconsin, another factor is considered when assessing alimony for purposes of a divorce in addition to the typical alimony factors (such as length of marriage and age and health of the parties). It is whether there was a prenup before marrying that concerns "any arrangement for the financial support of the parties." (Wis. Stat. § 767.56(1c)(h).) What this presumably means is that a trial court will weigh all the statutory factors for alimony along with the terms of the prenup, and presumably make some sort of calculus combining all these factors. It doesn't mean that a Wisconsin court will rubber-stamp an alimony waiver; a court might order alimony as appropriate after weighing the factors, including the existence of a prenup.

New Mexico law provides by statute that a prenuptial agreement may not adversely affect the right of a spouse to receive support. (N.M. Stat. § 40-3A-4(B).)

Iowa has adopted its own version of the UPAA. However, it does not permit any provision in a prenup that adversely affects the right of a spouse to receive spousal support. (Iowa Code Ann. § 596.5(2).) That provision states that "the right of a spouse or a child to support shall not be adversely affected by a premarital agreement."

South Carolina's Supreme Court held that prenuptial agreements waiving spousal support were not per se unconscionable, nor were they presumptively contrary to public policy. A court could enforce alimony waivers if certain protections were met and if the facts and circumstances hadn't changed since the time of execution to make its enforcement "unfair" or "unreasonable." *Hardee v. Hardee.* 355 S.C. 382 (2003). The *Hardee* court explicitly overruled an earlier case, *Towles v. Towles,* 256 S.C. 307 (1971), which held that a prenup that eliminated spousal support was void as against public policy.

Massachusetts is a state in which rules regarding prenups (including alimony waivers) are determined by case law. Until 2002, a prenup had to be both "fair and reasonable" at time of execution (the "first look") and at the time of enforcement (the "second look"). In 2002, the standard changed with the *DeMatteo* case. The standard at the time of execution remained the "fair and reasonable" standard, but at time of divorce, the "not unconscionable" standard now applied. *DeMatteo v. DeMatteo,* 436 Mass. 18 (2002).

This aligns Massachusetts with many other states requiring unconscionability at the time of enforcement, although many other states just have one standard applicable at the "first look" (time of signing the prenup), and that standard is that the agreement not be unconscionable at that earlier time.

With the *DeMatteo* case, the court noted the settled law that the prenup terms did not need to approximate terms of an alimony award or a property division a judge would make under the "fair and reasonable" standard at the time of a divorce. As it noted, many valid agreements may be "one sided," and a contesting party may have considerably fewer assets and "enjoy a far different lifestyle after divorce than he or she may enjoy during the marriage."

The *DeMatteo* court's view was that marriage confers a special legal status from which "certain rights and obligations" arise. The court said that it is not just a "mere contract between two parties," and concluded that the freedom to limit or waive legal rights in the event of divorce is not "appropriately left unrestricted."

The *DeMatteo* court held that a spouse must not be "stripped of substantially all marital interests." Otherwise the prenup would "essentially vitiate the very status of marriage." The court said it would not enforce a prenup that prevented a spouse from retaining his or her marital rights, of which maintenance and support is "most critical," however "disproportionately small" the retention of these rights were.

But what if both parties want to waive spousal support in their prenup?

Sometimes both parties to a prenup wish to waive spousal support in their agreement. In some of these situations, both parties are professionals or businesspeople with substantial incomes and/or assets. They appear to be highly employable. In these cases, there seems little risk to either party to agree to an alimony waiver. In some cases, they are later-in-life marriages, in which each of the parties is financially secure.

However, what if events change and a party becomes ill and can no longer work? What if there is a major business downturn or bankruptcy? When something unforeseen like this happens, the alimony waiver in the prenup could increase the instability of the marriage. The idea that support is impossible may trigger intensely negative emotions in the disadvantaged spouse, thereby derailing a marriage. Perhaps even with couples in a seemingly financially secure position, the prenup could include a provision to re-evaluate the waiver if there is a substantial change of circumstances.

For first marriages of young people embarking on careers, an alimony waiver is dangerous, because often things change during the course of a long marriage. Some of these couples may insist on an alimony waiver as a matter of self-pride and independence (particularly for the female partner). However, the attorney should counsel that client about the dangers of waiving support. After a review of the state laws, a spousal support provision could be drafted that is not as extreme as an outright waiver. The alimony waiver could be modified if there is a need at the time of divorce. And "need" can be described as something less than the "station during marriage" but something more than pure economic survival, as in Texas, or needing to go on welfare, which is the law in many states that have adopted the UPAA or the UPMAA.

In the preamble to the UPAA, the commissioners rosily state that the availability of prenups encourages marital partners "to take their interests into account before marriage." It further asserts that the result should be "better prepared marital partners and better marriages." But does striking a hard alimony bargain that is permitted under the UPAA create a better marriage? I'm not so sure. That hard bargain will likely be enforced at a divorce and will harm one of the partners. Will that really feel acceptable during the marriage?

How to structure alimony in a prenup.

It is clear that the "unconscionability" standard applicable in many states at the signing of a prenup is a different standard than the "fair and reasonable" standard applicable in a minority of states. Some but not all states require a "second look" at the alimony waiver at the time of a divorce to make sure it retains its intention at the time of the signing.

Although there is some overlap between the two standards, the "unconscionability" standard has been articulated by many courts as requiring a greater showing of inappropriateness than the "fair and reasonable" standard.

This is what the Massachusetts court stated in *DeMatteo* regarding the "unconscionability" standard at time of enforcement:

> The nomenclature attached to the standard of review – whether it be "fair and reasonable" or "conscionability" – is but a shorthand descriptor of what is of real moment: the content and meaning behind the label, and the careful analysis required of judges, case by case, of each antenuptial agreement and the circumstances surrounding its enforcement. Indeed, whether termed "unconscionable," "fair and reasonable," "inequitable," or something else, in jurisdictions that employ a "second-look" analysis, the vast majority direct trial judges to undertake an analysis that is remarkably similar in substance. *DeMatteo*, 436 Mass. at 35–36.

Judges do look at the impact of a prenup that is contested, including the impact of alimony waivers on the well-being of a contesting spouse. Often the typical alimony factors are brought in to a judge's calculus. Alimony waivers are one of those issues where states' public policy of supporting dependent spouses may override what is in a prenup.

At the time of a marriage, parties presumably care very much about each other and wish for each other's well-being. It is important and appropriate to think about an alimony provision that is workable and reasonable to be included in a prenup. There are a number of possibilities to consider, aside from a complete waiver.

Some parties to prenups address alimony by leaving the issue of spousal support silent or stating that the laws of support of the jurisdiction they reside in at the time of divorce will apply. A typical provision may state the following:

> Because the parties cannot now contemplate what might be fair and reasonable in terms of spousal support if their marriage ter- minates by divorce, the parties agree that unless mutually agreed otherwise, the laws of the spousal support in the jurisdiction in which they last lived together as a married couple shall be applied as pertaining to the alimony obligation of the spouses, as to both amount of support and duration, and any other issues contemplated by the said alimony laws.

In some prenup alimony provisions, it is stated that separate property and income from separate property will not be taken into account when deter- mining the amount of alimony awarded. Some prenups include (or don't include) income from marital assets that have been divided in determining the alimony amount. In some prenups, only a party's earned income through employment will count in the determination. This may or may not be drafted to include bonuses and stock options and similar forms of compensation.

But what if the payor has no earned income (because he or she volun- tarily does not work for money), but has, say, $10 million of separate assets generating income and the other spouse has little assets or income. A waiver of alimony on these facts may be very difficult for some courts to enforce, especially if at the time of the marriage the payor spouse had strong earnings.

Some prenups ensure that enough assets are conveyed to a dependent spouse (including perhaps a dwelling) to keep that spouse in a comfortable situation if the marriage ends in divorce. This settlement could begin after a certain number of years of marriage.

Another possibility is to draw a "fence" around the alimony issue, to have alimony paid for a shorter duration and/or for a lesser amount than the alimony laws would otherwise establish under the applicable state law.

For instance, one could base the limitation on the state's law that applies to your prenup, but reduces the payment amount produced by the state's formula by a certain percentage. Or the standard term of years for the payments could be reduced by a certain number of years or chosen percentage. A cap on the amount of alimony may also be set, perhaps adjusted for increases or decreases in a cost-of-living adjustment (COLA) index of the U.S. Bureau of Labor Statistics.

This may create a reasonable balance between the interests of one spouse who views himself as having been burdened by alimony payments in a previous divorce, and the potential needs of the new spouse if the marriage ends in divorce. One could balance this structure with protections for a dependent spouse that consist of ensuring a level of separate and/or marital property for that spouse before any such limitations take effect. Many prenups limit marital property and also deny alimony, which can put a dependent spouse in a very bad situation.

Prenups can also specify a "standard of living" be addressed by alimony and/or income from assets. It can be articulated as the standard of living prior to the marriage, the standard of living enjoyed at the end of the marriage, or somewhere in between. For a relatively wealthy ex-spouse to include the standard of living similar to that contained in Texas law – to meet the dependent spouse's "minimum reasonable needs" – seems rather harsh.

Articulating a particular standard of living could be very specific, including residential neighborhood or price range of house or condo that would be financially possible for an ex-spouse to reside in under the terms of the prenup if there is a divorce, and if it is possible for the more moneyed spouse to afford this. Cost-of-living adjustment (COLA) indexes promulgated by the Bureau of

Labor Statistics applicable for the geographic area can be used to change the amount of future spousal support as costs increase or decrease.

A prenup alimony provision may also address the efforts of the dependent recipient spouse in the workplace. Alimony laws typically encompass attribution of income if a party who could be employed is voluntarily unemployed or underemployed. Alimony can be based on what is needed in addition to income the other spouse can reasonably earn.

The alimony provision can specify a time period in which a spouse who has taken time off from the job market should re-enter it, and how, and at what level of employment. The spousal support could last for the minimal amount of time required to transition the spouse to be self-supporting, and can take into account other income, such as child support. The standard of living for the dependent spouse will need to be addressed here as well.

A reasonable projection of that person's ability to earn could be made. Support during a rehabilitation period of job training could be specified. Job-training costs could be contemplated as a term in the prenup. This provision can have exceptions for spouses who have reached a certain age at the time of divorce (such as 55 or 60), or spouses who are incapacitated and cannot work. If there are children of the marriage, the "go back to work" rule could apply when the youngest child reaches a certain age.

Sometimes a spouse who may be required to pay alimony has significant debt to pay off at the time of the divorce. The prenup could make an exception for debt payments when calculating the income base of that spouse which will determine support, until the debt is paid off. For instance, the amount of debt payment to be deducted from the income base for alimony could be the average of debt payments during the preceding two years.

Prenuptial agreements typically have a "choice of law" provision that says which state's laws will apply to the construction, validity, and enforcement of the prenup, and also to the determination of legal issues. There might be an impetus in a prenup that provides for alimony to follow the state law with the most restrictive (or most generous) alimony enforcement provision.

If the choice of law is the state in which the parties reside (or will reside at time of enforcement), there is likely no problem in enforcing that choice of law provision. But what if the choice of law is a state that has no current or foreseeable relationship to the parties to the prenup and no connection to where the spouses live at the time of divorce? This is a very important issue in prenups, because according to the U.S. census, the number of Americans moving to another state in 2015 was about 7.5 million people, at a time when the U.S. population was about 320 million. That's pretty significant. That means many people will be living in a different state when their prenups come up for enforcement.

The UPAA has an express "choice of law" provision, but this applies only to matters of "construction" of an agreement. See UPAA Section 3(a)(7). Construction of an agreement means interpreting the legal significance of unclear or ambiguous terms.

Some courts have held that Section 3(a)(7) includes decisions regarding validity and enforceability of prenups, and some courts have held that it does not. The issue seems to hinge on public policy. Many states view financial protection of ex-spouses (as well as children) as a matter of welfare of its residents to be determined by its own state law under its applicable public policies. This notion is contemplated by UPAA Section 3(a)(8), which permits any matters to be set in a prenup that are "not in violation of public policy . . . " This means that a choice of law provision that applies to alimony may be disregarded at the time of enforcement, as can the alimony provision itself, under the public policy doctrine.

Another issue in prenups is whether there can be an enforceable provision that requires settlement of alimony issues through an arbitration process. The issue of public policy arises here, too. Some states require that spousal support arbitration (whether or not in a prenup) not be binding for public policy reasons. That means a party would have the right to contest the result of the arbitration required by the prenup in court, even if the prenup purports to say (as it often does) that such arbitration is binding.

In some situations, an outright alimony waiver may be supportable, unless situations change dramatically. These would include situations where both of the spouses are financially protected with income and/or assets (including some elder marriages), and for prenups between two working professionals who have assets and where financial situations did not change drastically at the time of divorce.

As you can see, there are many ways for you to try to control the situation by adopting your own alimony provision. It's best to create a fair and reasonable outcome even if not required by law, as that will support its enforceability, as well as creating goodwill between the future spouses.

Can a prenup determine child support?

A prenup cannot include child support or child custody issues. The court has the final say in all child-related issues, which are determined based on a "best interests of the child" standard. Child support, child custody, and visitation are issues of public policy over which the court retains jurisdiction. This is similar to the view that courts often take regarding spousal support – that there are three parties to a marriage, each of the spouses and the state.

Having said that, there are ancillary child-related issues that may be resolvable in a prenup, such as maintaining medical insurance and paying for college. Another area relating to children that may be addressed in a prenup is support and gifts provided to children of prior marriages during the marriage.

CHAPTER 16

WHAT ARE THE DRAWBACKS TO PRENUPS?

I have written extensively about the many downsides to having a prenup. See my articles on huffpost.com, mediate.com and mediatingprenups.com. These articles are based on my many experiences with clients negotiating prenups over the years in my law practice. My aim in writing this book is to help educate people as to all the issues – legal and personal – that result from setting up a financial agreement at the beginning of a marriage.

But this book is not all about doom and gloom. I have been able to help people envision wider possibilities of what terms can be drafted into a prenup as my experience as deepened. In this way, this book is about discovering innovative possibilities that create fairness for both sides. A prenup can provide protection for the moneyed-spouse or businessperson spouse, and yet express mutual love and caring, some of which is reflected by offering or sharing financial security. (See Chapter 17 "Is There a Way to Make Both Parties Happy?" and other material in this book.)

My hope is that this book will help people embark on sound and loving marriages and avoid the pitfalls that lead to distress and shame when negotiating a prenup. If I can move the needle – just a little bit – away from harsh prenups to more thoughtful ones, I am doing my job.

When a loving couple starts to engage in creating a prenup, it's usually initiated by one side, the more moneyed future spouse. The interchange and resulting legal process in getting a prenup negotiated, written, and signed is generally brutal and harsh. You might call it cruel.

The result can be profound. The after-effects of prenups linger in the background of a marriage. Memories of a partner's empathy and generosity – or the lack thereof – remain embedded in both sides' memories. Depending on the terms of the prenup and the negotiating process, this can be very bad for a couple's marital health. A prenup is not a trivial thing. It is of crucial importance. It needs to be considered very carefully.

In this chapter, I'll outline and describe the major problems caused by having a prenup. Most of what I say pertains to prenups for first marriages of relatively young people. These days, among the "professional" or "educated" class (who would be more likely to consider having a prenup), an early first marriage takes place somewhere between the ages of 28 to 38.

The drawbacks I discuss here don't apply as strongly to second marriages or for older couples. But there are still drawbacks to prenups in these situations. People need to be aware of the implications in arranging financial affairs even if they are middle-aged or older and embarking on a second (or third) marriage and especially if they have children from previous marriages. Some of these future spouses need to consider protecting each other financially as well.

Prenuptial agreement terms are almost always inherently unfair.

When people are entering into prenups, they are almost always taking away marital rights that a spouse would have under the laws of their state. Otherwise, why enter into one? The rights taken away are often significant property rights.

It is reasonable to want to avoid a court battle at the time of divorce. However, I have never seen a prenup that simply defines the resolution process in case of divorce and does nothing else. This would be the most efficient way to achieve this goal. A "legal process prenup" might require negotiation, then mediation, perhaps followed by a collaborative divorce process, with a final resolution by binding arbitration and applying the state's divorce laws to the process.

But the initiator of a prenuptial agreement fails to trust state laws. That future spouse doesn't appreciate the balance of good common sense and experience embodied in these laws, which have been carefully developed over generations. In every state, divorce law is a law of equity intended to reflect fair and reasonable solutions for what happens at the end of a marriage.

Divorce laws have been designed to provide solutions to all aspects of divorce, including the financial elements, considering every fact and circumstance in the situation of that particular marriage.

Choosing a "private" law to apply to your marriage by writing a prenup leaves out flexibility for the future, and it also changes the marital relationship. The prenup also might change the nature of the marriage itself in ways that were not intended. Uncoupling state law from a marriage by means of a prenup can often restrict some possible good solutions if the marriage ends in divorce.

Divorce law is reflective of the future and can determine how to solve the puzzle of a divorce based on facts as they are at the time of divorce. What if a divorce occurs 25 years after a marriage? What if one of the spouses becomes a stay-at-home spouse with a part-time career? Should that spouse really have no spousal support, even if the other party can afford it? Should that spouse have no interest in a business that was built up during the marriage? And yet prenups can contain these terms.

Divorce laws are (or seek to be) fair and flexible. Yet courts routinely enforce prenups that often give a spouse a tiny fraction of what the spouse would be entitled to under state law. Isn't this proof that the deal made in the prenuptial agreement years earlier was unfair to that spouse who is contesting it (or would want to contest it)? By and large, a contesting spouse would be the losing party in this type of litigation.

Many things unforeseeable at the time the prenuptial agreement is signed will likely happen in the course of a long marriage. Applying these state laws at the time of divorce can be more sensible than making up the laws at the time of a marriage. If one spouse gets a "better" result than he or she would obtain under state divorce laws, why isn't that better result by definition unfair and the result of overreaching?

There is a severe imbalance present and a lack of *quid pro quo* in most of these agreements. These are bound to affect marriages. After all, why should the spouse who has been cut out of their rightful benefits feel good about it?

Prenups leave a future spouse with two bad choices

A typical client that I see in my practice has been part of a couple that has been together for some time. They love each other, and marriage is on the horizon. Sometime before (or even after) the proposal, the future husband (I'll use this gender in the example for simplicity, and also because it's the more typical situation) brings up the idea of a prenuptial agreement. The future wife wants to marry her fiancé, but when she finally gets a draft copy, she sees that the prenuptial agreement is complex and far-reaching, generally applying to so much more than the fiancé had told her it would.

When she actually reads it, it seems to block her access to everything the future husband currently owns, might own in the future, and any possible support rights. It also gives her fiancé sole and complete control as to any inheritance she would receive from him at his death.

This perception is confirmed by her reviewing attorney, who is aghast at the meanness of it all. But she still wants to go ahead and marry the person she loves and understandably does not want to throw away the investment she has made in building the relationship.

Her attorney tries to soften the prenuptial agreement through negotiation, but the lawyer handling the prenuptial agreement for her fiancé refuses to budge. The attorney for the fiancé says, "It's just a business deal," or "The prenup will stay in a drawer, and only come out if needed." But marriage is not just a business deal. That's why the state is concerned with the rules of divorce and inheritance between spouses. Yes, it will stay in the drawer, but when it is pulled out, it can have a devastating effect on one party – the least powerful one.

The client now has the choice of breaking up or signing the agreement. It's a Hobson's choice with no satisfactory solution. That person must end the engagement or marry with the prenup. Most often, the person will take the second choice. This is an inherently coercive situation.

Prenuptial agreements are generally one-sided but are "dressed up" to pretend that there is consideration for the contract on both sides. This is done by having the party who is being cut out of marital rights make untrue representations when he or she signs the prenup. One of these is that often there is a state-law requirement that the parties make a representation that they consider the prenup to be "fair and reasonable." A less moneyed spouse will sign this routinely; most times, that spouse does not believe it.

Another one that I hate to see (but see it often in a draft sent by the more moneyed spouse's lawyer) is "Neither of us would have married but for entering into this agreement." It's a patent untruth. The only one who wants the agreement is the more moneyed future spouse (or his parents). The other party generally does not want one and has made it known throughout the process, although that wish has been disregarded.

The prenup will probably state that there are no other oral or written representations or understandings outside of the contract that might vary it. Often there *are* verbal promises made by the more moneyed future spouse at the time of the signing that he or she will soften the terms of the contract during the marriage. These promises may well affect the willingness of the less moneyed future spouse to sign it. Beware – these promises do not need to be kept when and if the marriage ends in divorce (or death).

Young people in first marriages don't realize the importance of what they're signing.

At the heart of a prenuptial agreement is a financial contract. This contract generally involves the largest financial settlement you will ever make in your life. Bigger than most business deals. Bigger than buying a home. Bigger than the management of a retirement account. A prenup deals with all property – past, present, and future real property, businesses, retirement, investments, inherited, earned, and unearned. It deals with the entire financial aspect of the upcoming marital partnership, which might be ongoing for many years.

Marriage relies on several major components – among these are love and affection, financial sharing and building security, and a total commitment to each other. A prenup can weaken and take a heavy toll on all these factors. Young people embarking on their first marriages generally have no idea how important the role of money and security is in a long-term marriage.

Money is often the root of many, if not most marital breakups. Marriages can thrive or fail because of financial issues. The more mutually supportive the spouses are (in all ways, not just financial), the stronger and more enduring the marriage.

Remember, the financial aspects of marriage are called "rights" for a reason. The definition of the word "right" includes morally good, justified, or acceptable, or being in accordance with what is just, good, or proper. When the benefits of marriage are withdrawn from one party, the marriage suffers. That person is no longer receiving those "rights," that is, by definition, not receiving what is "just, good, or proper."

By derogating rights, a prenup creates a distortion in the marriage at its outset, which may flow through the marriage as it progresses. You might say that it festers. This is generally inappropriate for first marriages (which is why there are so very few prenups for first marriages). It also can be inappropriate for second marriages.

Another way that prenups may affect the marital state is that their aim is to lessen chance and make things predictable. This may be good risk containment, but marriage is a joint venture. By venture I mean "adventure." The dictionary defines "venture" as "a risky or daring journey or undertaking." That's what marriage is. By settling many economic issues of the marriage at the outset, a prenup fails to give the couple a chance to act together to fully experience the joint venture of their marriage. The excitement that keeps a marriage together might be lessened.

Marriages thrive on the ability to create something together. A good marriage often has an entrepreneurial feeling of joint partnership efforts as well as sharing the product of those efforts. There is an element of risk as in any joint venture. This can be seen as a positive aspect. Marriages are cemented by the bad things that happen, as much as and maybe even more so than the good things.

I often wonder how it would feel to get married without that sense of a future to be discovered, without its risk of loss or gain. I think that the future of that marriage would be bleaker. The day-to-day experience of such a marriage might be tedious and uninteresting. In a way, this can cause *disengagement* in the marriage. When parties don't continue to be "engaged," the marriage often fails. As a result, by settling financial issues in your prenup, you may be weakening your marriage.

A prenup gives a party a ready-made exit from the marriage.

A major foundation of marriage is commitment. Leaving aside the sexual meaning, marriage is the ultimate pledge of loyalty and fidelity to another person.

We read about celebrity divorces in the news almost every day. Often there are multiple divorces by one celebrity. Our current president has been married three times, each marriage preceded by a prenup.

Why do these celebrities get divorced so often? Because they can. Everyone who is or has been in a long-term marriage knows that marriage has its ups and down. Marriage is not a love affair. It's something else – for better or for worse.

Most people are bound to their marriages financially. They literally will lose their house and their standard of living if they get divorced. Everything will be cut in half. I work with people in this situation frequently as a divorce lawyer. The economic effect of a divorce can be profound, and this encourages many people to stick with their marriages during the tough times. If they do, often they will find contentment and added strength in their marriage when they reach the other side.

Another way to think about this is that when there is "skin in the game," a person is motivated to make the game work. In a marriage with a prenup, there is often no "skin in the game." One of the parties can leave the marriage without many financial repercussions if there is a divorce. There's nothing keeping that person in that sometimes difficult and frustrating institution we call marriage.

Prenups create a lifetime of corrosive memories.

During the engagement of a couple, love is at its most romantic level. The feelings between the couple are very affectionate and tender. Then the prenup process starts. There is usually an "initiator" spouse and a "compliant" spouse.

The negotiations will always be remembered as callous by the compliant spouse. The dynamics of the negotiations set up a bad pattern for the marriage. The initiator spouse is essentially controlling and overruling the wishes of the other. The idea of a prenup, the usually harsh first draft from the future spouse's attorney, which is generally especially hurtful, will never be forgotten.

Negotiating a prenup is a very painful and disagreeable process. People start to question their choice of a marital partner. The negative memories linger beyond the negotiation and signing. Can you imagine walking down the aisle in a big wedding having unwillingly waived many of your marital rights? Starting with mediation can greatly improve the process.

But it's really hard for both of the parties entering into a prenup. The less moneyed spouse feels discarded, unloved, and untrusted. The more moneyed spouse feels selfish – like a bully or a cad. The idea of a prenup and the prenup negotiations themselves throw water on the intense love that the couple was feeling. Many people never recover. Often the honeymoon ends right there. Not a good way to begin a marriage. Not a good way to show love.

Marriage relies on trust, good faith, and fair dealing at the outset and throughout the marriage. It expects that the parties will be committed to an effort to have a lifetime partnership. The future spouse who pushes for a prenuptial agreement demonstrates a lack of faith in the other and a lack of commitment to the marriage. That prospective spouse also presumes a lack of fairness from the other in the event of divorce.

Prenups often don't consider including kindness in the divorce terms. People who love each other should want the best for each other, even if the marriage ends in divorce.

There is often a silent party to the prenup who is controlling the process.

A high number of first-marriage prenuptial agreements are initiated by the parents of the more moneyed spouse. They are the elephant in the room who essentially coerce their son or daughter into having one. Often the marriage is at a time when the parents are relatively young (in their 50s or early 60s), and the child still doesn't have many assets or has assets given to him or her by the parents.

Almost all of these now wealthy parents have self-made wealth. They had a "real" marriage without a prenuptial agreement. They are now forcing their child into a lesser model of marriage than they enjoyed. They are probably making a huge mistake and forever alienating the new spouse and that spouse's family, thus making the marriage weaker from the outset. By trying to preserve assets for their child and reduce their child's risk, they have increased their child's risk of divorce. They have planted the seeds of marital destruction.

Prenups often damage the relationship between the families of the betrothed. In many cases, the other future spouse's family may be less wealthy than the other but is doing quite well, thank you. They often find the idea of a prenup very insulting. Often that future spouse's family are against prenups on theoretical grounds – as many people are. They might view them as marriage breakers, as many people do. They might view them as interfering with their child's free choices in life.

The parents who want the prenup are the "shadow" parties. They often control the behavior of their child, and they basically force their child to have one. The threat of disinheritance is often made. But even without that, it puts that child in an untenable conflict between his parents and his future spouse. Most often, as I have seen in my practice, the child will never go against his or her parents and will not take the step of eloping without a prenup.

This may cause many bad results. Can you imagine having a nice Thanksgiving dinner with the folks who made their grown child make you sign an agreement waiving your marital rights?

The less moneyed future spouse's family feels humiliated and disrespected and never forgets the rebuff. Can you imagine the interaction at the wedding shower, the wedding itself, and the many times during the marriage that the parents of the spouses are all at a family gathering? This is part of the extended family history that just doesn't go away.

As a result, a spouse and her family may lose respect for the spouse that was unable to stand up to his parents. The financial control of the marriage by one party's family (especially when a family business is involved) disturbs the delicate balance of a marriage. This imbalance makes it more likely for the marriage to fail.

Another detrimental aspect is that often the wealthy family requires their child to use their attorney as his prenuptial agreement attorney. This basically puts the attorney in a conflict of interest because the child's interest may be quite different from his parents. The child may want a generous prenup if he has one at all. The parent's attorney will follow the parent's lead and do whatever the parents require. After all, if the attorney acts independently, he will lose an important client – the parents. This is always a bad dynamic in creating prenups and in their negotiation, but in my experience, is often the case.

Many lawyers representing parties in prenuptial agreements seem to have no sensitivity to the harm they cause the couple and simply act (or pretend) as if marriage is purely a business deal. There is a culture among attorneys (especially older ones) that their job is "risk containment." But marriage is not just a business deal and the loss a party sustains when the prenup is taken out of that drawer is significant. Most people don't forget about that during their marriage. As a result, ironically, with the intent of reducing (financial) risk, prenups increase the risk of divorce by uncoupling the equitable state laws that regulate the financial aspects of marriage and divorce.

In my opinion, seeking to reduce risk by encouraging someone to have a very harsh prenup is not good lawyering. It fails to consider the most valuable part of the client's future – his or her marriage. It supposes that money is everything. Reducing risk should not be the focus of the period immediately preceding a marriage. Thoughts about supporting or fostering the upcoming relationship should be primary.

People entering into prenups generally have misconceptions or spurious information.

One of the main reasons people seek prenups is because of misconceptions as to what the law provides. Another major reason is a reaction to advice given by friends and relatives who say that they were "burned" or treated unfairly in their own divorces. A third major reason is people now think that prenups are frequent and standard operating procedure. They are not. It's a media myth. They are rare and seldom entered into. (See Chapter 5.)

One major area of misconception is the division of premarital property in a divorce. Community property states, such as California, make it clear that premarital and inherited assets are not marital assets and therefore not divisible in a divorce as part of the marital partnership assets.

Some equitable property states such as Massachusetts take an equitable view of the division of premarital and inherited property in case of divorce. Some equitable property states such as New York, Maryland, and Virginia have prenup-type provisions that consider premarital and inherited property to be separate property.

But even in a state without those prenup-like protections, a number of factors will determine whether premarital and inherited property are ulti-mately included in the marital estate subject to division. Some of these are whether the property was held in a separate account and not commingled with marital property. Another important factor is whether it was needed and used to support the marital expenses or expected to provide security for the couple's elder years. Other important factors are the length of the marriage, the ages of the parties, their earning capacities, and whether the other spouse reasonably needs part of the premarital or inherited assets for his or her secu-rity after the marriage ends. (See Chapter 7.)

People who are concerned about their premarital and inherited assets but don't particularly want a prenup would do well to investigate the law regarding premarital and inherited assets applicable to their state. Knowledge is a good thing. Application of that law may provide a satisfactory result. Maybe a prenuptial agreement won't be necessary.

Another misconception that people have is what happens to your estate when you die. It is not true in any state that a surviving spouse must be ben-eficiary of one's entire estate. You can write a will that has the provisions you want, subject to some state law protections for a spouse. It is true that a spouse has the right to "elect against" a will or estate plan when a spouse is excluded or receives very little upon a spouse's death. But these rights may be in alignment with what you (and your future spouse) intend, so you could draft your last will accordingly. (See Chapter 7.)

Another major reason that propels people toward thinking they want a prenup is what they hear from family members and friends who have been "burned" by their divorces. If you actually probe these circumstances, you will probably find in most cases the result was a fair divorce under the laws of that state. When someone says, "I had to give my ex-wife everything," that gener-ally translates into "I had to give my wife half of all marital property developed during the marital partnership." That's the law in every state. Don't believe everything you hear.

Prenuptial agreements that provide rules for divorce but often lack inheritance provisions.

Many prenuptial agreements have extensive provisions relating to what happens in the event of a divorce but may leave the issue of inheritance "open." These prenups lack any provisions on inheritance if the marriage is intact when one spouse dies. There are a number of problems with this approach.

Most prenup terms are one-sided, taking away potential marital rights from the other party. But if these people are getting married, and if it's a first marriage with an intent to raise children, it makes sense that the surviving spouse be the beneficiary of the other's estate, or at least be protected in the event of the death of a spouse. After all, when you marry, you are saying your spouse is *numero uno*.

People often forget after marriage that their parents or siblings are still beneficiaries of their non-probate assets such as life insurance and retirement accounts. Sometimes an ex-spouse is still listed as a beneficiary of one of these. This needs to be carefully reviewed and addressed upon marriage. When a couple does an estate plan, doing this due diligence is part of the process.

A prenuptial agreement can specify that the couple should complete an estate plan within a certain amount of days or months after their marriage. It can provide a "floor" level of what part of their estate will go to the surviving spouse upon death. Many prenups for first marriages have a minimum level of 80 percent (or more) to each other if the marriage is ongoing at the time of a spouse's death.

If the prenuptial agreement is silent on this, problems may arise. There is usually general language in prenups that say that each party cannot contest the other party's estate plan or take the benefit of spousal rights, such as taking the "elective" or "forced" share upon a spouse's death. These provisions and the lack of an inheritance "floor" level can leave a surviving spouse unintentionally without resources after an intact and happy marriage ends with the death of one of the parties. Oral promises to change an estate plan after the marriage are not enforceable.

People contract away their rights due to gender insecurities and values.

This problem goes both ways.

Men will often sign away their marital rights without giving it much thought or analysis. They do not want to appear "weak" and "unmanly" to their future spouse and her family. Men tend to be (or want to be) fiercely financially independent. Relying on a female spouse's assets or income upsets the usual expectation by both partners to the marriage that the male partner will be the primary support of the family unit and the more active money-maker in the relationship. As a result, male future spouses are often willing to sign the most restrictive prenups without negotiation. This can be a very big mistake.

Women will often sign away marital rights because they don't want to be seen as gold diggers.

In speaking with these women clients, it is clear that the future spouse's money is not the root of the relationship, although the power that money conveys may be part of the attraction to the fiancé. But the less moneyed spouse often over-compensates to prove she is not a gold digger. She does this by being willing to sign a prenuptial agreement that does not protect her rights. Often this type of prenup puts her in a worse position than if she had married someone with no money who was starting from scratch but would share everything with her (and she him) without a prenup. Ironic, isn't it?

Young millennial women often want to sign away their marital rights because they believe they should be forever financially independent from their husbands. They believe themselves to be putting forward a feminist vision of marriage. But by doing so, they are taking away one of the "legs" of the chair of marriage – the financial partnership.

These situations can, and often do, end up very badly.

At the beginning of a marriage, both parties to the prenup might be working and earning money, but things may change during a marriage. Working roles might change. Marriage is "for better or for worse," if you remember.

Prenups need to look into the unfathomable future to provide reasonable security for each spouse when the marriage ends. Attorneys counseling clients on prenups need to be very careful to describe the circumstances in which their client's waiver may come back to haunt them. That's what good legal counseling is all about.

These clients may be full of regrets if they've waived their marital rights without considering what their real needs and rights might be after a medium- or long-term marriage in an unknowable future. I have seen that happen.

Specific prenup provisions and their dangers.

There are some specific provisions that are included in many prenups that, in my view, fail to support marriages and can chip away at marital stability.

Ownership of the marital home.

In my opinion, one of the worst situations for first marriages is when a couple lives in a primary residence that they don't equally and jointly own. Having a shared house is a primal event for a married couple. It gives married people a closer marital bond if they live in a house that they both own. They both feel more invested in the sense of having close and warm personal connection in the place where they live. They will both want to work on the house to improve it and make it more of a "home." They will both willingly put "sweat equity" into it.

When "separate property" of one spouse is used for the primary residence, or if it is owned by a trust set up by the parents of one of spouses, it upends this vital sharing of a co-owned home. One of the spouses also loses the security that a house might eventually provide once it's paid off. It may be a "house," but not a "home" for one of the parties.

It's better to have the couple put a small down payment on the house and take out a mortgage. They can pay it off slowly with their own earnings (or gifted property). It's important that both parties equally own it – even if the couple could buy a more expensive house using separate property or parental property contributions that are tracked and remain separate.

Sharing gain when separate property is contributed into assets.

One provision often seen in prenups is how gain is shared when there is a separate property component to an asset. Some future spouses and their attorneys seek to use the "business" type result, where gain would be allocated proportionately to the investment of separate property in the asset. In other words, if one party contributed 90 percent of the purchase price and the other 10 percent, 90 percent of the gain upon sale would belong to the higher contributor. Thus the more moneyed spouse is the big winner.

While this makes sense in a purely business contract, it may not make such good sense in a marriage if you want your marriage to thrive. There are other ways to structure the gain that will help cement the marital relationship.

What about a return of the down payment to each, and then split the gain equally? Would that really be so averse to the more moneyed spouse? Doing this will increase the feeling of a participation in the joint marital venture, which is good for the health of a marriage. This also gives the other spouse an incentive to freely give sweat equity to increase the value of the property. Anyway, does the more moneyed spouse really need to retain all that gain?

Dangers of vesting trigger dates.

Vesting of separate assets and income into marital property can be very helpful in a prenup. (See Chapters 8 and 17.) However, trigger dates can have an intense effect on marital relations.

What happens if there is a major trigger of vesting at the five-year anniversary? Unless the couple is lobotomized, they (especially the more moneyed spouse) may start to ruminate about their marriage at about the fourth anniversary. That spouse may start to question it. Is it working, or is it not? Is it a good enough marriage or not? Will it survive or fail? Although vesting provisions might be very good, these trigger dates can also cause marital disruption. That's why I generally recommend that the vesting be done on a monthly basis rather than a yearly or multiyear basis.

Sunset clauses can be good or bad.

Sunset clauses can be a good thing. These are clauses that say something to the effect that "on the 15th anniversary of the marriage, this agreement shall be null and void and have no further effect." Sunset clauses can end the prenup after the marriage's durability has been tested by time. Yes, marriages end in divorce after 15 years. But after a certain number of years have elapsed, people acknowledge that they are in (or at least intend to be in) a lifetime marriage, and accept the normal financial consequences if they eventually divorce.

But sunset clauses have a downside, similar to trigger dates of vesting described above. The date the prenup self-destructs looms, encouraging a natural questioning of the marriage as the trigger date draws nearer. No marriage is perfect, but this trigger date puts more pressure on people to question their marriage. The result of a marriage that ends before the sunset date may be vastly different than the result if there is no longer a valid prenup. That's another reason to have gradual vesting of assets if the couple is considering a sunset clause.

There is another downside to sunset clauses. If the prenup is one that includes estate and death provisions, these will also be nullified by the sunset clause. A spouse will need to rely on the partner's good faith not to disinherit him or her, and will need to rely on the state law protections if disinheritance occurs or if a spouse is a beneficiary of a stingy estate.

Another downside of sunset clauses is that they can wipe out the couple's choice of procedures for divorce, which can be specified in a prenup. A couple can choose mediation, collaborative law, and/or arbitration as an alternative to litigation in their prenup. This binding choice is lost if the prenup is nullified by a sunset clause on a certain date. So, like with any marriage, you have to rely on the good faith and fair dealing of your spouse if you run into problems and eventually divorce.

CHAPTER 17

IS THERE A WAY TO MAKE BOTH PARTIES HAPPY?

I n writing this chapter, I reviewed the drawbacks to prenups that I described in Chapter 16. I then looked at ways to find a solution to each of the downsides described. There are indeed possible fixes for each of them. Analyzing the negatives of prenups and discovering what can make a prenup satisfactory to each of the parties is really one of the core messages of this book. That is not to say that everyone should have a prenup. There are very good reasons not to, as most marrying couples have decided.

Wanting to see what others had to say about how to make both parties happy when a prenup was in the works, I consulted Google. I was quite disappointed that my search pulled up very little on this topic. My search did pull up these articles: "How to Ask for a Prenup without Causing a Breakup" at BusinessInsider.com, and "How to Convince Your Fiancé to Get a Prenup" at GQ.com. Those were not exactly what I was hoping to find.

I think the information in this chapter will be of great interest to people thinking about prenups, their friends, their families, and their financial advisors. These techniques can help mitigate the harshness of many prenups.

Some of the questions addressed in this chapter include how to establish and balance and control issues between the spouses in a prenup, and how reasonable financial security can be established for the less moneyed spouse. Control, participation, and security are important in a marriage, whether or not there is a prenup. This chapter also addresses how to project into the future in a prenup and the importance of estate-planning commitments.

Remember, it's an agreement, after all.

First of all, people need to remember that a prenuptial agreement is an *agreement*.

That means the parties to the contract should actually agree. But that generally doesn't happen with prenups. The usual case (at least in first marriages) is that one party wants a prenup and the other party doesn't. If the parties don't agree and the contract is signed anyway, it will likely be an enforceable prenup, but it won't be a good contract.

This raises a problem in the negotiation stage if one party doesn't want the prenup. The party and his or her attorney might lobby for better terms, wanting to make the prenup satisfactory to that party. But often the resistance (usually by the attorney for the more moneyed fiancé) is fierce.

A very good strategy to avoid this situation is for the spouse who doesn't particularly want a prenup to start the process by sharing with the more advantaged spouse the various techniques in this book that can be used to reasonably meet the more moneyed spouse's desire for protection, but can also benefit the less moneyed spouse. Ask that future spouse to ask his or her attorney to build these provisions into a draft. Having provisions in the prenup that will cause their beloved to smile rather than weep is a good thing. (Read on to find out what these might be.)

If you are the less moneyed spouse and are faced with the prospect of a prenup, see if you can encourage your fiancé to get into the mediation process to mutually decide upon the terms. (See Chapter 20.) Share emails you receive from your attorney that talk about how to make the terms more conducive to supporting the marriage. Have discussions about these with your fiancé. If your fiancé's attorney fails to follow his client's instructions, keep raising the issue with your fiancé.

See a therapist together during the process. It's best to find a therapist who is very experienced with divorce, finances, and family issues. A good way to find one would be by searching your statewide Collaborative Law website. Therapists with this type of sensitivity and experience will be listed under coach, facilitator, or neutral process coach in the Collaborative Law organization's website.

What does consideration have to do with it?

The legal definition of a contract is that there must be mutual assent, consideration, and capacity to contract. The last requirement should be easy to meet for most people getting married. But what about mutual assent and consideration?

Mutual assent is one of the core problems with prenups if one party really doesn't want one. Assent might be given unwillingly by one of the parties, but not to the point where one could say the assent was "coerced" and therefore making the contract legally void.

Normally, a contract needs to be supported by *consideration*. That means something of value needs to be exchanged between the parties to make it a binding contract. Another way to put it is that a promise is made, and someone gets paid for the promise. Here's an example: "I will plow your driveway, and you will pay me $50 for doing it." In a prenup, it could be something like, "If you waive alimony, I'll divide marital property 75/25 percent in your favor instead of 50/50 percent."

But this doesn't happen in prenups. In fact, modern prenup law says that consideration is not needed to make a prenup binding. See Uniform Prenuptial Agreements Act (UPAA) (1983), Section 2, and Uniform Premarital and Marital Agreement Act (UPMAA) (2012), Section 6.

In the comment to UPAA, Section 2, the drafters note the "almost universal rule" that the marriage itself is the consideration for the prenuptial agreement. He agrees to marry you. In exchange, you give up marital rights. But you have also given him yourself as a spouse. Haven't you overpaid? It seems like you have paid him twice. Once by marrying him, and once by giving up your marital rights. It doesn't seem like a very good bargain. The lack of consideration causes a problem, because the person giving up rights often believes that they have been "had" or taken advantage of. Not a good way to start a marriage.

Remember that the word "consideration" has meanings outside of the contract meaning. It's derived from the word "consider," as in "taking into account" or "think" or "propose."

What does "consideration" mean?

The word "considerate" is a close cousin to that word. It's where the legal term "consideration" came from. The word's early meaning was "marked by deliberation," or the character of a "deliberate" or "prudent" person. But starting from around 1700, it started meaning showing care or empathy towards another person.

Here are some of the other meanings of "considerate" I found:

- Showing concern for the rights and feelings of others.
- Having regard for the needs of another.
- Aware of and respecting other people's feelings.
- Being respectful of others.
- Having regard for others.
- Being mindful of others.
- Characterized by consideration or regard for another's circumstances or feelings.
- Not heedless or unfeeling.
- Careful not to inconvenience or harm others.
- Paying attention to the wishes of another.
- Being kind.

Keep these in mind as you go through the process of formulating and negotiating your prenup. Reclaiming that core meaning of consideration as being *considerate* is of utmost importance in finding a way to make both of you happy, or at least content about your prenup and the process. After all, one of the hallmarks of a good marriage is for spouses to be considerate of one another. That's why prenups are often so jarring to the future spouses embarking on a marriage; it's because they are often inconsiderate.

This chapter describes the many things you can do to make the prenup more "considerate."

Some ways to make a generous prenup.

Create a signing bonus. If you intend to get married, you plan to have a lifetime relationship with your future spouse. If you are considering a prenup, you probably have enough money to be generous and to part with some of it.

You can create a signing bonus by making an outright gift to your fiancé upon the marriage, or by putting some funds into a joint account. A ring is a nice symbol (and generally much appreciated), but hard cash or a down payment on a home is even better. It may make your fiancé feel that you believe in the longevity of your marriage.

Pay off premarital debt or have a plan to do it.

Some future spouses going into a marriage may have accumulated some debt. In general, the more moneyed future spouse has the wherewithal to pay debts in full and is not burdened by them at the time of marriage.

I've run across situations where a fiancé cannot go on a vacation with his or her future spouse, because that person can't afford it and the fiancé will not pay for it.

People accumulate debt for many reasons. Often it is student loan debt for undergraduate education, graduate school, or both. The more moneyed future spouse likely had parents that financed their education, or at least the majority of it.

Often when you decide to marry someone, you may need to overcome the differences in family wealth or circumstances. The less moneyed spouse probably brings many things to the table that the other spouse may not. That's why you care enough about that person to marry him or her. Also, the education that person received (that caused the student loan debt) will (hopefully) benefit the marriage, either financially or in other ways, such as providing good companionship, which is an important aspect of marriage.

Often a person brings other types of debts to the marriage – credit card debts, tax debts, car loans, deferred dental work, and the like. Try not to blame the other for the accrued debts or feel guilty if you're the one with the debts. If you've accumulated debt, part of the reason (maybe most of it) is that you do not earn enough money to adequately support yourself and pay taxes. That is the plight of many people in this country. It's hard to make ends meet.

When people get married, they take each other as they are, with their good points and bad points. People getting married (perhaps luckily) are generally blinded to each other's bad points during their engagement, which probably aids in the perpetuation of the human race. As they say, "love is blind."

Perhaps one of the future spouses is not "that good with money." So what! That future spouse may be good at other things that you're not good at. There is no reason to punish that person for debt. Anyway, if you're in the market for having a prenup, money scarcity is probably not an issue for you.

A really good way to cement a marriage is to have a plan for the payment of a spouse's debt that's set forth in the prenup. View it as a form of a wedding gift. A gesture of good faith. But most prenups reflexively take the opposite tack and consider premarital debts solely as the problem of the debtor spouse. I believe this is a bad approach to prenups and a bad approach to marriage.

The debt can be initially the responsibility of the incurring party but then vest into marital debt during the course of a term of years. Or the prenup can be worded such that the debt is joint upon the marriage, and that if it is not fully paid off at the time of divorce, it gets divided equally (or in a different manner). The prenup might also have a payment plan saying that joint income will pay off the debt within, say, seven years and show a schedule of payment, or the payments could come from the wealthier spouse's separate assets or income from those separate assets. In other words, there are many ways to handle this other than putting the debt firmly on the shoulders of the less moneyed spouse, which is the boilerplate term contained in practically every prenup.

Some prenups may make the joint payoff of premarital debts "precatory," to use a legal term. This is aspirational language rather than a legal requirement. Attorneys don't generally like to use aspirational language in contracts, including prenups, because there might be an argument that the precatory language is enforceable rather than aspirational. But if someone doesn't want to make a commitment in the prenup, perhaps having precatory language is a good middle ground. It can be couched with the language in the prenup that "this does not create an enforceable right" or a similar phrase.

Considering the future spouse's debt as marital debt at the outset may make both parties feel better. And when it's all paid off, the original debtor party will have more funds to contribute to the household. If the debt can be paid off at the beginning of the marriage, so much the better. An intent to help one's spouse to relieve a spouse's financial burden is a strong gesture of love, commitment, and generosity in the marriage at the outset. It's a way of making both future spouses happy.

Make the process good.

Perhaps that should be rephrased, "Make the process as good as it can be." Nineteen times out of 20 that's very difficult to do since the prenup is usually wanted and initiated by only one of the parties to the marriage.

Here are some suggestions of how to make things somewhat better during the process of formulation and negotiation:

Give it plenty of lead time. I've seen many cases where parties begin to negotiate prenuptial agreements very close to the wedding and even after the invitations have been sent out. This is not conducive for arm's-length bargaining about a financial contract that may affect the next 50 years of your life.

"Meeting of the minds" is a commonly used phrase in contract law. It describes the doctrine that there must be a common understanding when two people enter into a valid contract. That understanding should be given freely and totally. When there is a wedding looming, people may not contract freely. Not going through with the wedding because there is no meeting of the minds would be socially embarrassing, as well as a huge disappointment. What usually happens is that one party gives in and makes financial accommodations in the prenup that he or she might not otherwise make.

Another problem that may arise is that a future spouse has often invested significant time in the relationship prior to the initiation of the prenup. People are generally unwilling to give up their investment in their relationship and will tend to accept a prenup instead of the very unappealing alternative – to break up.

But people don't bring up the idea of a prenup on the first date, or even the second date. It's a thought that might be brewing for months and years as the relationship grows more committed. Or it might be sprung on a party by his or her parents, usually as a demand and not just as a suggestion.

Once the parties begin to discuss it, they need to do it with care. Remember, a prenup is likely the most important contract that you will ever sign, as it affects finances during your entire marriage (which may be lifelong), and also changes the nature and dynamics of your lives together.

So make appointments together to talk to mediators, meet with therapists, and meet with pastoral counselors or ministers, priests, or rabbis, if you're so inclined. Get other professional people's views on prenups. Be wary of suggestions from lay people including parents, siblings, and families. Try to keep in mind your commitment to each other and your intent to make each other secure and happy in the marriage as you process the possibility of a prenup and its terms.

Choose your attorneys carefully. Resist the suggestion (sometimes an order) for the initiating party to use the family attorney of his or her parents. It's good to choose both attorneys together, although one attorney can't represent both parties. It's best if they are independent of the parties' families. Think about starting the process with mediation rather than with attorneys. (See Chapter 21 for more information on how to choose an attorney or mediator.)

Be knowledgeable.

Read everything you can about prenups. Do this together, as a joint reading process. Read out loud to each other before dinner. Make this a joint venture and a joint exploration. Remember, if you proceed, you can make it a customized plan, just for the two of you.

Be sure to find out what your state law would provide if your marriage ended in divorce. Find out the inheritance laws in your state if the marriage ends due to the death of a spouse. Evaluate your chances of relocating to another state at some point. Look at the differences in the laws of equitable distribution states and community property states. (See Chapter 7.) You can find out a lot about these laws on the internet.

It may make sense for the two of you to see a lawyer together for information on your state's laws. The lawyer will not (and should not) give you advice as to whether or not you need a prenup, because the two of you may have differing interests. This lawyer won't be able to represent each of you separately in connection with your prenup, but it would be a good place to start gathering information.

Don't believe the horror stories you hear. Sometimes people feel "burned" by their divorces, but the result they generally get in a divorce is fair and reasonable according to the laws of their state. The court systems are not some sort of demonic hell. They are places where judges are attempting to deliver equitable results to parties. Fairness is the aim. If your sister tells you that you should have a prenup because a friend of hers got "burned," process this with a healthy dose of skepticism. Or you can take the attitude of accepting the laws of divorce in your state that would be generated under the state's system if your marriage ends in divorce and decide *not* to have a prenup.

A major but semi-true misconception.

Some people enter into marriage with significant student loan and credit card debt. This may make a future spouse think he or she needs a prenup to avoid liability after the marriage on the other's pre-existing debt. But in most cases, married people are not liable for each other's separate debts (whether premarital or postmarital).

A debtor spouse's credit rating may impair the couple's ability to get joint loans on credit, including a mortgage loan on a home. This is not an insurmountable problem, but it's better if it's not a surprise. Then the new couple can work together toward the joint goal of debt reduction or decide to hold assets in one name until the debt and credit ratings are cleared up. (See Chapter 7 for more information on what assets separate debts can be collected upon.)

When viewing each other's finances, you can also get an understanding of the other party's use of debt, and in particular, credit card debt. Is the unpaid amount growing every year? What was the debt used for? What is the interest rate on the debt? Finding out this information is unromantic, but it's important to be apprised of each other's financial situations and fiscal behavior before you marry. You probably both still want to go forward with the marriage (because money isn't everything), but you will have a clearer sense of how to proceed financially in your marriage.

Make the prenup fair.

Both of you need to think about and analyze "What *is* fair?" Is it fair for the person who earns more money to keep more money in his or her name if there is a divorce? Is it fair for a person to keep his or her premarital assets under every circumstance? Is it fair for a person to keep an inheritance from her parents if it's a long marriage and the other person has no potential for inheriting from his parents?

What you need to do is to take every possible prenup term and test it against every factual situation that could occur in a long-term marriage. These include periods of joblessness, investment gains and losses, unexpected increases or decreases in income, financial setbacks, disability of one of the parties and caring for the disabled spouse, children that need financial help, disabled children, helping parents, etc. Spin all these possible scenarios and test the possible prenup terms. Does the prenup work? Might the prenup lose its vitality if any of these circumstances come to pass? Will it have a fair result under every conceivable circumstance? How can these situations be addressed in the prenup?

Following are just a few examples of future events that you would need to assess when considering the terms of your prenup, or if you are making the decision as to whether or not to have one.

The first one is typical. It happens often. What happens if one of you leaves the job market to care for the household and children? How do you assess the value of creating a home with all that entails? What do the terms of the prenup do if this division of labor occurs in the marriage?

Here's another one. What happens if one of you receives an inheritance at a time when the financial results of the marital venture have decreased? What if the marital property has decreased to levels not sustainable for old age of the non-inheriting party and there is a divorce?

And here's one more that comes up often. How will you treat the children

of your previous marriages if one of you dies? How will you balance your financial allegiance to the children from your first marriage with your care and loyalty toward your new spouse? What happens to the less moneyed spouse if
he or she is the surviving party? Does the agreement adequately provide for
that spouse?

Think about the effects that prenup terms have on control issues.

Be sensitive to the effect that terms of prenups have on the dynamics of
the marriage. Discuss them together as you embark on this journey.

For instance, many prenups have a monolithic rule that premarital property and proceeds and gains from premarital property are separate property.
What results is that a person with separate property will have a natural tendency to be aware of it and try to maximize it. It's human nature. I call it
"hoarding" behavior, like the old lady (or man) whose house is piled up with
newspapers, empty food containers, and a zillion cats.

This inclination is a predictable result of most prenups. Also, there's the
attention factor. A person with separate property will also spend time and
attention away from the marriage in thinking about and trying to maximize it.
That takes time from the marriage. Some of the thoughts can be quite petty.
For instance, imagine that you have just taken $100 in cash out of a separate
property bank account. You may actually think about it before you spend the
money on family food, and may choose not to. These types of thoughts are
detrimental to marriage.

Instead of a bright-line rule that isolates separate property, its gains, and
its proceeds from marital property, you can have a mechanism that puts some
of this into a joint account that is marital. Have it be a requirement, not just
voluntary – otherwise the more moneyed spouse may have too much control.
(See below regarding vesting regimens in a prenup.)

John Fiske, a lawyer/mediator practicing in Massachusetts, articulates
that the main issues challenging ongoing marriages come down to "control"
and "acknowledgment." In marriages, control needs to be shared or at least
alternated. A spouse's control needs to benefit the other spouse. Spouses
need to feel that their efforts are acknowledged and appreciated. If these two

things happen, the marriage will likely thrive.

But the terms of typical prenups often disturb the free flow of control and acknowledgment. One party has more financial control than the other. There is also an implicit decrease in acknowledgment of the efforts of the less moneyed spouse. Who is to say that a hedge fund manager is more valuable than an elementary school teacher even though he earns more? They both have jobs that serve a purpose in society. These two people married for a reason.

Lack of earned income sharing (which I've seen in some prenups) is generally quite destructive for these reasons. Some prenups (or marital arrangements) require payments of expenses proportionally to income earned. On the face of it, it looks fair, but it may not be.

The problem with this is that if one spouse's earned income is higher than the other's, even a proportional dividing of expenses may leave the lower earner with no excess funds for discretionary expenses. This can cause an imbalance in the lifestyle afforded to each spouse, and will create bad feelings and marital problems.

It is best to consider income earned during the marriage as shared, producing shared assets if any is left over after paying living expenses. This is what the law provides in all states (see Chapter 7) and for good reason. The sharing of the efforts underlies the generosity and contribution needed in a stable marriage and provides joint control, which is healthy for marriage. (See Chapter 4.)

Be a minimalist.

I can't count how many times I've heard a client say, "My fiancé said there'd only be one restriction in the prenup!" But then when the first draft is presented, more than just the inherited property was considered separate property. And many other unexpected rules were applied, such as a waiver of all inheritance rights and a waiver of spousal support.

This is a nasty surprise and has many repercussions.

One of the problems is that standard operating procedure of the wealthier spouse's lawyer is to provide the old-fashioned classic prenup, which separates everything, except maybe earned income during the marriage. That future spouse that engaged that attorney should be very clear about what his or her aims are prior to the first draft. That person should review the draft carefully before it is sent to the fiancé or the fiancé's attorney to make sure only those aims are addressed.

The draft should be returned to the attorney to be redrafted and not provided to the other future spouse until it actually reflects the intent of the initiating party. If there are changes in scope during the process of getting the first draft done, they should be discussed with the other future spouse before that spouse sees the first draft, so there are no surprises and there is a chance to negotiate changes before the terms are set in paper.

One of the biggest concerns for people wanting prenups is that they don't want to risk the chance of ugly, expensive, and drawn-out litigation in case the marriage doesn't work out.

Divorce litigation is serious business, and it's understandable that people embarking on marriage, especially those previously divorced or who witnessed their parents' ugly divorce, would like avoid this. There are so many examples of painful, protracted, and expensive divorce litigations in the media and among everyone's friends and families. That makes an interest in litigation avoidance reasonable (although it's also reasonable to trust the good faith of one's life partner).

A prenup does not have to have everything in it. A prenup can simply seek to determine how the divorce process would unfold. The most bare-bones version of a prenup is one that simply chooses the resolution process in the event of a divorce. As discussed in Chapter 6, many divorce methods are used to avoid litigation and resolve divorces. These include mediation, collaborative law, and arbitration.

Or a process can be set in the prenup where the parties can choose the method at the time of a divorce. If they cannot choose, binding arbitration would be specified as the default dispute resolution method. Even though there is a possibility of litigation even here (over the enforceability of the prenup or non-arbitrable issues), it would go very far in eliminating or reducing litigation if that dark day of the end of the marriage comes to pass.

Even if a prenup has other aims, such as protecting premarital property and inheritances, it should be written as narrowly as possible, and the other party should be on board after being advised by an attorney.

Don't use an off-the-shelf prenup.

Off-the-shelf prenups make people feel bad. I call them "cookie-cutter" prenups, because they vary so little and are often sent out by lawyers as the first draft to their clients who want prenups. Cookie-cutter prenups are like form letters. An off-the-shelf agreement may contain overstated and unduly restrictive provisions that do not reflect the actual aims of the contracting couple.

They are extremely negative and don't express the love and connection felt by the parties. They reflect the most negative possible aspects of a relationship. They put everything in dollars and cents. There is nothing individualized about the contract.

The prenups I draft always have a "Statement of Facts" section that is fairly long. It explains something about each party to the agreement, sometimes indicates the reasons they want to have a prenup, and can include their specific aims. It has room to express concern for each other and the kind of partnership that they want to have. It sets the stage for the "rules" in the prenup that follow. It allows each party to be "heard" in the prenup, and for them, as a couple, to be "heard" together by stating their mutual aims. It really softens and humanizes the process.

It's good for each of the parties to have "skin in the game."

One of the problems with having a prenup is that it can be so protective for one of the spouses that he or she can easily leave a marriage unscathed. It makes it much easier to leave a marriage when the going gets tough if you won't be financially hurt by a divorce. Most people who are married credit the word "commitment" as a big factor in the longevity of their relationship. That's why many people view prenups as a ready-made exit plan. It often is.

But it is possible to include a financial penalty for a breakup that will make a person think seriously about the financial ramifications of divorce. It would be for the sake of the marriage. In modern parlance, the person now has "skin in the game." A person with "skin in the game" will more likely endeavor to make the marriage work.

Drafting one of these "skin in the game" provisions as a penalty can be rather challenging. Does it apply only if the wealthier spouse files for divorce? Does it apply if there is a joint filing? What if abuse or addiction is leading to the divorce?

Fight against outside control by "shadow" parties.

One of the most hurtful aspects of the prenup process is when an outside party (usually the parents of the wealthier spouse) control the situation. These "shadow parties" often choose the lawyer for their child and specify the terms the prenup has to have. It's very difficult for their child to go against their parents, and yet by complying, he or she is not fully supporting the other future spouse or the marriage.

Young people in first marriages have strong connections to their parents and siblings. The love between the young couple may be strong, but financial allegiance has not built up yet. Often they come into the marriage with their siblings or parents named as beneficiaries of their retirement assets and life insurance policies and don't think about changing them to their new spouse after the wedding. The provision to re-designate is an important one to bring to the attention of these new spouses. It can be required in a prenup.

Many times, I hear that a child being controlled by the parents tells their partner that they can sign the restrictive prenup, but that the more moneyed spouse will do "better" in being generous to the other spouse during the marriage (and at divorce), even though they are not required to do so. This is an unenforceable side agreement that will be rendered a nullity by the boilerplate terms found in every prenup.

The child of the wealthier parents should think about advocating for his or her future spouse. The child can initiate joint meetings with his or her parents. The issues can be discussed openly, and perhaps less drastic means of "wealth protection" can be designed to satisfy the parents, their grown child, and the new family member.

Engaging an independent, non-family attorney at the outset is a very important step by the spouse from the wealthy family. Having some protective and generous provisions stay in the prenup can go a long way to making the other future spouse happy with the prenup and happy with the process. That other future spouse may not then feel so "burned" by the prenup. This will permit a good start for the marriage.

Provide something for what you are taking away.

To follow up on the earlier discussion about legal "consideration," most prenups don't require or have any. Rights are taken away but generally not conferred. But why is that? If someone is wealthy enough to have a prenup, why not give some consideration to their future spouse (other than the marriage)? It's good policy.

For instance, most "off-the-shelf" prenups have provisions relating to separate property, but they have no provisions regarding what happens if the marriage ends with the death of one of the spouses. The boilerplate provisions will make a waiver of inheritance rights binding. A spouse can disinherit you after a lifetime marriage.

Providing specified and generous inheritance rights (particularly in a first marriage) is one way of proving consideration. There are other techniques that can be used in prenups that provide some consideration for the rights a future spouse is waiving.

Vesting clauses: Having clauses and provisions that vest separate property into marital property is a very good way to soften the harshness of prenups and provide some consideration to a less moneyed spouse.

With vesting clauses, you slice and dice. It's like picking one from column A and one from column B from the old Chinese restaurant menus of the '50s and '60s.

You can vest income of separate assets and/or the separate assets themselves. Or you can vest some of the income and/or some of principal of the assets. You can also vest the gain in value of separate property and keep the principal with the party who owned it at the time of the marriage. Or you can give the owner of the separate property some return on principal and vest the rest into marital property. For instance, an imputed interest at the federal short-term interest rate defined by the Internal Revenue Service can be applied, or the actual return if less. Or you can use a cost-of-living adjustment

(COLA) index from the U.S. Department of Labor's Bureau of Labor Statistics. The possibilities are really endless.

The vesting can start in a certain year of the marriage and could go up to 100 percent, but it could also be some lesser amount. If 100 percent vested, this would mean all of that asset or income and/or gain from the asset, depending on your choice and agreement, would become marital property at some point. But remember, that means only forgoing half of it, as the original owner will retain half.

In a prenup, you have the option to decide how to divide marital property in case of divorce. You can divide it equally, you can divide it equitably, or you can divide it by some other method. You get to choose. If a spouse has $10 million in separate assets and the other spouse has $1 million, perhaps a 50-50 split of marital assets may not make sense.

For vesting schedules, you can choose trigger anniversaries or have monthly vesting. I've seen straight-line vesting with a certain percentage each year (or month) starting at a certain anniversary. I've also seen vesting where the percentages start out smaller and the applicable percentages increase as the marriage proves itself to be durable.

Having great changes in vesting at certain years of marriage are triggers that can put a lot of pressure on the marital relationship. For instance, if there is a jump in vesting percentages at five years or ten years or 15 years, the more moneyed spouse might start thinking about the financial ramifications of continuing the marriage a year before the triggers. It is possible that the couple has totally forgotten about the prenup and its terms. But more likely, the vesting anniversaries are clearly remembered by one or both of the spouses.

This second-guessing about the strength of the marriage can be softened by monthly vesting schedules and/or gradual increases of the percentage rates of vesting. When formulating the prenup, these need to be thought out carefully with some imagination as to how it will feel at each vesting point. It's good to create spreadsheets to see how this will work out in the future. A spreadsheet can be included in the prenup for clarity.

There is also the problem posed by vesting of inherited assets. What if there is bilateral vesting of inheritances, but one set of parents are considerably older (and maybe richer) than the other? Does it make sense for the vesting of this to take effect when all four parents of the married couple are deceased? Does the vesting start at the percentage level that the rest of the vesting has increased to? Or is there another way to look at this situation and make it fair, based on the actual facts that may be foreseeable about the inheritance? Can an adjustment for future sharing of inheritance be made *after* a divorce if some parents die afterward? What will it look like?

Sharing income: The healthy paradigm for first marriages is to share all income earned by the efforts of a spouse, no matter what the difference in earned income is. This would include income from employment, stock options, phantom stock, and other employee incentives, as well as income from self-employment and "business earnings" from a corporation, partnership, or limited liability company. It would also include additions to retirement and profit sharing during the marriage, including the employer contributions. This is consistent with state law.

For purposes of the prenup, it shouldn't matter whether this earned income is held in separate or joint accounts. It would be deemed a marital asset wherever it was. But surprisingly, many off-the-shelf prenups say that even this earned income during the marriage is not a marital asset unless it is put into a joint account. This sort of language gives one party to the prenup too much control as to what is separate and what is marital. It can cause resentment and hoarding.

As described above, in a prenup, one needs also to consider income from the separate property assets. A prenup can hold the separate property as separate and yet still share the income coming from the property. This is a very good way to make both parties happy. (See above for vesting possibilities.)

Thoughts of how business income will be addressed is very important in a prenup. This is particularly true if only one of the spouses is active in the business. His or her efforts in the business are marital efforts according the laws of every state. (See Chapter 9 for possibilities.) Income and increase in value from the business efforts of the spouse could be marital for the sake of the marriage. Defining what is the income or growth of the business due to a spouse's efforts can be challenging, but must be accomplished when formulating the terms of a prenup.

Sharing gifted assets: Often parents of spouses who can afford it, use

Internal Revenue Code Section 2503(b) to make gifts to family members that are not counted into their base for determining estate or gift tax. These are called "annual exclusion" gifts because they can be made once a year to each recipient and they are excluded from the gift tax base. The current limit (which is adjusted for inflation) as of tax year 2018 is $15,000 a year. A spouse's parents can collectively give $30,000 a year to anyone, including their children, children's spouses, grandchildren, and even non-related people, without lessening their credit shelter for estate and gift taxes.

Having a provision in a prenup that deems any of these annual exclusion gifts marital, no matter which spouse is the recipient, is a good way to create generosity and good feelings between the spouses. The prenup can also provide that larger gifts from a party's parents during the marriage are deemed marital. Or the prenup can put a dollar limit on what part of larger gifts would fall under the category of "marital" and what will remain separate property.

The importance of having a home you both own.

In first marriages especially, it is very emotionally important for the couple to live in a home they equally own. Creating a home is a very important aspect of marriage. When a home is not owned by one of the spouses, it tends to create bad feelings.

Sometimes when a couple gets together, one of the parties already owns a home. If the other party doesn't have the financial capability to buy into it, there can be a gradual vesting of the separate home into joint property. Or the couple can set a time line to purchase a new joint home together.

Often wealthy parents may want to make a financial contribution to the purchase of a home, but want to make sure that this source of funds doesn't become marital property in the event of a divorce. Or the parents may buy the house but put it in the trust that will never benefit the less moneyed spouse if there is a divorce or even if the marriage ends in the death of the more moneyed spouse. It might be better for a marriage to forgo this assistance and for the couple to do it on their own. This may mean the purchase of a less expensive house by taking out a bank loan. So you may need to look a gift horse in the mouth and say "no," when it comes to the marital residence.

Sometimes spouses may purchase a home, each with a different amount of a down payment. Perhaps one of them is able to pay $80,000 and the other $20,000 at purchase. Many of the people that pay the higher amounts may then feel that they are entitled to 80 percent of the gain of the house when it is sold. For the sake of the marriage, it's probably best to have the gain equally shared.

Sometimes it's simply best not to track separate property contributions into joint property at all. If a person puts $50,000 down on a house and the less moneyed spouse puts nothing down, maybe (for the sake of the marriage) the entire house should be marital from the outset. If he or she doesn't want this to happen, that person simply doesn't need to put the separate property into the house in the first place.

But think about it – people with money enough to want to have a prenup probably don't really need to keep most or all of the gain on the home if the marriage breaks up. The increase of goodwill in the marriage perhaps may be more valuable than retaining the $50,000 down payment and its "share" of appreciation. (Also, remember the basic meaning of the word "appreciation" and apply it to your marriage.)

Anyway, if it becomes marital property, the moneyed spouse only forgoes half of it because marital property is generally divided equally in the laws of many states and usually in prenups, too. This is a small price to pay to keep a spouse happy and satisfied. It may give your marriage more of a chance of working out. Terms that support this arrangement can be written in the prenup.

The benefits and drawbacks of "sunset clauses"

Don't box yourself in. You can think creatively about shielding premarital or inherited assets for a reasonable period of time and having some or all of the "separate property" vest into the marriage over a period of time. This can satisfy some of the concern over the financial results of a short marriage, similar to divorce laws, which in most states take into account the length of a marriage when dividing property.

There also can be a "sunset clause" in the agreement stating that after a period of time in the marriage the prenup simply self-destructs and the parties are then simply married, like everyone else. Sometimes that magical date is 15 years after the marriage, sometimes 20 or 25 years. There can be some gradual vesting before the sunset clause anniversary. The sunset clause can apply to different aspects of the agreement at different anniversaries. The future spouses are in control of what will work best for them.

There are a few downsides to sunset clauses. One is if the clause applies to inheritance by a spouse from the other. If there is a guaranteed floor set forth in the prenup (say 80 percent of assets for a first marriage), eliminating the prenup will eliminate this protection. A spouse will be relegated to what's in the estate plan of the other, the spousal forced share election, or the spousal intestate share if there is no last will. A sunset clause could be drafted to retain the inheritance provision and remove the other provisions pertaining to divorce.

Another downside is that the couple will lose the protection of requiring that, if they divorce, it will not be a litigated divorce. Again, the couple can retain the divorce process provision while eliminating other provisions.

And finally, there is the psychological effect of the trigger dates of the sunset clause. Let's say a couple experience average satisfaction with their marriage, with the typical ups and downs. Year 15 (the sunset clause year) is looming. As in vesting schedules, it may cause much rumination on the part of the more moneyed spouse about whether the marriage is good enough to continue or not. Think carefully about whether you want a sunset clause when drafting your prenup and whether it should be complete or partial.

CHAPTER 18

ARE ALL PRENUPS ENFORCEABLE?

The short answer to this question is no. But most of them *are* enforceable. It is very difficult to invalidate a prenuptial agreement. And they only get overturned in the most fact-egregious cases. If you are going to sign a prenup, you should assume that it will last for your entire marriage and will go into effect without change at death or divorce, even if the less-advantaged future spouse did not sign it precisely voluntarily.

Here's a typical scenario:

They are engaged. He has premarital assets and he stands to inherit quite a bit of money. Much more than she. He raises the issue of a prenup. She rejects the idea. He continues to insist, more strongly as the wedding day approaches. She continues to say no. He finally says, "I won't marry you unless you sign one." A draft is sent by his attorney six weeks before the large wedding. She doesn't like what's in it. She gets an attorney. Most of her and her attorney's suggested changes over the next few weeks are rejected. The prenup is signed, and they get married. Twenty years later after the marriage has produced two children, there is a divorce.

Does this scenario rise to the legal standard of coercion or duress? Does it rise to the level of overreaching? Most likely not. And some prenups contain a financial punishment for contesting the terms. In addition, there will be a huge legal bill for the person mounting the difficult and almost impossible lawsuit trying to invalidate it. And that person will likely have to pay the defense costs of the other spouse who succeeded in defending the terms, according to the terms in most prenups. As a result, under the very typical facts described above, she'll probably be stuck with the terms of the prenup.

This chapter addresses the major issues pertaining to enforceability of a prenup.

Coercion, duress, overreaching.

Extreme circumstances are required to prove *coercion*, *duress*, or *overreaching* in a court of law. The person claiming these grounds has the burden of proof, which means he or she must convince a court of their claim. Generally, the standard of proof to overturn a prenup is high – it needs to be proven by clear and convincing evidence. That means it must be substantially more likely than not that the evidence submitted is convincing. (In normal contract law, the burden of proof is generally "by the preponderance of evidence," in other words a 51 percent chance that the proof has been met.) The coercion, duress, or overreaching must have been present at the prenup's inception.

What is coercion? It occurs if someone tries to persuade another to do something by the use of force or threats. The force and threats do not have to be physical. They can be psychological, including harassment and intimidation. In a prenup, the threat is that if the future spouse does not sign the prenup, there will be no marriage. For coercion to exist, the party submitting to signing the contract must act in a way so contrary to his or her own interests that the person is not really able to act with free will. You can imagine how difficult that would be to prove in the context of someone signing a prenup unhappily.

Duress is similar to coercion. It involves restraint or danger, actually inflicted or threatened, so severe that it overcomes the mind of a person. It leads to choices against that person's best judgment that the person would not ordinarily have made. It is such great pressure that it basically destroys the free will of a party. Again, it is very difficult to prove in the context of a prenup.

If a person can prove coercion or duress, it shows that the person did not sign the contract voluntarily and that the prenup could be invalidated. But the cases indicate that even if a prenuptial agreement is presented to the other party for the first time one or two days before the wedding, it may not amount to duress or coercion.

But what if the future wife is from another country, and had "very poor" English skills? What if she had no money to retain a lawyer or translator, was pregnant, and had a visa that was about to expire? If her visa expired, she would have to leave the United States unless she married. Is that duress? According to an appeals court in South Carolina, this does amount to duress. See *Holler v. Holler*, 364 S.C. 256 (2005).

Overreaching is similar to coercion and duress. It is defined as taking unfair advantage of another's vulnerability. It happens where there is an inequality of bargaining power or other circumstances in which there is an absence of meaningful choice on the part of one of the parties. That does sound like the situation at the inception of many prenups. If one of the parties to the contract is the grossly disproportionate beneficiary of the transaction, it raises questions of overreaching. But as you will see below, the rules on enforceability generally make overturning a prenup on this legal ground very unlikely.

Undue influence is a concept often used in will contests, but sometimes in prenup litigation. It occurs when a person exercises influence on a vulnerable person, disrupting the person's normal decisions or impulses. In the will contest cases, this can lead the compromised person (often an elder) to leave assets to the person exerting pressure (such as a caregiver) rather than to the family. There is a fine line between "undue" influence and legitimate influence. In prenup cases, often the terms "overreaching," "coercion," and "undue influence" are used interchangeably.

Here's an example from Florida, where a court found there was overreaching and undue influence, and the prenup was judged unenforceable. In that case, on a Monday, the future husband said they would marry that week, provided they could book passage on an extended honeymoon cruise on the S.S. *Constitution*, scheduled to sail from New York that Thursday. As the court described it, the wife "ecstatically agreed."

They proceeded to make wedding plans. Friends and family were invited to the wedding, which was to take place at the Topflight Room of Northwest Airlines at O'Hare Airport prior to the couple's flight to New York to get to the cruise ship.

About 24 hours before the wedding, when they were at a jewelry store to finalize the sizing of their wedding rings, the husband took the prenuptial agreement out of his pocket and for the first time presented it to his soon-to-be wife. He gave her the ultimatum of "no prenup, no wedding." The wife had virtually no money or assets and signed reluctantly.

The court held that the circumstances surrounding the execution of the agreement and its disproportionate terms supported a presumption of undue influence and overreaching that affected the wife's ability to exercise her free will in executing the agreement. *Lutgert v. Lutgert*, 338 So. 2d 1111 (Fla. Dist. Ct. App. 1976).

How much time must you have to review the prenup, and must you have legal counsel?

In many cases, the time between presentation of the agreement and the wedding date is significant because it may bear on whether there has been a meaningful opportunity to obtain the advice of counsel before signing. This is true especially if the prenup provides disproportionately less than the party would have received in a divorce without a prenup.

No state statute requires a fixed a number of days between the signing of the prenup and the wedding. Many sound and enforceable prenups are signed the day before the wedding. But these are generally prenups signed by prepared, informed parties who have been represented by attorneys, where the prenup is not excessively one-sided and significant negotiations occurred prior to the signing.

California has a time rule that requires seven days between the time the agreement is presented and the time of signing. The aim is to permit parties to review an agreement and have an opportunity to obtain counsel prior to signing it. (Cal. Fam. Code § 1615(c)(2).) It does not require a certain number of days between the signing and the marriage. Also, the seven-day period may not apply if both parties are represented by attorneys at the outset of the negotiation of the agreement.

When one person is represented by counsel and the other is not, the burden of establishing the validity of the agreement may shift in some states to the party seeking its enforcement. See, for example, *Owen v. Owen*, 759 S.E.

2d 468 (W. Va. 2014). Some courts require attorney representation if the prenup is patently "unfair on its face." In one case, the wife first saw the prenup three days before the wedding, was not represented by separate counsel, and signed it at her husband's attorney's office after being there for just ten minutes. It was found to be unenforceable because of the "grossly inequitable distribution of property" and the "circumstances surrounding the execution of the agreement." *In re Estate of Robert J. Crawford*, 107 Wash.2d 493 (1986).

In general, courts may tend to require stricter scrutiny if a less sophisticated party is not represented by independent counsel. Negotiations are indicators of enforceability of a prenup, especially if they resulted in changes of terms in the agreement. The changes don't necessarily have to be substantial or meaningful. Some attorneys for more moneyed future spouses make sure that *some* changes are made, in order to make the prenup more likely to be enforceable for their clients.

When a party is represented and there are drafts sent back and forth, it is unlikely that the prenup can be invalidated. In one sense, then, it might be worse for the less-advantaged spouse to be represented by counsel.

And most prenuptial agreements have the parties make the representations that the agreement is free of coercion and that it was not signed under duress. However, if those elements are proven to exist, the contrary statement made in the prenup will have no legal meaning or effect, because the agreement itself will not be deemed to be made voluntarily by the less-advantaged spouse.

Fraud, fraud in the inducement, and fraudulent concealment.

Contracts, including prenups, can be invalidated if there is fraud that affects the decision of a party to sign it. Fraud or fraudulent inducement is defined as deception or false representation by words or conduct intended to deceive in order to result in financial gain. Fraudulent concealment arises if a party has a duty to disclose and that party conceals relevant and material facts not within the reasonably diligent efforts of the other party to discover them.

Lack of disclosure can rise to the level of fraud if it's intended to mislead the other party. Fraud and fraudulent concealment are very difficult to prove, and must be proven by clear and convincing evidence.

What if your future spouse promises you he or she won't enforce certain terms contained in the prenup if you just sign it? That happens often. If your spouse later breaks this promise at the time of the divorce, it will not rise to the level of fraud. All prenups contain a representation that there are no "side" agreements that are in addition to what's in the prenup. You signed it, so you are bound. You cannot have reasonably relied (an essential element of a fraud claim) on that side promise. As a legal matter, your reliance was unreasonable. You're simply out of luck.

Fraud can go the other way.

What if you sign a prenuptial agreement that permits you (as the less moneyed spouse) to receive a significant sum upon signing a postnup, or at trigger points during the continuation of the marriage? And then right after signing or after a major trigger point you file for divorce? That could be actionable as fraud. This is similar to the circumstances of an early Massachusetts case on postnuptial agreements, *Fogg v. Fogg*, 409 Mass. 531 (1991). (See Chapter 19.) In that case, the wife ended the marriage shortly after property was transferred to her under a postnuptial agreement. The court invalidated the postnup, leaving for another day whether agreements made after a marriage and not in anticipation of an immediate divorce are valid. *Fogg*, footnote 2.

Does engagement to be married create a fiduciary duty that affects enforceability standards?

Prenups are supposed to satisfy the requirements of a valid contract. But most states look at prenups as more than just a business contract.

In the commercial context, parties have no special duty to each other. They can treat each other "at arm's length" and the doctrine of *caveat emptor* applies (although fraudulent concealment is actionable).

But there are important differences between prenups and commercial contacts. You are not permitted to treat your fiancé as a stranger. States view prenups as contracts that have public policy requirements because the parties will marry. Marriage is viewed as a special relationship that the state wishes to protect and sustain that goes far beyond a business contract.

People who are already married have a fiduciary obligation (sometimes legally termed a "confidential" relationship) toward each other. This means that each of them has the duty and obligation to act in the best interests of the other party. That includes the best *financial* or economic interest. When you have a fiduciary duty, you are subject to a high standard of care toward the other person. For example, lawyers have a fiduciary duty to their clients. Trustees have a fiduciary duty to the trust's beneficiaries. People have reason to trust the financial actions of a person who is acting as their fiduciary. It's a much higher duty than owed to people negotiating standard business contracts.

But what if you're not yet married but are engaged?

In Illinois, an engaged couple are considered to be in a fiduciary relationship. *Kosakowski v. Bagdon*, 369 Ill. 252 (1938). In Ohio, also, an engagement to marry creates a confidential relation between the contracting parties. A prenup entered into after the engagement and during its pendency "must be attended by the utmost good faith." *Juhasz v. Juhasz*, 134 Ohio St. 257 (1938).

The New York Court of Appeals also found that there was a special relationship between engaged couples and noted the "unique character" of the inchoate bond between engaged couples. It called it a "relationship by its nature permeated with trust, confidence, honesty and reliance." *In re Matter of Greiff*, 92 N.Y.2d 341 (1998). These are indicators of the existence of a fiduciary relationship.

The *Greiff* court found that the burden of proof may shift from the more vulnerable spouse to the more moneyed one if the premarital relationship manifested "probable undue and unfair advantage" by a preponderance of the evidence. In order for the burden to shift, however, the spouse contesting a prenuptial agreement must establish "a fact-based, particularized inequality."

Note that in a "normal" breach of fiduciary duty case (not in the prenuptial agreement context), if the defendant has profited from the transaction, the burden of proof shifts to that party. The defendant then must rebut the assumption that a breach of fiduciary duty existed. That person will have to prove that he or she acted in the best financial interests of another. This might be very hard to prove in most prenup situations. However, in prenup law, the burden of proof is generally on the person contesting the prenup and making a claim that a there was a breach of fiduciary duty.

In New York, a court noted the "unique character of the inchoate bond between prospective spouses" and called it "a relationship by its nature permeated with trust, confidence, honesty and reliance." The court also cites other New York cases that hold that a fiduciary relationship can exist even in cases where the couple are not engaged but have been in a close relationship for many years as "romantic companions." *McKeown v. Frederick* (2013 NY Slip Opinion 50967 Monroe County).

So perhaps you don't have to be engaged for that "fiduciary" relationship to exist. For example, confidential relationships can exist between family members, partners in a partnership, and directors of a corporation and their shareholders. Doesn't it make sense that couples in a committed relationship as well as engaged couples might be in a confidential relationship in which fiduciary duties arise? Why should this status only become applicable the moment someone poses the question "Will you marry me?" or after the marriage takes place?

If a fiduciary relationship exists at the time of negotiating a prenup, should that change the content of a prenup? Is it still OK to have a one-sided prenup? Is it still OK for the more advantaged spouse to think about protecting only his or her assets and future financial situations and not to be concerned about the other spouse's future?

As you will see in this chapter, the rules of enforceability of prenups as they exist in law basically ignore the concept of fiduciary duty and the obligations it imposes. In reality, very few prenuptial cases are overturned under the breach of fiduciary duty doctrine. If you are entering into a prenup, don't count on this theory and argument to soften the effect of a prenup in the future when it is about to be enforced.

The influential Uniform Premarital Agreement Act (1983) (UPAA) and Uniform Premarital and Marital Agreements Act (2012) (UPMAA) were drafted by the National Conference of Commissioners on Uniform State Laws. They both provide lip service forbidding enforceability of prenuptial agreements that are in violation of public policy. See UPAA, Section 3(a)(8) and UPMAA, Comments to Section 2 (in which limited public policy protections are cited). However, both Uniform Acts allocate the burden of proof to the person challenging the validity of a prenup no matter what the circumstances. See UPAA Section 6(a) and UPMAA Section 9(a). That means that both uniform laws are very pro-prenup. UPMAA Section 9, however, provides an alternate template that, if adopted, shifts the burden of proof.

Prenups require full financial disclosure.

Full disclosure of assets, income, and liability are very important to the enforceability of prenups. When there is concealment of assets or debts at the time of signing, this can rise to the level of a fraud in inducing a party to waive marital rights, although successful litigation on this issue is extremely rare.

Standards of disclosure vary from state to state. The states that have not adopted the UPAA or the UPMAA generally require full disclosure. The parameters of the full disclosure requirement are set forth in case law, statutes, legal treatises, and in court practice in unreported cases.

The standard of disclosure as articulated in Massachusetts is whether "an intelligent, competent person did have or should have had a general, adequate and sufficient knowledge of the other's worth to make an informed decision as to whether they wished to consent to the terms of the proposed premarital agreement." C.P. Kindregan Jr., & M.L. Inker, *Family Law and Practice* § 20.8, at 654 (2d ed. 1996).

The law in Pennsylvania puts the burden on the contesting party who claims he or she was not provided with a fair and "reasonable" disclosure. That party must prove lack of disclosure by "clear and convincing evidence," which is a higher standard than just the weight of the evidence. (Pa. Cons. Stat. Dom. Rel. § 3106.)

Many courts have ruled that disclosure statements may *approximate* asset values if the other party has reasonable knowledge of the character and extent of the intended spouse's property. The standard applied is whether the information was adequate enough to enable the other party "by the application of ordinary intelligence" to verify the extent of the other spouse's assets. *Megginson v. Megginson*, 367 Ill. 168 (1937).

If the less moneyed spouse is represented by counsel, the standard may be different. There is less opportunity to argue that the disclosure was insufficient if that party was afforded the opportunity to review the financial statement with a competent attorney. *In re Estate of Robert J. Crawford*, 107 Wash.2d 493 (1986).

The UPAA and the UPMAA have lower standards than the case law relating to disclosure of assets. This reflects a more *laissez faire* treatment of the contracting parties, thus less protection for the disadvantaged party.

According to the UPAA Section 6, in order to overturn the prenup, the prenup must be "unconscionable" at the time of the signing (see below) and all of the following must be true: (a) the party was not provided a "fair and reasonable" disclosure of the property or financial obligations of the other party; (b) that party did not voluntarily and expressly waive, in right, disclosure beyond the disclosure that was provided; and (c) that party did not have, or reasonably could not have had, adequate knowledge of the property or financial obligations of the other party. This is a pretty difficult standard to meet.

The UPMAA in Section 9(d) has an even lighter standard for full disclosure because a party can *waive* financial disclosure in writing beyond what was provided. This permits extremely limited disclosure or no disclosure whatsoever. Otherwise, disclosure is satisfied if a party receives a "reasonably accurate description" and "good faith estimate" of the value of property, liabilities, and the income of the other party, or if the party has adequate knowledge or a reasonable basis for having adequate knowledge of the property, liabilities, and income of the other party.

The better practice is to provide full and complete financial disclosure at the beginning of the negotiation (or mediation) process. When the prenup is signed, the disclosure should appear as an exhibit to the prenuptial agreement. It should include an accurate list of assets, liabilities, income, and expectancies of future inheritances, as well as any anticipated changes in any of these areas and any contingent liabilities or reasonable expectations of additional assets or income. An example of the latter would be disclosure of ongoing negotiations to sell a business that would result in proceeds for the future spouse well above the business value stated in the prenup.

For purpose of the negotiations, it's important for the client and his or her attorney to look at actual documents. These will include personal income tax returns, business income tax returns, account statements, valuations, financial statements, and the like. This due diligence is needed in negotiating prenups, and you will need the assistance of counsel for this. On the part of the attorney, it requires sophisticated financial and tax expertise. It also requires an ability to explain complex financial issues to a client who may not be well versed with the financial issues and complexities involved.

The more disclosure and the more accurate the disclosure, the better. It protects both parties. The disclosure also helps to identify separate property and marital property as the marriage proceeds.

How do you waive your marital rights in a prenup?

Every prenuptial agreement requires a waiver of the laws that pertain to marriage, divorce, and inheritance that are applicable in your state. The intent of the prenup is to replace some of these laws with the prenup's terms. A waiver is important to substantiate the contract's enforceability. In order to be valid, a party who is signing must be exercising a meaningful and thoughtful choice when agreeing to the prenup terms. That's part of signing the agreement *voluntarily* – knowing the impact of what you are signing.

The waiver must be with full knowledge of what you are giving up. Your attorney should inform you as to what the state laws are being altered by the prenup are before you sign so you know what you are forgoing when you sign it.

This explanation needs to be done thoroughly and carefully and in a way that a non-lawyer client can understand. But it is often not done carefully and in detail. And a person who is presented with a prenup and wants to marry because they love the other person and have invested time in the relationship often does not want to hear it.

These are some issues affecting "meaningful" waiver. It helps if a party is represented by counsel and if there has been adequate time to review the agreement (and possibly negotiate terms). The key is to have a good understanding of the waived rights. But here again, you should be aware that it is very rare that a prenup is overturned on the basis of inadequate waiver.

How is a prenup different than a business contract?

A basis of contract law is the concept of "consideration." There must be consideration exchanged in every enforceable contact. That means one person gives something of value, and the other pays something in in exchange for it.

But with prenups, both the UPAA in Section 2 and the UPMAA in Section 6 provide that consideration is not required for a prenup to be enforceable. That's a glaring exception to standard contract law, which requires consideration (something exchanged) in every contract. It seems odd to have no consideration for the most important financial (and personal) contract for the most important relationship people have in their lives.

When looking at the commissioners' comments in both the UPAA and the UPMAA, the theory is that the *marriage* is the consideration for a prenuptial agreement. UPMAA makes it clear that no "additional" consideration is needed. It refers to the "almost universal" rule or "consensus" view that marriage itself is consideration for the prenup.

But is that realistic? After all, can't you view that both parties are providing consideration by marrying each other? Each of the parties is giving a lot to the other (besides the financial aspects) when they marry. Who is to say who gains more? By deeming the marriage as consideration only on one side of the equation, isn't that short-changing the other party who is also giving him- or herself in marriage, and who is also, *in addition*, relinquishing financial benefits?

What if a 45-year-old woman with no money marries a 65-year-old man with money? This is a common fact pattern in prenups. Where is the mutuality if there is a prenup protecting the 65-year-old's assets? It is likely that (if the marriage survives) the younger spouse may be actually nursing the elder spouse through infirmities as he ages. Where's the consideration for that? If they marry without a prenup, they each gave up something – potential sharing of his wealth at death or divorce with the eventual caretaking to be done by the younger wife. To add relinquishment of rights for less moneyed spouses seems unbalanced. She might understandably think that when the prenup is presented to her that she is being taken advantage of.

Even in a less extreme situation, how can you place a monetary value on the contributions people make in marriages? And how can you know who is going to provide value or services to the other in the future? How can you know that the value of the more moneyed spouse's income and assets is worth more than the contributions (monetary and personal) that the other spouse will be making? (See Chapter 4, contribution to marriage.) It could be that she is "selling herself" for an agreement resulting in a grossly disproportionate gain to the other party at the time the prenup is entered into, as one court bluntly put it. See *Lutgert v. Lutgert*, 338 So. 2d 1111 (Fla. Dist. Ct. App. 1976).

One of the arguments for not requiring consideration in a prenup is that a future spouse has protections through the other enforceability requirements. These include disclosure of assets and liabilities and, also, that the terms of the prenup are not permitted to be "unconscionable." (See below.) But how strong are these protections? In my experience, practically every less-advantaged spouse enters into the prenup unwillingly to a certain extent, often not wanting to lose the time and energy invested in the relationship with the future spouse by not signing the prenup.

The unconscionability standard.

The unconscionability standard is an important concept applicable in many states. Under this standard, in order to invalidate a prenup, it must be deemed "unconscionable." This is an extremely difficult standard to meet.

Marriage is not viewed as a mere contract between parties. States have an interest protecting the financial interests of spouses when they divorce. Marriage is, as the cases maintain, a legal status from which certain rights and obligations arise. See, for example, *French v. McAnarney*, 290 Mass. 544, 546 (1935). That's why most states limit the unfettered freedom to limit or waive legal rights in the event of divorce. *Osborne v. Osborne*, 384 Mass. 591 (1981).

But most states (both those that have and have not adopted the Uniform Acts) go much further in letting future spouses make contracts with each other before a marriage that severely lessen marital rights and obligations. The standard often in effect in order for a prenup to be invalidated is that the agreement or the terms must be "unconscionable." (See below for the legal definition of "unconscionable.")

Both the UPAA and the UPMAA state that a prenup can be held to be unenforceable if the terms are "unconscionable" at the time of the signing. The UPAA states that the entire agreement would be unenforceable. Section 6(a)(2) of the UPAA provides that aside from the agreement being unconscionable at the time of the signing, there must also be a lack of a "fair and reasonable" financial disclosure, or a party must have waived disclosure, and that the party "did not have, or reasonably could not have had, an adequate knowledge of the property or financial obligations of the other party."

The UPMAA decouples disclosure and unconscionability. It provides that a court "may refuse" to enforce a term of a prenup if, in the context of an agreement "taken as a whole," the term was unconscionable at the time of signing. (Section 9(f)(2).)

Many states, even those that have not adopted the UPAA or UPMAA, have adopted the doctrine of unconscionability at the time of the signing in their prenup statutes.

But what is unconscionability? Both the UPAA in Section 6(c) and the UPMAA in Section 9(g) state that the issue of unconscionability will be decided under state law. The word, of course, is derived from something that is antithetical to someone's (or a court's) conscience. It is *un*-conscionable. Some definitions tie it to a lack of sense of morality of what is right and wrong. It's the opposite of "conscience," which entails a strong sense of right and wrong and an urge to do the right thing.

Here's what the courts say:

- The inequality must be so strong and manifest as to shock the conscience.
- The terms must be so extremely unjust, or overwhelmingly one-sided in favor of the party who has the superior bargaining power, that they are contrary to good conscience.
- An unconscionable contract is held to be unenforceable because no reasonable or informed person would otherwise agree to it.
- The perpetrator of the conduct is not allowed to benefit, because the consideration offered is lacking, or is so obvi-

ously inadequate, that to enforce the contract would be unfair to the party seeking to escape the contract.

- The agreement must be such that no reasonable or informed person would agree to it.
- An agreement is unconscionable when the "inequality is so strong, gross, and manifest that it must be impossible to state it to one with common sense without producing an exclamation at the inequality of it."
- An unconscionable agreement shocks the conscience of the court.
- An unconscionable agreement requires a greater showing of inappropriateness than a contract that is merely unfair and unreasonable.
- And from an eighteenth-century English case, the classic lawyer's definition: An agreement that "no man in his senses and not under delusion would make on the one hand and as no honest and fair man would accept on the other." *Earl of Chesterfield v. Janssen*, 28 Eng. Rep. 82, 100 (1750).

The determination of whether a prenup is "unconscionable" or not reminds me of that U.S. Supreme Court case in which the issue was the definition of obscenity. The case involved whether Louis Malle's film *The Lovers* should be banned under Ohio's obscenity laws. As Supreme Court Justice Potter Stewart so famously wrote:

> I shall not today attempt further to define the kinds of material I understand to be embraced within that shorthand description [of hard-core pornography], and perhaps I could never succeed in intelligibly doing so. But I know it when I see it, and the motion picture involved in this case is not that. *Jacobellis v. Ohio*, 378 U.S. 184, 197 (1964).

Unconscionability does not exist just because you make a bad deal or made a mistake in judgment. It doesn't exist merely because in retrospect you now think that some of the provisions were improvident or one-sided. A prenup can be very "unfair," but that doesn't make it unconscionable. Prenups can and do result in a marital property settlement that a judge would not think right under a decree of divorce. But that doesn't make them unconscionable. The same is true about inheritance provisions in a prenup – they are often much more parsimonious than the laws would otherwise allow.

In light of this exacting standard, there are very few cases in which a contesting spouse prevailed in a lawsuit contesting the terms of a prenup on the basis of unconscionability.

The "fair and reasonable" test.

At present, a minority of states require that the terms of a prenuptial agreement be "fair and reasonable" at the outset rather than "not unconscionable." This is distinguished from the almost universal requirement of a "fair and reasonable" disclosure of assets, liabilities, and income before signing a prenup. An even fewer number of states require that the same "fair and reasonable" standard be met at the time of enforcement.

For instance, in New York, a prenuptial agreement must be "fair and reasonable" at the time of its execution and "not unconscionable" at the time of its enforcement. (N.Y. Dom. Rel. Law § 236(B)3.)

As a New York court explained, it would not invalidate a prenup merely because some of its provisions were "improvident or one-sided," or because a party relinquished more than the law would have provided. In that case, the terms of the prenup were not found to be "manifestly unfair" in light of the financial benefits the wife would receive pursuant to the prenup. *Gottlieb v. Gottlieb*, 138 A.D.3d 30 (N.Y. App. Div. 2016).

Massachusetts does not have a prenup statute enacted in its general laws. The laws of prenups have been defined by case law. The state has struggled with the "fair and reasonable" standard. Prior to 2002, that standard had been applied to prenups as a two-step process, so that the terms of a prenup had to be "fair and reasonable" both at the time of execution and at the time of enforcement. *Osborne v. Osborne*, 384 Mass. 591 (1981). These testing points have been termed the "first look" and the "second look" in Massachusetts law. As you will see below, there is a possibility of "second look" in the UPMAA and in some other states' statutory laws and case law.

In *DeMatteo v. DeMatteo*, 438 Mass. 18 (2002), the Massachusetts Supreme Judicial Court saw no reason to replace the "fair and reasonable" standard at the time of the signing with the unconscionability standard. The "fair and reasonable" standard sounds like a similar standard that Massachusetts (and many other states) require for divorcing couples who do not have prenups – the agreement must be fair and reasonable in relation to the facts and circumstances of the marriage at the time of divorce. This is generally based on the various divorce factors set forth in the states' statutes in equitable distribution states. See, for example, Mass. Gen. Laws chapter 208, § 34.

But the fair and reasonable standard for prenups is not the same as a fair and reasonable standard in a divorce agreement or in a divorce decree made by a judge. As the *DeMatteo* court said, if the standard was the same, ". . . the parties' right to settle their assets as they wish in a prenuptial agreement 'would be meaningless.'" The court goes on to say that many valid prenuptial agreements "may be one sided" and a contesting party may enjoy a far different lifestyle after a divorce than he or she enjoyed during marriage.

In addition, the court determined that it was only when a future spouse was essentially "stripped of substantially all marital interests" that a judge may determine that a prenup was not "fair and reasonable" at the outset. So the fair and reasonable standard for prenups is lighter than what one might expect.

Maryland, like Massachusetts, has no prenup statute. The test there in determining validity of a prenup is whether, in the "atmosphere and environment" of the confidential relationship, there was unfairness or inequity in the "result of the agreement, or in its procurement." *Cannon v. Cannon*, 384 Md. 537 (Md. Ct. App. 2005) citing *Hartz v. Hartz*, 248 Md. 47 (1967). That means that it had to be fair and reasonable in the effect of its terms at the time of enforcement, and also in the process of signing the agreement, e.g., disclosure, absence of duress, willing waiver of rights. The *Hartz* case held that a prenup could be upheld if it is fair and equitable under the circumstances even if there had been no financial disclosure at the outset, as long as there is adequate knowledge of "what a frank, full and truthful disclosure" would reveal.

Similarly, in the state of Washington, a prenuptial agreement, by case law, must be found to be "procedurally" and "substantively" fair and reasonable at the inception to be valid. That means the process must be fair and reasonable and also the terms must be fair and reasonable. *In re the Matter of the Marriage of Gloria Bernard*, No. 803480 (2009). The court added that even if the agreement is not "substantively fair" (i.e., if it didn't have fair and reasonable terms), the agreement would be upheld if it was procedurally fair.

The *Bernard* court said that procedural fairness depends on full financial disclosure and whether the agreement was freely entered into with independent advice from counsel and full knowledge by both spouses of their rights.

The "second look" to determine if a prenup is still enforceable.

While maintaining this "fair and reasonable" standard at the "first look," the *DeMatteo* court articulated a new standard for the "second look" standard to be applied at the time of enforcement. The new standard, in line with many other states, is now the higher "unconscionability" standard. *DeMatteo*, 436 Mass. at 33. The court describes this standard as requiring a "greater showing of inappropriateness" than the "fair and reasonable" standard.

The purpose of the "second look" in Massachusetts (and in the other states that have adopted it) is to make sure that the prenup retains its vitality or intended spirit at the time of divorce. If circumstances have changed so far beyond the contemplation of the parties when they signed the prenup, the result may not be what the parties intended at the time it was executed. This "second look" is intended to protect a spouse that has been left without sufficient property, maintenance, or employment to support him- or herself.

The *DeMatteo* court admitted that there is much overlap between the fair and reasonable standard and the unconscionability standard used in many states and in the UPAA and the UPMAA. It said that a standard of unconscionability generally "requires a greater showing of inappropriateness."

Another state that has a "second look" is Minnesota. According to the Minnesota Supreme Court, a prenup must be substantively fair and procedurally fair at the time of execution and must not be unconscionable at the time of enforcement. *McKee-Johnson v. Johnson*, 444 N.W.2d 259. (Minn. 1989).

The Minnesota Supreme Court noted that while many states only adopt protective standards at the time of execution, a prenup may have become "unconscionably unfair" as a result of circumstances originally not foreseen by the parties. The circumstances must be quite extreme. The contract must be so one-sided as to be oppressive.

Wisconsin is another state that has adopted the "second look" doctrine in its interpretation of its prenuptial agreement statute, which provides that the terms must not be "inequitable" as to either party. (Wis. Stat. § 767.255 (3)(l).)

The terms of the prenuptial agreement dividing property upon divorce are required to be "fair" to each spouse, both at execution and at the time of divorce. This is to protect parties if circumstances have significantly changed since the agreement was signed. The court is to make a discretionary determination that must be the product of a "rational mental process" where the facts and law are considered for the purpose of achieving a "reasoned and reasonable" determination. *See In re Marriage of Button*, 131 Wis. 2d 84 (1986).

In Ohio, a prenup might not be enforced if there are changed circumstances that rise to the level of unconscionability. These might include an extreme health problem requiring considerable care and expense, change in employability of the spouse, and changed circumstance of the standards of living occasioned by the marriage, where a return to the prior living standard would work a hardship upon a spouse, among other reasons. *Gross v. Gross*, 11 Ohio St. 3d 99, 106, and footnote 11 (1984). The critical factor is if the changed circumstances render the provision unconscionable at the time of divorce.

By statute, a number of states, including New Jersey and Connecticut, require that the prenuptial agreement be "not unconscionable" at the time of enforcement. (N.J. Rev. Stat. § 37:2-38(b); Conn. Gen. Stat. § 46b-36g (a)(2).) The statutory standards vary among these states. Words like "fairness," "hardship," "undue burden," and "substantial injustice" are used in the cases to flesh out the notion of "unconscionability." Facts are also important.

For instance, different conclusions might be made for short-term marriages versus long-term marriages. Extreme changes of standard of living as a result of the prenup terms might be important. Another factor could be the disparity between what the parties would receive under the agreement and what they would likely have received under state law in the absence of an agreement. If the parties did not anticipate a change of circumstances or its impact at the time the agreement was signed, that would be an important factor in leading a court to not uphold a prenup.

The UPAA in general does not permit court mitigations of prenup terms based on changed facts existing at the time of enforcement. Section 6 "Enforcement" provides no exception for change of circumstances, except in a very limited scope pertaining to alimony if a former spouse becomes a public charge, that is, receives federal or state benefits for people lacking income or assets.

However, even without a "second look," a change of circumstances may come in through the back door by asserting that the prenup was unconscionable at the outset. The argument would be that the drastic economic circumstances resulting from the prenup could have been foreseen as a possibility when the terms were initially set.

The UPMAA has some alternate language that can be adopted by a state when it considers adopting the act. This would allow for a "second look" at time of enforcement. If this additional term is adopted, there would be the option of refusing enforcement if there was "substantial hardship" at the time of enforcement because of a material change of circumstances after the prenup was signed. See bracketed portions in Section 9(f)(2).

It is unclear from the commissioners' comments to Section 9 whether they intend this to be a less stringent standard than the unconscionability standard. Section 9(g) provides that the question of "unconscionability" and "substantial hardship" will be decided by the (state) court "as a matter of law." (Note that the UPMAA, promulgated in 2012, has to date been adopted in only two states, North Dakota and Colorado.)

See Chapter 15 for discussion of whether alimony waivers are enforceable.

Contesting prenups.

Caveat emptor (buyer beware) to the spouse who is giving up rights in a prenup. That less moneyed partner needs to be aware when signing a prenup that it will be extremely difficult – nearly impossible – to successfully contest it in a lawsuit. If negotiation or other interest-based processes (such as mediation and collaborative law) fail to produce results at the time of enforcement, the less moneyed spouse will need to engage in litigation, which is extremely expensive. That party will need to bear the cost. In addition, some prenups contain a financial penalty for spouses who contest prenups, similar to an in *terrorem* clause in a last will. And most prenups have a clause that provides that the losing party in the litigation has to bear the legal cost of the prevailing party. Except in the most egregious cases, the party contesting the prenup will lose.

As you have seen in the above discussion, state laws tend to be very protective of prenups, so if you sign one, you should expect that it will be enforced, unless the factual situation at the time of the signing was so extreme as to "shock the conscience," or in some states, your situation at the time of the divorce is extremely dire, that is, you are on public assistance.

Sometimes prenups are challenged after the death of a spouse by the widow or widower. In these cases, the survivor may face a choice between what the prenup provides for him or her under the estate plan of the deceased spouse, or what the survivor would receive if the will or estate plan is invalidated. (See Chapter 7.)

A contesting spouse may be left with a lesser amount of assets (or income derived from assets) under the laws of intestacy or by a spousal election to take a forced share than if that spouse accepts the benefits conferred in the prenup (or in the deceased spouse's last will and testament if greater). Many prenups align to the state law statutory provisions that set permissible minimums for spousal distributions at death in order to prevent enforceability challenges.

It's good for both parties entering into a prenup to be aware of this: A prenup that is not extreme or economically harsh at the time it is signed and as it plays out over time during the marriage will be more acceptable by the less moneyed partner. As a result, (aside from a possibly more felicitous marriage) that partner will have less incentive to attempt to contest it or a portion of it.

CHAPTER 19

THE POSTNUP:
A POWERFUL TOOL TO BE
HANDLED WITH CARE

ostnuptial agreements are essentially prenuptial agreements that are signed *after* the marriage. Postnuptial agreements are a relatively new area of law. They have been around for about 20 years, although they are little known and have been barely utilized. Prenuptial agreements are rare. Postnups are even rarer.

Courts and state laws have been gradually accepting them in a process similar to the gradual acceptance of prenups (the latter which started in the early 1970s). The rules of enforceability, though, are often quite different than those pertaining to prenups. Each state has different requirements for enforceability. Most states now permit them, either by case law or by statute.

Many lawyers are advertising postnups on their websites as a cure-all for marital woes. Today I found 332,000 hits for the search term "postnuptial agreements" and 224,000 hits for "postnuptial agreement attorney" on Google. (This was an increase from the year before, at which time my search for "postnuptial agreements" found 209,000 results.)

I have Google Alerts set for the terms "postnuptial agreement" and "post-marital agreement." I get links to typical lawyers' ads on postnups almost every day. Here's a recent one I received:

> If you're already married and would like to create a written postnuptial agreement to settle your assets and income in the event of divorce, the attorneys at [our law firm] can help you create an agreement that meets all of your specifications. You may include all

personal and business assets, as well as other stipulations to be followed in the event of a divorce. Our experienced attorneys can make this process easy and stress-free for parties looking for a practical solution to sharing assets.

It sounds easy, but postnups are a powerful tool and should be handled with great care! Because people are already married when they consider a postnup, higher state standards of enforceability often apply. These laws are intended to protect each spouse who is engaged in an ongoing marriage. These protections often get stronger as the couple gets closer to retirement age.

This is very different from the laws of prenuptial agreements, which on the whole are very unrestrictive and end up being much less protective of spouses. Because the marital relationship is established by the time a postnuptial agreement is negotiated, the courts view the relationship as a confidential/fiduciary relationship imposing a requirement of loyalty. (See Chapter 18.) As a result, courts are very concerned when enforcing postnups and may find them unenforceable more frequently than is the case with prenups.

Often postnuptial agreements are required to be more "generous" than prenups, and more like a divorce settlement agreement than a prenuptial agreement. The general rule is that postnups are more protective of marital rights than prenups. In general, prenups permit a greater degree of financial separation and allow the parties to change the rules of divorce to a greater degree than is generally possible and enforceable in a postnuptial agreement.

How postnups can help an ongoing marriage.

At this time, postnuptial agreements have been found enforceable by almost all states. Courts have recognized that being married should not mean that married parties should give up their right to contract during their marriage. Courts understand that these contracts can help marriages survive through difficult times. They can serve a useful function in permitting married parties arrange their financial affairs as they best see fit, even after the marriage. Some postnups address marital conduct issues, such as fidelity. (See below on "Lifestyle Postnups.")

Postnups can provide binding terms for solving something that has come up to disturb the marriage and shake its equilibrium. Often that something has to do with finances or having some type of security put in place. People in medium- and long-term marriages are increasingly affected by these issues. The idea of having a postnup generally arises in long-term marriages of people who are middle-aged or older. Sometimes they arise in first marriages, and sometimes in second (or subsequent) marriages with blended families.

Most, but not all, of these situations when people are wondering about having a postnuptial agreement are financially based. Say, for instance, a spouse who was the major breadwinner has lost his job. This happened to many "breadwinner" spouses in the Great Recession of 2008. Many of these (mostly) men were unable to get re-employed with earnings commensurate with their pre-2008 earnings. Many had to take jobs at lesser salaries. Some of them chose to go into business for themselves.

Often one spouse is risk-averse and doesn't want to put marital money into a business venture. That person may want their spouse just to get a job and not start their own business. In a postnup, that spouse may want to be assured that the other spouse's business venture won't interfere with the security that was built up during the marriage. The risk-averse spouse may be understandably concerned about financial resources for eventual retirement and old age.

When thinking about a postnup for an ongoing marriage, especially with spouses in their 50s and older, protections and security for both spouses need to be considered and embodied in the postnuptial contract. If these needs are not taken into account, the agreement might be found to be unenforceable, aside from it being potentially unfair to one of the spouses.

Even if there is not an unemployment (or underemployment) problem, perhaps one of the spouses wants to start a new business that requires a substantial amount of seed money. There is a danger that the business will not be successful and that the money or assets will be lost. That "money" or those "assets" in a medium- or long-term marriage often consist of "marital" money, that is, assets that belong to both of the spouses. That's because in general, all money earned after a marriage and assets purchased with that money are "marital," no matter whose name it is titled in and whether you're in an "equitable distribution" state or a "community property" state.

The new venture may require so much money that if the business goes under, the couple will be left with a financially challenged retirement (if they can retire at all). Potentially facing an impoverished old age is a serious decision for both spouses to make. It's a decision that needs to be made together, with much reflection. When one spouse makes that decision alone, it is often a recipe for marital failure.

If the business fails, will there be money to protect the non-business spouse? What happens to the business-owner spouse if it fails? Will a court enforce a postnup that leaves either spouse of a long-term marriage in a precarious financial condition due to a business failure? The implications of leaving risk of loss totally on the "business spouse" needs to be carefully thought out.

Also, there is the question of gain and profit from the new business. Will that "upside" be shared between the spouses? Or will it belong to the business-owner spouse who took the risk of being left with less access to marital property and security? And what do these financial agreements in mid-marriage lead to? Will it help the couple stay together, or will it drive the couple apart?

Other reasons people might want postnuptial agreements.

Sometime a postnuptial agreement is sought because of very harsh prenuptial agreement negotiations and interactions (with parties and legal counsel) that ended up in a very painful signing of a prenup prior to the wedding. Often parties report that their lawyers did not do what they asked them to do when the prenup was negotiated and drafted. A postnuptial agreement (especially when created with a mediator's help) can often undo the harm that resulted from the earlier negotiations and the resulting agreement.

Often the negotiation and signing of a prenup before a marriage is very hurried, leaving both parties dissatisfied and putting a damper on the joy of the wedding. Letting some time elapse is good, even several years after the wedding. This hiatus can give people time to process what they might have done had they had more time. Thoughts about what is appropriate in their prenup may change during the years immediately after the marriage. This, too, is a good reason to reconsider the terms of a prior prenup even if the process was relatively good.

Some prenups have trigger dates for vesting of property and income. As the trigger dates approach, marriages may become troubled. There might be second thoughts about the health of the marriage around the time of the trigger dates. Sometimes couples want to change or omit the trigger dates because they may sense potential conflict when these dates approach. A postnup will take into account the progressing marital economic (and personal) relationship that may be more reflective of the spouses' current wishes than the triggers originally conceived by the parties' attorneys.

Postnuptial agreements are supposed to help maintain a marriage and not be a divorce agreement. But knowing what the financial result would be if there were to be a divorce can help a spouse stay in a marriage even if the marriage has suffered a damaging event, such as infidelity. In these cases, a postnuptial agreement can be a very effective tool, perhaps allowing the marriage to continue.

Some people enter into second marriages without adequate thought of how they would balance their financial allegiance to their children of a previous marriage with the allegiance to their new spouses. This can be a disturbance to the new marriage. A thoughtful postnup process can be very helpful in finding a pathway to navigate through these competing loyalties.

The prenup-postnup.

A postnup that is deliberately created during an ongoing marriage is a completely different animal than the postnup that is created because the couple ran out of time to finish their prenup. This type of postnup (which I call the "prenup-postnup") occurs fairly often. People are continuing to negotiate their prenup and want some time to enjoy their upcoming wedding, rather than hashing out divorce (and death) terms with each other and their lawyers. They simply stop and put the prenup on hold for a while. They want to rest from the bad interactions they have been having trying to construct their prenup right before their marriage.

Putting off a prenup until after the wedding requires trust between the future spouses, especially if one of them is not so keen on the idea. They essentially make a promise to get back to it. That promise needs to be supported by good faith and trust.

But when they get back to it, it is a *postnuptial* agreement. Do different standards of enforceability apply to the "prenup-postnup" because it was intended to be a prenup, or do the prenuptial agreement rules of enforceability (which are generally more *laissez faire*) apply? I have not found the answers to this question in the case law.

Having a postnup that does not comply with your state's laws can be the subject of extended lawsuits on enforceability. It may be best to play it safe and follow the rules of postnups if you didn't have time to complete your prenup. Or one can rely on the good faith of your partner to reaffirm the terms of the "prenup-postnup" (without litigation) if there is a divorce. If the terms are fair and equitable, then there is a good chance that the enforceability issues won't arise.

"Lifestyle" postnups.

Sometimes there has been an infidelity issue that a spouse wants to address in a postnup. Or the parties may decide to put a clause in to punish a party that has started drinking, using drugs, or gambling. There may be a financial penalty clause in the postnup in case it happens again. Is that an enforceable term in a postnup?

Sometimes people want to put penalty clauses in postnups that specify different results depending on which one of them calls it quits on the marriage. Whether this is enforceable is highly questionable in today's no-fault divorce environment.

A prenup contract that financially penalizes a spouse who strays from the marriage has enforceability issues that need to be weighed by attorneys to see if a legal contractual solution in a postnup will hold up. All these lifestyle provisions bring with them questions of enforceability if tested in court. (See Chapter 14 for enforceability of lifestyle provisions.)

Postnups as a result of an inheritance.

Another situation that may make people think about a postnup is if a spouse is about to receive, or has received, an inheritance from his or her parents. Having received a great deal of money, a spouse may not want to share it with the other spouse. One reason could be that the existing marriage is less than "happy." Or the inheriting spouse may want additional security in old age or wishes to make sure the money stays within the bloodlines.

Inheritance brings up many issues, some having to do with security and the health of the marriage, some having to do with emotional and family-of-origin issues. These issues can be addressed in a postnup. The first step is to look at what your state law says about inherited assets in a marriage. The second step is to look at the projected needs of both of the parties, especially in a long-term marriage. This is important in determining the terms of a postnup in order for it to be equitable for both parties. In some cases, the analysis will affect whether or not the postnup will hold up in a court of law if it is questioned later.

Estate-planning postnups.

A couple may wish to have a postnup in order to guarantee that certain estate-planning actions are taken if the marriage ends with the death of a spouse or even in case of a divorce. Sometimes these might benefit children of previous marriages. But even in a first marriage situation, at times this planning commitment is desired and may be done by means of a postnup. The terms of the postnup are essentially contracts to make a will, and they will be followed up by an actual signed estate plan. If the estate plan doesn't get done, the contractual provisions in the postnup can serve as a contractual liability assessed against a party's estate, payment of which can be enforceable by process of law.

Some people in a long-term marriage decide to stay legally married but live separate lives. A postnuptial agreement can determine how this would work financially, and also can put reasonable jointly determined requirements for how each of their estates will be distributed after their deaths. Often, unlike the situation with divorces, these parties may wish all or part of their estates to go to their surviving spouses, even if they are separated from them. I have seen this happen in my law practice.

This type of estate planning, although rare, can also be done in the case of actual completed divorces. People don't think about this often, but estate planning benefitting the ex-spouse is sometimes desired and can be written into divorce settlement agreements.

The role of marital mediation.

Marital mediation is an emerging field of mediation. It is a process in which a couple is assisted by a neutral mediator to identify and discuss financial problems and other issues that may be causing the marriage to be troubled. The process sometimes (but not always) ends up with a written postnuptial agreement. Often this postnuptial agreement will focus on establishing financial rules of the marriage and what will happen in the event of a divorce.

If both of the spouses truly want to stay together, marital mediation can be a very helpful process. If a postnuptial agreement is sought by the couple, careful consideration and evaluation of all the potential terms of a postnup during the mediation process are important.

Non-financial issues are often best handled by marriage counselors and therapists. Financial issues are sometimes better handled by lawyers and mediators who can inform the couple about legal issues and standards. Importantly, lawyers by experience and training have a deep understanding of financial issues and various forms of business and investment assets. Marital mediators who work with couples on financial issues are often divorce lawyers who have strong knowledge related to finances.

Sometimes there is a marital issue of perceived differences in "contribution" to the marriage that is bothering a couple. "Contribution to marriage" is a standard divorce law concept and is very important to the health of a marriage. (See Chapter 4.) An attorney can teach a client and a marital mediator can teach a couple how the law addresses financial and non-financial contributions to a marriage.

An analysis of the relative "contributions" of the couple to the marriage can be very helpful to them in marital mediation sessions. Often there is a perceived imbalance of contribution that turns out not to be the case. Sessions like these can help clarify mutual misunderstandings of the marriage and the parties' interactions.

Another major assistance a marital mediator can give a couple is helping them analyze their communication skills. Often, even in a very long marriage, people do not communicate with each other clearly. A third-party mediator who observes the couple's verbal dialogue can very quickly observe and identify miscommunications and disconnects and share that information with the mediation clients. This turns out to be very helpful.

The marital mediation process can often lead to increased mutual understanding so that the marriage can go forward on a healthier basis. When couples are able to obtain a better understanding of what is troubling their marriage, they are better able to make changes and move forward. Often, they do that without a written agreement. (See Chapter 20 for more on marital mediation.)

Problems with postnups.

Parties seeking to overturn postnups have made arguments in courts that they should be void. They put forward a contention that postnups are "innately coercive." Or they argue that postnups usually arise when a marriage is already failing, and that they may "encourage" divorce because they provide a ready-made exit plan or provide a way to benefit a party in a future divorce. See discussion in *Ansin v. Craven-Ansin*, 457 Mass. 283, 290 (2010). *Ansin* is the seminal Massachusetts case in which the court found postnuptial agreements to be enforceable, with protections both at time of signing and at enforcement. It's been quoted by many other postnuptial agreement cases all over the country. It's good reading for anyone (even if not living in Massachusetts) who is interested in knowing more about postnuptial agreements.

Another concern is that a postnup may offer an "illusory promise" of remaining in a failing marriage.

For instance, in an earlier Massachusetts case, the Supreme Judicial Court shot down a postnup in which the husband transferred a great deal of property to the wife, hoping that the transfer would make the marriage more viable. Shortly thereafter, the wife filed for divorce. The judge found that the agreement was not free from fraud, because the wife, while outwardly pledging to preserve the marriage, was simply concerned with arranging a favorable financial settlement. *Fogg v. Fogg*, 409 Mass. 531 (1991). A postnup will be carefully reviewed by a judge to make sure that fraud in the inducement did not play a part in its execution, as in the *Fogg* case.

Another issue that is raised in a postnup when compared with a prenup is the fiduciary duty married spouses owe each other. This means married spouses are supposed to act in each other's best financial interests. This is different than the current law on prenups, which does not generally impose a fiduciary duty on contracting future spouses.

Here's another difference: Generally, courts take the position that the future spouse who doesn't like the prenup terms can simply walk away and decide not to go through with the marriage. But married couples are legally and morally bound to take care of each other. As a result, postnuptial agreements are not considered to be the product of classic arm's-length bargaining, which is the standard that applies in ordinary business contracts and, to a great extent, to prenups.

As a Connecticut court articulated it in the context of a post-divorce fraud claim:

> Courts simply should not countenance either party to such a unique human relationship [marriage] dealing with each other at arms' length. *Billington v. Billington*, 220 Conn. 212 (1991) quoting *Grayson v. Grayson*, 4 Conn. App. 275 (1985) (Judge Borden, dissenting).

But are postnups necessarily coercive? What if a business owner spouse told his wife that he would divorce her unless he retained sole ownership of the business that he had developed during the marriage? The wife may sign the postnup because the property and support she would receive if there was a divorce may not be adequate to support her and the children, even if she is working outside of the home. In this way, she may be a hostage to the marriage.

This type of postnup obviously has coercive undertones. But there are many situations in which postnups can be fair and evenhandedly negotiated between spouses and can have an extremely positive effect on the marital relationship. Postnups can be freely entered into if both sides perceive the agreement as fair and addressing their concerns in a reasonable manner and taking into account future foreseeable situations.

Courts look at the issue of coercion very carefully when assessing the enforceability of postnuptial agreements (sometimes called "marital agreements" or "mid-marriage agreements"). Most states require that postnuptial agreements be "carefully scrutinized" by the court. Many states have adopted different standards for prenups versus marital agreements. Often the "fair and reasonable" test is used for postnups both at inception and enforcement, rather than the common "not unconscionable" standard for prenups at one or both points in time. See, for example, *Ansin v. Craven-Ansin*, 457 Mass. at 296-297.

In addition, unlike the analysis for prenups in most states, a judge might consider the magnitude of disparity between the outcome under the postnup and what would happen under divorce laws *without* a postnup. This analysis might be especially acute in the case of long-term marriages.

Typical property division factors in a divorce (such as length of marriage, ages of parties, parties' health, and parties' employability) might come into play. If a postnup satisfies the requirements of a divorce settlement agreement, a court would uphold it. If it does not, then enforceability may be in question. If a party is represented by experienced and able counsel and the parties are sophisticated in financial affairs, the agreement would more likely be enforced.

In a postnup, the burden of proof might shift from the party seeking to invalidate it to the party that seeks to enforce it. This burden shifting is part of the "heightened scrutiny" that some courts believe is appropriate at the time of enforcement to provide additional protections to spouses who are already married and therefore bound to act in each other's best interests.

Examples of enforceability in various states.

Most states now permit postnups with varying degrees of protections. Ohio is one of the few states that at present categorically disallows postnups. In fact, it may be the only state at the time of this writing. Ohio law provides that a husband and wife cannot alter their legal relations by a contract except to agree to an immediate separation and to make provisions for the support of either of them or their children during the separation. (Ohio Rev. Code Ann. § 3103.06.)

New Hampshire is one of the states that permits enforceability of marital agreements, but with greater protections than with prenups. *In re Estate of Wilber*, No. 2012-368, Supreme Court of New Hampshire (2013). In *Wilber*, the court noted that the state has a special interest in protecting marriages but saw no reason not to enforce the agreement in question. In finding the postnup to be fair to the wife, the court stated that:

> Because of the fiduciary nature of the marital relationship, the parties must exercise the highest degree of good faith, candor and sincerity in all matters bearing on the terms and execution of the proposed agreement, with fairness being the ultimate measure.

The Kansas Supreme Court put it this way: "[P]arties entering into a post marital agreement are in a vastly different position than parties entering into a premarital agreement." *Davis v. Miller*, 269 Kan. 732 (2000).

The Connecticut Supreme Court stated that postnups are consistent with public policy because they realistically allow two mature adults to handle their own financial affairs. The court distinguished enforceability standards for prenups with those of postnups, stating that unlike prenups, a postnup must be fair and equitable at time of execution and "not unconscionable" at the time of marital dissolution. *Bedrick v. Bedrick*, 300 Conn. 691 (2011). This provides the stricter scrutiny generally required in a "mid-marriage" contract at its inception than in a prenup.

As the court explained in *Bedrick*:

Because of the nature of the marital relationship, the spouses to a postnuptial agreement may not be as cautious in contracting with one another as they would be with prospective spouses, and they are certainly less cautious than they would be with an ordinary contracting party. With lessened caution comes greater potential for one spouse to take advantage of the other. This leads us to conclude that postnuptial agreements require stricter scrutiny than prenuptial agreements. In applying special scrutiny, a court may enforce a post-nuptial agreement only if it complies with applicable contract principles, and the terms of the agreement are both fair and equitable at the time of execution and not unconscionable at the time of dissolution.

Under *Bedrick*, the issue of unconscionability is to be made on a case-by-case basis, "taking into account all of the relevant facts and circumstances." The court said that in determining whether a particular postnuptial agreement is "fair and equitable" at the time of execution, the court may consider "the totality of the circumstances" surrounding the execution, as well other various factors, including:

> . . . the nature and complexity of the agreement's terms, the extent of and disparity in assets brought to the marriage by each spouse, the parties' respective age, sophistication, education, employment, experience, prior marriages, or other traits potentially affecting the ability to read and understand an agreement's provisions, and the amount of time available to each spouse to reflect upon the agreement after first seeing its specific terms . . . [and] access to independent counsel prior to consenting to the contract terms.

The *Bedrick* court went on to say unfairness or inequality alone does not render a postnuptial agreement unconscionable; spouses may agree on an unequal distribution of assets at dissolution. It connected the determination of unconscionability to whether enforcement of an agreement would "work an injustice."

This is similar to the standard for both prenups and postnups as set forth in Section 7.05 of the 2002 Principles of the Law of Family Dissolution (ALI Principles) (American Law Institute), which provides that a court should not enforce a term in an agreement where enforcement "would work a substantial injustice." However, one person's (or a court's) "substantial injustice" may be another's "fair and equitable."

Interestingly, there was a discussion in *Bedrick* as to whether a postnuptial agreement requires legal "consideration" to be binding. The *Bedrick* court concluded that the postnuptial agreement in that case failed, without having to reach the issue of whether the agreement could have failed for lack of consideration. See *Bedrick*, footnote 5, which contains an extended discussion about the issue of whether consideration is required in a Connecticut postnuptial agreement. It says that under current Connecticut statutory law (unlike the situation for prenuptial agreements), adequate consideration *would* be required. (See Chapters 16 and 18 for further discussion of consideration.)

Providing mutual consideration, other than the mere continuance of the marriage, would be a helpful way for people entering into postnuptial agreements to ensure a greater chance of enforceability. In addition, the consideration will help each party be satisfied with the agreement as being fair and equitable.

What about a premarital agreement that is later amended after marriage? That's an issue that arises often, and it always raises the question as to whether prenuptial or postnuptial agreement standards of enforceability apply. At least in Connecticut by statute, the legislature has made it clear that an amended *prenuptial* agreement does not require additional consideration. (Conn. Gen. Stat. Chapter 815e, § 46b-36f.)

In New York, an agreement between spouses is seen as unlike an ordinary business contract because it involves a fiduciary relationship requiring the utmost of good faith. That means there must be a heightened level of fairness to each other in order for it to be upheld. *Petracca v. Petracca*, 101 A.D.3d 695 (N.Y. 2012). The case confers a "cloak of protection" that must be thrown over postnuptial agreements to make sure they are arrived at "fairly and equitably." The *Petracca* court said it would set aside or refuse to enforce those prenups "born of and subsisting in inequity."

If, at enforcement, a court finds that results of the postnup are so one-sided that they are "manifestly unfair," the burden shifts to the proponent of the postnup, who must disprove fraud or overreaching."

In California, courts will assess a postnup to see if it was meant to provide a hoped-for reconciliation of a marriage, or if it is intended (by one party) as a way to coerce a spouse into an unfavorable divorce settlement. If a party contemplates an imminent dissolution of a marriage, then a postnup is inappropriate because it raises the issue of whether it was made in good faith. *In re Marriage of Burkle*, 139 Cal.App. 4th 712 (2006).

California statutory law specifically requires that transactions between spouses, although permitted, are subject to the rules governing fiduciary relationships. This law provides that this confidential relationship "imposes a duty of the highest good faith and fair dealing" on each spouse and that "neither shall take any unfair advantage of the other." (Cal. Fam. Code § 721.)

The leading New Jersey case on postnuptial agreements (termed "mid-marriage" agreements), stated that they must be closely scrutinized and carefully evaluated. A mid-marriage agreement also must be "fair and equitable" both at the time of signing and at the time enforcement is sought. Changed circumstances may make the enforcement of a postnuptial agreement inequitable. *Pacelli v. Pacelli*, 319 N.J. Super 185 (App. Div. 1999).

In *Pacelli*, one of the parties wanted the marriage to survive. The other also wanted to continue with the marriage, "but only on his terms." The husband had presented the wife with an ultimatum. The court noted that the cost presented in the postnup was not only monetary but would have been "the destruction of a family and the stigma of a failed marriage."

In another (unpublished) New Jersey case, the court held that all mid-marriage agreements are unenforceable as "inherently coercive" if only one of the parties wanted the marriage to survive and the other spouse did not. *Gallagher v. Gallagher*, Docket No. A-1261-09T31261-09T3 (2010).

Indiana, by case law, will allow postnuptial agreements as valid and enforceable contracts if they are entered into for the purpose of extending a marriage that was otherwise facing divorce. *Hall v. Hall*, 27 N.E.3d 281 (Ind. Ct. App. 2015). In that case, the wife was adamant about dissolving the marriage. The husband told her he would do "anything to make her more comfortable with him." She agreed to no longer pursue a divorce in exchange for such an agreement. This was unlike the *Fogg* case (see above), because the wife stayed in the marriage for an additional eight years. The court found that the agreement was supported by adequate consideration and that the pressure upon signing did not rise to the level of duress. He was *not*, in essence, deprived of the free exercise of his own will.

Practitioners engaged in drafting, negotiating, or mediating postnups need to be very aware as to whether a postnup is meant to extend and improve a marriage or whether it is being negotiated by one party to gain advantage in an imminent divorce. Valuable consideration mutually given and received by each of the spouses (other than the mere continuation of the marriage) may take it out of the zone of questionable validity.

Postnuptial agreements and the Uniform Laws.

The Uniform Premarital Agreement Act (1983) (UPAA) does not address postnuptial agreements. This means that for the many states that have adopted the UPAA without adding a provision about postnuptial agreements, the enforceability of postnups would be addressed by case law. It's difficult to pass legislation, and most of the UPAA states have not enacted specific terms that apply to postnups.

The Uniform Premarital and Marital Agreements Act (2012) (UPMAA) specifically addresses postnuptial agreements. The UPMAA treats premarital agreements and postnuptial agreements (the latter are termed "marital agreements") with exactly the same principles and requirements. As a result, it takes a very *laissez faire* attitude toward postnups; it does not put a higher burden on those wishing to enforce postnups than those entering into prenups. It views the general requirements of enforceability as being sufficient to protect parties in both types of marital contracts.

Section 9(c) offers an adopting state the option to adopt bracketed language which would allow a court to refuse enforcement of a postnup (or a prenup) if enforcement would result in "undue hardship" because of a "substantial change in circumstances arising since the time that the agreement was signed." Another ground for invalidating a postnup (or prenup) is unconscionability at time of signing. Standard contract law regarding duress is incorporated in Section 9(a). There are also optional provisions that can be adopted in Section 9 that can place the burden of proof on the party seeking enforcement of a postnup. (The default is to place the burden of proof on the party who is trying to overturn the agreement.)

By the number of states that have adopted the UPMAA (to date only two), it could be that not many states agree with this approach. A concern may be in the identical treatment between prenups and postnups. More likely, legislatures may be just too busy to consider this revised uniform act, especially if they had enacted the earlier UPAA or another prenup statute.

The ALI Principles also takes the position, like the UPMAA, that prenuptial agreements and postnuptial agreements (termed "marital agreements") should follow the same set of rules. While acknowledging that different types of risks may predominate in the various types of "marital" contracts, the ALI Principles view the resources available in the principles and the common law relating to contracts that is incorporated in the principles as being capable of addressing different situations and problems that develop in either type of contract. But it does note that opportunities for hard dealing may be greater in the context of marital agreements than with prenups.

The drafters' comments to the ALI Principles describe a situation in which a spouse has changed their position to their detriment in reliance of the marriage in making choices having to do with employment, child care or householding. In that situation, as it says, a divorce can impose a particular burden on that spouse. The other spouse's threat to divorce may be a tactic to "extract one-sided marital terms." It notes that this pressure is often heightened if there are children of the marriage. (Comment (e) to ALI Principles Section 7.01(4) and Illustration 2.)

The problem can be addressed through a claim of duress under Section 7.04(2). It also permits courts to examine the impact of an agreement at the time enforcement is sought if enforcement would work a "substantial injustice" and there was an unanticipated change of circumstances that had a substantial impact on the parties. See Sections 7.05(1) and (2). But the burden of proof is on the party seeking to invalidate the agreement. (Section 7.05(3).)

Is a written postnuptial contract required?

Postnuptial agreements are just that – agreements. Agreements can be oral understandings or written. Many postnuptial agreements are made during the course of every marriage without attorneys, without writing, and without fanfare. People change their financial relationships during their marriages as their situations change. They do this by discussing the issues and making adjustments. Even when parties seek the advice of attorneys or see a mediator to discuss postnuptial issues, they may decide to not memorialize their post-marriage agreements with a written contract. But as a general proposition, oral agreements are not legally binding.

As discussed in Chapter 7, there are plenty of unwritten contracts that are binding on married couples already relating to marriage and divorce. These are embodied in the statutes and case law in all the states. People in marriages know that situations change and spouses need to adjust. There is a natural tendency to fear imposing rigidity by applying written contract provisions to a fluid situation – a long-term marriage.

If a written contract is desired by the spouses, the level of what is written can vary. It can be as simple as a note put on the kitchen table. Or it can rise to a "term sheet," a numbered or bulleted set of sentences written by the attorneys or mediator that summarize the spouses' agreements. Or it can be a "Memorandum of Understanding" that is signed and perhaps acknowledged in front of a notary, but may not have the enforcement power of a full-blown postnuptial agreement.

A postnuptial agreement, even if mediated, is generally reviewed by each party's separate attorney, who will likely provide suggested changes, advice, and input on behalf of their respective client as to the terms of the agreement. Attorney review is generally not a requirement of an enforceable postnuptial agreement, but it will make the agreement have a greater chance of being enforced if litigation ensues. The attorney will also presumably give the client good advice. This is another advantage of having legal representative. A full-blown postnuptial agreement should also include detailed financial summary statements of each of the parties to provide full financial disclosure and prove that full disclosure was made. The agreement and the financial statements will be signed before a notary public.

Because enforceable postnuptial agreements often vary the laws of marriage, divorce, and death, they should be undertaken with great care. The more equitable they are and the more they resemble separation (divorce) agreements in their terms, the more likely they would be enforceable if the marriage ends in divorce. In addition, it is more likely they will be acceptable to both of the parties. That means they will be more likely to support the marriage rather than serving to undermine it.

CHAPTER 20

WHAT ARE THE WAYS TO BEGIN THE PROCESS?

I started practicing law in 1987. During the past 30 years, there has been a sea change in the style of lawyering. Lawyers are now, in general, cooperative rather than adversarial. The new view is that our clients have a problem and we lawyers work together to solve it. It has become an interest-based collaboration rather than a zero-sum process where "I win and you lose."

Thankfully, today the field of law is populated largely with a newer type of attorney who functions as a collaborative problem-solver and not a warrior, a transition that may bode well for prenup negotiations. Unfortunately, this is not universally the case in the field of prenuptial agreements. In that segment of legal services, attorneys for the more moneyed spouses often harken back to the older adversarial model.

The prenup process often begins when the more moneyed future spouse tells his or her fiancé that a prenup will be required before the marriage begins. The parties then each hire an attorney. The first draft is usually drafted by the attorney for the more moneyed future spouse and is generally restrictive and one-sided, offering the other spouse very little in terms of generosity, financial participation, or control.

This is followed by painful negotiations, always resulting in bad feelings. Often the attorney for the more moneyed spouse refuses to listen to his own client and puts what the attorney thinks is "right" in the prenup, rather than what the client actually wants. That especially happens if the attorney is also the attorney of the "shadow party," the parents of that future spouse. Tears (by the less moneyed spouse) are usually shed. The other future spouse feels pangs of guilt and self-reproach. Sometimes the process is so rancorous that the couple abandons the idea of having a prenup. Sometimes the process is so bitter that they decide not to get married and break off the relationship.

Sometimes the prenup gets signed, but at great cost. There are the memories of the self-interest and lack of caring demonstrated right before the wedding in the negotiations and drafting of the prenup that are unromantic and can weaken the bond. The terms that are often entered can be harsh and one-sided and will cause additional resentment later if they create an imbalance of rewards for marital efforts and decreased security for one of the spouses. The terms of prenups often fester in the background of a marriage.

The advice we give clients as attorneys is bound to be partly based on our personal experiences.

Often, but not always, when I encounter extremely non-collaborative behavior from another attorney in prenup negotiations, I start to wonder whether the attorney on the other side had a bad divorce experience of his or her own. A Google search will sometimes find that the attorney is, indeed, in a second (or third) marriage. Many attorneys recommending prenups, and particularly restrictive ones, have a history of divorce.

Sometimes the other attorney is young and/or single and has had no long-term marital experience. This can also be a detriment to the negotiation process, because how can a young attorney understand what a long-term marriage entails if that person has never been in one?

What does positive psychology have to do with it?

There is a type of psychology called "positive psychology." It seeks to improve the level of happiness and positive emotions, and it is a subset of a field of academic research now called the "science of happiness." It theorizes that negative or positive thoughts become self-fulfilling prophecies and take on a life of their own as reality.

The concepts of positive psychology have ramifications in the creation and negotiation of prenups. In order to think about your prenup and work on its potential terms, you must create negative fantasies of all the things that might happen in a marriage. That's why I tell my clients that in order to create a prenup for them, I need to divorce them and kill them (figuratively speaking, of course).

Formulating a prenup requires one to intently envision a marriage that ends in divorce. People negotiating prenups must live these negative fantasies at the time they are in love and planning their wedding. It's not a very nurturing or encouraging way to begin a marriage. So if you are going to have a prenup, there should be a very good reason for it. Try to make sure the process is a good one. And mediation may be the best way to begin. (See below.) Leave enough time between the prenup negotiations and the wedding so that you can have some relatively blissful time before the marriage to just enjoy your happiness at getting married.

What are the lawyer's ethical responsibilities in representing clients in connection with prenups?

Lawyers are trained to be paranoids. It's our profession. We are duty bound to try to think of every possible thing that can go wrong for our clients. We see it as our obligation to try to protect our clients from harm. Practicing law, in a way, is like playing chess. You have to attempt to see eight moves ahead in order to solve the legal problem. At each of those moves, as attorneys, we try to see all possible danger for our clients and try to protect them from harm.

The Hippocratic Oath for medical doctors is to "do no harm." It equally applies to attorneys. But sometimes our duty to protect our clients from harm is in opposition to our duty to advise and provide appropriate counsel to help clients make sound lifelong decisions. This quandary is especially prevalent when an attorney represents a client in connection with negotiating a prenuptial agreement.

The ABA Model Rules of Professional Conduct for Attorneys (the Model Rules or Rules) adopted in almost all states discuss the "lawyer as advisor" role. It states that in representing a client, a lawyer should render "candid" advice. It further states that in rendering advice, a lawyer "may refer not only to law but to other considerations, such as moral, economic, social, and political factors, that may be relevant to the client's situation." (Model Rule 2.1.)

The official comment to Rule 2.1 ("Scope of Advice") elaborates on this. It explains that advice "couched in narrowly legal terms" may be "of little value to a client," especially where the legal advice has predominant effects on other people. It goes on to explain that it is therefore "proper" for a lawyer to bring in moral and ethical considerations that may "impinge" upon legal questions. These extra-legal considerations may "decisively influence" how the law will be applied. Purely technical advice can sometimes be inadequate, the comment states.

The flip side of the lawyer's ethical obligation is contained in Rule 1.3 of the Model Rules. This rule requires a lawyer to represent a client "zealously within the bounds of the law." But the preamble to the Model Rules ("A Lawyer's Responsibilities") says that a lawyer is not only charged with providing a client with an understanding of his or her legal rights and obligations, but also has a duty to explain their *practical implications*. [Emphasis mine.] (Preamble, paragraph 2.)

What kind of advice in accordance with the conflicting moral and ethical considerations described in Rules 1.3 and 2.1 is appropriate for prenuptial agreement clients? And what does it mean to represent a client "zealously" in negotiating a prenup with a future spouse? What should be "zealously" protected? The good health of the marriage or one of the spouse's separate financial goals, protection of which might damage the marriage? How can these two somewhat conflicting ethical requirements be integrated in prenuptial agreement representation? Which of the roles should be emphasized? The zealous advocacy, or the lawyer as ethical counselor explaining practical implications of prenups?

Lawyers are called "counselors" for a reason. Counseling a prenup client on the broad effects of a prenup should always be part of the process.

How it starts.

Generally, the negotiations of a prenup start with a draft written by the lawyer for the more moneyed spouse-to-be. There might be some discussion between the future spouses prior to the draft, but the discussion may be fairly vague.

Protecting that client from financial loss generally comes front and center. The loss, of course, would come from a future divorce. Generally, these drafts are quite "zealous" in protecting a client from this loss. The irony is that people who are wealthy enough to need a prenup probably can be more generous in its terms than they often are.

The typical first draft is generally very one-sided. This is what prenup lawyers are trained to do. The couple is in love and getting married. The first draft is bound to create waves of unhappiness and anxiety for the couple. Almost always, both future spouses are upset by it. They think, why do lawyers do this? But the cat is out of the bag, and the prenup takes on a life of its own.

The typical first draft seems to gloss over what makes a good marriage and is largely concerned with "risk containment" and spousal control by the more moneyed future spouse. Sometimes a "bone" for the less moneyed spouse is put in. But now the couple needs to intensely contemplate divorce and its terms – at the very start of their life together.

To help mitigate the negative aspects of this process, I recommend that the attorney for the less moneyed spouse write the first draft. Better yet would be for the spouses of the upcoming marriage to decide on a term sheet in a mediated process conducted by a neutral mediator. (See below.)

But out of the ashes of the death and divorce discussions inherent in formulating a prenup, one can resurrect a financial relationship that strengthens rather than weakens the marital bond. One piece of advice for lawyers is to view "the marriage" as the client, in a sense, while still trying to balance reasonable protections for your client with terms that will help a marriage flourish.

For instance, the vesting options described in Chapter 17 go a long way toward addressing a client's anxiety about the financial results of divorce. Requiring arbitration, if there is any dispute at the time of a divorce, can address concerns about litigation. Making sure the agreement is not one-sided and recognizing the non-monetary contributions of each spouse is important. Having a plan to build marital security through marital property is vital to the emotional well-being of a marriage, especially in first marriages, but even in marriages of older people as well.

As a lawyer, you should be able to balance the sustenance for the marriage with reasonable protection for your client.

Best to begin with a term sheet.

As described in Chapter 17, I don't recommend that an attorney start with a standard "off the shelf" prenup form. This will not generally reflect the particular situation and aims of the clients. Reflecting the particular couple's situation in a prenup is very important to having them fully embrace the terms. And that is the goal for a sound prenup.

Remember, the prenup is (or at least should be) an agreement. Note the word "agree" in the term, and remember it. The first draft can express that agreement of both parties, and can make both future spouses – the less moneyed spouse and the more moneyed spouse – feel that his or her needs and aims are reflected in the draft.

My recommendation is that the prenup should always start with a term sheet and not a draft contract. The term sheet is an outline of the agreed-to terms of the prenups. Once agreed to, the terms will be imbedded in the final document.

The term sheet is usually one or two pages long and very simply stated. No legalese is involved. The terms will be discussed between the future spouses, who will also get input from their respective attorneys. Terms can be read and understood more easily than in the full-blown agreement, and changes and adjustments in terms can be made clearly and easily. It is very tiring for clients (and attorneys) to go through draft after draft of a complete agreement in order to negotiate and change the imbedded terms that can more easily be seen and adjusted on a term sheet.

Entering into a mediation process with a trained neutral mediator is a good way to start to formulate a term sheet. There will probably be mutual adjustment of the terms as advice, information, and agreements between the spouses are made based on their own thoughts and feelings, as well as their separate attorneys' review and advice. When the terms are finalized, it's time for one of the attorneys (or the mediator, if he or she is an attorney) to draft the full-blown agreement incorporating the terms that the parties have mutually agreed to. Sometimes the reviewing attorneys enter the picture after the mediation, and the drafting of the contract by a lawyer/mediator is based on the clients' term sheet. The draft prenuptial agreement will have the requisite

334 / LAURIE ISRAEL

legal language required in such an important contract.

A prenup is likely the most important contract a person will sign in his or her lifetime. It's not only important financially, but it can change the nature and dynamics of your marriage. That's why it's important to do it carefully and (generally) have your own counsel to advise you.

Getting a prenup form (readily available on the internet) or creating one with one of the self-help books on the market (including this one!) is not the way to create a prenup. Entering into a prenup is a very important step in your marriage by which you may be changing the essence of state laws that embody marriage values and protections. These laws have been developed through generations of human and societal experience. Much thought needs to be given to the prenup if you decide to circumvent or contradict existing laws.

There are several types of attorneys who have experience in working with prenuptial agreements. Family (divorce) lawyers, estate-planning lawyers, and business lawyers are the primary providers. They each have different points of view as to what prenups should achieve. Sometimes in complicated situations involving vast wealth or significant business interests, there might be more than one prenuptial attorney representing a client or consulting on the prenup.

I prefer to refer to divorce attorneys for representation in prenuptial agreements in most cases. Through their experience as divorce lawyers, they tend to be sensitive to the dynamics of marriage, the role of money and contribution to marriage, and what makes marriages work. This can be very helpful to a client who is formulating a prenup. Because much of the prenup contract deals with the terms of a possible future divorce, I think divorce attorneys have the requisite experience in divorce law and can better consider and draft these provisions.

As described in Chapter 8, many attorneys representing the more moneyed spouse are the family attorney of that future spouse's parents. That "family" attorney will follow the marching orders of the parents – otherwise that attorney would lose a very important client (the parents).

There is an inherent conflict of interest situation when a party engages his or her parents' attorney. The independence of the future spouse's choice and the advice of the counsel can be questionable. It's best to start with an attorney engaged independently by the more moneyed party.

Some couples, in fairly complicated situations, use the collaborative law process to negotiate and formulate their prenups, with good success. Although this process is mainly used for divorces (see Chapter 6), it can also be advantageous to formulating prenuptial (and postnuptial) agreements.

Collaborative law involves face-to-face sessions with the two clients and their attorneys, generally with the addition of a neutral process facilitator to keep everyone in line. Sometimes even in a divorce, the collaborative divorce process can result in preserving the marriage rather than finding the terms for a divorce settlement. It can happen after a series of these "team" sessions, and can end with a postnuptial agreement that embodies the terms of the newly ongoing marriage rather than a divorce settlement agreement. Because of its potential for healing, collaborative law can serve very well as a beneficial process for some couples who are negotiating a prenuptial agreement.

Mediating a prenuptial agreement.

As we have seen, there are many problems in the way most prenups are negotiated. The role of attorney and the adversarial nature of the process often lead to increasing premarital disharmony right before the wedding. If at all possible, mediating a prenuptial agreement is an excellent way to start the prenup process and, in my opinion, often the preferred method. The same holds true for mediating postnuptial agreements.

Starting with mediation, one can reduce or eliminate damage to the relationship when a prenup is certain or even likely to happen. This process lets the parties (not their lawyers) decide the terms for themselves. Mediators can help level the playing field and help the couple come together with a solution that is acceptable to both.

Here's how it works:

The first step for couples thinking about having a prenup is to know that mediation is available. People often don't realize that this is an option. Many mediators are now mediating prenups with great success. People are searching for non-conflictual ways to negotiate prenups. If you search "mediation" and "prenuptial agreement" in your geographic location, you will find many professionals working in this area of mediation. Today my Google search of "mediation prenuptial agreement" found 516,000 hits, and my search of "mediation prenuptial agreement Boston" turned up 74,200 results.

One of the future spouses can encourage the other not to have one of their attorneys work on a first draft. That first draft, if received, is usually a very harsh and unwelcome way to start the process. It can make the negotiations turn bitter very quickly. If a party has received that type of draft from his or her attorney, perhaps he or she should start by putting it in the shredder, unread. Reading it and sharing it with the other future spouse may be very counterproductive. It's important to start fresh when you are trying to figure out prenup terms that work for both of you.

I often see mediation clients after they have experienced a very negative negotiation process led by their two attorneys. A mediator can open a new door and create an entirely new chapter by means of mediation.

The idea of mediation is for the parties to think about and mutually set the terms of their prenuptial agreement with the mediator's guidance. They are getting married, so the terms should reflect mutual love and caring. Hopefully the process won't be contaminated by the thoughts of their previous lawyers or their parents who are often the shadow parties behind a prenup.

At the first meeting, the mediator should become familiar with each of the parties' factual situations. How long have they been together? What is their sense of the marriage? Is it a first marriage or is it a second one? Are there children from the first marriage? Are either of their sets of parents divorced? If the clients have been divorced, what was their experience? Have they been struggling over the prenup? Have they had a bad experience with attorneys that have previously represented them in connection with the prenup?

If a party has an ongoing business, it is very important to clearly understand its financial aspects. This will take some time and require review of additional documents. Some questions that you should consider would be the following:

How is the income the business generates characterized – as salary or business income, or as both? Who controls the earnings that might remain in the business? What is the fair market value of the business? If there is a recent financial statement of the business (such as in connection with a loan application), that statement should be part of the package to review. Look at the past two or three years of business income tax returns (if typical) and personal tax returns. A full understanding of the business by the mediator and by the parties (including the non-owning party) is crucial to formulating a sound prenup plan.

Often the idea of a prenup comes from the moneyed parents of one of the future spouses. In the case of parental wealth, a spouse may be asked to waive all rights of the other to gifted and inherited money coming from a spouse's parent to their son or daughter, forever. That party needs to know what he or she is waiving. Accordingly, in some reasonable manner, the assets of those parents need to be revealed in order to ensure waiver by the less moneyed future spouse. Oftentimes this includes review of the applicable instruments (trusts, etc.) to review the terms. Some way of understanding the monetary value of what a party is waiving is also important. (Is the future spouse's parents' net worth $1 million or $100 million? It does make a difference.)

All the information that is provided should be shared between the parties so they have full disclosure and understanding of each other's assets and income, including financial information on the wealth of the parents, if that is what's driving the prenup. The understanding of each of their finances and the reasons for the prenup should be probing and precise. Terms addressing the reasonable protection interests of a future spouse should be as narrowly drawn as possible.

A good mediator should also find out what the clients' plans are. Do they expect to have children? At what point? Do they expect to have more than one? Do they expect the mother (or the father) to leave the job market? If so, for how long? If it's a second marriage, how do they plan to provide for the children of the first marriage? How do they envision providing for their own and their spouse's needs as they age? These goals should be accommodated in a "gray" prenup. (See Chapter 11.)

It's important that each of the parties knows what the applicable laws of divorce and inheritance are in their state. (See Chapter 7.) That way they know what they are waiving. Waiver is a very important aspect of prenuptial agreements. In certain aspects, a prenup may even expand the rights a spouse would have under state law. There's nothing wrong with that, especially if that person is giving up other rights.

Sometimes, after going over the applicable laws, the parties decide that they want the state law to apply and abandon the idea of a prenup altogether. Never assume the mediation (or legal representation) will end up with a prenup, especially when it's a first marriage of relatively young people. It sometimes doesn't.

Remember, mediators are allowed to provide legal information (but not legal advice). A mediator can and should provide information on state laws relating to divorce, marital rights, and inheritance, as well as laws determining the enforceability (and non-enforceability) of prenups. That means you need to engage a mediator (lawyer or non-lawyer) who is fully versed in the laws relating to prenuptial agreements and the laws pertaining to divorce and inheritance.

Different people have different conceptions of what a marital partnership is and what its financial aspects should be. In mediation, it is also important to find out the two mediation clients' respective views on prenups, which might be quite divergent. Part of leveling the playing field is hearing from the person who doesn't really want a prenup. That person often is concerned or fearful about expressing his or her concerns. Having those concerns expressed and dealt with is very important to having a sound prenup.

In mediation, the clients can air their views on all the substantive issues that would be in the prenup. If someone is concerned about receiving a potential inheritance, the mediator can encourage the parties to fully discuss it. Any concern should be viewed through the filter of all the other financial information obtained and foreseeable (and unforeseeable) future financial circumstances.

What if the other party will receive no inheritance? How old are the parents of the party with the expectancy? What if the marriage is long-lasting? Does it still make sense to forever isolate an inheritance as separate property? Some states and community property jurisdictions do that, but many states take an equitable view based on the then existing financial situation, health, age, and any other considerations that may apply at that time.

In mediation, the parties can mutually decide to have terms that are not "all or nothing." Any issue can be sliced and diced. For instance, gains and income derived from separate property can be always considered separate property, or not. Income as well as gains from separate property can be shared as marital property. Or the sharing can be staged in percentages. The sharing percentages don't have to be fixed – they can start at some point after the wedding and accelerate as the marriage grows longer and proves itself as durable. Or there can be no sharing at all, and separate property (and its income and gains) can remain separate. It's important, though, for people to know and consider what the options are.

Parties in mediation can seek to address every financial issue. However, due to public policy considerations, child-related provisions (and sometimes spousal support) may remain subject to court jurisdiction and oversight. A prenup could take the opposite tack and be as bare-bones possible. For instance, it can just talk about divorce process, leaving all other issues to be decided by the parties at the time of divorce and, if they cannot decide, require arbitration and not litigation.

It is understandable that a person coming into a marriage with great wealth would want to protect him- or herself from loss or uncertainty through divorce litigation, especially if it turns out to be a marriage of short duration. And yet being overly protective about money may diminish the strength of a marriage. One must ask themselves, "What's more important, money or the marriage?" and "How much money is enough?" It's good for the marriage if a balance is struck. Mediation is a good way for the future spouses to have this conversation with a neutral third party and create a mutually acceptable balance.

If the mediator is an attorney who is admitted to the bar in the state where the couple resides, it is often preferable for the first draft to be written up by the mediator. It should reflect the terms agreed to by the mediation clients clearly and accurately, but also reflect their situations and aims. After all, they are getting married, and this is not just a financial business contract between two unrelated people. I don't believe in having a prenuptial agreement that is difficult for clients to understand, even though the "legalese" language might seem elegant to the attorneys. Much of the agreement can be written in plain English.

The "Statement of Facts" I use in my prenups is an important part of the document. It describes the parties' factual situations, including information on families of origin, the client's educations, and their livelihoods. It will provide the facts sufficient enough to draw the inference, often subtly, of the reasons that this particular couple has decided to have a prenup. It's important, because the couple is reflected in these facts. It's not a "one-size-fits-all" document.

When written this way, the agreement seems softer, more loving, and less harsh, as is the impersonal template often used by attorneys. This makes a big psychological difference for people signing prenups. They can truly "sign on" to the document. They're "all in." Many times, when attorneys do prenups for their clients, one of the clients is not "all in."

When the draft is approved by both of the parties, it can be sent to their respective attorneys for review and input.

If the mediator is not an attorney, it would probably be best to refer it to one of the attorneys to write it up, based on the term sheet. (Each of the parties should be separately represented.) It's probably best to have the parties agree that the attorney for the less moneyed spouse write up the first version. That will help level the playing field. It will be good if the parties permit the mediator to have a chat with the attorneys to explain the process and the goals of the couple before the draft is written up.

Feedback from the reviewing attorneys can be very useful. They can make the document better and find places where the drafting needs to be clarified. Reviewing attorneys can also find issues that were not adequately addressed or were omitted. They will provide independent advice to their client, which is very important. The clients, of course, can choose their attorneys at the outset and consult with that attorney before and during the mediation process.

It's the clients' choice as to whether they want the mediator to be copied on the drafts as they are generated by the reviewing attorneys. The mediator is sometimes in a good position to pick up on what the parties intended as the attorney drafts come through. Sometimes the reviewing attorneys (or the mediation clients) need to consult with the mediator on an issue. Sometimes an issue may find its way back into mediation to be resolved.

Are caucuses appropriate in prenuptial agreement mediation?

In a caucus, one of the parties to the mediation meets in a private session with the mediator. They are often used in business mediation and divorce mediation to help parties come to a compromise. In these types of mediations, individual meetings are sometimes used as a last-ditch effort by a mediator trying to resolve an impasse. These private sessions can be very helpful having the parties come to an agreement. I do not recommend them for prenuptial agreement negotiations for the following reasons.

In a caucus, as a general rule, the mediator is obligated to maintain the privacy of information given by to him or her by a mediation client. The mediator would have to hold private information gained in a private caucus session with one of the future spouses as confidential.

Perhaps the other party may then meet with the mediator and impart other confidential information on the same topic that the mediation is addressing. Secrets, especially financial ones, are incompatible with marriage.

The two mediation clients are embarking on, hopefully, a very long marriage. If there are secrets (and these would likely be financial or personal secrets relating to prenup terms), they could well be detrimental to the marriage. If they are big enough secrets to call them "secrets," that seems quite ominous. Having important facts unrevealed detracts from the honesty and full disclosure needed by the future spouses as they negotiate the financial terms of their marriage. If they hide things, they are not working with a full deck.

Also, imparting information to be held secret by the mediator in a caucus puts the mediator in a very compromised position. The mediator has gained confidential information that the mediation client doesn't want shared with his or her future spouse. How can a mediator pretend he or she has not heard that information when there is an ensuing discussion involving the content of that information in a three-way mediation session? Keeping the secret would be tantamount to the mediator committing a fraud on the party who doesn't know the real facts.

It puts the mediator in a grave conflict. That's why mediators generally advise clients in writing before the mediation begins that he or she will not hold secrets or confidential information imparted to the mediator by the clients.

As a result, I do not think caucusing is appropriate for clients mediating prenuptial agreements or postnuptial agreements. For the same reasons, I don't think caucuses are appropriate to marital mediation. (See below.)

Where does marital mediation fit into prenuptial or postnuptial agreement mediation?

Marital mediation is a new area of mediation in which a mediator (rather than a marital counselor or therapist) helps clients resolve problems in their marriage. It is often used to address financial issues in an ongoing marriage. (See Chapter 19.) The mediator uses standard mediation techniques to work on marital issues such as "contribution to marriage," planning for financial security and making financial decisions, and parsing and giving feedback on marital communication and interactions.

I view prenuptial agreement mediation as a form of marital mediation (pre-marital mediation, if you will).

Prenuptial agreement mediation encourages generosity, truthfulness, and clear communications. It's about money and security, which are deep concerns in marriages. It helps a couple with their ability to discuss and resolve difficult issues. This is identical to marital mediation where couples are struggling over difficult issues, often money issues, which are extremely common in marriages. Prenuptial agreement mediation is good training for the upcoming marriage.

People sometimes come to mediation during an ongoing marriage because they are considering a mid-marriage change in their relationship (often financial). They are seeking some resolution of a difficulty that is continuing to upset their marriage. They would like a mediator's help in order to proceed harmoniously. Terms reflecting the needed changes can be worked out in medi-ation sessions and can be written up in a formal postnuptial agreement.

In my experience as the mediator for these couples, more often than not, the mediation helps them to come to financial terms. They believe they can incorporate these terms into their ongoing marriages. They ultimately do so, often without the need for a formal, written postnuptial agreement. In other words, the postnuptial agreement mediation becomes a marital mediation process that transforms the marriage into something more workable.

Mediators work in all types of contexts – in workplace disputes, divorces, business relationships, and in other situations involving people in disputes. Marital mediation is simply another application of mediation in a different context. Although very helpful to many people, most people don't yet know about its availability or may wonder about its utility. But there is no sound reason to disqualify mediators from working with people who are in the relationship of being married.

Marital mediation is different than marital therapy or counseling. It focuses on the here-and-now to help couples resolve ongoing disputes. It tends to be very practical and short term. It deals with discrete problems and issues. It does not delve into family histories, personal pasts, or psychology.

Marital mediation often occurs contemporaneously with the couple seeing marital counselors or individual therapists. When a mid-term marriage is having problems, it makes sense to obtain as much professional help with the situation as possible. People often want to preserve and improve their marriages at this point and are willing to try everything they can to make it work.

Mediators (including marital mediators) are very good at ascertaining whether people are understanding each other. The mediation techniques of identifying overt and covert messages, questioning assumptions, and determining the basis or "interest" of a spouse in what they want (rather than their stated "position") is extremely important in helping married couples.

Even people in long-term marriages tend to incorrectly interpret each other's words and behavior. Mediators are very good at being able to observe these misunderstandings and share them with the mediation clients. They can drill down to deconstruct some of the misunderstandings, which can lead to a very transformative change in a married couple's interactions with each other.

If you are in mid-marriage and things are not going the way you would like, a good step for you might be to find a postnuptial agreement mediator or a marital mediator. You may find that this type of outside help may aid you in moving forward in your marriage in a positive way.

CHAPTER 21

LAWYER OR MEDIATOR — HOW CAN WE FIND A GOOD ONE?

O ne of the most important decisions you will make in the process of getting a prenup is choosing your lawyer. Lawyers come in all different types and with different personalities. We're not all the same. We have diverse values and experiences. We have differing philosophies about marriage, divorce, and prenuptial agreements. Our personal life experiences also play a part in the advice we give our clients. In other words, lawyers are not indistinguishable.

How to find a good fit.

People say that clients pick lawyers that are similar in outlook to themselves. I think there is a lot of truth to that. Litigious people tend to choose litigious lawyers. New Age people tend to pick New Age lawyers. The attorney-client relationship is, in a certain way, quite intimate. Usually the relationship begins when the client has a difficult personal issue to resolve, often a painful or embarrassing one. The client needs to feel personally comfortable with their lawyer and feel like their life values and their attorney's are well-aligned.

The attorney will (and must) keep professional boundaries in order to properly serve the client. That means that the relationship is about listening to the client and understanding the client's needs, wishes, outlook, and difficulties. The relationship is not about the personal life or needs of the lawyer.

That's what I mean by boundaries. We are here to serve our clients in whatever way we can.

Before lawyers give advice to clients, we must listen first, and listen carefully. Although we as lawyers are trained to act (and act assertively) to render help to a client, the listening part is important. We need to know what our clients' worries, fears, and past experiences are before we apply the legal filter.

When you find a good fit with a prenuptial agreement attorney, you'll know it. It's a crucial first step in the process. You want someone who will listen to your goals (and your future spouse's), as you will convey them to your lawyer. The most destructive choice you can make is if you choose someone who lacks the outlook, style, and experience that can make the process, if not delightful, at least constructive and not corrosive. This will require some thinking and research on your part (and on the part of your future spouse), as well as your monitoring of the prenup process as it unfolds.

But what screening questions should you ask in order for you to find a good match?

What to look for in a prenup lawyer.

It's important for you to find a lawyer who can explain the underlying law clearly and plainly to you. This will consist of the laws of divorce, marriage, and inheritance in your state. Since you will be varying the law of your state in the prenup when you sign it, you need to understand exactly what you are waiving. Your attorney also should explain to you the laws of prenuptial agreements in your state and give you parameters about the enforceability of various terms.

Asking your attorney to give you input on all the terms you and your spouse are thinking of adopting can be very helpful to you. Often prenup clients are on the youngish side and haven't experienced a long-term marriage. The attorney may have had more life experiences, including as a spouse in an ongoing marriage. That attorney may be able to advise you as "counselor." (See Chapter 20.)

The attorney may be in a good position to explain the ramifications of some of the terms you may think you want to include. For instance, if your initial thought is to keep all property and income separate forever and never have any possibility of spousal support under any scenario, an attorney can provide real-life input and counsel to you on why this may not be such a good idea in your situation.

A written prenup has a lot of legalese in it. This is for two reasons. First, the legalese has many important terms that are needed to make the contract enforceable. Secondly, legalese is very efficient. It has been shown that if were written in plain English, most contracts would be two or three times the length of the same one written using legalese. But the legalese does need to be explained by the lawyer. A great deal of the agreement can (and should) be written in plain English. Many attorneys don't do this, and this might be a good screening question to ask.

Look for a lawyer that is a good communicator. Also, you'll want an attorney that enjoys his or her job. You may be able to tell that by the attorney's voice and energy level when you speak with him or her. You'll want someone who is flexible and creative. You may be able to get a sense of this by visiting the attorney's website and reading what that attorney has posted online.

Being creative is really important in prenups, as there are many choices and many directions that can be taken in every decision that ends up in a prenup. You can perhaps test this by asking the prospective attorney a single question: "How would you address _____?" or "What are your thoughts about _____?"

You will also get a sense of whether or not the lawyer is personally compatible with you in values, style, personality, and often background.

What if your attorney doesn't reflect your views or intentions?

Attorneys do not (and should not) rubber-stamp everything a client wants, but rather they are obligated to exercise their independent judgment. That means providing the client with information and feedback on the terms proposed by the client. But that doesn't mean the attorney should control what's in the prenup.

This is an issue that often comes up is when your lawyer doesn't reflect or communicate your views and intent in the drafting of the prenup, or in the negotiation process. A client may want a particular term in the prenup, and the draft from the attorney may have the opposite of what the client wanted. Surprisingly, this is a very common situation that causes many problems.

In the field of prenuptial agreements, many attorneys have a fixed view of what a prenup should be and what terms should be in it. An attorney may fail to put a certain provision in place, even when requested by a client to do so, after receiving the attorney's contrary advice. This causes a lot of unnecessary stress in the negotiation process. It may be a draft with a term in it that the other future spouse had specifically asked the fiancé not include. And yet it appears in the draft, even though he had instructed his attorney not to include it. This happens fairly often.

The client may have a very strong opinion about what should go into their prenup that is against the independent judgment of the attorney. A lawyer can try to convince the client to include the provision the lawyer thinks is correct and appropriate. But if the client insists on his own version, the lawyer should put that term in the prenup, perhaps with a side letter (also known as a "cover your a— " letter) warning the client of the dangers, or the attorney should withdraw as the client's counsel.

Lawyers' billing practices.

Lawyers usually bill at an hourly rate for time spent. This method tends to be the most equitable for both the client and the lawyer.

Lawyers with more experience usually bill at higher rates, but they also tend to generally get the job done more quickly. Less time means a lower bill. In addition, the experienced attorney tends to have more insight, which will be very helpful to you and your future spouse as you embark on a prenup. Lawyers at large firms (or lawyers who formerly worked for large firms) bill at the highest hourly rates. They tend to have expertise in complex business and financial matters that may be needed in certain cases.

So in the long run, you might not necessarily save anything by choosing an attorney with a low hourly rate. There are also problems if you and the attorney agree to a fixed amount to complete the prenup (i.e., a "flat fee" for the job). Someone offering to do an entire prenup for $1,250 is probably not experienced but is trying to become experienced. Also, the resulting document will essentially be a form of an "off-the-shelf" document rather than a customized prenup that reflects your values and aims and supports your marriage. Remember that a prenup is generally the most significant financial agreement most people will sign in their lives, so treat it seriously. The money you spend on it should be worth it.

Solo and small firm practitioners who are actively engaged in representing prenup clients will be good choices in most cases. Remember what the term "practicing" law means. Lawyers get better at doing their jobs with more practice. The more prenups they do, the more experience they acquire. A legitimate question to ask is how many prenup clients the attorney represented in the past year or two. It would be good to find someone for whom prenuptial agreements is a significant portion of that attorney's practice.

An experienced lawyer's billable rate may be $300 an hour. But it's not really $300 an hour; the lawyer does not keep all of it. An average of 50 percent goes to overhead. That leaves $150 an hour as the rate. But lawyers spend an average of half their time doing administrative work, client development, meetings, and engagement in professional groups such as bar associations. They also spend time increasing their knowledge by reading cases and legal newspapers and attending seminars. That leaves a net of $75 an hour for the actual lawyer's work. That's something like the typical rate of an electrician or a plumber. So don't be scared, angry, or feel you're being taken advantage of if your lawyer charges $300 an hour. Put it in perspective.

Busy, competent, successful lawyers tend not to agree to be "interviewed" by clients. Often an attorney will not accept a client who even asks for an interview at no charge. You can really find out all you need from the attorney's online presence, plus an initial short phone call, which almost all attorneys are willing to do. If you would like an extensive interview, be prepared to pay the attorney his or her hourly rate. You will benefit from the information imparted by the attorney, even if you decide to go somewhere else.

You certainly have a right to ask the lawyer for an estimate of his or her work. What I say to people (once I find out what's involved – prenups with business interests or great family wealth are more complicated than more simple ones) is an average cost. (My average time spent on a prenup, whether I am the mediator or acting as counsel for one of the parties is 15 hours.) I ask for that amount to be paid as a retainer. If the hours worked amount to less, the excess retainer balance will be refunded; if more, then additional funds will be requested as a retainer in order to complete the work.

Try to get an honest estimate, not one low enough just to acquire you as a client. Most potential clients understand and respect the estimate, even if they are given a lower estimate by another attorney. Prenups are complicated agreements, and they take time to formulate and draft. Don't expect to find one at a very low cost.

How to choose an attorney from attorney websites.

Doctors are different than lawyers, in that there is a tradition for physicians not to advertise. There is an almost complete blackout of online advertising of physicians' backgrounds. You can hardly find out anything about a doctor online, except a phone number, the doctor's area of practice, and perhaps the medical school they attended. Doctors seem to take the position that they are virtually identical – fungible, in legal language. There is no way to get any sense of who they are, their experience, or what they say about their practices and philosophy of practicing medicine.

My brother, a retired physician, is very familiar with this phenomenon. He says that within the medical profession, medical doctors operate as a "guild." He calls it a historic and long-standing view. One of the guild's jobs is to protect the livelihoods of its members by protecting its secrets, creating a lack of price competition, and creating a monopoly for their services. Another major difference between physicians and lawyers is that doctors' fees are mostly paid through medical insurance. This prevents doctors from needing to go out into the market to drum up business, as lawyers have to do.

Lawyers have had experience in advertising for more than 30 years. Advertising content is subject to lawyers' ethical rules. The ABA Model Rules of Professional Conduct require that a lawyer not make a "false or misleading" communication about a lawyer's services. The drafters give examples of what "false or misleading" is. It includes statements that would create unjustified expectations as to the results a lawyer could achieve. (Rule 7.1 and Comment.)

But lawyers are specifically permitted to advertise in print and online, subject to this requirement. (Rule 7.2.)

Because lawyers don't get paid by insurance companies (as doctors do), the legal profession is quite competitive. As a result, lawyers can and do advertise in every way possible, within the boundaries of these ethical requirements. This applies to big-firm attorneys as well as small and medium-size firms.

There is much information about almost every lawyer on the internet. In fact, if you cannot find an internet presence for a lawyer, you have reason to be wary of that person when you are choosing an attorney to represent you. You may conclude that this person does not have an active, thriving practice. The more actively engaged in the practice of law and the more experienced that attorney is, the better for the client. The actively engaged attorneys generally have a significant internet presence, and you can find out a lot about them if you take a look online.

Other things to think about when choosing a prenup attorney.

When you are engaging an attorney, you should verify who actually will be doing the work. Will it be the attorney you engaged or someone else in the firm? If an associate attorney, that person may never have met with you in person. He or she might be quite young and may be inexperienced in the law. It is very possible that you might want to work with someone close to your age, particularly if you are embarking on a "gray" prenup. And believe it or not, you can get a good sense of the person by looking at the photo of the lawyer online. You know what they say – you can know a person by looking into their eyes. You want to find someone who is compatible with you. You and the attorney will be partners in the endeavor of formulating a prenup.

I don't believe it is appropriate for paralegals (or inexperienced lawyers) to work on prenups, other than to perform administrative work. A prenup thoughtfully done is not like a house closing or routine litigation work. It involves a great deal of discretion at every step. It also requires a deep level of legal knowledge encompassing many areas of law. It also requires a great deal of personal life experience as well as legal knowledge to do it properly.

Every lawyer is different, and each has different interests, strengths, and weakness. Also, each lawyer may have a different view on what marriage is and what the effects of prenup terms might be on the upcoming marriage. Some are concerned with how to draft a prenup that can support the upcoming marriage. Some are more concerned with asset protection and risk containment. You will have the opportunity to choose the attorney with the outlook that most closely aligns with your views and goals.

At best, the lawyer-client relationship is, and feels like, a partnership. The attorney is a resource to their client. He or she should provide counsel as to real-life situations and legal consequences as would be appropriate in thinking about the terms of the prenup and their effect on the upcoming marriage. But the attorney takes his or her lead from the client. The clients express their own views and priorities. The more intelligent and thoughtful the client, the better the partnership between attorney and client works.

What law background and experience should a prenup attorney have?

There are several interrelated areas of law that are important to know if you are a prenuptial agreement attorney. They are divorce law, probate law, estate planning, business law, elder law, and tax law, as well as the law of prenuptial agreements. As a result, your attorney probably should be a generalist in knowing at least a great deal about each these areas of law. The knowledge base would be similar to that of a primary care physician or an internal medicine physician.

My view on prenups (perhaps a minority view) is that they are not solely documents for the purpose of asset protection, as some attorneys view them. They are that, yes, but they also should create a reasonable financial structure for a marriage. Marriage is a particular relationship that goes beyond that of business partners or arm's-length buyer-and-seller commercial transactions. The prenup should reflect this special relationship. Having said that, in many situations, the structure and certainty determined by the prenup can help people relax as they enter marriage. At the outset, they have solved the question of what will happen if they break up or if one of them dies.

If the level of complexity is beyond that of a "generalist" prenup attorney, that attorney (and the client) can consult with another specialist. In general, it probably is a not good idea to start with a specialist lawyer, such as a business lawyer, as your primary prenup lawyer. That lawyer may know a lot about business, but he or she may know little about divorce law (or marriage). Sometimes a corporate attorney, or a sophisticated estate-planning attorney, should be called in. Don't disqualify a generalist prenup attorney because that attorney doesn't know what QTIPs, GST, IDGTs, or ILITs are. Others can be brought in with this knowledge base as consultants if it's relevant to the work.

Another aspect that you might be looking for is someone who understands and knows how to support long-term marriages. That's the aim of most everyone getting married, including those entering into a prenup.

Some attorneys who have been through "bad" divorces will probably have a mindset toward asset protection and away from asset sharing. This may be inappropriate, especially for first marriages of young people. Someone who has never been married may not fully understand the dynamics and the importance of developing financial security in a long-term marriage and how easy exit plans sometimes inherent in prenups may weaken the marital bond.

What if the more moneyed spouse's lawyer is his or her parents' family lawyer? Then an inherent conflict of interest exists. (See Chapter 8.) Often the attorney for one of the upcoming spouses is the family lawyer or business lawyer of his or her parents and the parents are the driving force behind the prenup. It's best to start with an "outside" attorney freely chosen by that future spouse if possible.

Personal referrals are another way that people can find appropriate prenuptial agreement attorneys. But make sure the referral is a prenuptial agreement attorney and not a personal injury lawyer. It may be wise to avoid litigation attorneys when choosing someone to represent you in a prenup. Having this type of attorney may make the negotiations more negative than you may want them to be. Some divorce lawyers are primarily litigation attorneys. You can often tell from their websites the types of law they practice. Perhaps choosing a divorce lawyer who is active in a mediation association or the collaborative law bar might be a better choice.

A good source of referrals may be a referral from the attorney that has been engaged by one of the future spouses. Perhaps the two attorneys have a good history of working together on cases. They might be compatible and have good communication between each other. Finding a "team" like this is similar to putting together a collaborative law process team – you want to find professionals that work well together as the terms of the agreement are worked out. Synergy and cooperation between two lawyers bodes well for the clients.

What search strings to use to find a prenup lawyer on the internet?

It is generally quite easy to find prenup lawyers who are appropriate for you on the internet.

Starting with a Google search would be good. The search string I use for the type of prenup attorney I'm looking for when I'm making out-of-state referrals is the following in one search string:

> prenuptial agreement collaborative law mediation marital mediation [your geographic area]

This pulls up divorce and family law attorneys who are experienced in prenups and also in mediation and collaborative law. (My preference is for the attorney to have a deep knowledge of divorce law, since divorce terms are so important in a prenup.) Some of these attorneys might be working in marital mediation (see Chapter 20), which is a good skill set for representing people in prenups. If both of you find lawyers who practice in these fields, it may enable a harmonious prenup process where there might be much flexibility on terms. Decisions can be encouraged to be made collaboratively rather than unilaterally.

Prenuptial agreement lawyers who call themselves "matrimonial lawyers" (rather than "divorce lawyers") have a somewhat different approach. They are generally very skilled divorce lawyers who often emphasize a primary interest in the asset protection aspects of a prenup. Many of these attorneys are in large firms or medium-size firms. Litigation tends to be an important part of their practice. Some of these attorneys are members of the American Academy of Matrimonial Lawyers (AAML). AAML is a selective lawyers' association that only accepts lawyers with significant litigation practices. Its attorneys often deal with high-asset clients. If your aim is primarily asset protection, you could do the following internet searches:

> prenuptial agreement matrimonial lawyer
> [your geographic area]

or

> prenuptial agreement matrimonial lawyer AAML
> [your geographic area]

After you've done your initial screen, you can find out much more about each of the attorneys returned by your search string by looking at their websites. You can find out even more about an attorney by an internet search for them outside of their firm's website. These searches would look like this:

> [Name of attorney] attorney [state]

or the more general one:

> [name] [state]

These searches may bring up some of that attorney's activities outside of their law practice, such as community activities. You might find that the attorney was a plaintiff or a defendant in a lawsuit, or other personal information about the attorney that may also help you to come to a decision. You might even find information about the attorney's own divorce.

By looking at attorney websites, you'll find a list of their publications (print and online) and the types of cases they are involved in.

You can also search for that attorney on Facebook, LinkedIn, and Twitter. These are also good ways to research your future spouse's attorney, too. In most cases, if you want a peaceful prenup, you and your fiancé should create a list together and each choose an attorney on the mutually developed list.

I would not put too much credence in Google, Yelp, or Avvo reviews. They may (or may not) be accurate, depending on who has posted reviews. One dissatisfied client with a single (perhaps anonymous) review can skew the results. There is generally not enough information on each lawyer to make a rational assessment.

Finding a postnuptial agreement attorney.

Postnuptial agreements are different than prenuptial agreements and follow different legal rules and requirements. This is a relatively new area of law. Because of that, postnups are even rarer than prenups. It would be very important to find a lawyer with experience in drafting and representing people in connection with postnups, if that's what you and your spouse are looking for. There are fewer lawyers experienced in that field, but you should be able to find them.

As described in Chapter 19, because the marriage is already in existence, great care and sensitivity need to be taken when formulating the terms of a postnup. Different enforceability standards are often in effect. Finding an attorney who also is a mediator, and specifically a marital mediator, might be helpful to the process as well.

Here's a search string you might use:

> postnuptial agreement attorney marital mediation
> [your geographic area]

How to find a mediator.

Mediation is often the preferred way of beginning the process of getting a prenuptial agreement done. Parties to most mediated prenups also have attorneys in the wings, advising them along the way. These attorneys review the terms formulated in mediation. They can add value by making changes and improvements in the concepts developed in mediation. These attorneys are called reviewing attorneys, and they serve a very important function. (See Chapter 20.)

An important question to ask yourself when looking for a mediator is whether to choose an attorney mediator or a non-attorney mediator.

Non-attorney mediators come from various professional (and non-professional) backgrounds. Mediation is an unregulated field, unlike law, where attorneys must pass competency tests and whose practices are regulated by the state bar associations and the Rules of Professional Responsibility.

Some mediators come from mental health backgrounds, ranging from master's degrees to PhDs and PsyDs. They are psychologists, counselors, social workers, and family therapists. Others have educational degrees or business degrees or experience. There is no requirement for any specific degree, educational background, training, or registration in almost all states to be a mediator. There are some mediation organizations that have "certified" mediators who have to satisfy certain rules of education or experience, but basically it's an unregulated field.

I like to call lawyers "money doctors." When it comes right down to it, that's what we are. Most lawyers have a lot of experience in reviewing financial documents, no matter what areas they work in. Even divorce lawyers – in fact, especially divorce lawyers – have a great deal of financial expertise. Divorce is the termination and unwinding of a financial partnership between two spouses. Sometimes, especially in longer marriages, the finances inherent in the breakup of this marital partnership can be quite complex.

Working on prenups (or postnups) involves finding out everything you can about a couple's financial situation and assets. That's because prenups and postnups almost always have to do with money – sometimes a lot of it. So a mediator needs to be able to intimately understand the finances of the couple.

If there is an ongoing business, the tax returns, financial statements, and organizational documents of the business need to be reviewed and understood by the mediator. In all cases, review of a party's personal tax returns is important. Every asset on the asset list needs to be understood. Asset statements and reports need to be provided and reviewed.

There may be complex estate-planning documents set up by the clients (or their parents) as well. These need to be obtained and reviewed as part of the due diligence, and the terms explained to the mediation clients. Account statements of the underlying trusts or other arrangements (such as family limited partnerships) need to be reviewed and understood. This requires estate-planning knowledge and income and gift/estate tax law knowledge.

All this requires much financial sophistication on the part of the parties' mediator. The mediator must have an ability to understand and explain these complex financial issues to the client. Because a prenup is largely a financial contract, the finances must be deeply and thoroughly understood by the mediator if the mediator is to help the clients set terms for their prenup. Many non-lawyer mediators are not in a position to be able to do this.

Three different approaches to mediation.

Different mediators approach the practice of mediation differently. These different philosophies of mediation will affect the process.

There are three main conceptual frameworks for mediation: facilitative, evaluative, and transformative. Many mediators blend two or three of these approaches into mediation sessions. (See also Chapter 6.)

Facilitative Mediation is the form most frequently practiced. It consists of focusing on clients' needs, values, goals, and fears. The primary aim is to help parties come to agreement. Facilitative mediators use standard mediation practices such as finding the interests behind the parties' positions, reframing, active listening, validating points of view, defusing "hot" speech, and helping to clarify communication misunderstandings.

Some facilitative mediators believe that the "law" is irrelevant to the dispute, and that clients should not necessarily make decisions "in the shadow of the law." This means they shouldn't necessarily have to follow closely how legal precepts would resolve the issues they are dealing with in the prenup. Some facilitative mediators believe that the clients should control all of their decisions without much input from the mediator – that the process should be completely "client driven." Nowadays, most facilitative mediators have substantive knowledge in the field they are mediating, and are willing to share that knowledge with their mediation clients.

Facilitative Mediation (with guidance from the mediator) is a good mediation style for prenuptial agreements. A mediator is allowed to share legal information – and should do so. But a mediator is not allowed to provide legal advice. However, it is reasonable for a mediator to describe to the mediation clients the ranges and types of solutions the mediator has encountered in his or her practice.

Evaluative Mediation is the second type of mediation. In this type of mediation, the mediator evaluates the dispute presented through the lens of existing law and predicts how the dispute would be decided by a judge or a jury if brought to court. Although not generally appropriate in mediating prenups, the issue of whether or not a prenup (or postnup) would hold up in court is an important issue.

If asked by the mediation clients, the mediator might well refer that question to the reviewing attorneys, although the mediator should know the law of enforceability and seek to formulate (by a term sheet or a draft) an agreement that will be enforceable. It is certainly appropriate for the mediator to refer the clients to cases that address relevant enforceability issues. The mediator may even summarize them as part of giving "legal information" to the mediation clients. But giving an opinion of the enforceability of a prenup is giving legal advice, which a mediator should not do.

Transformative Mediation is the last major type of mediation. Transformative Mediation originated to provide a means to affect deeper changes in people than just the resolution of specific disputes. The originators of this type of mediation (Joseph Folger and Robert Bush) articulated the key to transformative change as "empowerment" and "recognition."

According to Bush and Folger, "empowerment" comes from gaining clarity through understanding options, choices, goals, and preferences. The other aspect, "recognition," involves considering, acknowledging, and having empathy for the other person in the mediation. Transformative Mediation can be very useful in mediating postnuptial agreements, which you could view as a form of marital mediation.

Sometimes after the mediation, a couple will decide not to have a written, signed postnuptial agreement, but will have had "transformed" certain aspects of their marriage by the mediation process. If a written postnuptial agreement results, it will be sounder and have a better chance of working to secure and improve the marriage because the document and the process has resulted in increased "empowerment" and "recognition." Empowerment would include a deeper understanding of the options, goals, and choices the spouses have and why they chose the options they did. Mutual recognition can grow if the process results in increased compassion for one another and mutual acknowledgment of their efforts and contributions. (See Chapter 4, Contribution to Marriage.)

Mediator as neutral versus mediator as truthsayer.

Some mediators hate to give their views in the mediation process. This is because mediators are supposed to be neutral and unbiased. And yet, at times, there may be a big, giant, hairy elephant in the mediation room. It might be a small but very important fact that has revealed itself, but as yet has been unsaid. It lingers in the background, infusing the entire mediation with an element of mendacity. It is poisonous to the mediation process.

That elephant may need to be acknowledged and discussed openly in order to have all the relevant information available for the clients to make a thoroughly considered agreement. Sometimes it's the mediator's job to smoke out and lead a discussion about the elephant in the room.

My experience as a mediator is that it is usually helpful to be honest, and to tell the truth as you see it, at certain points in the process. Clients don't generally simply want a rubber stamp as a mediator. They want someone who can provide input and helpful comments and insight. A mediator needs to be trusted by the mediation clients, and if it becomes clear that the mediator is not being truthful, then his or her ability to effectively mediate will be greatly diminished.

But being truthful as a mediator can be dangerous, too. Sometimes you may appear to support the position or view of one of the mediation clients over the other. Sometimes you can say something one of the clients doesn't like or can readily accept. But if you can demonstrate support and respect for that client, they sometimes can change their minds about an issue when the feedback comes from a mediator who is perceived as neutral. These truthful moments can go a long way toward getting to a peaceful and civilized mediated prenuptial agreement.

How to find a mediator online.

Most states have statewide mediators' associations, which is a good place to start. You can find these online. Look through the listings and follow up by looking at the websites of the ones that attract your interest.

A typical search for a mediator might be:

> mediator prenuptial agreement divorce marital mediation and [your geographic area]

The search will pull up both lawyer mediators and non-lawyer mediators. To find a lawyer mediator, add the terms "lawyer" or "attorney" and perhaps "collaborative law" to the search.

A good question to ask a mediator on the telephone for screening might be how that mediator would address a particular issue. Give the mediator one that is likely to come up in your mediation, such as, "I want to have a prenup, and my fiancé doesn't want one. How would you address that?" or, "My fiancé and I are not in agreement on how we want our estate to be distributed after our death. We both have children from previous marriages." Or you can ask the question as to how the mediator would address an impasse, without giving an example. You can ask the mediator about the mediator's philosophy of mediation, his or her opinion on prenups, and the mediator's sense of the interplay between prenups and marriage. Another reasonable question is how many prenups they have mediated in the past year or two.

Mediating across state lines.

At times, mediation clients may seek the services of a mediator who is not practicing within their state. Or the couple may each reside in different states, and one of those states (or even a third state) is where they initially plan to reside after they marry. Another variable is the "choice of law" provision in the prenup, which could be still another state.

With the availability of Skype, Facetime, Google Hangouts, and other free digital video-conferencing programs, clients in various locations can meet with their attorneys and with mediators without being constrained geographically. The choice of which state's law to apply is a question to be addressed when creating the prenup. The state should have a "nexus" or connection with the marriage, at least at the outset. But sometimes people start their marriages in one location and end up living in another.

Mediators are supposed to be process facilitators, and they are not permitted to give legal advice. Having said that, mediators do need to be substantively informed of the laws of the jurisdiction that will apply to the prenup and/or the laws of the jurisdiction in which a party lives, as the parties may be waiving some state laws. This applies to non-attorney mediators as well as attorney mediators.

If you do choose an out-of-state mediator because of the qualities you seek in the mediator, do expect that the mediator will spend some billable time getting familiar with the law of the states that are relevant to your prenup. The mediator needs to have the appropriate knowledge of such laws to capably assist you in determining the terms of your prenup.

Choosing mediation reviewing attorneys.

Not every couple that enters the mediation process engages their own attorney to provide advice, review the process, or provide input on the final agreement. However, having separate counsel is recommended in all but the simplest of situations.

Lack of separate reviewing counsel in divorce mediation is somewhat more common. This may occur if the situation is quite straightforward. Short marriages, no children, few joint assets, and each party gainfully employed are some of the situations in which clients sometimes forgo reviewing counsel.

Prenups and postnups are different. Prenups change the very template of marriage existing far into the future. Postnups change legal rights of married couples in ongoing marriages. Both these situations are rife with the possibilities of overreaching, unfairness, and coercion. They all have enforceability issues. It is best to engage a reviewing attorney for these contracts. But how should you go about choosing one?

If you are mediating prenups, your mediator can and should provide you with a list of recommended review attorneys. I refer to so-called mediation-friendly lawyers. These are generally lawyers who are also experienced and active mediators and usually practice in the field of collaborative law, as well.

My referral list includes attorneys who are very experienced in divorce law and prenuptial agreements and who have a similar philosophy to mine in making prenups as generous as possible under the facts and aims of the couple in order to support the marriage. Most of these are attorneys I've worked with a number of times. Some of them have strong business backgrounds and are good to engage if there is an ongoing business in the asset pool of the couple. The bottom line, though, is that all of my referral attorneys are excellent lawyers who can provide value to the process.

My view is that divorce lawyers tend to have more sensitivity to the role of money and marriage than other types of attorneys. They deal with these issues every day in working with clients whose marriages are breaking up. Since much of the prenup contract deals with the terms of a possible future divorce, divorce attorneys have the requisite experience in divorce law. They can more easily think about and provide input into these provisions.

Reviewing attorneys can and should be consulted after (and maybe also before) each mediation session, to analyze the progress and the issues that still remain to be resolved. It is very rare in prenuptial agreement mediation for the attorneys to accompany the clients to the mediation sessions, although there is no proscription against this.

If you contact your reviewing attorney before the mediation begins, it's probably a good idea to share the content of that talk with your fiancé.

Who should do the first draft of the prenup?

One of the issues when there is a mediated prenup (or if there is a mediated prenup with two reviewing attorneys) is who should write up the first draft. In the typical situation, as described in Chapter 20, the attorney for the more moneyed future spouse creates the first draft. This tends to have many negative consequences to the process and to the upcoming marital relationship. I suggest that if there is a mediator, and the mediator is an attorney, that the mediator create the first draft based on the term sheet negotiated by the clients. If the mediator is not an attorney, I would suggest that the attorney for the less moneyed future spouse create a first draft based on the term sheet.

If the prenup is not mediated, my preference is for the clients themselves to create a term sheet by conferring with each other with the assistance of their respective attorneys. After the term sheet is set, I would suggest that the attorney for the less moneyed future spouse create the first draft.

What if we decide not to use a reviewing attorney?

Some mediation clients decide not to engage reviewing attorneys. Perhaps they have sought mediation because they had a previous bad experience when they each hired a separate attorney to start the process of getting their prenup. This happens surprisingly often.

Sometimes, mediation clients simply do not want to risk having the provisions that they carefully and thoughtfully agreed to in their mediated prenup overturned or questioned by an attorney. This is indeed a risk when you send a mediated prenup to a reviewing attorney.

Sometimes, the idea of sending the prenup draft to reviewing attorneys seems superfluous, as in the prenup of two income-earning professionals who wish to put structure around their financial relationship once they are married.

Engaging a reviewing attorney is probably a step each partner to a mediated prenup would be well advised to take. Having a competent attorney who is providing legal advice to you (which a mediator cannot do) is important. For the more moneyed spouse, having reviewing attorneys (or being represented by attorneys) makes a prenup have a greater chance of enforceability. In many of the instances in which prenups have been invalidated by courts, the less moneyed future spouse did not have an attorney or did not have sufficient time to consult with one.

Additionally, you and your future spouse can ask the mediator to be active during the attorney review process. The mediator can help you choose mediation-friendly attorneys, explain the term sheet and your mutual intentions to the reviewing attorneys, and monitor the process as it unfolds. If there are changes, the changes can be assessed during a continued mediation process, if that becomes helpful.

• • •

My aim in writing this book is to change preconceptions about prenuptial agreements. Part of this is by suggesting the concept of a "generous prenup" developed over my years in private practice as a divorce attorney and mediator. For decades, prenuptial agreements have been divisive tools that have often harmed marrying couples, pitting spouses against each other at a time when love should rule the day.

In this book, I first presented information and tools that help couples decide if a prenuptial agreement could actually benefit them. I then showed how it is possible to vastly improve the prenup as we know it. This is done through ideas on how to change the tenor of the negotiations between future spouses and their attorneys and also improve the content of prenups.

I have included comprehensive source material and laws relating to prenups. Part of this is to show how prenups affect and change state law. Part of this is to present ideas on how to make a prenup more customized. What people don't know is that there is a multitude of financial choices that a couple can make when formulating the terms of a prenuptial agreement.

Importantly, the book talks about money and marriage, and how prenups can decrease marital harmony. I hope that to some extent I have succeeded in these goals. I hope you, my readers, are now better prepared to make informed decisions on the many options available to you as you embark on your marriages.

ACKNOWLEDGMENTS

Many thanks to Mary Dearborn, Eric Laursen, and Elaine Sidney, who read early drafts of my proposal, provided comments and supported me throughout this project.

I am grateful to the following people who generously provided input into *The Generous Prenup*:

Massachusetts attorneys Devlin Farmer, Joyce Kauffman, Jason Giannetti, Jonathan Korb, John Hope, Natalie B. Choate, William Coyne, and Jeffrey Fink; California attorneys Ron Rosenfeld, Elizabeth Potter Scully, Frisco Fayer, and Jill Cohen; Pennsylvania attorney Rosadele Kauffman; and New York attorney Rachel Fishman Green, all of whom provided valuable input and assisted me greatly.

Maggie Weems of Oregon, and Kenneth Cloke and Peter Spelman of California, generously put me in touch with others to assist me in my work. Mediator colleagues Jon Kent and John Hoelle provided thoughtful comments that guided me in the process. Mari Hall, Ben Israel, and Michael Gross provided perceptive comments and guidance.

Many of my writing friends from Western Massachusetts helped me formulate the title of this book. Their input and support throughout this project was invaluable. They are Mary Bagg, Robert Bagg, Alice Schertle, Susan Pearson, Gordon Massman, Mary Dearborn, Eric Laursen, Bill Latimer, Lina Bernstein, Wilmot Hastings, Frances Henry, and Patty Kimura.

My friends Ed Rogoff and Perry-Lynn Moffitt of New York provided astute comments and connected me with Mike Shatzkin of Ideolog, who was my consultant in connection with this project, and who connected me with David Wilk of Booktrix, who is handling the publishing aspects of the book.

To editors Deanna Brady of California and Bill Latimer of Massachusetts, who assisted me in reading and editing the book.

I also give many thanks to my law partners, Karen Van Kooy and Laura E. Days, who have supported me during this project by giving me the time and solitude during these last two and a half years to combine book writing with my firm-based legal and mediation work. My thanks also to Victoria Ellsworth and Philippina Loh at my law firm who greatly assisted me in my law practice so that I had time to write this book. My grateful appreciation also to Venezia VanDerZyde, a legal assistant in our law firm, who read every chapter of this book and who served as an excellent copy editor.

Any errors or deficiencies that remain in *The Generous Prenup* are solely mine, and not those of the people who have so generously helped and supported me throughout this project.

And for my clients, who have taught me so much, and to whom I dedicate this book.

If I have moved the needle a bit, I will have done my job.

The information in this book may not be current and is subject to change without notice. The author cannot guarantee that the information is accurate, complete, or up-to-date. The author makes no claims, promises, or guarantees about the accuracy, completeness, or adequacy of the information contained in this book.

INDEX

Del Vecchio v. Del Vecchio, 143 So. 2d 17
(Fla. 1962), 57
DeMatteo v. DeMatteo, 436 Mass. 18
(2002), 181, 243–244, 245–
246, 304, 305
DePaulo, Bella, 65
deceased spouse unused exclusion
(DSUE), 149–150
Diosdado v. Diosdado, 97 Cal. App. 4th
471 (2002), 219–220, 222, 245–
246
discretionary trusts, 120–121
disinheritance, 36, 97, 99–101, 110, 116,
140–141, 158, 165, 259, 266,
282
dissipation of marital assets, 81, 88, 217
divorce rate, 60, 65–66
domicile, change of, 96
double-counting (alimony), 96
Drew, Jeffrey, 42

E

Earl of Chesterfield v. Janssen, 28 Eng.
Rep. 82, 100 (1750), 302
Eason v. Eason, 384 S.C. 473 (2009), 225
elective share, 99–100, 108, 160–161,
261, 263
elephant in the room, 258, 359
emotional affair, 219
English language proficiency, 22, 206–
207, 290
equitable distribution laws, 57, 85, 87–
90, 92, 93, 178, 261, 304
Employee Retirement Income Security
Act (ERISA), 164–165
estate freezing techniques, 136–139
estate plans in prenups, 158
ethical rules for lawyers, 71, 72, 116,
172, 275, 330–331, 349
evaluative mediation, 74–75, 358

F

5 × 5 power, 153
facilitative mediation, 74, 357
fact pattern, 4, 9, 20, 24, 28, 29, 36, 40,
226, 233, 299
fair and reasonable standard, 243, 245,
303–305
family lawyer representing more
moneyed spouse, 107, 116,
260–262, 334, 352
Family Limited Partnership (FLP), 137–
138
Felder, Raoul, 105
fiancé visa, 196, 198, 203
fiduciary duty, 130, 293–296, 310, 318,
320, 322, 323
financial disclosure, 296–298, 336–337
finding a mediator, 335–336, 355–357,
360 (web searches)
finding an attorney, 334, 344–346, 350,
351–352
postnuptial agreement attorney, 355
web searches, 349–350, 353–355
first draft (who should prepare), 339,
362–363
Fiske, John, 277
flat fee prenups, 347–348
Florida statutes, 235
Fogg v. Fogg, 409 Mass. 531 (1991),
293, 318–319
Folger, Joseph, 358
forced share, 99–100, 108, 160–161,
261, 263
fraud, fraudulent inducement and
fraudulent concealment, 292–
293
fraudulent conveyance (transfer) laws,
136, 172
French v. McAnarney, 290 Mass. 544,
546 (1935), 300
frequency of executed prenups, 62–65

 Laurie Israel is a lawyer and mediator located in Brookline, Massachusetts. A founder of Israel, Van Kooy & Days, LLC, she has been practicing law for 30 years. Her writings on prenuptial agreements have appeared in the *New York Times*, the *Wall Street Journal*, and the *Huffington Post*. Laurie has been interviewed by a number of other publications, including *New York* magazine.

Laurie's significant work in the area of prenuptial agreements – in representing clients individually and in serving as a mediator for couples formulating the terms of their prenup – made her aware of the dangers prenups pose, both in process and in content, especially in first marriages. *The Generous Prenup: How to Support Your Marriage and Avoid the Pitfalls* is the result of her experience in this field.

Laurie's divorce practice led her to an interest in marriages – what makes them succeed and what makes them fail. She is one of the leaders in the emerging field of marital mediation, in which the mediation process is used to help married couples improve their relationships.

For more on the author, visit www.laurieisrael.com and www.mediating-prenups.com. To read her articles on law, marriage, and other topics, visit www.ivkdlaw.com, www.huffpost.com, and www.mediate.com.